Information Systems Engineering

Distributed Systems: Application Development

September 1994

Edited by R. Duschl and Dr. J. Stewart

Authors: Dr. M. Breu, A. Aue, J. Hall and K. Robinson

LONDON: HMSO

© British Crown / Siemens Nixdorf 1994

Applications for reproduction should be made to HMSO

First published 1994

ISBN 0 11 330623 7

For further information regarding this volume and other CCTA products please contact:-

CCTA Library
Rosebery Court
St Andrews Business Park
NORWICH
NR7 0HS

01603 704704

Preface

The **Information Systems Engineering Library** provides guidance on managing and carrying out Information Systems Engineering activities. In the IS life cycle, Information Systems Engineering takes place once the IS strategy has been defined. It is concerned with the development and ongoing improvement of information systems up to the operational stage, and their maintenance whilst in operational use.

The Information Systems Engineering Library complements other CCTA products, in particular the project management methodology, PRINCE, the systems analysis and design methodology, SSADM and the IT Infrastructure Library on operational issues.

This volume on application development for distributed systems comprises 2 main parts: part 1 which provides method independent guidance; and part 2 which shows how to use the European Methodology and System Center's BOS Engineering Method and CCTA's SSADM for the development of distributed information systems.

CCTA welcomes customer views on Information Systems Engineering Library publications. Please send your comments to:

> Information Systems Engineering Group
> CCTA
> Rosebery Court
> St. Andrews Business Park
> Norwich
> NR7 0HS
> United Kingdom

Information Systems Engineering Library
Distributed Systems: Application Development

Contents

Chapter			page
	Preface		3
	Foreword by German Editor		9
	Foreword by British Editor		11
	Acknowledgements		12
Part 1	**Method Independent Guidance**		
1	**Introduction**		15
	1.1	Purpose of this volume	15
	1.2	Who should read this volume	16
	1.3	Structure of this volume	16
	1.4	Structure of Part 1	17
2	**What is a 'Distributed System'?**		19
	2.1	Introduction	19
	2.2	Introduction to EU-Rent	19
	2.3	What do we mean by a 'distributed system'?	21
	2.4	Issues in distributed systems development	25
3	**Approach/Philosophy**		29
	3.1	Introduction	29
	3.2	3-schema Specification Architecture for information systems	29
	3.3	Overview of general notion of services	37
	3.4	Design approach	45
4	**Distribution concepts**		59
	4.1	Introduction	59
	4.2	Actor/business location concepts	60
	4.3	Data/object concepts	64
	4.4	Trigger/processing concepts	66
	4.5	DP location concepts	70
	4.6	Data implementation concepts	72
	4.7	Process implementation concepts	74
	4.8	Volumetrics	76

5	Cooperation services and architectures	83
	5.1 Introduction	83
	5.2 Abstract cooperation services	85
	5.3 Architectures for distributed systems	89
	5.4 Mapping of services to architectures	99
	5.5 State of the technology	99
6	Decisions specific to distributed systems	109
	6.1 Introduction	109
	6.2 Generic development process	109
	6.3 Types of decision	111
	6.4 Heuristics	125
	6.5 Guidelines for mapping conceptual processes to service architectures	132
Part 2	Tailored versions of BOS Engineering Method and SSADM	
7	BOS Engineering Method extensions	137
	7.1 Introduction	137
	7.2 Related Guidance	138
	7.3 Mapping of common decision points	139
	7.4 Representation of distribution concepts	140
	7.5 Method specific heuristics and rules	147
	7.6 Extensions to GRAPES	165
8	BOS Engineering Method applied to EU-Rent	167
	8.1 Introduction	167
	8.2 Business Context Model	167
	8.3 Business Service Model	172
	8.4 Business Organisation Model	185
	8.5 Technical Distribution Scenarios	193
9	SSADM extensions	217
	9.1 Introduction	217
	9.2 Related guidance	219
	9.3 Mapping of distributed systems guidance to SSADM	220
	9.4 Changes to modelling steps and techniques	225
	9.5 Changes to current SSADM techniques	243
	9.6 Additional SSADM techniques	273
	9.7 Mapping from specific requirements to services	278

10	**SSADM extensions applied to EU-Rent**		**287**
	10.1	Introduction	287
	10.2	Current System	287
	10.3	Preparation for Design Options	299
	10.4	Option 1 - Centralised Option	326
	10.5	Distributed Options	333
	10.6	Option 2 - Fully Distributed Option	335
	10.7	Option 3 - Partially Clustered Option	356
	10.8	Option Sizing & Costing	367

Annexes

A	**Meta model of distribution concepts**		**381**
	A.1	Meta modelling notation	381
	A.2	Meta model of distribution concepts	382
B	**Checklist for cost estimation**		**385**
	B.1	Costs per location	385
	B.2	Inter-location communication costs	388
	B.3	Support infrastructure costs	389
	Bibliography		**391**
	Glossary		**395**
	Index		**417**

Foreword by German Editor

Today, IT-solutions must be derived from business structures and processes in order to be profitable and successful.

With the tendency of modern enterprises and organisations to globalise their activities across trans-national markets, a new level of complexity is introduced into business organisation and processes. IT-systems must be able to cope with this challenge.

It is of crucial importance that control over business processes is guaranteed when work flows are spread out over locations in different countries or even on different continents. The spatial distance between activities requiring co-ordination is an issue which must be carefully addressed in the development of widely-distributed information systems.

Already underlying technologies to facilitate the co-operation of people working in different locations are well established:

- *Telecommunications technology* has progressed dramatically. This is typified by the availability of cellular networks, the increased speed of message transmission and the increased choice of services.

- *Multi-media conferencing* has the potential to overcome the spatial separation of organisational units by using modern office communication technology and multi-media services.

- *Multi-lingual systems* facilitate multi-national co-operations. The automated translation of texts, as for example supported by the METAL system, is a strategic issue in the European multi-national community.

- *Work group computing* and the enabling technology are evolving more and more, as the paradigm naturally supports the way people work together.

Besides that, an ongoing range of international standardisation activities have also pushed the development of distributed systems:

- *X/Open* defines a standard that allows interoperability of software on any hardware platform.

- *ISO standardisation* defines distributed transaction processing and remote database access.

- *EDIFACT* standardises the exchange of business data via networks, ensures co-ordinated decision making processes, and thus helps to save valuable resources.

- *Euromethod* takes into account the nowadays multi-national character of IT-projects from a procurement point of view.

The architectural view on information systems development has also progressed. The transition from host-systems to client/server architectures and the integration of isolated IT-islands in networks are current trends. In this context, techniques for the modelling and simulation of different configurations of distributed information systems can be used to predict the benefit of a system without running the risk of implementing the wrong solution.

But, in order to exploit all these technical opportunities for building the right distributed system, a sound methodological approach is required. The time has come to extend the underlying concepts of existing methods like SSADM and GRAPES to handle the additional dimension of distribution, and to plan and model the effective use of technological opportunities.

This volume is another successful step in the collaboration between CCTA and the EMSC. It defines common extensions to the two specific methodologies: SSADM and BOS Engineering Method/GRAPES.

The volume has used the synergy of the collaboration to provide advanced methodological guidance including a common architecture, common distribution concepts and an approach for the successful development of distributed applications.

R. Duschl   Munich, September 1994

Foreword by British Editor

Technological advances in the IT industry over recent years have resulted in a widespread adoption of distributed systems, with their potential for good price / performance characteristics and improved local facilities. The industry's application development methodologies have unfortunately not kept pace and developers of distributed applications have been largely left to fend for themselves. The industry is now faced with the challenge of explaining how to use these methodologies to develop distributed applications.

Within the European Union there is a growing need for government administrations and commercial organisations to coordinate their activities across national boundaries. This requirement will increase demand for information systems that are not just distributed but also span national boundaries. Building such systems presents the further challenge of coordinating development activities based on differing approaches and methodologies.

This volume is a major step forward in addressing the requirement for guidance on how to develop distributed applications. The volume has been developed as the result of collaboration between the European Methodology and System Center and CCTA, the UK Government Centre for Information Systems.

The EMSC and CCTA are also participating in larger EU-funded collaborations to address the second challenge. The first of these collaborations is developing EUROMETHOD, a major EU initiative to provide a public domain 'framework' for the planning, procurement and management of services for the investigation, development or amendment of information systems. The second collaboration is developing a common European Modelling Language which will enable different developers to use different development methods at each stage of the development process, but require the IS experts acting on behalf of the customer of the information system to be familiar with only the European Modelling Language.

Dr. John Stewart   Norwich, September 1994

Acknowledgements

EMSC and CCTA gratefully acknowledge the help of the following organisations in the preparation of this volume:

Model Systems (UK)
Edinburgh University Computer Services (UK).

Valuable review comments were provided by:

Siemens Nixdorf Informationssysteme AG (D)
Avis (D)
National Health Service Information Management Centre (UK)
Inland Revenue (UK)
Ministry of Defence Procurement Executive (UK)
British Computer Society Data Management Subgroup (UK)
International Business Machines (UK)
Learmonth and Burchett Management Systems (UK)
Cray Systems (UK).

Part 1:

Method Independent Guidance

1 Introduction

Developing distributed information systems in a systematic, cost-effective way is one of the major challenges for the software engineering community in this decade. Appropriate hardware and system software is available, but stringent methods for developing distributed information systems are not.

There is a rapidly-increasing desire for information systems which range over very wide areas. The European Union and single market spur demand for systems allowing Europe-wide exchange and administration of information, eg EURES (EURopean Employment information System) and EDIS (Electronic Data Interchange for the Social domain). Each of these systems requires a considerable number of cooperating data processing systems. Currently, island solutions are connected by ad-hoc approaches. But methods are needed that support the comprehensive planning and construction of distributed information systems.

1.1 Purpose of this volume

The purpose of this volume is to bridge the gap between traditional systems engineering methods for centralised systems and the available or expected technology for distributed IT solutions. Thus it is intended as a supplement to both BOS Engineering Method/GRAPES and SSADM.

However, its purpose is not restricted to developing applications with these methods. Rather it elaborates the general concepts behind the design of distributed information systems. These concepts are to be considered when developing any distributed information system whether they be in commercial or administrative domains.

The volume covers the requirements analysis, and the conceptual and logical design of a distributed information system. It does not cover facets of analysis and design already treated in the context of centralised systems.

The volume restricts its coverage to distributed applications; it does not cover the design of distributed technical platforms.

In the remainder of this volume, apart from Chapter 4, 'distributed information system' will be abbreviated to 'distributed system'. The term 'method' is used in two senses in this volume and in each case the intended sense should be clear from the context. Both senses are defined in the glossary.

1.2 Who should read this volume

The intended audience of this volume are IS development practitioners and project leaders dealing with the development of distributed systems who require support for:

- systems analysis and logical design with distributed solutions

- decisions as to whether a particular distributed architecture is appropriate.

On a more general basis it gives guidelines to technical decision makers for:

- decisions at a general level on whether a distributed solution is appropriate

- 'infrastructure' management for distributed systems (eg maintainability).

1.3 Structure of this volume

This volume is divided into two parts:

- method-independent guidance (Part 1)

- method-specific guidance (Part 2).

Part 1 provides method-independent guidance on the development of distributed applications. This guidance is relevant whatever specific development method is used.

Part 2 shows how the method-independent guidance of Part 1 can be used to tailor two specific application development methods:

- BOS Engineering Method/GRAPES

- SSADM.

Part 2 also separately summarises the application of the tailored versions of the two methods to the same case study.

Annexes provide:

- a meta model of distribution concepts (Annex A)

- a checklist for cost estimation (Annex B).

1.4 Structure of Part 1

The remainder of Part 1 consists of the following chapters:

- what is a 'distributed system'? (Chapter 2);

- approach/philosophy (Chapter 3);

- distribution concepts (Chapter 4);

- cooperation services and architectures (Chapter 5);

- decisions specific to distributed systems (Chapter 6).

Chapter 2 introduces the case study, explains what is meant in this volume by a 'distributed system' and highlights three key areas where development of distributed systems differs from development of 'centralised systems'.

Chapter 3 introduces the 3-schema Specification Architecture which simplifies the move from a centralised to a distributed system and makes it easier to compare distribution options. The chapter provides a simplified overview of services in distributed systems. Finally, it describes the approach to designing distributed systems.

Chapter 4 describes the six categories of concepts which are needed to describe a distributed system during its development.

Chapter 5 describes, in abstract, services needed to support the cooperation of distributed applications and the architectures which provide interfaces between applications and various combinations of these services. It also discusses the current state of technology in this area.

Chapter 6 introduces a generic development process, describes the types of decision which must be considered when developing a distributed system, gives heuristics on which to base provisional decisions and provides guidelines for mapping conceptual processes to service architectures.

Navigation

Readers interested in an overview of the approach taken in this volume to the development of distributed applications should concentrate on Chapters 2 and 3.

Readers interested in the details of the approach - how to analyse the requirements and how to design a distributed system - should also read Chapters 4, 5 and 6.

If the guidance contained in this volume is to be applied in a project, then it is recommended that the whole of Part 1 is read followed by either Chapters 7 and 8 where BOS Engineering Method/GRAPES is to be used or Chapters 9 and 10 where SSADM is to be used.

2 What is a 'Distributed System'?

2.1 Introduction

This chapter introduces some of the main concepts and ideas presented in this volume. Specifically, the chapter:

- introduces an imaginary car rental company, 'EU-Rent', which is used throughout the volume to provide examples of the concepts being discussed (Section 2.2)

- clarifies what 'distributed system' means in the context of this volume (Section 2.3)

- highlights three of the key issues to be borne in mind when developing distributed systems (Section 2.4).

2.2 Introduction to EU-Rent

The business of EU-Rent is car rentals, but this is largely irrelevant; it merely provides an easily understood context for illustrating examples in this volume. Many of EU-Rent's characteristics are common to other types of business; for example, health care, vocational training, social security, policing, retail chain stores, branch banking etc.

EU-Rent's business

The car rental company EU-Rent has 1000 renting branches and 200,000 cars in towns all over Europe. At each branch cars, classified by car group, are available for rental. Each branch has a manager and booking clerks who arrange rentals and reservations for future rentals.

Cars rented from one branch of EU-Rent may be returned to any other branch. The rental period and the car group are specified at the time of reservation. The renting branch must ensure that the car has been returned to some branch at the end of the rental period. If a car is returned to a branch other than the one that rented it, the car is assigned to the new branch.

At the end of each day cars are assigned to reservations for the following day. If no car of a requested group is available, a branch manager may ask other nearby branches if they have cars they can transfer to him or her.

EU-Rent has 400 service depots, each serving several branches. Cars may be booked for maintenance at any time provided that the service depot has capacity on the day in question.

For simplicity, only one booking per car per day is allowed. A rental or service may cover several days. There are about 20,000,000 rental bookings and 800,000 service bookings per year.

A customer can have several reservations but only one booking at a time. EU-Rent keeps records of about 5,000,000 customers, their rentals and bad experiences with customers. This information is used to decide whether to approve a rental. Customer records are kept until ten years after their last rental.

Current IT system

The EU-Rent business is moderately successful, but has two problems:

- each branch and service depot has a local IT system based on PCs and a file server. The equipment is obsolete and limited in capacity (especially RAM). Hardware failures - screens, disk drives and power supplies - are increasingly frequent.

  The application programs have been maintained over several years. Small amounts of RAM in the PCs has necessitated intricate, complex programs which makes amendments progressively more difficult and expensive

- each location operates almost independently of others:

  - communication between locations is mainly by phone and fax and coordination is very variable. Sometimes, when a car is dropped off at a branch different from the pick-up branch, the drop-off branch will not inform the pick-up branch. Branch managers tend to cooperate in small groups and not to look for 'spare' cars outside those groups. EU-Rent management feels that some capacity is wasted, but does not have reliable estimates of how much.

- scheduling of service bookings in branch and service depot files is coordinated by phone and fax between branch and depot. Sometimes service bookings are not recorded in the branch files, and cars booked for servicing are rented. Service depots sometimes do not get to know that cars have been transferred to branches served by other depots until another depot requests service history.

New IT system

EU-Rent management has decided that a new IT system is needed. Business activity is not expected to change significantly - locations, volume and pattern of rentals, and staff are expected to remain about the same as at present. The new system is justified on two grounds:

- the current system cannot be kept going much longer

- better management of numbers of cars at branches and better coordination between branches is expected to increase utilisation of cars slightly - the same volume of business should be supportable with fewer cars. Each car ties up about 8,000 ECUs in capital and loses about 3,000 ECUs in depreciation, so significant savings are possible from small reductions in numbers of cars needed.

Role of EU-Rent in development of this volume

EU-Rent has been used as the basis of two case studies on which the concepts presented in Part 1 of the volume were used and refined. The extensions to BOS Engineering Method and SSADM presented in Part 2 were abstracted from the results of these case studies. EU-Rent has been checked for credibility with AVIS.

2.3 What do we mean by a 'distributed system'?

It is important to establish what we mean by a 'distributed system' in the context of this volume. The problem is not so much what 'distributed' means - we know it is to do with different elements of functionality and data residing in different locations - but what 'system' means in this context.

When activities in different locations are cooperating with each other, in what circumstances should they be regarded as a single system? Or in what circumstances should we regard them as distinct systems with a capability of communicating with each other? It seems that different design considerations should apply in each case.

An important characteristic in determining whether a system is distributed is the degree of coordination between activities in different locations.

Tightly-coordinated activities

With tightly-coordinated activities we expect that what happens in one activity should be consistent with what happens in another activity, when viewed by an external observer, independently of where those activities are located. We take a set of tightly-coordinated activities to be a single system. Design of such systems is addressed by this volume.

For example, in EU-Rent we would expect that a car's return from rental would update a customer's data and a car's data at the same time, and that the update would succeed for both or fail for both. It should not matter that perhaps the customer's data is updated at head office and the car's data is updated at a branch.

Benefits of developing a system of tightly-coordinated activities are:

- we produce a system that implements the user's business requirements in the most coherent way

- we eliminate all problems of inconsistency between locations, provided that the hardware and communication equipment operate fault-free.

A tightly-coordinated system costs more and takes longer to develop than several uncoordinated systems. Uncoordinated systems are less complex - they do not have to manage consistency between locations - but the users have to accept the inconsistencies. There is also a risk that a tightly-coordinated system will be less fault-tolerant.

Uncoordinated activities

By uncoordinated activities we mean that locations can inform each other about what they are doing, but each location is free to take notice of the other's communication when and if it decides to do so. In this volume we consider the locations as having separate systems. Design of such systems is outside the scope of this volume.

For example, in EU-Rent:

- each branch may maintain its own version of customer data

- head office may periodically collect the changes that each branch has made to its customer data, collate that data and send consolidated changes back to each branch

- a branch may then apply those changes back to its own customer data.

Potentially, this is an unreliable process; head office may not wait for every branch to make a return before it collates and distributes the data.

The benefits of this approach are that, except for the coordination of data definition etc, activities for branches and head office can be designed and implemented separately. The risks are that there will be operating problems: bad customers may be allowed to rent cars, out-of-date data may be transferred to rental documents from out-of-date files. Nevertheless the benefits may outweigh the risks: simpler development against low levels of car abuse, re-keying of out-of-date customer information, or customer dissatisfaction with longer waiting times.

We take systems with uncoordinated activities to be separate systems: in the example, a branch system and a head office system. In this volume we do not regard this as a distributed system, but as two communicating systems in different locations. The benefit is in not having to analyse the communication and synchronisation between the locations.

As part of the development of a distributed system, analysis of existing uncoordinated systems may be necessary. Development of uncoordinated systems is not covered in this volume as it is not a distributed systems problem. Integration of separately-developed systems could be regarded as a distributed systems problem but is outside the scope of this volume. It is addressed for example in the *ISE Library Volume: Application Partitioning and Integration with SSADM*.

| Loosely-coordinated activities | Loose coordination of activities allows parts of the system to become temporarily inconsistent. We take a set of loosely-coordinated activities to be a single distributed system. The design of such systems is within the scope of this volume.

For example, in EU-Rent, when a reservation is submitted the customer's status is checked. If the customer is blacklisted the reservation is rejected. If customer data is held only at head office and communication lines are down, the reservation can be put in suspense and accepted or rejected when communication is re-established.

A walk-in customer wants a car immediately. His reservation has to be accepted or rejected immediately. We need a local reservation acceptance for those times when lines to head office are down. When communication is re-established, we may find out that the customer is blacklisted; had this been known, the reservation would not have been approved. EU-Rent management accepts the trade-off of occasional risky rentals against the ability to take walk-in rentals when lines between branch and head office are down.

Checking of customer status and acceptance of reservation are loosely-coordinated only with respect to the originally-stated business rules. What we have done is to compromise the business rule, blacklisted customers are not allowed to rent cars, as a trade-off between the desire to take walk-in rentals and the limitations of technology. With respect to the relaxed business rules the system is still tightly-coordinated. But we need two levels of description:

- the description of the semantics of the desired tightly-coordinated system

- the description of the relaxed semantics of the loosely-coordinated one to be implemented.

We also need a statement of the relationship between the two. This should include external processing constraints to be applied to make the relaxed semantics approximate the tightly-coordinated semantics; for example although it is possible under the relaxed semantics to accept a reservation without checking customer status there should be a constraint that if it is possible to check the customer status then it should be done.

Benefits of developing a system with loosely-coordinated activities are:

- we produce a system that implements an acceptable compromise between the most desirable semantics of the user's business and the achievement of an acceptable level of fault-tolerant operation

- we eliminate problems of inconsistency between locations (although we have redefined what we mean by consistency).

The risk is that analysis and design is more complex than for a tightly-coordinated system because we have to define:

- the tightly-coordinated semantics

- the relaxed semantics (usually more complex than the tightly-coordinated semantics)

- the relationship between the two.

2.4 Issues in distributed systems development

There are three key areas, where distributed systems development is different from development of uncoordinated systems.

Consistency and functionality versus robustness

Distribution provides a way of making remote locations less dependent for their operation on the availability of a system at a central location. But transactions that require data at several locations are still compromised if one of the involved locations is out of communication. Indeed the risks of failure for some transactions are likely to be higher if more than two locations are involved; the probabilities of failure are multiplicative, not additive.

For transactions reliant only on the data at single locations the risks of failure are smaller; even if one such location is out of action most transactions will continue as other locations will still be running.

Clearly, if single location transactions are overwhelmingly dominant and if multi-location transactions can be rescheduled until communications have been re-established, distribution can, by itself, provide a robust operating environment.

But what if the dominant or important transactions are multi-location? There are several solutions. It may be possible to reorganise the location of data so that the transactions become single location transactions, or so that data is available in several locations. If this cannot be done, it may still be possible to split a transaction into several pieces, one of which can be done locally. The remote pieces either need not be done at all (providing a degraded service) or may be done later, making the overall system temporarily inconsistent as described in the preceding section.

There is a trade-off to be made; the only person who can decide is the customer of the system, although he will need some support for analysing the impact. To this extent at least, distribution issues must be raised early in the system requirements analysis process.

Visibility of geographical distribution facts in requirements and code

Suppose that we have built a system that is centralised and we wish to distribute it. Or suppose that the system is distributed in a particular way and we wish to redistribute it in a different way for example for business reengineering purposes. If all or most of the facts about geographical distribution pervade the systems description it will be very expensive to rework the systems description and implementation.

But it should be possible with modern systems development methods to buffer the geographical distribution decisions from most of the rest of the systems description. To a large degree this buffering is achieved in the EU-Rent case studies.

Our assumption in this volume is that such a separation of concerns is desirable and achievable. The case study developments and proposals are founded on this assumption. But there is a limit to what is achievable. If the new geographical distribution compromises robustness, even that part of the system description that manages the system semantics will have to be changed.

Technical architecture and platforms

The logical design approach used in this volume generally assumes a suitable implementation platform that provides capabilities for:

- reliable communication between locations (messages do not get lost or corrupted)

- distributed commit management (including deadlock resolution).

By this we do not mean that we have a particular kind of implementation platform in mind, but that the logical level of analysis and design stops at the point of describing the semantics; the procurement or implementation of platform facilities is a subsequent step in the system's development.

In the absence of a suitable implementation platform, one would have to be designed and built by the system's implementors - clearly a significant cost. Implementors may disguise the fact that they are building such a platform, or, perhaps, not consciously be aware that they are doing so if they implement ad-hoc solutions to these requirements. But we think it better that the process of implementing these facilities be kept separate from that of specifying the system to run on top of them.

Information Systems Engineering Library
Distributed Systems: Application Development

3 Approach/Philosophy

3.1 Introduction

This chapter:

- introduces the 3-schema Specification Architecture for information systems (Section 3.2)

- explains how the 3-schema Specification Architecture maps on to network components, each providing different kinds of services, and gives a simplified overview of services in distributed systems (Section 3.3)

- describes the approach to designing distributed systems (Section 3.4).

3.2 3-schema Specification Architecture for information systems

The design of a distributed system consists of description at different levels of abstraction. The 3-schema Specification Architecture is a general approach to buffering the main part of the system description from information about the system's geographical distribution. This has the benefit of simplifying redesign when moving from a centralised to a distributed system and also makes it easier to compare different distribution options.

The *ANSI Sparc 3-schema database architecture* identifies three different views of data. It describes the conceptual, external and internal schemata. Broadly speaking, the role of the conceptual schema is to define the meaning and interdependencies of the objects, whereas the role of the external schema is to define how the objects are organised to suit a particular end-user purpose. The internal schema is concerned with the physical implementation of the data.

The publication *SSADM & GRAPES* describes a way of extending the ANSI-Sparc 3-schema database architecture to incorporate processes. This is further developed in the discussion that follows.

3.2.1 What do users want from information systems?

For most systems developed with BOS Engineering Method or SSADM, users require simulation of what is happening in their business based on databases. They can then use information obtained from the databases to support decisions that are applied to the real world of the business. It is easier and more effective to obtain information from the simulation than to deal directly with the real world.

In EU-Rent, for example, customers want to rent cars. It is easier for EU-Rent branch staff to check the car-rentals file and assign a car to the customer in the database than to walk around the parking lot to see which cars are available, and stick a label on a car saying 'Reserved for Mr. Smith'. But that decision reflected in the database leads to real-world action - a real customer gets a real car and will drive it away, bring it back and pay for the rental. See Figure 3.1.

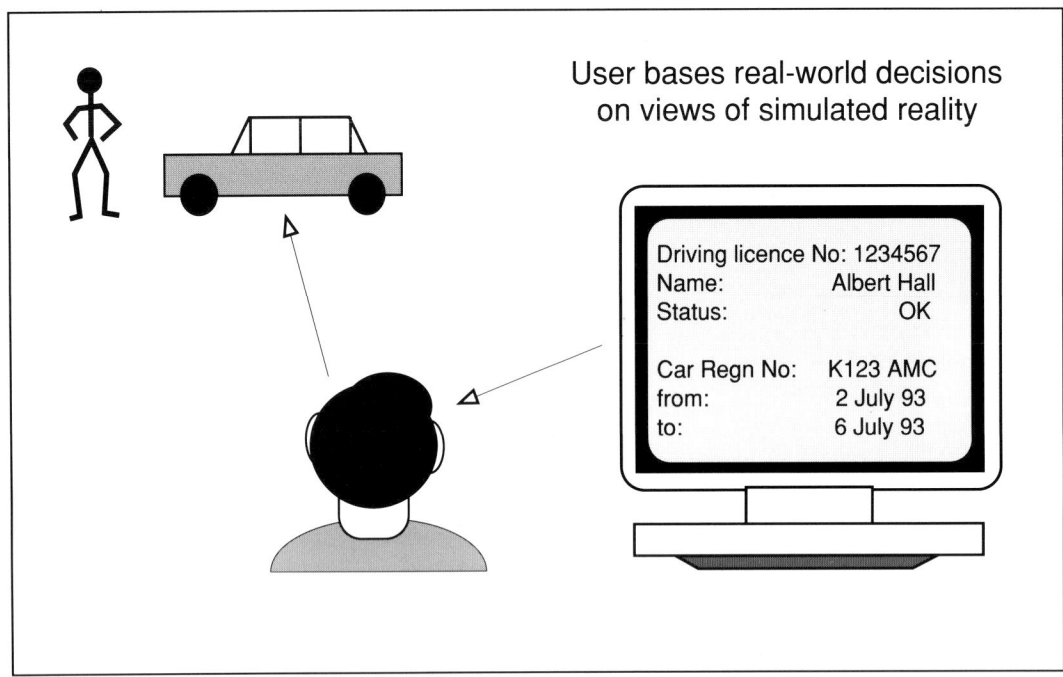

Figure 3.1: Real world and simulated reality

Users do not want the entirety of their business to be simulated. Many facets of the real world are not relevant to the business activities that need information support. The scope of an IT system is determined by:

- describing the Business Process View (BPV). How we develop a BPV is outside the scope of this volume, but processes in the BPV are real-world activities. In EU-Rent they would include: making sure there are enough cars available to fill the next day's rentals, moving cars from one branch to another, allocating specific cars to rental reservations, deciding whether to blacklist an unreliable customer, and so on

- defining the support that *actors* need from the IT system. (Items which are italicised the first time they appear in this chapter are described in more detail in Chapter 4.) We define functional requirements by developing detail for two facets of this support:

  - defining what information is needed to support each BPV process

  - deciding whether any BPV processes can be wholly or partially automated. For example, in EU-Rent, the automated system might allocate specific cars to reservations when there are cars of the requested group available at the branch, and refer the problem to the booking clerk when there are not. The booking clerk could then decide whether to offer an upgrade, arrange for the customer to be taken to another branch, and so on.

3.2.2 A conceptual schema for information support

The scope of the required IT system is defined by the information support needed for the BPV. See Figure 3.2.

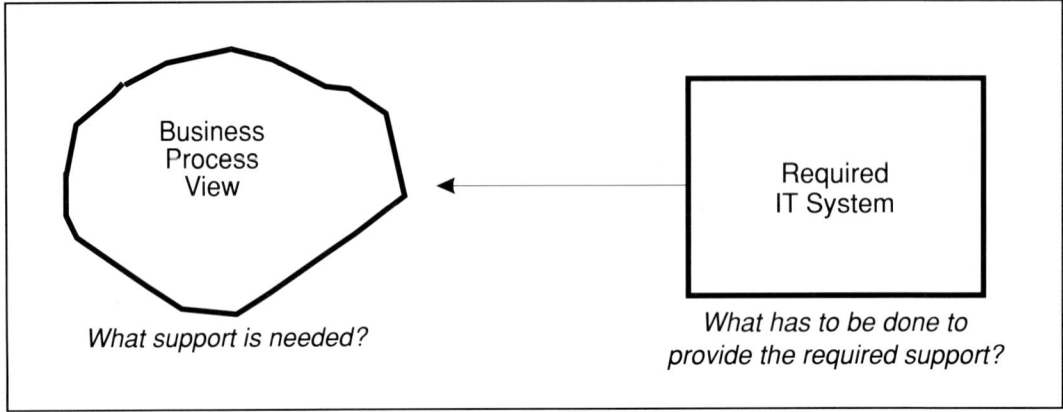

Figure 3.2: The information needed to support the BPV determines the scope of the IT system

In IT system development, we define provision of information support by:

- developing a data model from the entities and their relationships within the scope of the BPV processes. We shall, eventually, turn the data model into one or several databases that provide a basis for the simulation of the behaviour of those entities and relationships

- testing the data model for capability of providing information support - ie validating the data model - and documenting the access paths that describe how the required outputs can be extracted from the data model.

We can build up the attributes of entities in the data model as a result of this validation, either informally (by asking for each entity as we validate the model, 'what attributes would be needed to support this output') or formally, using data analysis on the output specifications.

For the data model to provide useful information support, it must be kept up-to-date. We need to identify the changes in the business that have to be reflected in the data model.

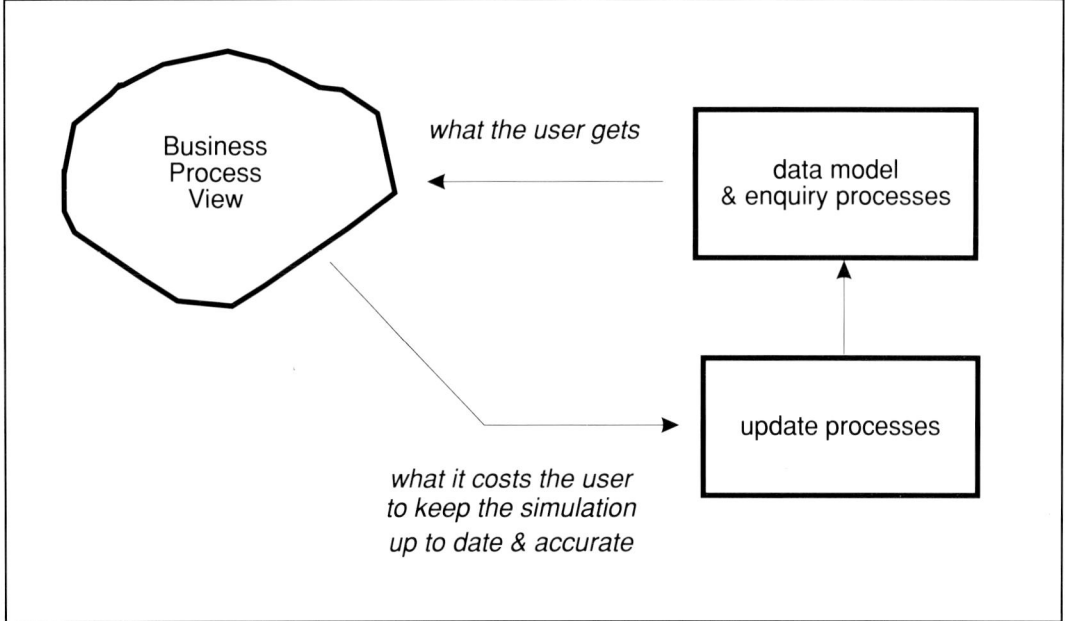

Figure 3.3: The simulation's usefulness to the business is dependent on it being kept up-to-date

If we know what has to be in the data model we must determine how it can be kept up-to-date. See Figure 3.3.

We must ensure that inputs are identified for:

- creation and removal of each entity type
- swapping of changeable relationships
- making and breaking of optional relationships
- updates of every changeable attribute
- imposing and removing constraints by setting states of entities.

We must also ensure that we know which actor roles provide which inputs.

The important thing about this process is that it is one of discovery - we need to find out what information is needed to support business activities, how it could be provided from the data model, what is needed to keep the data model up-to-date and where we can obtain the inputs.

This part of the system description - data model, update and enquiry processes and their input and output specifications - we call the conceptual schema. It defines the scope of the IT system.

Reusability of the conceptual model

The services in the conceptual model are enquiries to support business activities, automated execution of business activities, updates to record data needed to support business activities.

Some services may support more than one type of business activity. For example, in EU-Rent, the enquiry on availability of cars in a given rental group can support a booking clerk allocating a car to a rental reservation or a manager redistributing cars between rental branches.

3.2.3 A 3-schema processing architecture

In addition to the conceptual schema we also have to be concerned with an external schema, that determines how users can access the system, and an internal schema, that maps the data model on to an implementation technology and provides access to the stored data. All three schemata lead to code at the technology level, as shown in Figure 3.4. These three schemata could be thought of as a 3-schema processing architecture, but we will refer to them collectively as the 3-schema Specification Architecture.

Chapter 3
Approach/Philosophy

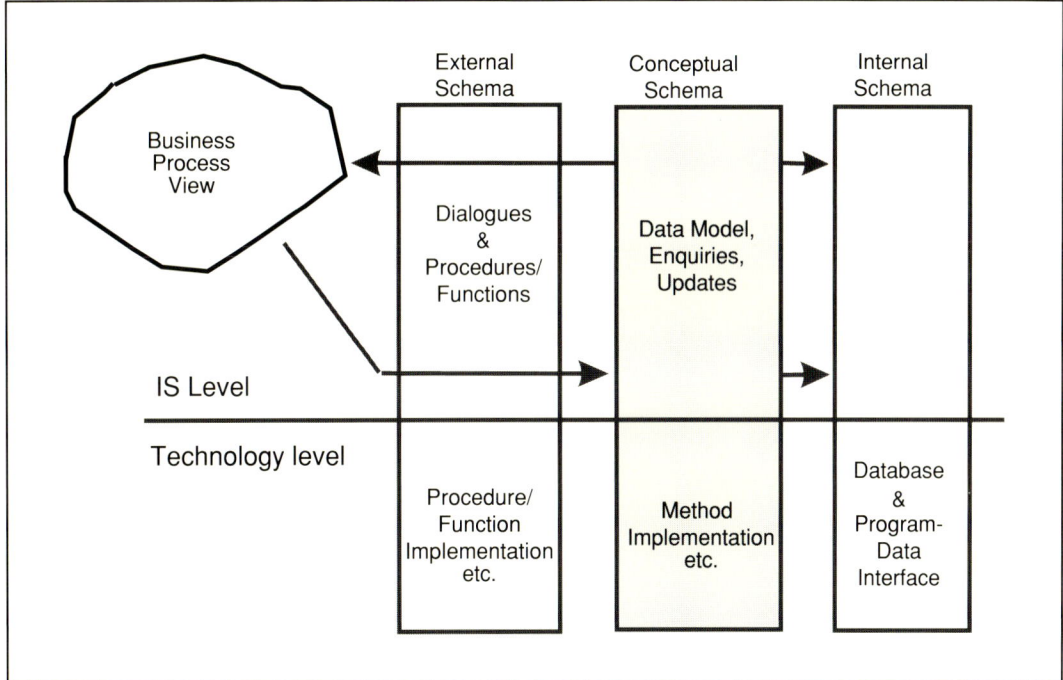

Figure 3.4: A 3-schema processing architecture

3.2.4 External design

The external schema is defined in:

- procedures (derived from DFDs and Requirements Catalogue Entries (SSADM) or Business Transactions (BOS Engineering Method) and ad-hoc enquiry specifications)

- dialogues (which may have been developed via prototypes)

- the batch input-output subsystem.

The external schema passes update data and enquiry triggers to the conceptual schema, and receives update and enquiry output in response.

The external schema has three major elements:

- a packaging of the outputs provided by and inputs needed by the conceptual schema into procedures/functions that serve actor roles

- processing:

    - to convert external DP-input messages to update data and enquiry triggers

    - to convert update and enquiry responses to outputs for actors

    - to detect and diagnose syntactic errors

    - to report semantic errors notified by processes in the conceptual schema

    - to navigate between the elements of a procedure/function and between procedures/functions

- a mapping of the external schema logical specification to an implementation technology.

The external schema differs from the conceptual schema in two significant ways. First, it is developed by design and engineering, not by discovery. Second, there could be several different external designs for a single conceptual schema.

Design versus discovery	There is, within fairly narrow boundaries, a 'right' answer, based on the conceptual schema, that simulates the entities and relationships in the business and the business behaviour to some required level of precision and currency. Once we know what BPV processes have to be supported, developing a conceptual schema is a process of discovery.

There is no 'right' answer for an external design. There are many factors outside the designer's control - allocation of user responsibilities within the business, level of ability and training of users, constraints on technology to be used, interface style guides, arbitrary rules and preferences, legislation. The designer has to make trade-offs between conflicting requirements and constraints, and construct a workable external design that is acceptable to all users.

Multiple external designs for a single conceptual schema	There could be several external designs for the same conceptual schema. This is obviously true at the technology level. More-or-less the same external services could be delivered via, for example, Motif, MS Windows, text menus, SQL-supported forms or batch input-output. In a distributed system these could all exist concurrently.

But the differences could be more fundamental. The information support provided by a conceptual schema could be packaged in different ways into functions, to serve different organisational structures and users roles. |
| 3.2.5 Internal design | Similarly, the internal schema is a constructed system, and there could be several internal designs for the same conceptual schema. There are many DBMS technologies available to implement the data model of a conceptual schema, and many ways to use their facilities to meet the physical design objectives. In a distributed system the same data model (or submodel) could be implemented (with replicated or partitioned instance data) at different locations, using different DBMSs. |

3.3 Overview of general notion of services

This section explains how the 3-schema Specification Architecture maps on to network components or IT facilities, each providing different kinds of service. The section also provides a simplified overview of services in distributed systems. More formal descriptions are provided in Chapters 4 and 5.

3.3.1 Mapping of 3-schema Specification Architecture on to IT facilities	The 3-schema Specification Architecture maps on to three kinds of IT facility, as illustrated in Figure 3.5, each providing different kinds of service. Note the IT facilities are not separate physical networks, but three kinds of component in the same network.

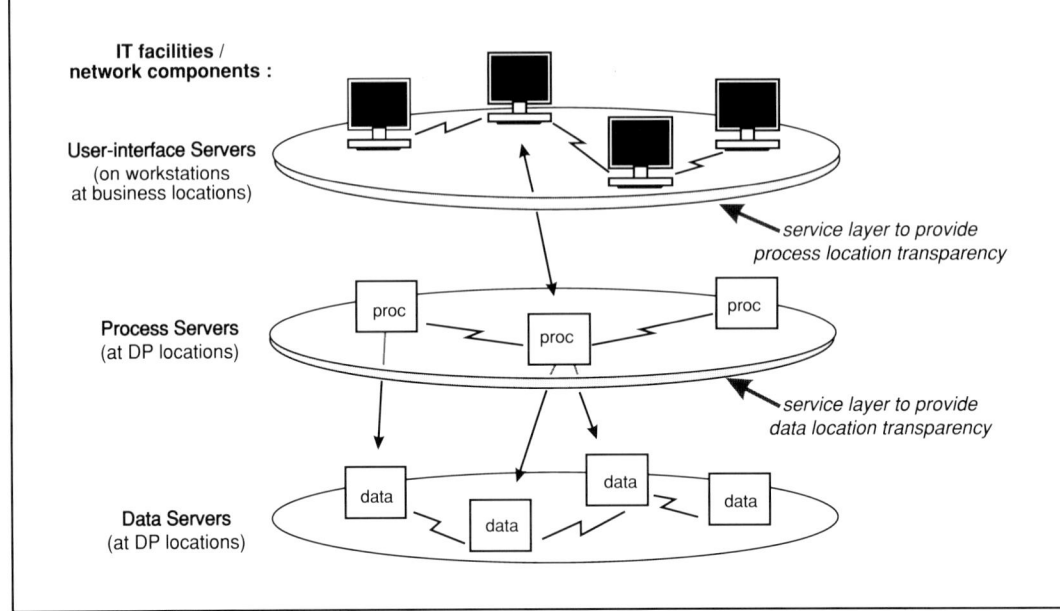

Figure 3.5: IT facilities and service layers

Figure 3.5 illustrates two simple client/server relationships, where:

- the conceptual model (plus some network services to provide process location transparency) serves the external design

- the internal design (plus some network services to provide data location transparency) serves the conceptual model.

As described in 3.2, the services provided to users by the IT system are defined in the conceptual model. However, the services are delivered to the user via the external design, as shown in Figure 3.6. In a distributed system the external design is implemented as a set of dialogues provided on *workstations* at *business locations*. The external design may be implemented in different ways on different types of workstation.

Actor roles are authorised to use workstations to carry out *procedures/functions*. People at business locations who use the system are *actors*; their job specifications include actor roles. The external schema serves their business activities.

Chapter 3
Approach/Philosophy

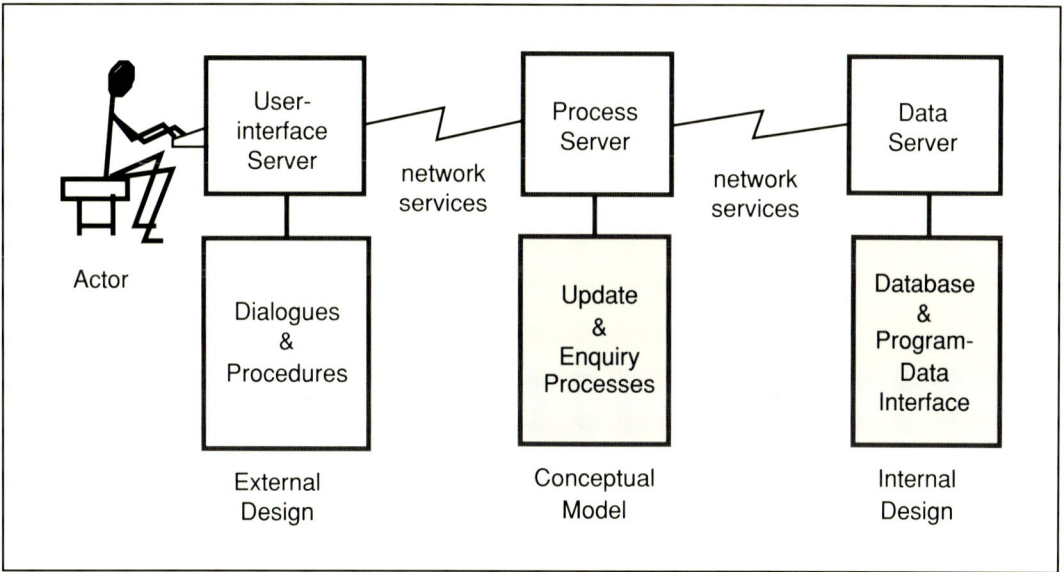

Figure 3.6: Services are delivered to the user via the external design

A network of *process servers* serves *user-interface servers* (or, more precisely, the external schema as implemented on workstations) by providing the functionality specified in the conceptual schema. Process servers are available at *data processing locations*.

Note that in this volume we assume that update and enquiry processes are developed in the form of *commit units*. Although 'commit unit' is normally used in respect of database changes, not enquiries, we have assumed that the data used by an enquiry will be locked to ensure consistency within the enquiry. The lock may also be carried forward into an update following the enquiry. This mechanism is so similar to that required for a database change that we have extended the usual meaning of 'commit unit' to accommodate it.

Procedures/functions in the external design invoke commit units, stored on process servers at data processing locations. Ideally there should be a service layer that provides location transparency - user-interface servers should not have to know where processes are located in order to invoke them.

The internal design is implemented as databases on *data servers*. Commit units are implemented independently of data management technology, and use data servers to access the required record instances. Location of data and replication of data should not be visible to the commit units (although robustness requirements may partially override this).

User-interface servers can communicate with each other without going into the conceptual schema, by means such as EMail. Conceptual processes can invoke other conceptual processes. Note that there are not separate physical networks, simply different modes of communication across a single physical network, and a computer may have more than one role - it may be a user-interface server and a process server, a process server and a data server, or all three.

In products currently available, the service layers that provide transparency are not very sophisticated; developers will often have to develop some middleware themselves.

3.3.2 Services provided by technology to enable implementation

The kinds of service required for implementation are:

- remote data access

- remote procedure call

- 'client/server'

- distributed object-oriented database.

These services are introduced here and are described in more detail in Chapter 5.

Remote data access

Commit units can be stored on user-interface servers with the procedures/functions that invoke them. Process location transparency is trivially preserved - the external design does not need to know where commit units are located, because it only calls processes on the same processor (see Figure 3.7). However, it is important to preserve the separation between the two types of processing component, to support portability and reusability.

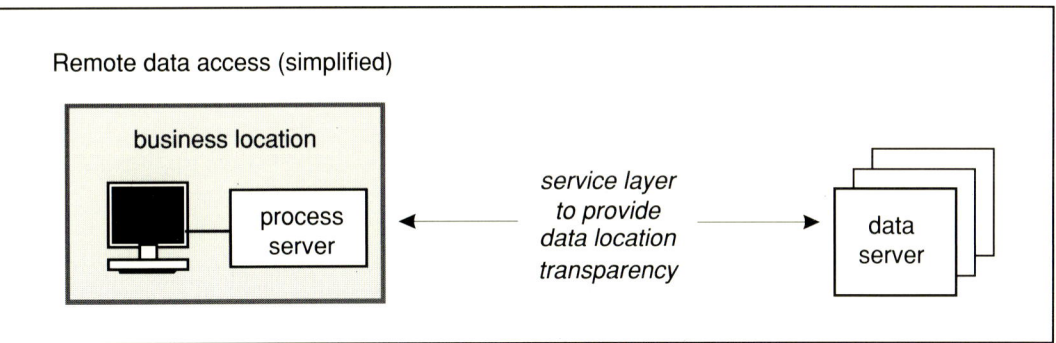

Figure 3.7: *Remote data access - user-interface server and process server on the same platform*

When data is needed the commit unit requests it from the data server. Ideally, this would be a distributed DBMS that keeps track of where the required entity instances are. In practice, almost all current products need location information. Access to entity location indexes can be hidden inside a program-data interface, to preserve data location transparency for the commit units.

It may be necessary for reasons of robustness or performance to replicate data at different locations. This should also be masked by the service layer or hidden inside a program-data interface.

Remote procedure call

Commit units can be stored with the data they use. See Figure 3.8. Not all the data needed might be stored at the same location as the methods in the commit unit, in which case process servers will have to issue remote database calls, as described in the preceding section.

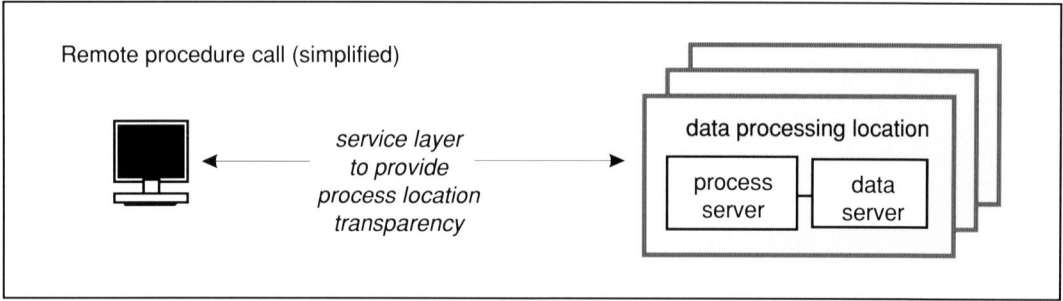

Figure 3.8: Remote procedure call - calls to complete commit units at the same locations as data

If the instances of an entity type have been partitioned horizontally (ie by row - for detailed description see Section 6.4.2), and partitions placed at different locations, there are two strategies for placing conceptual processes:

- place one copy of the relevant commit units at one data storage location, and access other locations remotely. This would be necessary if the process had to treat all selected instances as a single set

- place a copy of the relevant commit units at each data storage location that stores a partition of the required entity type(s). This could be done if copies of the process could work independently on local partitions. This allows parallel working, and reduces the scope of locking in the system.

Most currently-available DBMSs or network managers will need to know which nodes to access to invoke the methods. This could be hidden from the external process in an external-conceptual interface, analogous to a program-data interface. However, this concept is not very well-developed in practice.

'Client/server' A commit unit as described in both BOS Engineering Method and SSADM is hierarchical, with the externally-input data at the top of the hierarchy. Sub-hierarchies may be cut off from the main structure, and placed on one or more process servers, or perhaps on the same platform as the data server for the relevant data. See Figure 3.9. This can also be done with partitioning of data either horizontally (by row) or vertically (by column).

The high-level structures of the commit units are retained at the workstations and they, not the procedures in the external design, act as the clients.

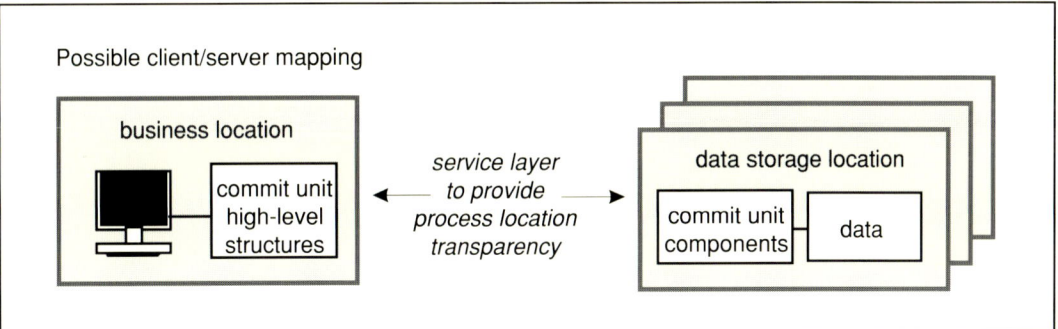

Figure 3.9: 'Client/server' - lower-level commit unit components placed on one or more process servers

Process servers that serve user-interface servers may themselves be clients of other process servers.

Distributed object-oriented database

We can extend the idea, introduced in the previous section on 'client/server', of implementing the commit unit as several related processes. The lowest unit of decomposition is the method (the effect of one business event or one enquiry on one object class).

Methods can be encapsulated with their object classes; the commit unit then becomes a network of invocations of object classes. See Figure 3.10. Note that methods need to be encapsulated with the object class - the instance variables could be stored elsewhere.

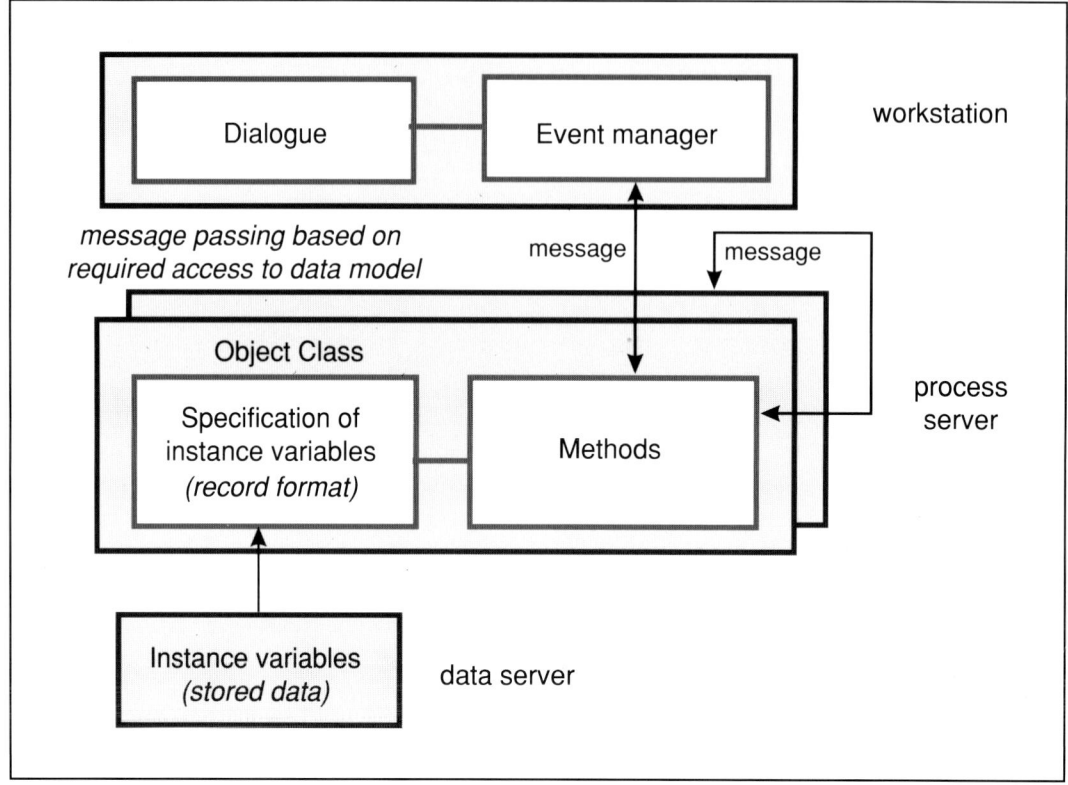

Figure 3.10: Commit unit split between event manager and smallest possible units, ie methods

We don't have to have an object database to implement this. It could be implemented on a client/server platform, or on a conventional network or relational database. The 'event manager' is a process that handles the externally-input data, breaks it down into messages used to invoke objects, and consolidates the responses into the output expected by the external design. See Figure 3.11.

Chapter 3
Approach/Philosophy

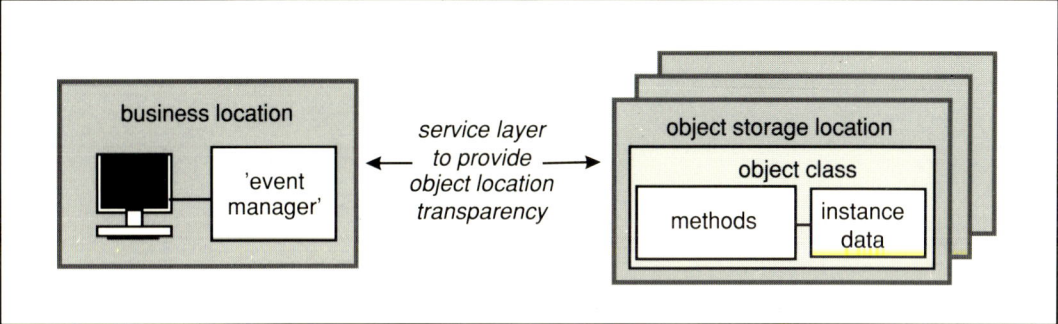

Figure 3.11: Distributed object-oriented database - conceptual process distributed by object class

3.4 Design approach   This section:

- summarises the design principles which underlie the approach to designing a distributed system (3.4.1)

- describes the design principles (3.4.2 - 3.4.8)

- lists the decisions which address distribution requirements (3.4.9)

- summarises the design approach (3.4.10).

3.4.1 Summary of design principles   The design principles can be summarised as follows:

- concepts of distributed system design are defined in terms of a 3-schema Specification Architecture (3.2)

- a distributed system is a coordinated system (3.4.2)

- systems that serve different location types can be coordinated on entity aspects (3.4.3)

- logical design should be independent of architectures (3.4.4)

- data location should be transparent up to the limits imposed by robustness requirements (3.4.5)

- process location should be transparent to the user

- technical architectures are packages of required services (3.4.6)

- logical requirements are mapped to architectures via required services (3.4.7)

- distribution-related concepts are identified in logical requirements (3.4.8).

3.4.2 A distributed system is a coordinated system

A distributed system requires that related activities be coordinated - ie that what happens in one activity should be consistent with what happens in other related activities when viewed by an external observer, wherever those activities are located.

The coordination of activities may be:

- **tight**: if communication is not possible between locations for a group of related activities, then none of the activities in the group can succeed

- **loose**: if communication is not possible between locations for a group of related activities, then some activities may succeed; the other activities in the group must be carried out, and consistency established when communication between locations is again possible.

It is possible to have both tight and loose coordination in the same system.

Some systems that operate in several locations are uncoordinated - locations can inform each other about what they are doing but each location is free to take notice of the other's communication when and if it decides to do so. They are regarded as separate systems that can communicate with each other. Design of uncoordinated systems and the communication between them is not addressed by this volume.

3.4.3 Systems that serve different location types can be coordinated on entity aspects

An entity aspect is a view of some more-widely-defined entity type. We define aspects so that we can develop separate specifications (attributes, relationships, events, enquiries) for an entity type that appears in more than one context - different projects, different subsystems, different location types etc. There may be requirements for different contexts to communicate, eg an enquiry that spans different location types, a common server for several projects. How this is handled in BOS Engineering Method and SSADM is described in Part 2.

Logical data modelling accommodates aspects fairly easily; they can be treated as if they were entities in one-to-one relationship. And although aspect modelling is a useful extension of logical data modelling, it is applied only to entity types that are shared between different contexts.

Corporate entities and project aspects

Suppose, for example, that EU-Rent is one of three businesses - car rental, hotels and an airline. They are run separately and have their own business and IT systems, but share their customer base; many of the car rental customers also fly EU-Fly and stay at EU-Stay hotels.

EU-Corporation may decide to manage customer data at corporate level. It makes sense for all three business areas to have consistent customer information on current address, telephone number, credit rating etc. It may be useful to know in each system when there are problems with a customer in other systems. And it may be possible to run promotions in one system, based on what we know about customers from other systems.

The entity defined in the EU-Rent project data model is an **aspect** of the corporate customer. It models customer behaviour in the car rental business. See Figure 3.12.

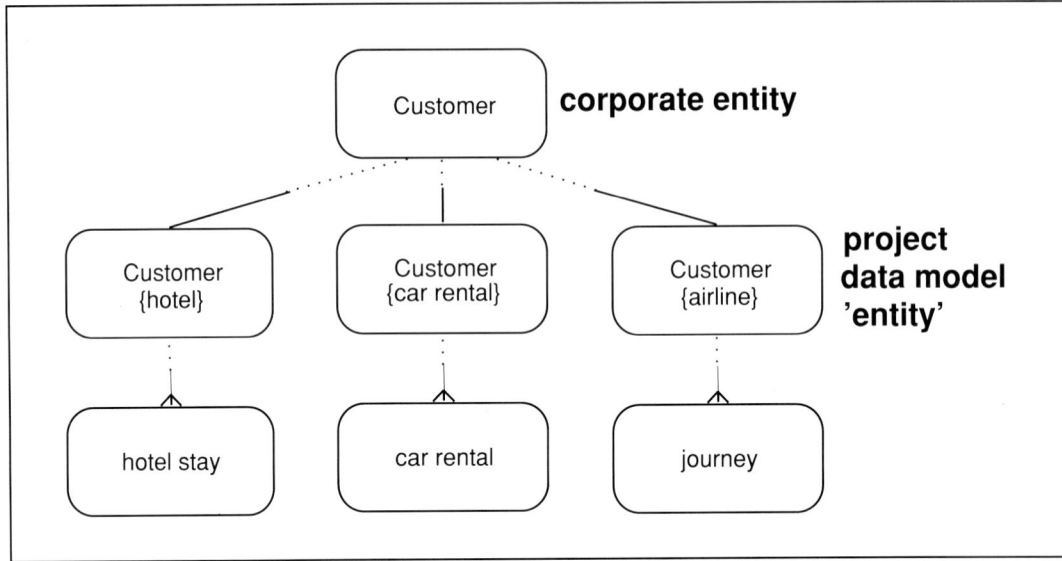

Figure 3.12: Aspects of the corporate entity 'customer'

Whether use of corporate aspects affects distributed system design depends on the implementation (decided as part of a strategy, not within a project). There are, broadly, two approaches:

- to copy down the corporate attributes into the project database. This leads to some replication of customer information across projects but leaves each project self-contained, with one exception. When 'corporate' attributes are updated, a message must be fired off to the other systems, and similar messages may be received from other systems

- to have a corporate server for customer information, serving all three systems. We have to take communication with the server into account when calculating costs, estimating performance and analysing robustness.

Project partitioning

Within a project, we may want to divide the data model into more-or-less self-contained subsets. There might be three reasons for doing this:

- to allow detailed analysis and specification to proceed in parallel (this is an extension of the 'corporate entity' concept)

- to divide the project into parts to be delivered at different times (even if it is to be installed all in one place). We might call this 'distribution over time'

- to map the database (and invocations of event and enquiry processing) of the project on to different location types; subsystems for different types of location could, of course, be delivered at different times.

Where an entity type is needed in more than one subsystem we can separate it into aspects.

The approach we take is:

- identify entity types that are shared between two or more types of location.

  For example, in EU-Rent, customers are used by head office and branch, car service bookings are used by branch and service depot

- separate shared entity types into aspects, each modelling the behaviour of the entity type at a location type.

  For example, in EU-Rent, the head office view is that a real-world person is a customer at some car rental branch(es); if airline and hotel systems are integrated with car rentals, the head office view is that a real-world person is a customer of at least one car rental branch, hotel or flight. The branches view of customer is that he rents cars.

For example, in EU-Rent, one of the options considered is to hold basic customer data at head office and manage rentals at branches. See Figure 3.13. If we define head office and branch aspects we can analyse them (in terms of attributes, enquiries and updates) as if they were separate entity types in one-to-one correspondence.

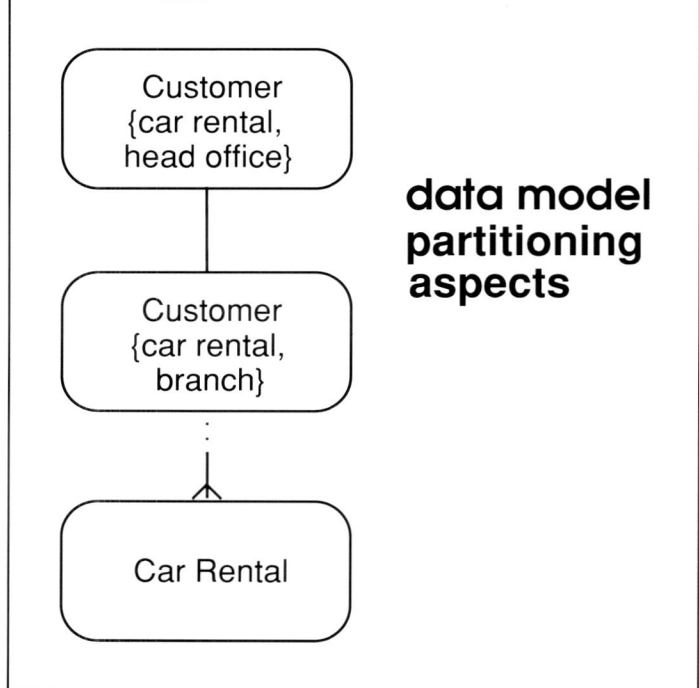

Figure 3.13: Head office and branch aspects of customer

Separating the customer into head office and rental aspects simply separates the specification of customer behaviour (attributes, relationships, enquiries and updates) into two parts that can be located independently of each other. It does not commit us to a physical mapping. There are several possibilities for physical management of customer processing that originates from branches:

- the customer-rentals data and processes might be stored at the branch

- the customer-rentals data and processes might be stored at head office, with remote procedure call from the branch

- the customer-rentals data might be stored at head office, and the processes at the branch, with remote database access to head office.

Aspects and inheritance

Using aspects gives a consistent way of modelling entity behaviour from corporate model to entity within subsystem.

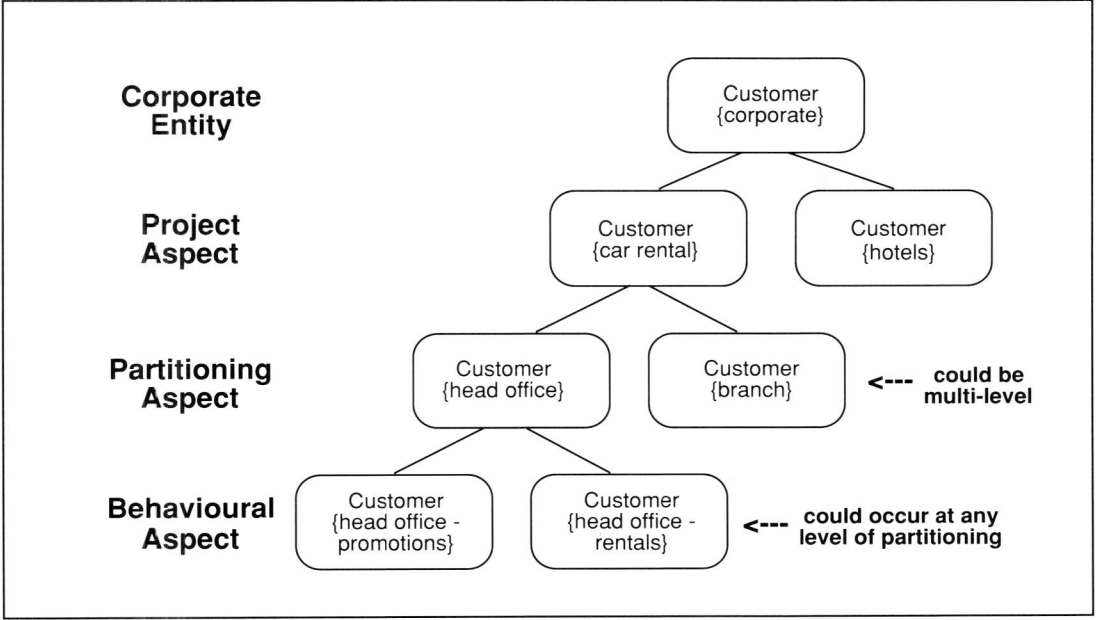

Figure 3.14: Concurrent aspects of same real world entity

It is easy to visualise how an aspect within a project could inherit the data and processes of its corporate entity, or how a branch aspect could inherit the data and processes of its head office entity. However, pictures like that in Figure 3.14 should not be confused with subtype hierarchies (class hierarchies in OO).
One-to-one relationships 'coming down' a subtype hierarchy are mutually exclusive.

All aspects of a single entity instance can exist concurrently. And (in theory, at least) an entity aspect can invoke any other aspect of the same entity in event or enquiry processing. This goes beyond the usual concept of inheritance.

3.4.4 Logical design should be independent of architectures

When a decision has been taken to develop a coordinated system, a common approach is taken to the specification of requirements and logical design. Technical architecture(s) for implementation are selected after the logical design has been developed.

The design approach is described as an extended version of BOS Engineering Method and as an extended version of SSADM in Part 2 of the volume.

3.4.5 Data location should be transparent up to the limits imposed by robustness requirements

Ideally, location of data should be completely transparent. When an application accesses data in a distributed system it should not be apparent whether the data is held locally, or retrieved from some other location. There should be a software service layer that maps data requests to the appropriate location. It should be possible to move data from one location to another without the need to modify the application.

Robustness of a distributed system is defined in terms of the services each type of location must provide when communication with other types of location is not possible. Some of these services will be provided in degraded form if data from other locations is not accessible. This degradation must be designed into the applications - they must be able to work even when some of the data they would normally access is unavailable.

There is no rule on how to reconcile these conflicting requirements; it is a trade-off. The approach taken in this volume is to maximise transparency of data location, then gradually compromise it until robustness requirements can be satisfied.

Part of the solution may be to replicate data at different locations. If so, data replication must also be transparent to applications. If replicated data is not always synchronised (ie some copies may be older than others), applications may need to recognise the currency of data (without needing to know where it is stored) and report it on end-user outputs.

3.4.6 Technical architectures are packages of required services

The technical architectures assumed to be available are:

- distributed database management systems:

    - remote database access without distributed commit

    - remote database access with distributed commit

- distributed transaction processing

- object-oriented distributed transaction processing

- electronic mail.

They are described in Chapter 5.

Technical architectures are not the starting points for system architectures. They are seen as ways of providing services needed to support requirements defined in the logical design, and reflecting the business needs.

Where technologies have been imposed on the system (because of procurement policy or already-installed hardware, software and network) it may be necessary to implement additional services needed to support logical requirements but not provided by the technology.

3.4.7 Logical requirements are mapped to architectures via required services

The types of service needed to support distribution-related concepts are assumed to be:

- information exchange services:

    - remote database access

    - transparency of data location

    - transparency of data replication

    - message exchange

- process cooperation services:

    - remote processing

- distributed commit management

- security services.

They are described in Chapter 5, together with a table indicating which technical architectures support which services.

After requirements, including the distribution-related concepts (see 3.4.8), have been defined at a logical level, the services needed to support them are identified. Then, technical architecture(s) are selected which can best provide the required services.

The choice of technical architecture may be constrained by hardware and software procurement policy, or by requirements to be compatible with already-installed technology.

3.4.8 Distribution-related concepts are identified in logical requirements

The major distribution-related concepts used in this volume are:

- business-related:

  - distributed system

  - business location type and instance

  - actor type & instance

  - role played by actor (at business location)

- data-processing-related:

  - distributed data processing system

  - data processing location type and instance

  - workstation (linking business location instance to data processing location instance)

- mapping of data and process to location:

- support for user activity by user-interface server (to be used by actor at business location)

- availability of automated process at data processing location

- storage of data at data processing location.

They are described in Chapter 4.

Distribution-related concepts are included in logical requirements before technical architectures are considered.

3.4.9 Decisions which address distribution requirements	BOS Engineering Method and SSADM both provide guidance for development of a system at a single data processing location. When either method is used (as extended in this volume) for a distributed system, additional decisions are needed that address distribution requirements. These decisions are described in detail in 6.3, but can be briefly summarised as:

- decisions taken before the project, perhaps as part of a strategy. They include:

  - whether to use already installed technology, (or accept a procurement policy that constrains the choice of technology)

  - recognising the effect of external requirements, such as legal constraints on where data may be held

- whether to build one coordinated system or several uncoordinated systems. Factors that need to be taken into account include:

  - functional requirements

  - cost

  - stability of design

- robustness vs. consistency

- distribution of data:

  - partitioning of data

  - replication of data

- distribution of processing (using the 3-schema processing architecture):

  - assignment of internal processes to data processing locations

  - assignment of external processes to user-interface servers (at business locations)

  - replication of processes.

The mapping of these decisions to BOS Engineering Method and to SSADM is described in Part 2.

3.4.10 Summary of design approach

The approach for design of a distributed system can be summarised as:

- decide on a coordinated distributed system. Note that:

  - this decision may have been taken at a strategic level

  - a distributed system may be an option to be compared with a centralised system

- use BOS Engineering Method or SSADM to develop requirements and a logical design. Define data and processing specifications as if for a single, integrated system, with the addition of:

  - business geography (business locations and actor roles)

  - data processing locations

  - estimates of traffic between locations

  - robustness requirements

- map external processes to user-interface servers and, further, to workstation types at business location types, duplicating processes as necessary

- partition the data in the system across data processing locations (heuristics are provided to support this), and allocate the corresponding conceptual processes to those locations

  Assume initially that (at the instance level) there is no replication of data

- carry out a robustness analysis. Introduce compromises into the design to satisfy robustness requirements:

  - replicate data

  - specify degradation in some services when part of the required data is not accessible

  - identify services that will not be available when communication lines are down

- identify the services needed to support logical requirements, and select the technical architectures that best provide them:

  - the selection may be constrained by installed technology or procurement policy

  - the project may have to develop software for some of the required services

- specify the physical design (detailed guidance is outside the scope of this volume)

  - map the logical design on to the selected technology

  - analyse performance and modify the design to reduce/remove performance problems

  - produce component specifications for implementation.

4 Distribution concepts

4.1 Introduction

During the analysis and design of a distributed system we record facts that describe distribution on several levels of abstraction. In this chapter we define abstract concepts needed to classify and record these facts. We define these concepts and their relationships in a meta model.

Most of the concepts defined in the meta model are specific to distributed systems. However, we have included some concepts that have a particular importance in the context of distribution, even though they are equally applicable to centralised systems.

Concepts in the meta model can be classified into business concepts and data processing concepts. Both categories can be subdivided into location concepts, processing concepts and object/data concepts. Figure 4.1 shows the categories of concepts and how they fit into the 3-schema Specification Architecture. Each category is defined in one section of this chapter. (The full meta model is provided in Annex A). The final section, Section 4.8, specifies the concepts needed to record volumetric information for logical and physical design.

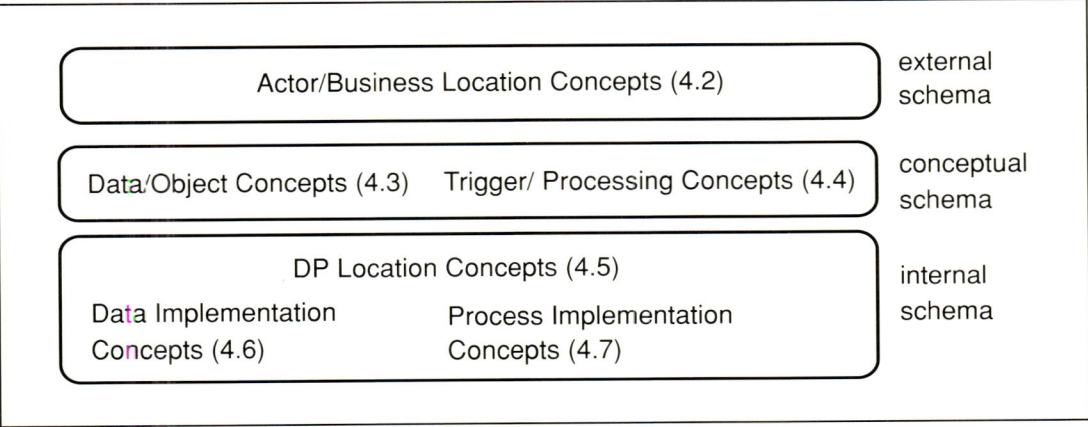

Figure 4.1: Categories of distribution concepts mapped on to 3-schema Specification Architecture

The meta model contains the important concepts that classify the facts used to describe a distributed system. Usually the described system will be designed to be robust against component failures. The meta model concepts could also describe a non-robust version of the system. We do not discuss the relationships between robust and non-robust descriptions of the same system.

The meta model is not intended to define a repository structure: it should, nevertheless, provide a good starting point.

In the following sections meta model concepts are italicised where they are defined, which is not necessarily where they first appear.

4.2 Actor/business location concepts

A *Location Instance* is a location that can be identified uniquely and usually corresponds to a site whose position on a map, postal address and possibly position within that address can be specified. *Business Location Instances* and *Data Processing Location Instances* (*DP Location Instances*) need to be distinguished. See Figure 4.2. However, at some Location Instances both business and data processing take place. Such a Location Instance corresponds to a Business Location Instance and a DP Location Instance.

For example, the EU-Rent branch at Munich Airport and the EU-Rent head office in London are Business Location Instances. See Figure 4.3. In Frankfurt there is a DP Location Instance that provides computing power to the branch at Munich Airport. There is a computer at head office in London, therefore the head office in London is also a DP Location Instance.

A *Distributed Information System* (*DI System*) is a set of coordinated Business Location Instances. A *Distributed Data Processing System* (*DDP System*) is a set of coordinated DP Location Instances.

A DI System is usually supported by a DDP System. In some cases, it may be supported by more than one. For example, a just-in-time logistics system may be supported by several companies' DDP Systems. On the other hand, a DDP System may support more than one DI System. For example, a production planning system and an accounting system may be supported by the same DDP System.

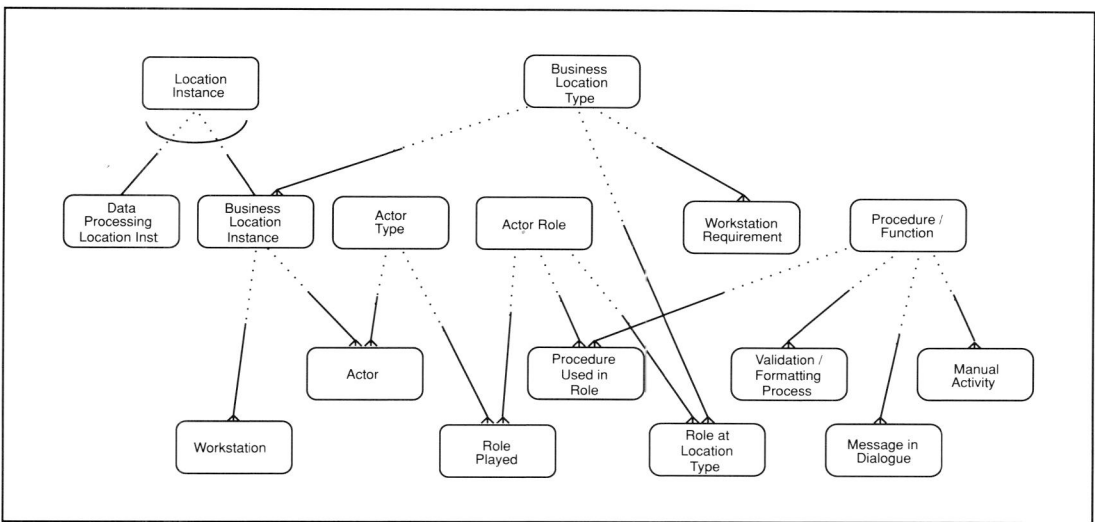

Figure 4.2: Actor/business location concepts

An *Actor* is an agent that carries out a task in an enterprise at a Business Location Instance. An Actor may be a human, a User and a DDP System, or in extreme cases a DDP System only. For example, in Figure 4.3, Mr. Schmidt is an Actor at the EU-Rent office at Munich Airport.

Usually an Actor will be a User, ie a human who executes a set of Procedures/Functions with the aid of a DDP System, and a DDP System. Each Actor is uniquely assigned to a Business Location Instance.

Humans who work at several Business Location Instances are treated as several Actors, each of whom can be assigned uniquely to a Business Location Instance. (This simplification is made because having actors who can move between Business Location Instances would complicate the meta model without contributing to the discussion of distributed systems.)

The processing in a business is carried out in units called Procedure/Functions. A *Procedure/Function* is a set of business activities that is seen as a unit from the business point of view. It is carried out by a single Actor in a relatively small time interval. For example, reservation of a car and pick-up are Procedures/Functions.

From a data processing point of view a Procedure/Function consists of a set of Manual Activities, a set of Messages in Dialogue and a set of Validation/Formatting Processes, and defines their possible sequences.

Actual business takes place at a Business Location Instance such as the EU-Rent office at Munich Airport. At a Business Location Instance, Actors do their job by carrying out Procedures/Functions. For this, Actors generally need the services of a DDP System, ie automated Procedures/Functions and stored Data.

The services of a DDP System are provided at a Business Location Instance by a set of *Workstations*, which enable Users to invoke automated Procedures/Functions and to use Data stored by the DDP System.

A DI System usually involves a large number of Actors and Location Instances. We need classifications that allow us to talk about properties of whole sets of Actors and Location Instances.

The Procedures/Functions carried out by an Actor are classified by Actor Role; ie an *Actor Role* is a set of Procedures/Functions. Actor Roles are not arbitrary sets of Procedures/Functions; they contain Procedures/Functions that satisfy closely related tasks. Common tasks in similar jobs are amalgamated into single Actor Roles. For example station management, rental processing and maintenance processing are Actor Roles.

Chapter 4
Distribution concepts

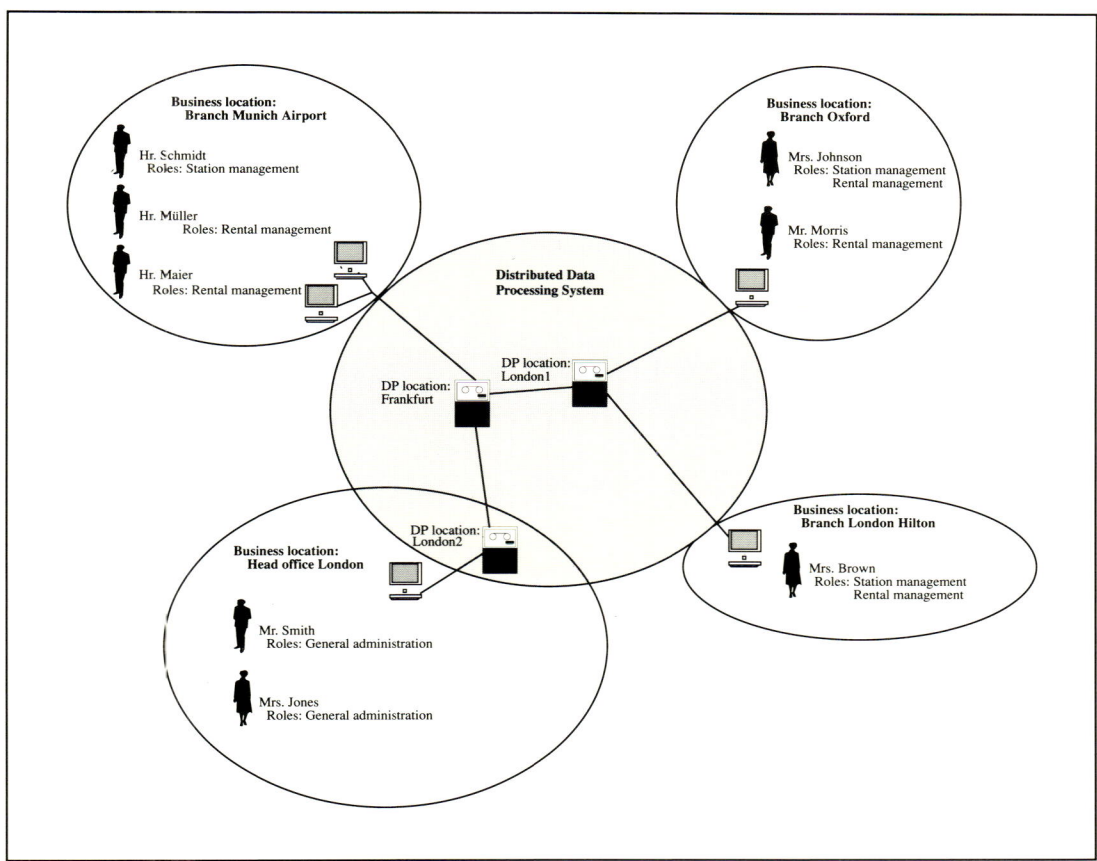

Figure 4.3: Examples of actors, business and DP locations

Actors are classified by Actor Type. An *Actor Type* is a classification of Actors according to similar tasks or jobs. An Actor Type is defined by a set of Actor Roles. For example, station manager is an Actor Type. Two of his or her Actor Roles are station management and rental processing. Another example is the Actor Type business clerk with the Actor Roles rental processing and maintenance processing. The jobs of Actors may overlap, ie Actors of different Actor Type may carry out the same Actor Roles.

Business Location Instances are classified by Business Location Types. A *Business Location Type* denotes a set of Business Location Instances where the same Actor Roles are played. Examples of Business Location Types are depot, branch and head office in EU-Rent.

The Actor Roles assigned to a Business Location Type indirectly specify the set of Procedures/Functions and Data that is needed in a Business Location Instance of this Business Location Type.

Each Business Location Type has a set of *Workstation Requirements* that result from the Actor Roles that make up this Business Location Type.

4.3 Data/object concepts

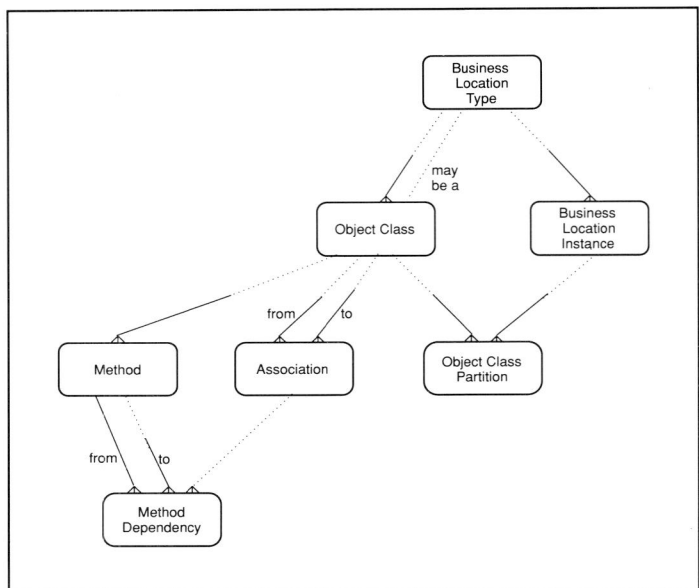

Figure 4.4: Data/object concepts

A DI System manipulates Object Instances. An *Object Instance* is something, whether concrete or abstract, which is of importance to the DI System being investigated. An Object Instance has a state, a behaviour and an identity. For example each car group, car booking and branch are Object Instances.

Object Instances are represented in the DDP System by Data and a set of Methods that manipulates this Data. In the simplest case, an Object Instance corresponds to a single entity in a conventional database environment. It may, however, correspond to several entities.

In this meta model, *Data* is a representation of information in a formalised manner suitable for communication, interpretation or processing by human beings or automated means.

Object Instances are classified by *Object Class* according to similarity of structure and behaviour. See Figure 4.4. The structure of an Object Class is defined by the structure of the Data of the Object Instances in the Object Class. A set of Methods defines the uniform behaviour of Object Instances in an Object Class.

A Business Location Type may correspond to an Object Class. For example, the Business Location Types branch and depot correspond to Object Classes.

In a conventional database environment an Object Class corresponds to an entity type or a set of closely related entity types.

An *Association* is a relationship type between two Object Classes (or one Object Class and itself). Each instance of an Association, which relates Objects, has to conform to its relationship type. In relational data modelling, an Association is called a relationship. In most object-oriented literature the term Association is used.

A *Method* is a function on the Data of an Object. Changing the Data of an Object changes the state of the Object. As a side effect, a Method may cause the data of other Objects to change by calling Methods in those Objects. If this is the case the Method depends on other Methods, because if they fail then it must also fail. Such a *Method Dependency* may correspond to an Association between Object Classes.

An Object Class may naturally belong to a Business Location Type. For example in EU-Rent it is business policy that cars are owned by branches. Therefore, the Object Instances representing cars in the EU-Rent DI-System naturally belong to the Business Location Type branch. However, not all Object Classes naturally belong to a Business Location Type. For example, the Object Instances representing customers in the EU-Rent DI-System do not naturally belong to a Business Location Type.

The distribution of Objects amongst Business Location Instances is described by Object Class Partitions. An *Object Class Partition* is a set of Object Instances of a given Object Class that belongs to a Business Location Instance.

An Object Class Partition may result from the fact that an Object Class naturally belongs to a Business Location Type. For example, in EU-Rent cars are owned by branches and so each branch owns a partition of the Object Class car. Usually each Object Instance of such an Object Class has an attribute that denotes the Business Location Instance to which it naturally belongs. All of the Object Instances of such an Object Class, which belong to the same Business Location Instance, make up an Object Class Partition.

Other Object Class Partitions result from design decisions, which define the Business Location Instance to which a set of Object Instances, of a given Object Class, belong.

4.4 Trigger/processing concepts

The details of a Procedure/Function are specified by a set of Manual Activities, a set of Messages in Dialogue and a set of Validation/Formatting Processes. See Figure 4.5. A *Manual Activity* is a part of a Procedure/Function to be carried out manually by a human Actor or User. A User communicates with a DDP System by a set of Messages in Dialogue. This communication is supported by a set of Validation/Formatting Processes.

The Messages in Dialogue are classified into DP Input Messages and DP Output Messages.

A *DP Input Message* is a set of Data entered together into a DDP System via an input device. For example, a User might type in a request for reservation of a car (see Figure 4.6). Thus a *Message in Dialogue* is always a set of Data that has a direct meaning in the application context. Usually, low level input and output, for example a pressed key or a scanned character, are not treated as self-contained Messages in Dialogue.

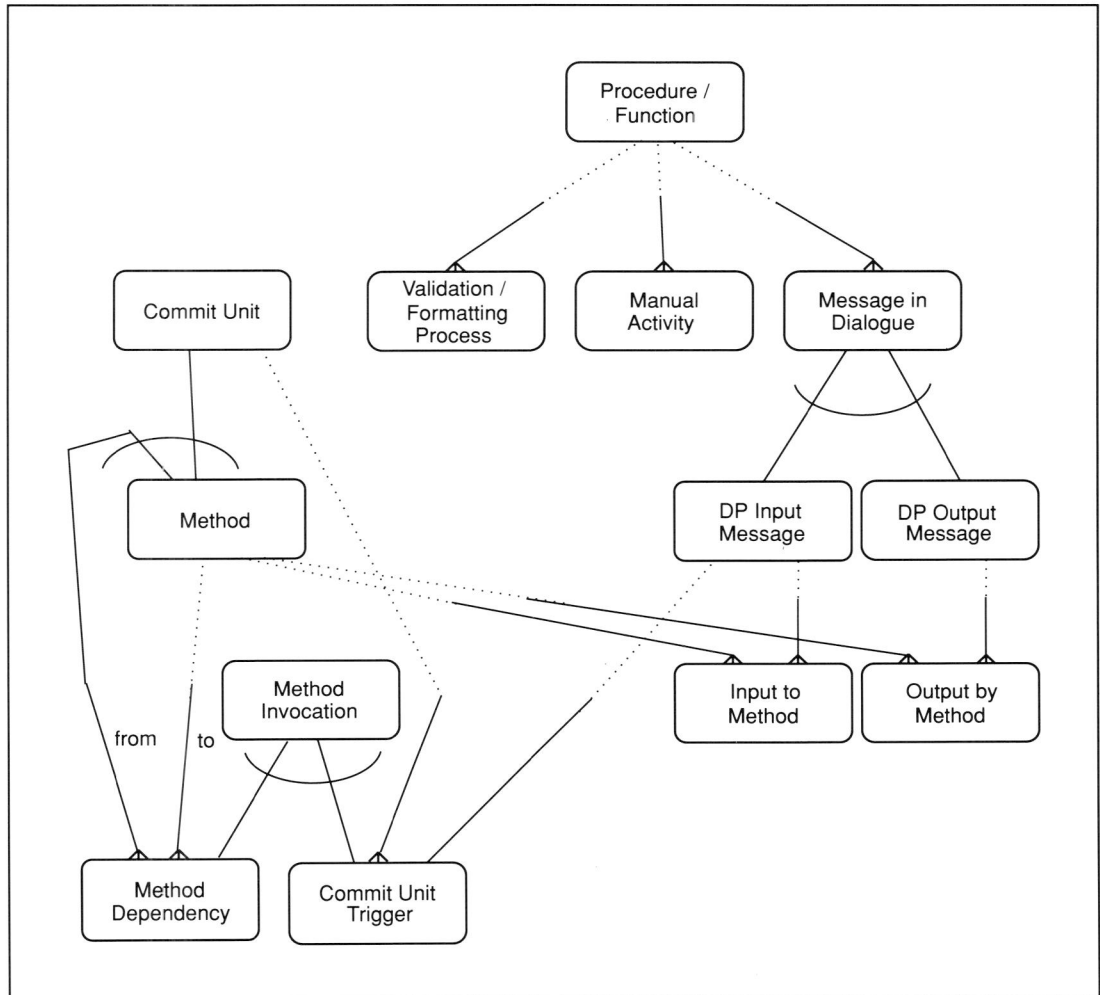

Figure 4.5: Trigger/processing concepts

A *DP Output Message* is a set of Data that is sent together to an output device of the DDP System, for example an acknowledgement of a car reservation (see Figure 4.6).

A *Validation/Formatting Process* covers the processing required at the user interface for a part of a Procedure/Function which validates input, by for example checking syntax and type, and which presents output. A typical example of a Validation/Formatting Process is the processing carried out by a graphical user interface.

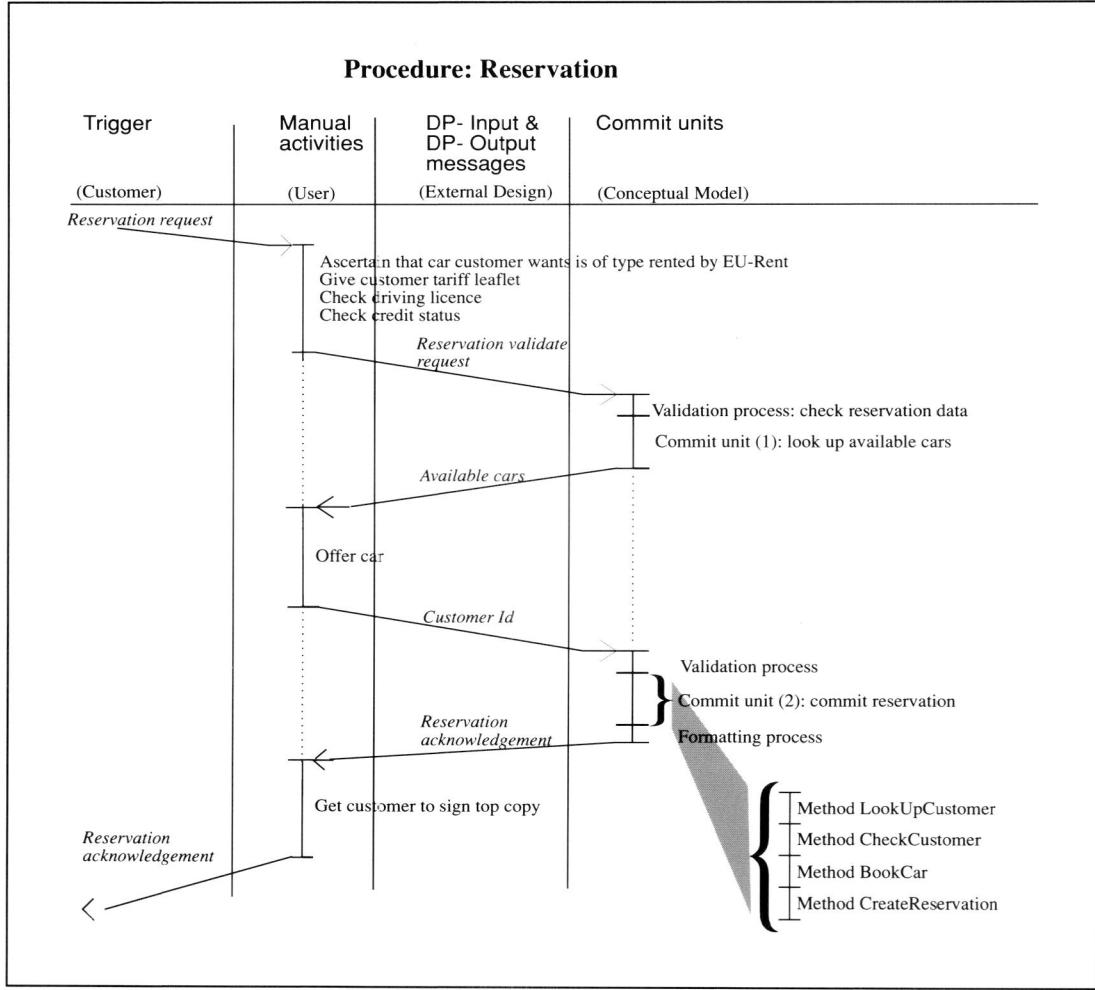

Figure 4.6: Examples of procedures, commit units and methods

Most DP Input Messages are required for the execution of Methods; they correspond to *Inputs to Method*. Other DP Input Messages may be required by the system software. Most DP Output Messages result from the execution of Methods and correspond to *Outputs by Method*.

Users invoke DDP System processing via DP Input Messages. DP Input Messages that result in invocation of Commit Units are called Commit Unit Triggers. Some DP Input Messages do not correspond to a Commit Unit

Trigger. For example, a note sent to the screen of another User.

A *Commit Unit* is a set of Methods to be executed in accordance with the ACID properties, ie the set of methods should be atomic, consistency preserving, isolated and durable:

- atomic means that either all the Methods in the Commit Unit are executed or the Commit Unit is not executed at all

- consistency preserving requires that a Commit Unit either brings all the affected Objects into a new valid state or, if the Commit Unit is terminated, returns the Objects to the states they were in before the update started (by a process known as 'rollback')

- a Commit Unit is isolated if during its execution the state changes imposed on to Objects are not visible to other Commit Units. Only if a Commit Unit is completed successfully is its impact on the Object states visible to other Commit Units

- a Commit Unit is durable if the changes made by a successfully completed Commit Unit are not lost because of system breakdowns. In a conventional database environment a Commit Unit corresponds to a transaction.

Each Commit Unit has a start Method, which is the Method invoked by a Commit Unit Trigger. A Commit Unit may have a set of Commit Unit Triggers. A *Commit Unit Trigger* can be the arrival of a DP Input Message, a defined point in time, or a change in the internal state of the DDP System.

A Commit Unit Trigger starts the execution of a Commit Unit by invoking the start Method in the Commit Unit. The start of a Method is called a *Method Invocation*. This usually involves the passing of input parameters and transfer of control to the invoked Method.

Methods do not have to be invoked by a Commit Unit Trigger. A Method Invocation may be initiated by another Method; there is a Method Dependency corresponding to this Method Invocation.

The set of Methods that make up a Commit Unit is defined by the start Method of the Commit Unit and all Methods on which the start Method depends, either directly or indirectly.

4.5 DP location concepts

The services of a DDP System are provided by DP Location Instances. Hardware and system software are located at a DP Location Instance. Data may also be stored there.

A *Workstation* is a set of devices that allows a User to interact with a DDP System at a Business Location Instance. See Figure 4.7. Typically a Workstation consists of a keyboard, a mouse and a screen, sometimes a printer and a scanner.

Each Workstation is connected to a Data Processing Location Instance that provides computing power. Thus a Workstation links a Business Location Instance to a DP Location Instance. Both the Business Location Instance and the DP Location Instance may correspond to the same Location Instance, ie the processing power might directly be provided at the Location Instance where it is needed. An example of this is the London Headquarters of EU-Rent in Figure 4.3. A Workstation might also coincide with a Data Processing Location.

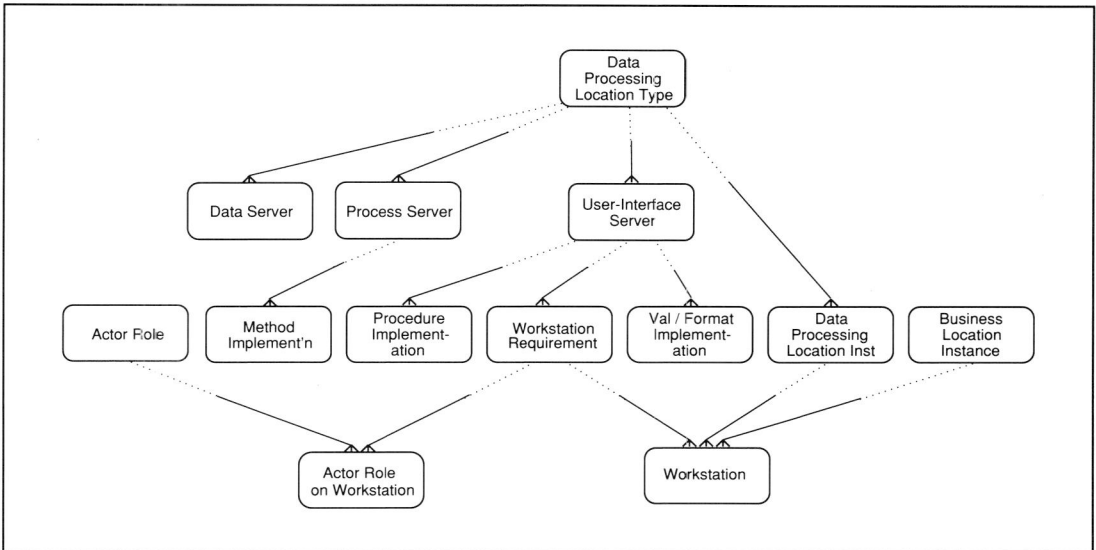

Figure 4.7: Data processing location concepts

Workstations are classified according to their potential to support Actor Roles. A *Workstation Requirement* is a set of Workstations that are capable of supporting the same set of Actor Roles. This classification of Workstations helps to abstract from hardware details that are irrelevant to the application under consideration. For example, a terminal with a 43 cm screen might be as good as a terminal with a 51 cm screen for a rental clerk in EU-Rent. Therefore in EU-Rent they belong to the same Workstation Requirement.

DP Location Instances are classified by DP Location Types according to their capability to store Data and execute application-specific processes. A *DP Location Type* is defined by:

- Data Server capabilities:

  - a set of Record Types the DP-Location Type is able to store

- Process Server capabilities:

  - a set of Method Implementations

- User-interface server capabilities:
    - a set of Procedure Implementations
    - a set of Validation/Formatting Implementations.

The definition of a DP Location Type specifies minimal hardware and system software capabilities that must be available at the DP Location Instances of that DP Location Type. Requirements for a DP Location Instance can be derived from:

- the data and processing needed by Actor Roles at the DP Location Instance
- the data and processing provided by the DP Location Type of the DP Location Instance.

A DP Location Type supports a set of Workstation Requirements.

4.6 Data implementation concepts

Data is stored by a DDP System in the form of Record Instances, where a *Record Instance* is a tuple of attribute values. Each Record Instance conforms to a *Record Type*, which is a named tuple of attribute names. If a DP Location Type is capable of storing a set of Record Types it acts as a Data Server. See Figure 4.8.

A *Data Server* is a software product that is capable of managing and storing Data, and providing access to this Data via an interface. For example, a relational Database with an SQL interface is a Data Server.

Each Data Server has the capability to store Record Instances of certain Record Types.

The set of Record Instances stored on a Data Server is given by its associated *Record Population Partitions*.

In the DDP System each Object Instance is represented by instances of one or more Record Types. The numbers of Object Instances and instances of Record Type are usually so large, that the mapping of Object Instances to instances of Record Type is defined at type level and not for individual instances.

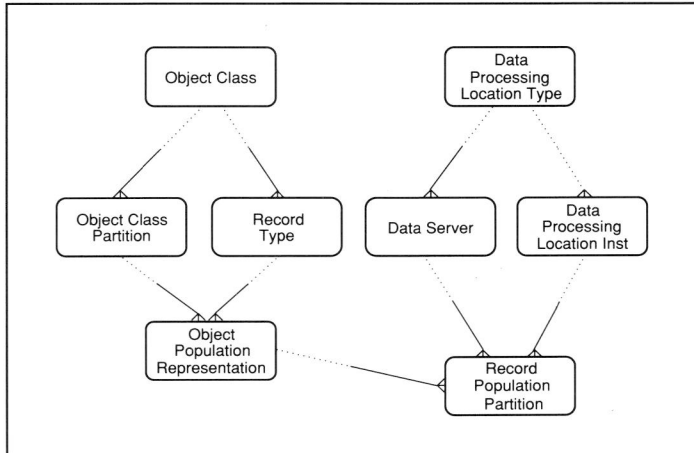

Figure 4.8: Data implementation concepts

Each Object Class is represented by one or more Record Types (see Figure 4.9). Record Types with the same tuple attribute names that represent different Object Classes are treated as separate Record Types. Representing one Object Class by several Record Types corresponds to vertical partitioning.

Details of the mapping of Object Instances to Record Instances are described at the *Object Class Partition* and Record Population Partition level by Object Population Representations.

An *Object Population Representation* is a mapping of an Object Class Partition on to a Record Population Partition. An Object Instance in a given Object Class Partition may map on to a set of Records, each of which may be stored at a different Data Processing Location Instance, ie belong to a different Record Population Partition.

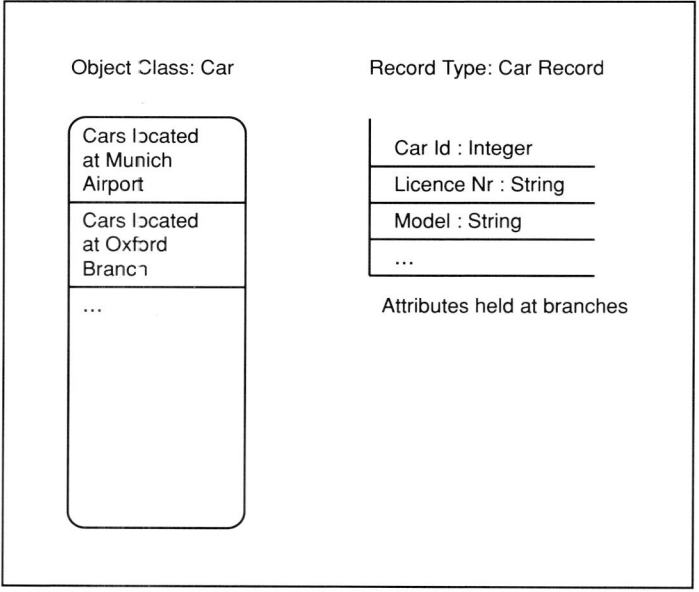

Figure 4.9: Example of the partitioning of the object class car

4.7 Process implementation concepts

A Data Processing Location Type may implement two types of processing capabilities (see Figure 4.10):

- Process Server: Implementations of the Methods as well as Method Invocations

- User-Interface Server: Implementations of the Functions/Procedures and Validation/Formatting Processes.

The parts of the code that implement the abstract Trigger/Processing concepts can be identified. A *Procedure Implementation* is the program code that implements a Procedure/Function. A Procedure Implementation mainly implements the chaining of the Messages in Dialogue and Validation/Format Processes that are assigned to a Procedure.

A *Validation/Format Process Implementation (Val/Format Implementation)* is the program code that implements a Validation/Formatting Process.

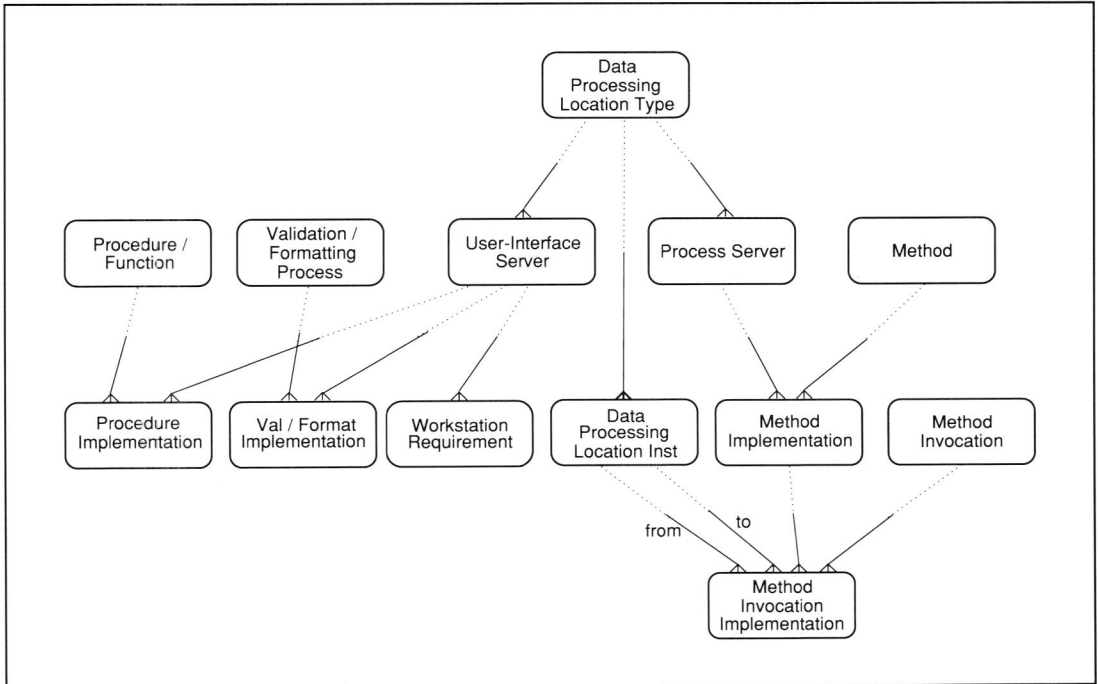

Figure 4.10: Process implementation concepts

A *Method Invocation Implementation* is the realisation of a Method Invocation on the implementation level, ie implementation of a Method Invocation. Possibilities include:

- a message passed by a message exchange service from one DP Location Instance to another

- a set of variables which contain the input parameters of the Method to be invoked

- a procedure call, either local or remote.

In all these cases mechanisms are needed to transfer control to the invoked Method.

4.8 Volumetrics

Important design decisions are guided by costs. In order to assess the costs of a design, volumetric information needs to be recorded.

The volumetric information that needs to be gathered depends on the project. Gathering volumetric information is time-consuming and costly, and is dependent on the availability and accessibility of the information. In some cases, only broad estimates may be possible.

Volumetric information can be gathered across a range of levels of abstraction and granularity. In Sections 4.8.1 and 4.8.2 we describe concepts for which volumes may need to be collected. In general, a distinction needs to be drawn between logical and physical design volumetrics.

4.8.1 Potential logical design volumetrics

Logical Design Volumetrics describe the size of the DI System in terms of the number of Business Location Instances and their activity profiles.

The number of Business Location Instances per Business Location Type can be counted. For example, we can count the number of EU-Rent branches.

The activity levels of Business Location Instances of a given Business Location Type are not usually uniform. Subclasses of Business Location Types, called *Business Location Type Activity Levels* (Business Location Types with defined Activity Levels), are identified. See Figure 4.11. These support, for example, the distinction between the number of airport branches and the number of hotel branches, which have different activity profiles.

An activity profile is defined by the frequency of Procedure/Function use and the associated numbers of Object Instances and Actors.

Actors can be counted by Actor Type. For example, we can count the number of booking clerks there are in EU-Rent. An *Actor Type at Location Type Activity Level* gives the number of Actors of a given Actor Type assigned to a Business Location Type Activity Level. For example, we can record the number of booking clerks per airport branch.

Chapter 4
Distribution concepts

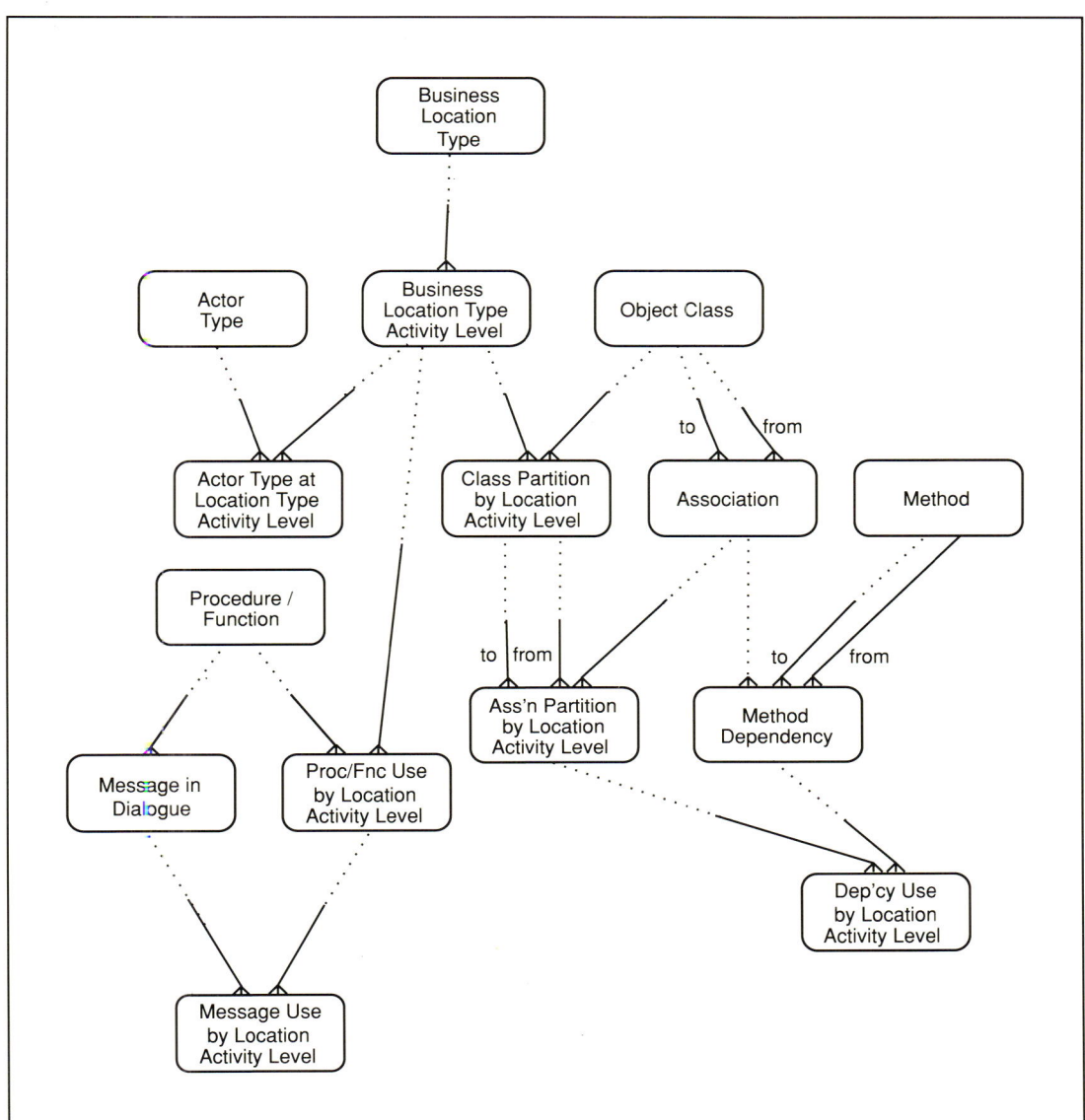

Figure 4.11: Potential logical design volumes

Object Instances can be counted by Object Class. For example, we can count the number of cars owned by EU-Rent. The number of Object Instances of a given Object Class per Business Location Type Activity Level is given by a *Class Partition by Location Activity Level*. For example, we can record the number of cars per airport branch is a Class Partition by Location Activity Level.

The frequency of Procedure/Function use per Business Location Type Activity Level is given by *Procedure/Function Use by Location Activity Level*. For example, we can record the number of walk-in rentals per airport branch.

The number of Messages in Dialogue per Business Location Type Activity Level is called Message Use by Location Type Activity Level. The *Message Use by Location Type Activity Level* depends on the number of Messages in Dialogue per Procedure/Function and on the Procedure/Function Use by Location Activity Level. The number of Messages in Dialogue per Procedure/Function is given in the Procedure/Function definition. The Message Use by Location Activity Level holds a count of, for example, the number of Messages in Dialogue per walk-in rental at an airport branch.

Cardinality of Associations, for example how many bookings there are per car, can be worked out from the number of Object Instances per Object Class providing the relationship is mandatory at both ends. An *Association Partition by Location Activity Level* gives the number of Associations relative to a Business Location Type Activity Level. The Association Partition by Location Activity Level depends on the Class Partition by Location Activity Level. For example, the number of bookings per car at airport branches is an Association Partition by Location Activity Level of the booking car Association.

Some Method Dependencies correspond to Associations; they hold counts of the frequency of use of an Association per Method Execution and can be counted. For example, we can count the number of times the booking car Association is used in pick-up.

The number of times an Association Partition by Location Activity Level is used per Method execution is given by *Dependency Use by Location Activity Level*. For example, we can record the number of times the booking car Association in an airport branch is used in pick-up.

Note that volumes given by Association Partition by Location Activity Level and Dependency Use by Location Activity Level need only be collected if

Association dependent volumes and Method Invocations are unevenly distributed between Business Location Type Activity Levels.

4.8.2 Potential physical design volumetrics

Physical Design Volumetrics are about requirements for storage and processing capabilities, and network capacity for a DDP System to support a DI System. See Figure 4.12. They also include data about the number of Workstations required at Business Location Instances.

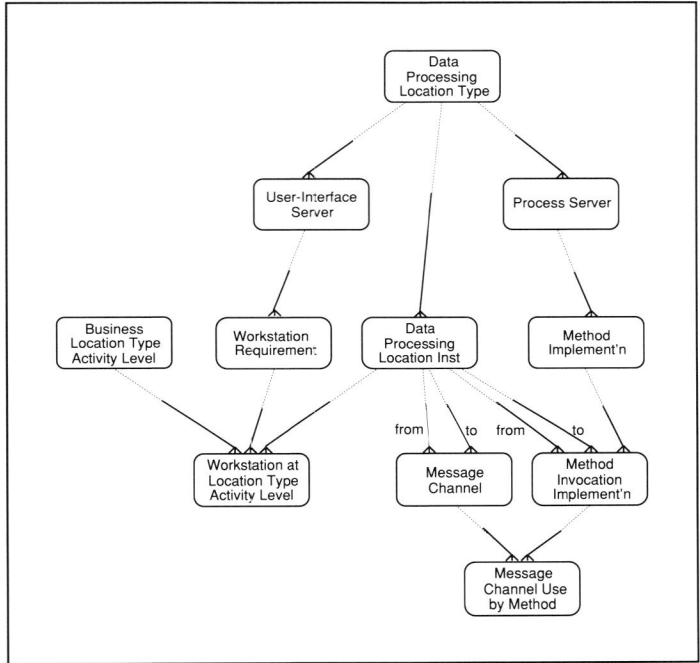

Figure 4.12: Potential physical design volumes

The number of DP Location Instances per DP Location Type can be counted. For example, the numbers of big branch DP Location Instances, depot-branch cluster DP Location Instances, branch cluster DP Location Instances, head office DP Location Instances and depot DP Location Instances.

To assess the hardware requirements of a DP Location Instance of a given DP Location Type, the amount of storage needed and the required processing speed have to be estimated.

The amount of storage needed at a DP Location Instance is given by the number of Record Instances that need to be stored there.

The number of Record Instances, of a given Record Type, can be worked out from the number of Object Instances per Object Class. For Object Classes that are not represented uniformly the partitioning of Object Classes by Location Activity Level and the different Object Population Representations have to be taken into account.

The required size of Data Servers is worked out by assigning to Data Servers, the number of Record Instances, of a given Record Type, that need to be stored at a DP Location Instance of a given DP Location Type. For example, the number of car Record Instances at a depot-branch cluster, ie a DP Location of EU-Rent that provides services to a certain number of depots and branches.

The required processing speed at a Business Location Instance, of a given Business Location Type depends on the number of executed Method Invocations.

For each Business Location Type the number of executed Methods can be assigned to the supported Method Implementations. This figure can be worked out from the number of executed Commit Units, ie start Method Implementations, called at a DP Location Instance of the given DP Location Type, by following the Method Invocation Implementations for the Method Dependencies.

The communication costs have to be based on communication volumetrics at the DP Location Instance level, because they depend on the topology of the communication network.

From a logical point of view, each DP Location Instance must be able to communicate with any other DP Location Instance. Physically, a message transfer may proceed via several intermediary DP Location Instances from the sending to the receiving DP Location Instance. Ideally, at physical design we would consider the traffic between each pair of DP Location Instances individually, but realistically we will only be able to consider traffic between DP Location Types.

Messages are transferred between two DP Location Instances by a Message Channel. A *Message Channel* is a point to point connection between two Data Processing Location Instances, via for example modems or a Datex-P connection, that is capable of transferring messages. The communication topology of a DDP System is defined by its set of Message Channels. (Message Channels have attributes which specify the DP Locations at either end.) A Message Channel is characterised by its transmission rate and transmission cost. Thus the utilisation of the Message Channels is the basis for assessing the communication cost.

The number of times each Method Invocation Implementation is called at a DP Location Instance has to be determined. This number can be determined from the number of Method executions at a DP Location Instance.

A Message Channel Use by Method records how many times a Message Channel is used for a Method Invocation at a DP Location. Message Channel Use by Method can be worked out from the type of Method Invocation Implementation.

The Message Channel utilisation then results from the sum of its associated Message Channel Uses by Method.

The number of Workstations needed is given by the Workstation Type Activity Levels. A Workstation Type Activity Level is the number of Workstations, corresponding to a given Workstation Requirement, at a Business Location Type Activity Level. For example, 10 terminals with 43 cm screens are needed at each airport branch of EU-Rent.

5 Cooperation services and architectures

5.1 Introduction

This chapter gives an overview of the basic technical facilities used to link data processing systems together.

Since there are many technical solutions available or under development Section 5.2 concentrates on different cooperation services that support the interaction of data processing systems. These are:

- information exchange services like remote database access together with location and replication transparency and high level message exchange

- process cooperation services like remote processing, and distributed commit management

- security services that gain more importance in the context of distributed systems.

In Section 5.3 different architectures of technical solutions are discussed. These architectures provide interfaces between applications and various combinations of cooperation services.

Section 5.4 summarises the mapping of abstract services to system architectures.

Finally, Section 5.5 discusses the current state of technological support for distribution services and architectures.

Architectures and cooperation services

A distributed data processing system is the automated part of a distributed system. We implement it on individual data processing locations which interact with each other. There are several architectural approaches to supporting the cooperation of these dp-systems. Each architecture provides, among other things, basic services for the application programs running on the dp-systems.

Application software is built on top of such an architecture; it consists of application programs providing application-specific processes. Some application programs have direct control of the user-interface. They are supported by other application programs that for example control access to the databases. A service-providing layer, via internal interfaces, maps requests to a hardware layer (see Figure 5.1):

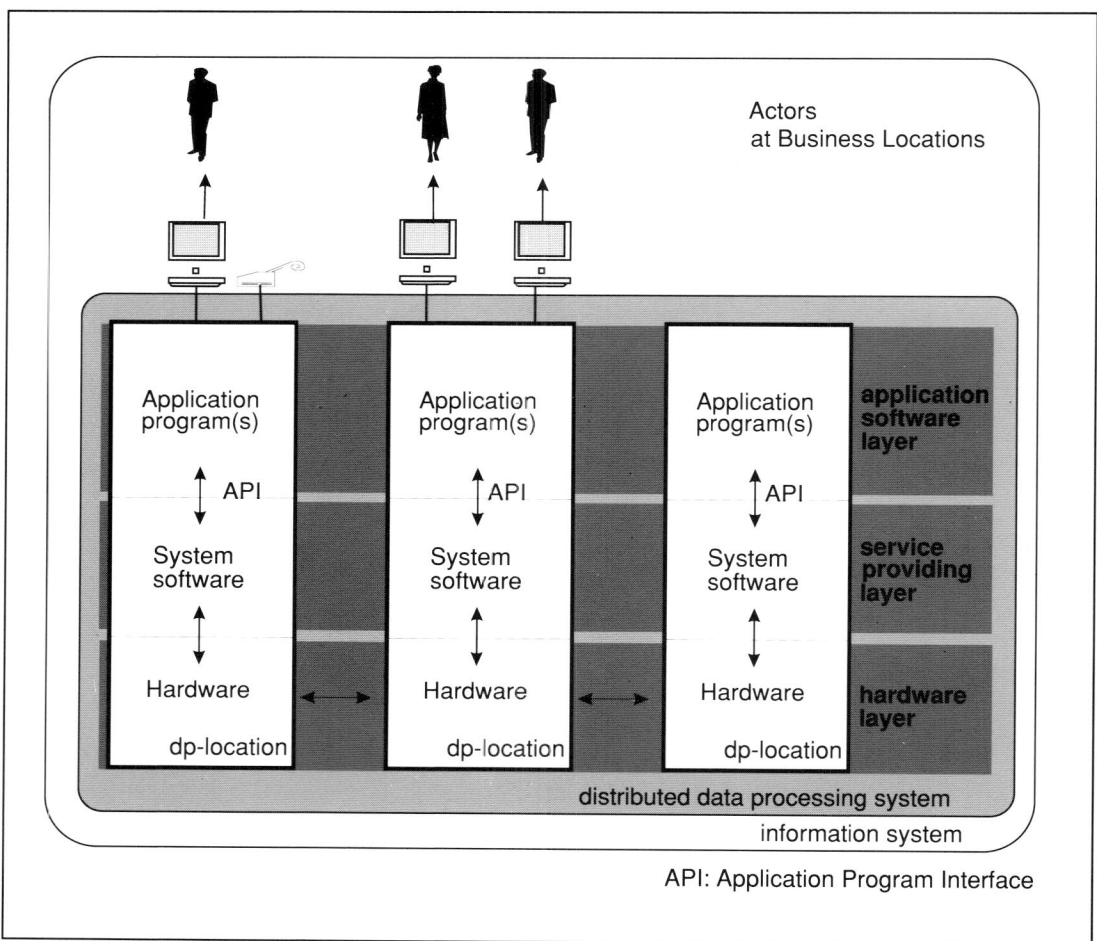

Figure 5.1: *Structuring of an information system with respect to system layers*

Application programs contain implementations of the processes of the conceptual model and the external design. (The conceptual model and external design were introduced in Section 3.2.) We consider the processes of the internal design to be part of the system software. In situations where internal design processes are required to support the application and are not provided as part of the system software they may need to be implemented explicitly. We do not discuss them further.

We do not attempt to define a single architecture suitable for all distributed systems. Instead, we describe in this chapter, in abstract, the types of cooperation service needed for implementation of distributed systems. Then we list typical architectures for distributed systems and the services they provide.

5.2 Abstract cooperation services

A server (here, one or more dp-systems) provides services to a client (here, an application program). An application program may not know which dp-systems are its servers; we describe a service-providing layer that is accessible via an application program interface (API) (see Figure 5.1).

Rather than going into the detail of specific implementations, we describe abstract services. They support interaction and coordination between application programs and the service-providing layer. These high-level cooperation services are mapped by system software to lower-level communication facilities, such as dial-up telephone lines or package switching connections (eg *CCITT Recommendation for X.25*). Application programs do not need direct access to these low-level facilities.

During logical design of a distributed system we need to consider services in two areas - information exchange and process cooperation.

5.2.1 Information exchange services

Remote database access (rda)

Remote database access provides access at one dp-location to data stored at another dp-location.

Typically, there is only one difference between accessing remote data (eg by using the *X/Open CAE Specification for SQL Remote Database Access*) and accessing local databases - the application has to specify where the data is in the former case. If the architecture supports data location transparency then, as far as the application is concerned, there is no difference.

Rda may also support data location transparency and replication transparency.

Data location transparency (dlt)

For data location transparency the service-providing layer manages the location of data. An application program will access data without specifying where in the distributed system it is. The service-providing layer maps the data requests to the appropriate locations. Data may be moved to other locations without affecting the application program.

Location transparency may also apply to mapping of process invocations to the processes at dp-locations.

Replication transparency (rt)

For efficiency and robustness we may need to store copies of the same data at several dp-locations. Updates must be propagated to all copies. Replication transparency means that the service-providing layer does this; application programs do not know that data is replicated.

Message exchange (msg)

Different activities in the system may be coordinated by exchange of messages. Message exchange provides reliable transmission of a message from a sender to a receiver.

Message exchange can be used in different layers. We have assumed that implementations of abstract services are based on message exchange in lower layers of software or hardware. In this volume message exchange is concerned only with exchange of application-specific messages between different application programs, or the exchange of text messages between system users.

5.2.2 Process cooperation services

Remote processing (rp)

Remote processing supports initiation and control of execution of an activity on another dp-system.

Rp may be necessary in order to delegate some processing to another dp-system; for example, for reasons of efficiency (in a situation where access to data stored at that location is complex) or for balancing the processor load in the distributed system.

Remote procedure calls such as *X/Open's Preliminary Specification for Remote Procedure Call* or *Open Software Foundation's (OSF) Distributed Computing Environment (DCE) Remote Procedure Call*, and so-called peer-to-peer connections between two application programs such as *X/Open's Snapshot on Distributed Transaction Processing - The Peer-to-Peer Specification* are typical rp mechanisms.

Distributed commit management (dcm)

A distributed data processing system includes requirements for consistency of data at different dp-locations. When cooperating activities manipulate data at different locations, consistency must be preserved; the activities form one commit unit. If any of them fails, changes initiated by all the others must be undone.

With distributed commit management the service-providing layer handles the 'all succeed or all fail' mechanism. Several application programs can thus participate in the same commit unit. If any of the application programs aborts the commit unit, all application programs involved receive a failure indication and their changes to the databases are rolled back. If each application program requests normal completion of the commit unit (and providing the data changes can be committed in the databases) all applications receive a success indication.

Typically the service-providing layer uses a 2-phase commit protocol. In this, every dp-location affected by the commit unit first makes the required change, then reports back on success or failure. If all locations report success, they are all instructed to commit their changes (ie make the changed part of the database available to other programs). If any location reports failure, then all locations are instructed to undo their changes.

Commit management does not include resolution of deadlock, where two applications are each waiting for the other to release data before they can complete their commits. We assume that there are (local) database locking mechanisms to resolve deadlock.

5.2.3 Security services (sec)

Where confidentiality and integrity of data are important, we need specialisations of several security services which are also important in the context of centralised systems. For example we need specialisations of:

- audit functions which monitor interaction with a data-processing system and collect information about it

- access control which prevents unauthorised access to the system or to particular data within the system

- non-repudiation functions to ensure that an actor cannot deny having participated in an interaction with a dp-system.

We do not discuss the specialisations of these security services in any further detail.

5.2.4 Further cooperation services

Distributed systems also involve more complex mechanisms for system administration. Other cooperation services, such as network management and distributed user management, are important in operating a distributed data processing system. However, they are of only limited relevance when discussing the coordination of data processing systems on the logical level.

In this volume we do not address low level cooperation services, such as distributed time synchronization, calendar functionality or distributed file systems.

Chapter 5
Cooperation services and architectures

5.3 Architectures for distributed systems

We take 'architecture' to mean the structure of the system software components that provide basic services to applications. We are interested specifically in properties, components and services of architectures that support distribution of processes and data.

The architectures discussed in Sections 5.3.1 to 5.3.6 are typically off-the-shelf components (or subcomponents) of system software. We might choose system software with an architecture that lacks a service we need for a distributed system. We would then have three choices:

- implement the required service specifically for this application

- redesign the system so that it does not need such a service

- weaken the business requirements that lead to the requirement for this service.

For example, we might implement data location transparency as an extension of the remote database access service. We could develop a component that maps data requests to the appropriate dp-system so that the application program would not have to specify the location of the data.

5.3.1 Distributed database management systems (DDBMS)

Several distributed database management systems on the market support management of a set of separate local databases as a single logical database. Typically all the local databases are from the same vendor and are therefore homogeneous.

A DDBMS provides an interface to access the set of local databases as one virtual database. See Figure 5.2. An ideal DDBMS would provide remote database access (rda), commit management for each database transaction (dcm), location transparency (dlt), and perhaps also replication transparency (rt).

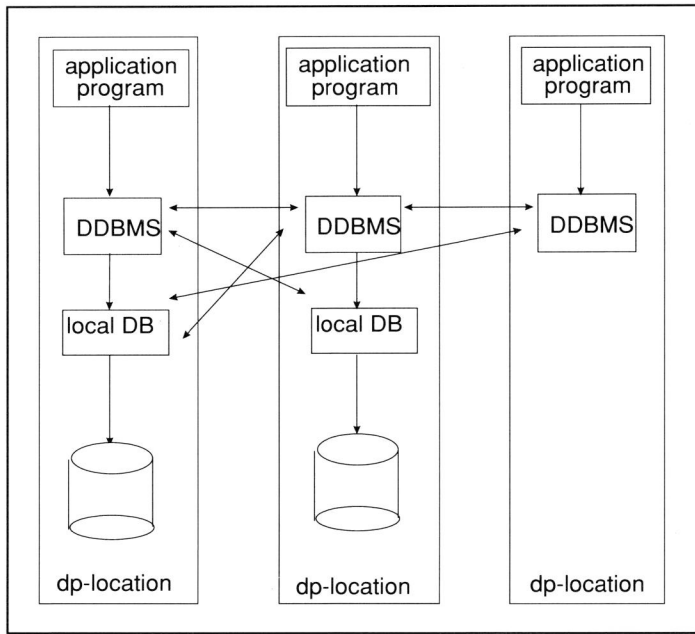

Figure 5.2: Distributed database architecture

The application programs contain the implementations of the external and conceptual processes. The processes of the internal design are either provided by the DDBMS or built as an additional layer on top of it.

In EU-Rent use of a DDBMS might be the solution that requires least implementation effort. For example, all customer records could be held at head office; car and reservation records could be held at the branches they are currently assigned to. Update and enquiry processes would be implemented locally on each workstation, and would use standard SQL calls to access data. The SQL requests would be mapped by the DDBMS to the appropriate databases at the local branch, head office or other branches. Commits would be handled by the DDBMS.

A technical trade-off is that distributed database management requires communication lines with a broader bandwidth, because of additional coordination effort.

Chapter 5
Cooperation services and architectures

5.3.2 Remote database access (RDA)

Remote database access is another basic architecture. Application programs have to know which databases hold the data they require as they must explicitly access the databases via the rda service. See Figure 5.3.

Commits are managed locally. An application program would have to coordinate local commits to ensure consistency across the system.

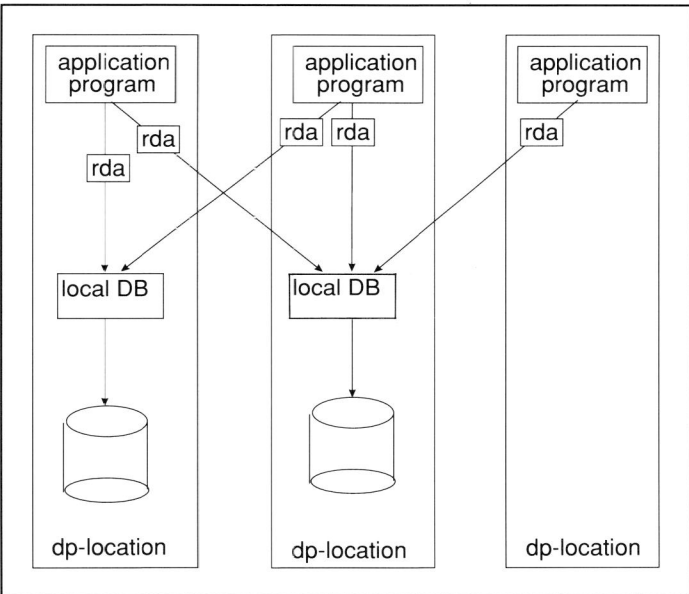

Figure 5.3: Remote database access

SQL remote database access as defined in *X/Open CAE Specification for SQL Remote Database Access* is an example of RDA.

Again the application programs contain the implementations of the external and conceptual processes. The processes of the internal design are either covered by the rda service or built as an additional layer on top of it.

In EU-Rent, use of RDA would also require less implementation effort. A central database server could store customers, cars and rentals. Update and enquiry processes would again be implemented locally on each workstation, and use SQL calls to access the central data. The central database server would have a lighter processing load.

A client could even access databases at several dp-locations simultaneously. However, if these database accesses needed to be carried out in one commit unit then RDA would have to be extended by distributed commit management.

5.3.3 Remote database access with distributed commit management (RDA+)

This architecture is similar to RDA but includes the dcm service and thus ensures consistency of data at different dp-locations. The ISO standard *ISO/IEC 9579 for Remote Database Access* supports this architecture. See Figure 5.4.

Within EU-Rent RDA+ would also support distributed data storage. Consider the same data distribution as in the DDBMS scenario. Update and enquiry processes would be implemented locally on each workstation, and use SQL calls to access data. The SQL requests would need to be explicitly directed to the appropriate dp-location.

Distributed commit management would be required where for example the pick-up of a car updates both the local booking database and the central customer database.

5.3.4 Distributed transaction processing (DTP)

Distributed transaction processing supports cooperation of application programs on different dp-systems and the definition of common commit units.

The *X/Open Model for Distributed Transaction Processing* is a common reference for DTP.

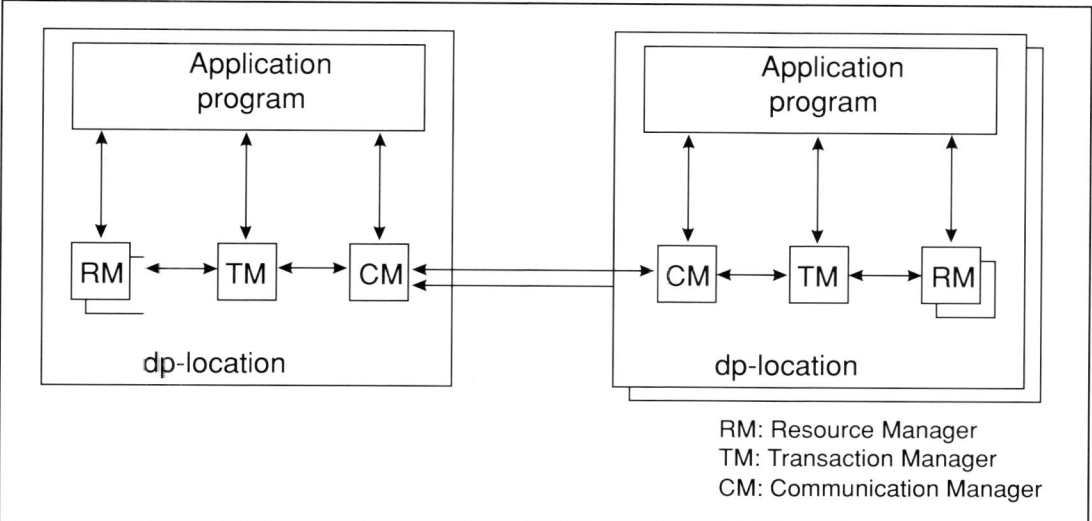

Figure 5.4: X/Open model for distributed transaction processing

As well as the application programs running on the dp-system, the DTP model recognises three other components and their interfaces:

- a resource manager provides the interface between an application program and a shared resource, typically a database or ISAM-file

- a transaction manager defines the boundaries of commit units and commits or rolls back effects on the resource managers

- a communication manager enables communication with or invocation of application programs on other dp-systems. Two or more application programs connected via DTP are in the same commit unit; they must commit or fail together. DTP achieves this by coordinating the respective transaction managers.

Distributed transaction processing is required where conceptual schema processes and external design processes, participating in the same commit unit, are implemented at different dp-locations.

For example, the return of a car to a branch might require the registration of the car return at the pick-up branch and an update of the central customer account database. Suppose the dp-systems are not just simple data-servers, but also provide a restricted set of methods for manipulating the data, then the procedure car_return must trigger a method register_car_return at the pick-up branch and a method account_update at head office. See Figure 5.5. A distributed transaction processing system is required if these three processes are in the same commit unit.

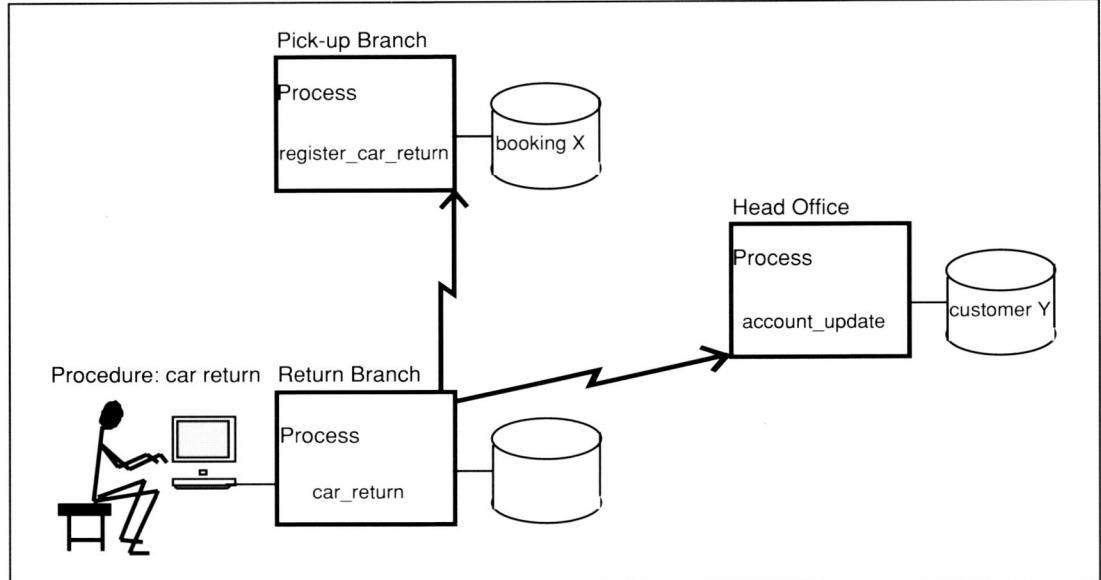

Figure 5.5: Distributed transaction processing for car return

5.3.5 Electronic mail (EMAIL)

Electronic mail enables the exchange of messages between application programs or between users. Email provides the abstract service mess. See Figure 5.6.

Messages can hold unstructured text, formalised text, or even have documents with a complex internal structure attached. Users are able to compose messages, attach documents and send them to other users by giving their addresses. Upon receipt of a message, the recipient can read the message and detach the attached documents.

Chapter 5
Cooperation services and architectures

The ISO adoption of the *CCITT Recommendation for X.400* defines an architecture of this type; it is already supported by public networks. *ISO/IEC 9735:1990 Electronic Data Interchange for Administration, Commerce and Transport (EDIFACT)* for electronic data interchange is also relevant in this context.

The car return procedure from the previous example could also be handled as follows with the email service. At the return branch the booking clerk branch sends a message to the pick-up branch to inform them about the car return. When the booking clerk at the pick-up branch receives the message he or she triggers the registration of the car return and the updates of the databases. See Figure 5.7.

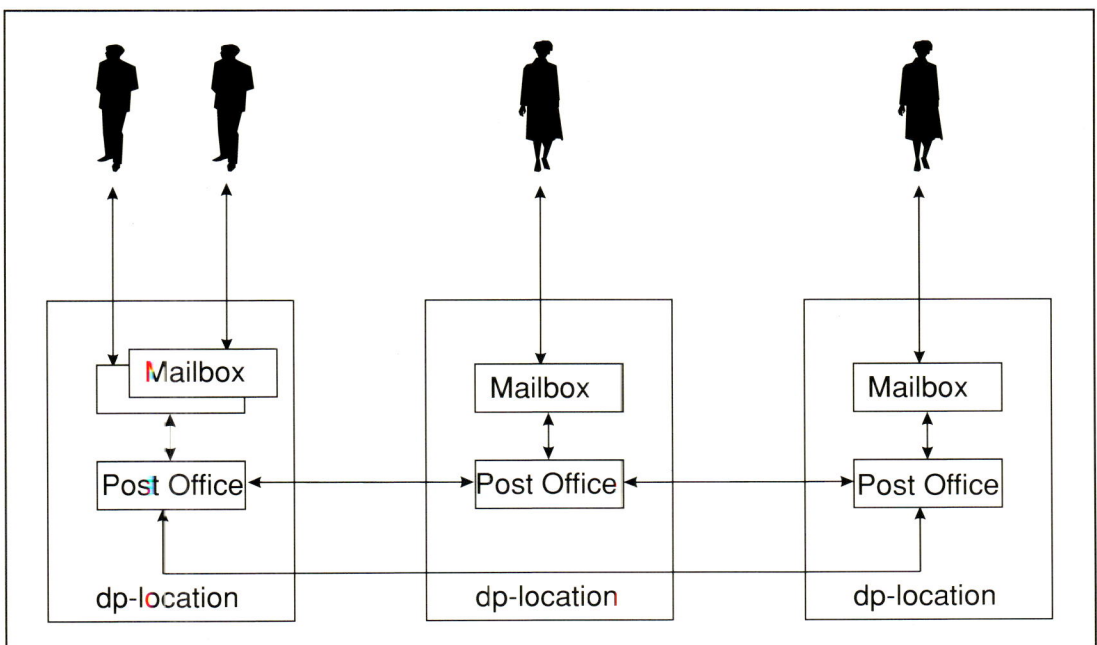

Figure 5.6: Electronic mail exchange

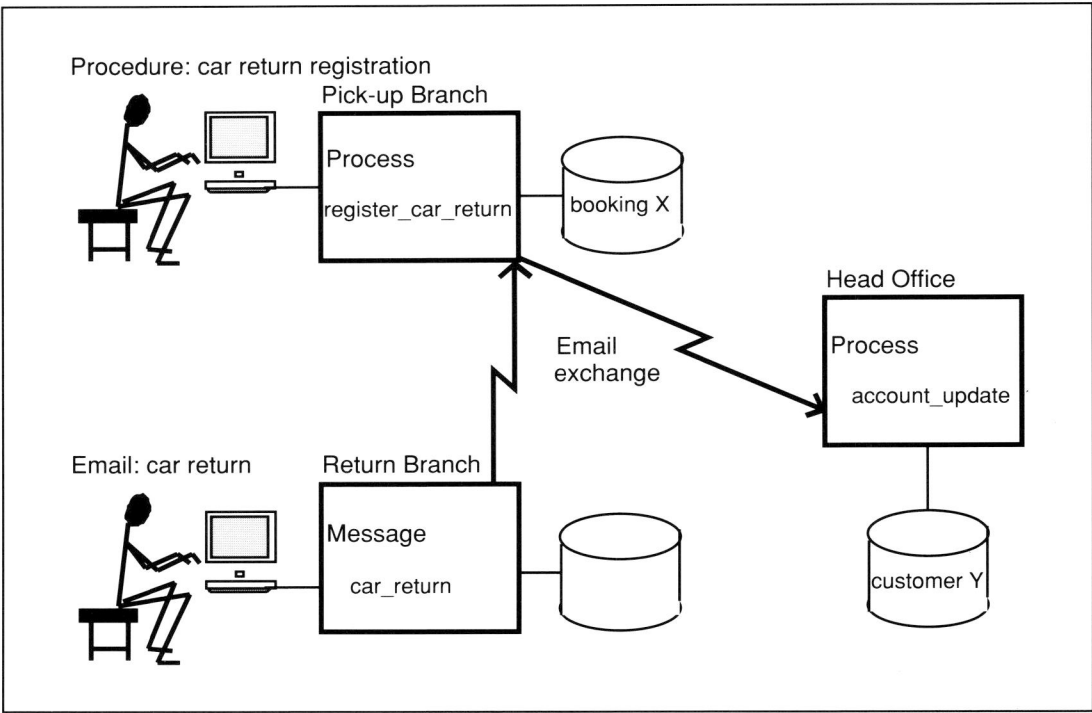

Figure 5.7: Email supported processing for car return

5.3.6 Client/Server (CS)	Several architectures are promoted under the label 'client/server', but the essential concept is a supply-demand relationship between distinct client and server processes. The client is the 'driver'; the server responds when invoked by the client.
	The simplest client/server mapping of the 3-schema Specification Architecture is for the user-interface server to be installed on workstations, and the data and process servers to be installed on some central configuration, as in figure 5.8. Note that a client/server configuration does not have to be distributed; the server could, for example, be on a LAN with the workstations.

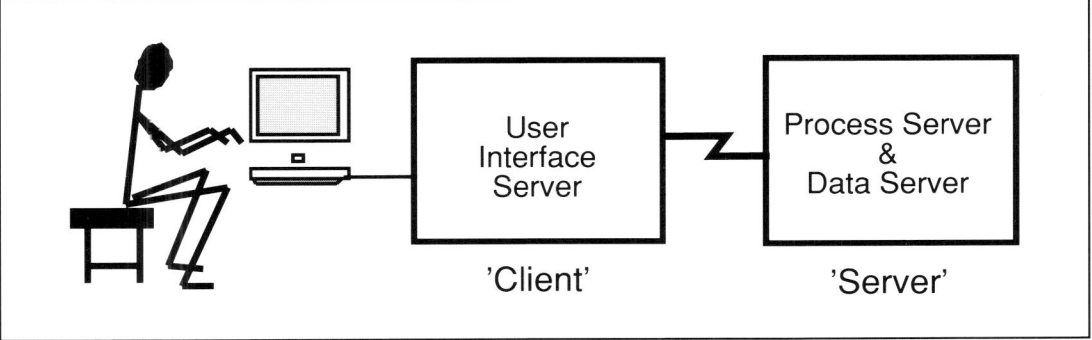

Figure 5.8: Simple client/server mapping

The server could be a central mainframe, so that transaction and database management is centralised. Each dp-input message would result in a remote procedure call invoking an enquiry or update at the server. Alternatively, the logical design for this kind of system could be implemented on a central mainframe with dumb terminals.

Client/server architectures can have more than two layers. For example, the process and data servers could be structured hierarchically as in figure 5.9. The user-interface server is the ultimate client; it invokes servers at the middle layer, which than act as clients to invoke servers at the next layer.

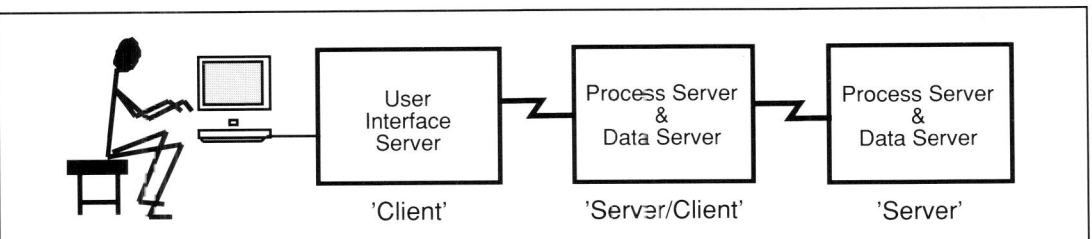

Figure 5.9: Layered client/server architecture

For example, in EU-Rent the external design could be installed at branch workstations. Servers supporting processing of cars and bookings could be installed at major branches (each major branch supporting itself and a number of smaller branches). These servers could then be clients of a central server that supported customer and account processing as in figure 5.10.

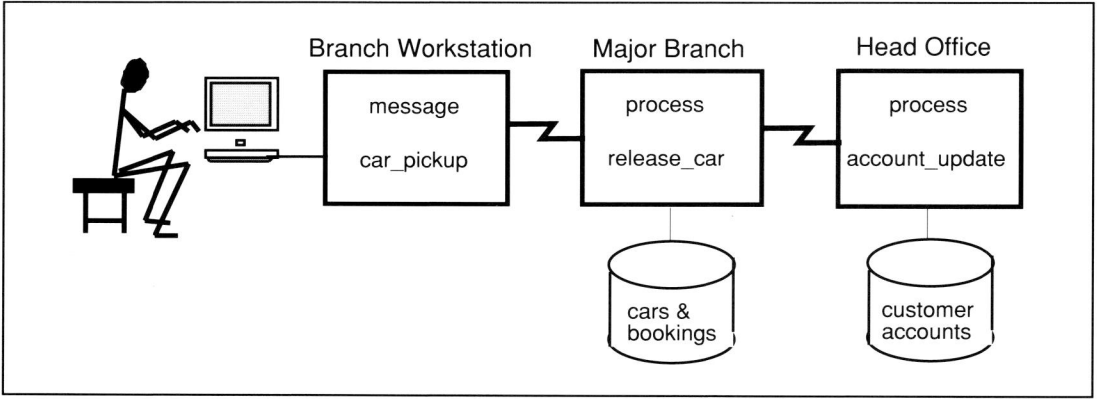

Figure 5.10: Processing of car pick-up in a client/server architecture

More complex mappings could be made. For example, the user-interface server could be layered, with, say, screen and window handling and syntactic validation handled at the workstation, but management of output (sorting, removing duplicates, calculating derived items etc.) handled by an intermediate server. Intermediate client/servers could be designed and coded as separate components, but installed on the same computer.

5.4 Mapping of services to architectures

The table in Figure 5.11 summarises the mapping of abstract services to system architectures.

Services/ Architectures	dcm	dlt	rt	rda	rp	msg	sec
DDBMS	o	o	o	–	-	-	o
RDA	-	-	-	–	-	-	o
RDA+	+	-	-	–	-	-	o
DTP	+	-	-	-	+	-	o
EMAIL	-	-	-	-	-	+	o
CS	+	o	o	o	+	-	o

Legend:
+ service is provided,
- service is not provided,
o service may be partially included

Figure 5.11: Summary of services and architectures

5.5 State of the technology

This chapter has discussed cooperation services needed for distribution and architectures that will, to varying degrees, support those services. Architectures have been discussed in terms of standards such as X/Open RDA (for remote access of relational databases using SQL) and OSF DCE RPC (for invocation by a procedure on one processor of a procedure stored on another, perhaps remote, processor).

However, individual technology vendors are adopting these standards with varying degrees of enthusiasm, speed and consistency, and important questions for a project are:

'If we want select a particular architecture, to what extent is it supported by products we can buy now? How much middleware will we have to develop ourselves?'

For example, suppose that a project is considering:

- groups of local workstations on LANs

- each LAN served by an application server containing the database updates and enquiries

- a distributed relational database on data servers not directly connected to the LANs.

Will the vendor's version of SQL serve as the PDI, or will a more elaborate PDI have to be developed? (Currently, for some vendors, an application making a remote database access has to specify where the instance data is. Using SQL as the PDI would mean that data location would not be transparent to the update and enquiry programs. Projects will have to make trade-offs in this area until distributed DBMSs are better able to manage data location transparency).

The purpose of this section is to provide an overview of what was available in 1994 (when this volume was developed), to help determine projects' expectations of the technology. The content provides input to the definition of criteria for comparing and evaluating products, but it does not go into details of individual products or vendors and, of course, the technology is developing; vendors are continuing to implement and support standards.

5.5.1 Standards for distributed systems

The two major organisations developing open standards for distributed systems are the Open Software Foundation (OSF) which offers the Distributed Computing Environment (DCE), and UNIX International (UI) which offers Open Network Computing (ONC). OSF and UI are each supported by a group of hardware and software vendors. DCE and ONC are fairly similar in most aspects; the major difference is the way in which remote procedure calls are handled.

X/Open is a standards-promoting organisation supported by vendors and some major users (vendors are in the minority). Its strategy is to adopt industry standards, both established and de-facto, which are promoted in the X/Open Portability Guide (XPG).

In addition, several of the major vendors have proprietary standards for distributed systems. Almost all of these are being extended for compliance with DCE, ONC or both.

5.5.2 Remote database access (RDA)

Simple remote database access has been available from many vendors for several years, and is generally well-tried and robust. The application program can access tables at remote locations, but has to know where the tables are. Views may be restricted; for example, with some DBMSs, a joined view may be defined only of tables at the same location.

Commit is generally available at the transaction level - the application program does not have to coordinate commits for individual tables, even when they are at different locations.

5.5.3 Distributed database management systems (DDBMS)

Data location

Data location transparency is often supported at the table level (application programs do not have to specify a table's location).

Data fragmentation

Transparency of horizontal partitioning - in which a table is partitioned by row across several locations - is becoming increasingly common. However, some DDBMSs do not yet support it; they require a separately-defined table at each location. The SQL UNION of the tables at different locations can be defined as a single view for application programs, but in most cases it will only support queries; each update will have to be made to a base table or a view of a single base table.

For most DDBMSs, vertical partitioning (by column) is not transparent. A joined view of the partitions can be defined but, as above, in most cases it will support only enquiries.

Data replication	It is fairly rare for data replication to be transparent, except for 'disk-mirroring' (replication of entire disks). Several DDBMSs support read-only local copies of tables (sometimes called 'snapshots') that can be automatically refreshed at specified intervals.
	Where replication is transparent, it is at the table level; entire tables or horizontal partitions of tables are replicated. Currently-available DBMSs (at least those from the major vendors) cannot manage row-level replication transparently; i.e they cannot manage a horizontally-partitioned table in which some rows are replicated in more than one partition and others are not.
Query optimisation	One area that needs careful investigation is automatic query optimisation. Most implementations of SQL include a query optimiser, but these have generally been developed for a database at a single location, using rules based on factors such as table size, existence and size of indexes, clustering, block size and packing density. Query optimisation across multiple locations is often weak; single-location optimisation rules applied to distributed data without taking account of location may actually degrade performance.
	Some vendors are developing cost-based, rather than rule-based, optimisers. If optimisation is rule-based, distributed application programs may have to issue SQL calls that minimise the effect of the query optimiser; for example, by using distinct selections rather than a join which might be spuriously 'optimised'.
Multiple DBMSs	Most DDBMSs provide gateways to DBMSs from the major vendors, so that it is possible to distribute data across different DBMSs; this kind of facility is important when some of the data needed is in legacy systems. Transparency of data location, fragmentation and replication is generally not available across different DBMSs. The application may have to manage commits separately for each DBMS.
	As more DDBMSs move towards a client/server architecture (see 5.5.6) and comply more closely with

distribution standards, it should be possible to increase transparency to applications of database services.

Stored procedures   Increasingly, DDBMSs support procedures stored with the data, so that part of the database processing is done at the data location, which may be remote from the application program. The stored procedures may be invoked explicitly from the application (this is the basis of the client/server model - see Section 5.5.6) or implicitly as a trigger process that is invoked, when specified conditions occur, as a side effect of a data access.

Administration   Facilities that are becoming generally available in DDBMSs include:

- user authorisation profiles: 'packages' of access privileges can be defined and assigned to users, rather than creating access privileges at the level of individual tables or views

- remote database administration: the alternative is to provide DBA expertise for all data processing locations, either on-site or by means of a travelling team

- backup and recovery of partial databases at individual locations without the need to take the location off-line.

5.5.4 Electronic mail (EMAIL)

EMail is a well-developed technology for human-initiated activity. For example, a workstation user can send files to another workstation; the files could be text, data or programs.

One possibility is that EMail could support services for non-interactive remote procedure calls and transaction shipping. A workstation user could send a request and parameters for a stored procedure, or the procedure itself, to a remote station and receive the reply by EMail. Using a third-party network (such as a public subscription EMail service) this approach could provide a robust low-throughput service that is instantly available, with no requirement for the project to develop or maintain the network.

The problem is that most EMail services assume human activity at both ends of the communication. Those automated interfaces that do exist are generally fairly restricted; examples are gateways to other EMail networks or to systems supporting services such as electronic shopping and public databases. What is needed is a facility to connect data processing locations as another type of user, with automatic interaction with the EMail service. Some user organisations have developed their own interfaces of this type; network owners are following.

If it is possible for a data processing location to be plugged in anywhere and then handle large numbers of transactions automatically, local performance may be a problem. Increasing network speed, increasing throughput capability and technology for managing network loading are gradually overcoming this.

5.5.5 Distributed Transaction Processing (DTP)

Currently, distributed transaction processing is not so well-developed as distributed database. It is generally handled better within vendors' proprietary environments than in open systems products. The proprietary environments have grown up over many years; there is a lot of experience in using them and some very large distributed systems have been developed within them. Most proprietary environments offer industry-standard communication protocols as alternatives to the vendor's own, and provide support for gateways to some other vendors' systems.

Open systems standards for distributed transaction processing have been accepted only recently. The main focus in developing open systems transaction monitors has been program-to-program communication (including remote procedure calls), access to multiple DBMSs, distributed commit, and programming language support (including distributed debugging). Proprietary environments often provide more comprehensive facilities for network performance optimisation and end-user interfaces.

Facilities of open system transaction monitors are well-suited to the client/server model. For example, in DCE-compliant environments, stubs can be created for the client (taking the place of the server procedure) and the server (taking the place of the client); the two stubs are then connected by the transaction monitor, hiding the underlying network from the client/server communication. This can support process location transparency.

Transaction monitors for open systems and those that have evolved from proprietary environments are converging. No currently-available transaction monitor has a complete solution for automated two-phase commit over multiple DBMSs.

5.5.6 Client/server architecture (CS)

In the architectural model of client/server presented by most vendors, what we have called (in Section 3.3) the user-interface server (supported perhaps by the highest level structure of process servers) would be the 'client' and the process and data servers together would be the 'server' component of the architecture.

There are many client/server product families currently available. As well as the distributed database features described in Section 5.5.3, they typically support a range of graphical front ends; gateways to other DBMSs; cost-based optimisation; binary large objects (BLOBs) for image, graphics and sound; disk mirroring; some degree of parallel processing. They are often used in LAN-based architectures. For high-performance databases, major products can be installed on symmetric multiprocessor platforms (tightly-coupled multiple processors sharing memory) which provide good scalability for different throughput requirements at different locations, and easy expansion as volumes increase.

Most vendors of client/server products encourage a hierarchical architecture for data access, partly for performance but mainly to avoid complex interactions for locking and commit.

For example, suppose that:

- a client needed to access a server at location type A, and the stored procedure at location A needed to call another server at location B

- the data at location type A was partitioned across several location instances, A1, A2 etc with a copy of the server at each

- the client invoked the server at every instance of location of type A that held relevant rows.

There could be a locking problem if:

- the stored procedure at, say, location A1 needed to invoke the server at location B. The relevant row at location B would be locked until completion of the two-phase commit

- the stored procedure at location A2 needed the <u>same row</u> at server B; it would invoke the server at B, but could not have the row (because it was locked for A1's request)

- the two-phase commit could not be completed without a positive response from A2.

The result is a deadlock that cannot be resolved by the timeout mechanisms used by most transaction monitors.

Most client/server vendors encourage one of three solutions to the problem, all ensuring that the server at B is called by only one A server in any one transaction:

- the client should make a separate call to each of the A servers; this does not mean that the client has to know where the data is, but it has to know how the data is logically partitioned

- the client's call should be directed to one of the A servers (perhaps the one on the same LAN as the client), which will make further calls to other A servers to process rows that are not local to it, and will make all calls to the server at B. This makes for more complex design of stored procedures

- the client's call should be directed to one of the A servers, which will process all the relevant rows, using remote database access for any rows that are not local to it, and will make all calls to the server at B.

Client/server vendors are beginning to recognise the need for event- or transaction-level locking in a network of invocations (so that all messages for the same transaction are allowed to access a locked row, but messages for other transactions are locked out) but it is not yet well-supported. It is possible to develop middleware to handle the locking.

5.5.7 Object-oriented distributed transaction processing

Object-oriented databases are relatively immature and have only just begun to address the requirements of distributed data. There seems to be a widely-held assumption among vendors that instance data will be stored at the location where their object class is implemented. Transparency of partitioning and replication of instance data are generally not addressed.

However, it is possible to develop a distributed system that has strong OO characteristics using distributed client/server technology. An overview of the approach is given in Chapter 3. The networking problem for distributed commit described in 'client/server' above has to be resolved.

5.5.8 Middleware

Note that when vendors' products do not provide the required transparency automatically, it is worth considering development of middleware that isolates application code from concerns of location, fragmentation and replication. Such middleware does not have to be complex or elaborate.

6 Decisions specific to distributed systems

6.1 Introduction

During the development of distributed systems specific decisions must be taken to select between different variants of distribution that differ in assumed construction and operational costs, fulfilled functional requirements, robustness, stability of design etc. In this chapter we describe these decisions. In general, we do not discuss decisions common to the development of both centralised and distributed systems.

Section 6.2 introduces a generic development process to provide a framework for the decisions.

Section 6.3 defines the types of decision that need to be taken. For each decision, we describe what needs to be decided, factors which need to be weighed and when the decision has to be taken.

Section 6.4 provides heuristics on which to base provisional decisions

Finally, Section 6.5 provides guidelines for mapping conceptual processes to service architectures.

6.2 Generic development process

The generic development process is derived from the customer-supplier transformation and decision point concepts produced as part of the Euromethod project. The Euromethod decision point concepts were carefully chosen to allow compatibility with the development processes of existing European methods.

The *Euromethod Delivery Planning Guide* describes the circumstances under which other more iterative or evolutionary sequences of decision points can be put together. The products referred to in Sections 6.2.1 to 6.2.7 are defined in the *Euromethod - Deliverable Model*.

The term 'study' is used to refer to the work done to define requirements during the life of an IS development, from its inception as a consequence of strategic planning, onwards.

6.2.1	Agree the basis of an IS project in an application area	For this decision, an organisation, or specifically the customer within an organisation accepts that the study which was undertaken:

- accurately reflects the strategic information needs of the organisation, to an appropriate level of detail

- has defined a suitable strategy and policies under which information systems can eventually be developed to meet these information needs.

The basis of an IS Project in an application area is established and the content of the project initiation document is decided. |
| 6.2.2 | Agree the information system requirements | The customer agrees that the study:

- accurately reflects the customer's system requirements, particularly the business and information needs. (Products which need to be evaluated: business information view, business process view)

- describes the existing system to an acceptable level of detail and accurately reflects the problems that exist within the current situation. |
| 6.2.3 | Agree the information system architecture | The customer:

- agrees that the study considers all the appropriate information system options which meet the information system requirements. (Products which need to be evaluated: scope of computer system data view, scope of computer system function view)

- selects the most appropriate information system architecture for the organisation. (Product which needs to be evaluated: work practice view). |
| 6.2.4 | Agree the information system specification | The customer agrees that the study:

- completely and consistently specifies an information system which meets the requirements of the |

Chapter 6
Decisions specific to distributed systems

information system option selected. (Products which need to be evaluated: computer system data view, computer system function view).

6.2.5 Agree the IT system architecture and the user/machine interfaces

The customer:

- agrees that the study considers all the appropriate computer system options which meet the computer system requirements

- selects the most appropriate computer system option for the organisation. (Product which needs to be evaluated: technical environment of computer system architecture view).

6.2.6 Agree the specification of the computer system and manual procedures

The customer agrees that the study:

- completely and consistently specifies a computer system for the option selected. (Product which needs to be evaluated: computer system architecture view).

6.2.7 Agree the information system adaptation

The customer agrees that:

- the implemented computer system was satisfactorily completed and installed on the customer's premises.

The customer may also:

- agree that the information system is operationally satisfactory

- specify how ongoing enhancement and maintenance of the system should be managed.

6.3 Types of decision

The following types of decision must be considered when developing a distributed system.

6.3.1 Pre-project decisions

Strategic decisions, requiring a distributed solution, may have been taken ahead of a project. For example:

- machines and network may already be installed. The emergence of GUIs has considerably changed the demands placed on computer system hardware. GUIs like X-Windows or MS-Windows require relatively high speed processing and large amounts of storage for bit maps. This, together with lower communication costs than for centralised solutions, has led to the appearance of networks of workstations for highly interactive tasks, such as text processing or computer graphics. With such distributed systems already in place, users are likely to demand more and more applications to run on them.

  Alternatively, there may be a plan to manage island solutions already installed on pockets of workstations in a consistent way.

- external requirements originating outside the organisation, such as legal constraints, may demand distribution. For example, certain data may have to be stored separately for reasons of data protection. Fiscal information relating to the national parts of an international organisation, such as balance sheets, may have to be stored in national computer systems even if an international information system is used by the total organisation.

6.3.2 Single coordinated system vs. multiple uncoordinated systems

What is to be decided

This decision is between developing a single coordinated system in one project or a number of uncoordinated systems in several projects. (The further possibility of developing a single coordinated system in several projects, through incremental or parallel development is considered in the *ISE Library Volume: Application Partitioning and Integration with SSADM*.)

Chapter 6
Decisions specific to distributed systems

Factors to be taken into account

Reasons for developing as several projects:

After we have defined a syntactical interface between projects, we can separate the development into two or more independent projects. In this way, we get individually implementable packages which can be delivered earlier than with one large project. The reduced complexity can lead to a decrease of unit costs for the development. If however, the separate developments have to be coordinated then the sum of the complexities of several small projects is likely to be considerably higher than the complexity of a single large project. (For guidance on special measures - equivalent to incremental development - to take in that circumstance, please refer to *ISE Library Volume: Application Partitioning and Integration with SSADM*).

Reasons for developing as a single project:

There is a risk of consistency problems between systems when they are developed through several projects. The underlying assumption when developing a set of uncoordinated systems through several projects is that there are no overall consistency requirements. This can lead to islands of automation being produced. A later requirement for integration may force complete redevelopment.

When to decide

This decision must be taken during *agree the basis of an IS project in an application area*.

6.3.3 Distribution on grounds of functional requirements

What is to be decided

The decision is between developing a centralised or a distributed system because of functional requirements. Robustness issues, especially, might lead to a decision in favour of a distributed system.

This decision is closely related to that described in Section 6.3.6, which is to be made once it is clear that we want to develop a distributed system. There we discuss the detailed trade-off between consistency and

113

robustness. Here we are concerned with more superficial considerations that might lead to the decision to develop a distributed system.

| Factors to be taken into account | When the network is down in a centralised system, then it is impossible for users to progress work at any location. But in a distributed system there may still be processing that can be carried out locally. The processes would either be intra-location processes (processes requiring local data only) or reduced versions of some inter-location processes (processes requiring data from other locations).

When one of the components in a distributed system fails, most of the work in progress need not be interrupted. Even functions that require resources from the failed component can still continue if there is sufficient redundancy in the system.

When to decide: If robustness is a dominant requirement, this decision has to be taken during *agree the basis of an IS project in an application area*.

At the latest, the decision to distribute or centralise on the grounds of functionality must be taken when *agreeing the information system architecture*. At this early point in the analysis process the automation boundary and raw functionality of the data processing system is fixed. However, as consistency and robustness influence the user's perception of the system, this decision cannot be deferred.

6.3.4 Distribution on the grounds of cost

What is to be decided: The decision between centralised and distributed solutions may be based on cost considerations. In the absence of overriding political or other reasons for adopting a particular technical solution, costs are likely to be used to help decide between solutions involving varying degrees of distribution. This means that we must make a business case for the option to be chosen.

Factors to be taken into account	Usually when comparing computer system costs, 'lifetime' costs are used; that is the cost of the initial system, together with estimated costs over the system's expected life. However, accurate lifetime costing of any system is difficult. Regardless of the effort and care put into their derivation, cost predictions may become inaccurate because of unpredictable and uncontrollable external factors. Nevertheless, such inaccuracies do not invalidate the costing exercise. Market forces usually dictate that any significant changes in cost factors for one technical solution are likely to be applicable, in some degree, to others.

Apportioning costs to a particular system development is further complicated when some of the technical infrastructure is already in place or is to be shared at a later date with other systems. In such circumstances, selecting a particular technical solution for one system can have a significant effect on the costs and even the feasibility of other systems.

It must be stressed that for a distributed system, there are important strategic decisions to be taken relating to how distributed support, such as for maintenance and upgrades, is to be provided. In particular, these decisions can have a significant impact in terms of cost. These decisions involve personnel, organisational and financial considerations as well as technical matters.

Amongst the cost factors which contribute to the total cost of a distributed system are:

- communication costs - the capability to do a considerable amount of processing locally reduces the communication cost in a distributed system

- hardware costs - in a distributed system resources can be shared between several locations. For example, database servers with large amounts of backup storage

- operational costs - the cost of operating a distributed system includes the costs of updating software and repair of hardware at all locations. The software updates can be done through the network, but

- maintenance of hardware requires either local or travelling maintenance engineers

- software costs - software for distributed systems is inherently more complex than for centralised systems because of the need for supporting communication, the need to synchronize processes across locations and the need to maintain data consistency. Thus the cost for system software as well as the cost for application software will increase.

Annex B provides a checklist of subjects for which costs should be considered. Note that the list is not necessarily complete for all business or technical environments; neither will all the items on the list be relevant for all environments. In particular, very large distributed systems are likely to require special considerations whereas small distributed systems will probably require a much smaller, less formal, support infrastructure.

When to decide

There are several points in the generic development process where this decision might be taken. These include *agree the information system requirements* and when formulating options for *agree the information system architecture*.

In general, the cost estimates become more reliable the further the development proceeds. Early cost estimates for a distributed system are unlikely to be any more precise than those for a centralised system.

6.3.5 Distribution on the grounds of stability of design

Apart from robustness and cost considerations, there are other benefits that might lead to the choice of a distributed solution. We summarise these under the heading 'stability of design'.

What is to be decided

The decision is between a distributed and a centralised solution because of stability issues.

Chapter 6
Decisions specific to distributed systems

Factors to be taken into account

A distributed system tends to be more stable with respect to each of the following:

- load fluctuation - in a distributed system where a lot of the processing can be done locally at a user's location, the response is faster and more predictable than in a centralised system where the response depends on the workload of the network and the mainframe, ie on the work of other users

- system changes - a distributed system can be extended as the demand for service grows either without replacing any existing components, or by just replacing components at some locations. It seems easier and more economical to add or upgrade locations in a distributed network than to expand a large central computer. But it might also be more complex to upgrade software in a distributed scenario

- data theft - if unauthorised access to data is gained, the potential for loss or damage is greater with a single centralised location than where data is spread across many locations, since in the latter case the unauthorised user would have to navigate the network to reach other locations.

When to decide

These considerations are hard to quantify. Therefore, we believe that in most cases the decision to develop a distributed or centralised system will not be based solely on stability of design. However, stability issues may add weight to the robustness or cost arguments in favour of a distributed system. The decisions will be taken at the same points as the decisions about distribution on grounds of cost.

6.3.6 Robustness vs. consistency

Once the decision in favour of a distributed solution has been made, we have to decide on the detailed trade-off between consistency and robustness.

What is to be decided

The decision is about the degree of autonomy of the locations of the system.

One extreme is where the locations have no autonomy, thus none is able to work independently of the others. In this case, data consistency across all locations is nearly always guaranteed.

The other extreme is where locations have total autonomy, ie they do not need any communication with other locations to fulfil their duty. They maintain a locally consistent set of data independently of any other location.

In distributed systems we usually need a solution somewhere between the two extremes in order to satisfy the users' robustness and consistency requirements.

The relationship between autonomy, consistency and robustness is shown in Figures 6.1 and 6.2.

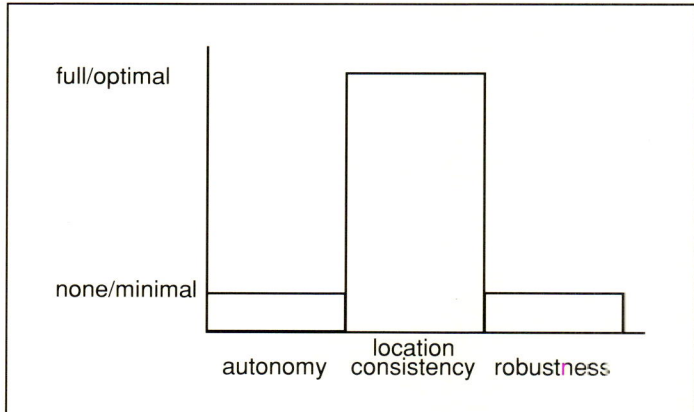

Figure 6.1: Multiple locations, one system

Chapter 6
Decisions specific to distributed systems

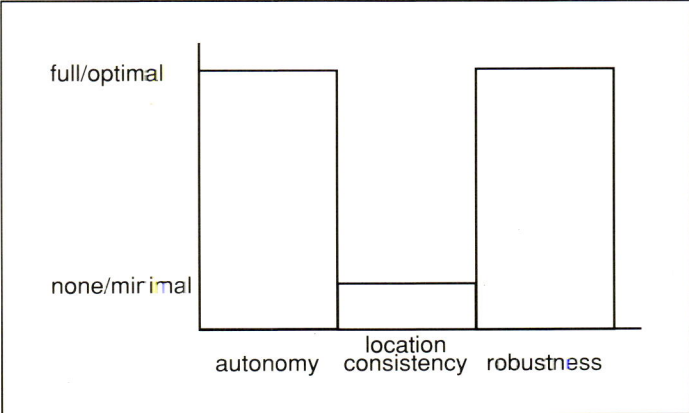

Figure 6.2: Multiple locations, multiple systems

Factors to be taken into account

The decision on the importance of robustness and consistency relative to each other can be guided by the robustness which is inherent in the business and the risks to the business in the case of consistency violations.

In every distributed system there is some inherent robustness because of the possibility of doing some work locally or of involving only a subset of all locations. This level of robustness is there even in the case of maximal constraints on consistency.

Additionally, the risk of the system's ceasing to work has to be weighed against the risk of using inconsistent data.

It has to be decided what the system is to do in the case that it cannot guarantee data consistency because of network or location failures. In particular, we need to decide what minimum level of consistency we require for the system to continue working and what reduced level of functionality the system should provide in the case of failures. We also need to decide how the system should recognise inconsistent states and then reach a consistent state again. In some cases the user might have to be informed to take some action such as starting compensating transactions.

When to decide

Decisions about the level of service in case of failure cannot be made before business locations and locally-

119

needed functionality have been identified, ie before we have fixed the organisation of the business. However, robustness requirements are constraints on the design of the data processing system. The decision about the level of robustness and consistency is therefore part of *agree the information system architecture*.

6.3.7 Distribution of data

When developing a distributed system, we have to decide how to distribute data, representing the states of objects.

The ANSI Sparc 3-Schema Database Architecture, introduced in Chapter 3, describes three different views of data - conceptual, external and internal. Distribution of data is about defining the internal schema, with the conceptual schema as the starting point and the external schema providing some guidance.

What is to be decided

The decision on where to store objects physically has two dimensions, partitioning and replication.

By partitioning we mean the separation of data representing an object class into proper subsets which are assigned to separate locations. We distinguish horizontal partitioning where we separate the rows of a table (see Figure 6.3) and vertical partitioning where we decompose a table by columns (see Figure 6.4).

In contrast, replication means storing copies of objects or parts of objects at more than one location (see Figure 6.5).

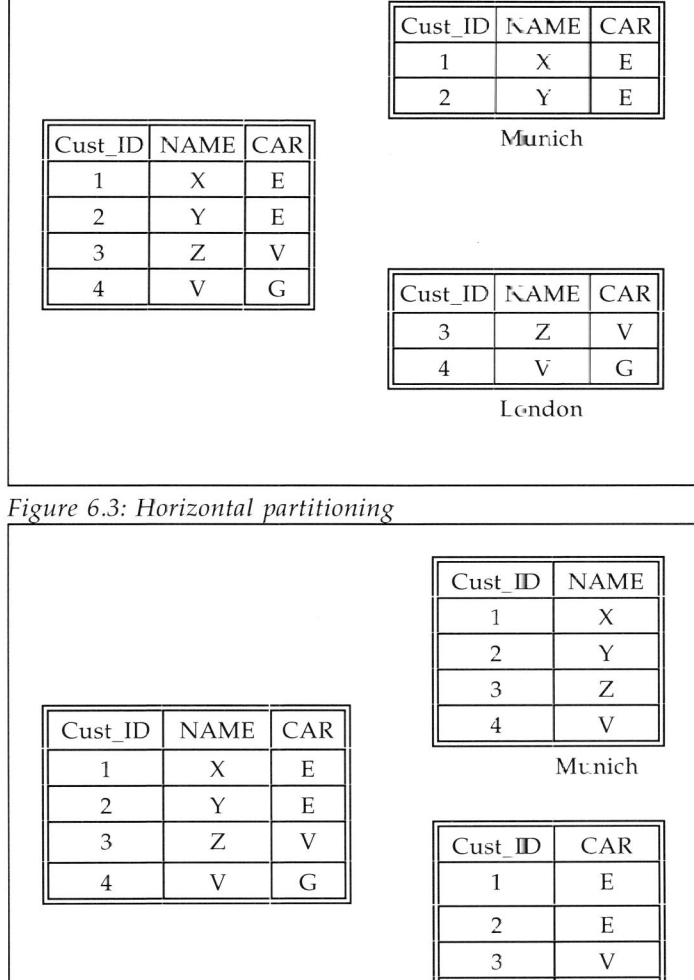

Figure 6.3: Horizontal partitioning

Figure 6.4: Vertical partitioning

Cust_ID	NAME	CAR
1	X	E
2	Y	E
3	Z	V
4	V	G

Cust_ID	NAME	CAR
1	X	E
2	Y	E
3	Z	V
4	V	G

Munich

Cust_ID	NAME	CAR
1	X	E
2	Y	E
3	Z	V
4	V	G

London

Figure 6.5: Replication of a table

Guidance

The default principle in distributing data is to store data at the locations where it will be accessed most frequently (this information is recorded in the external schema). Other considerations like security, data integrity or cost may outweigh this principle.

Partitioning the data facilitates:

- efficiency. Data can be stored where it is used and separated from other data used by other users or applications
- local optimisation. Data can be stored to optimise performance for local access
- security. Each location controls the access to local data, only giving access to other locations via secure interfaces.

Partitioning has the following disadvantages:

- inconsistent access speed. When data is required from several locations, access times can be significantly slower than with local-only data access

- back-up vulnerability. If data is not replicated, and the location at which the data is stored becomes inaccessible then no process will be able to use that data.

Horizontal partitioning is particularly useful in a situation where a function is replicated at several locations and each location is responsible for a subset of the objects. Vertical partitioning supports functions, at different locations, with reasonably separate data requirements.

Replication of the data facilitates:

- reliability. If a location becomes inaccessible, a copy of the data can be found at another site

- fast response. Each site that has a copy of the data can process queries locally, without communication delays.

Replication has the following disadvantages:

- storage requirements. Each site that has a full copy of the data must have the same storage capacity that would be required if the data was stored centrally

- multiple updates. All copies of the data must be updated. This requires additional processing capacity and increases network load

- synchronization. If updates are not carefully synchronized different copies of the same data will be inconsistent

- propagation of corrupt data. If the data at one of the sites becomes corrupted, then there is a risk that the corrupted data could become replicated to other sites.

Replication is particularly recommended for data which is updated relatively infrequently. For example, catalogues, train schedules and telephone directories.

	When to decide	Having identified data distribution as a matter of the internal schema, it is clear that these decisions have to be taken in defining the *information system architecture and computer system architecture*. Distribution of data might also be the subject of tuning during the maintenance of a distributed system.
6.3.8	Distribution of processes	When developing a distributed system, we have to decide how to distribute processes, including procedure implementations, method implementations, and validation and formatting process implementations.

In the 3-schema Specification Architecture, described in Chapter 3, the conceptual model is both a static and dynamic model of the business world and captures all of its semantics, ie all of the necessary business knowledge about the system to be built. The conceptual model processes are implemented as methods at data processing locations, which may be distinct from data servers and user-interface servers. The external design is a model of how the user interacts with the data processing system, ie a model of the procedure implementations. The internal design includes the program-data interface between method implementations and data servers. |
| | What is to be decided | Procedure implementations, and validation and formatting process implementations are allocated to user-interface servers. Method implementations are allocated to process servers.

What is then needed is a mapping of user-interface servers, process servers and data servers to dp-locations. As in the case of data distribution, the decision of where to locate the processes has the dimensions of partitioning and replication. By partitioning we mean the assignment of servers to locations. A process server might invoke processing at other locations.

Replication of servers means the same functionality is offered at more than one location. |

Chapter 6
Decisions specific to distributed systems

Guidance	The default is to place user-interface servers at the same locations as their users. We recommend replication of user-interface servers at each business location according to the users located there. This choice enables parallel activity on relatively low cost equipment and increases robustness.
	The problem of distributing process servers is of a different nature. For the decision on partitioning we can take the location of the data, which is needed by the processes, as the default. When we partition data horizontally, by default we locate a copy of the process server with each partition of the data. In the case of vertically partitioned data, there will be different types of process server for each partition, because each partition typically corresponds to another set of functionality.
	Nevertheless, how do we know we have partitioned the data in the right way? We might have to change the distribution of the data to increase performance or robustness, or to reduce cost. If we did, then we would still locate a copy of the process server with each partition.
	If the necessary network bandwidth is higher than for a centralised solution, then there is something wrong with the distribution of the data and/or processes. We could consider separating process servers from data to reduce network load, distribute processor load or reduce cost.
	Note: A widely used phrase is 'client/server' architecture'. In the most commonly presented model the user-interface servers (the 'clients') are distributed to local workstations and the data server together with the process servers reside on a central dp-system (the 'server'). If you want to distribute the database in a 'client/server' environment among several 'servers' the considerations about distribution as above apply.
When to decide	This decisions have to be taken when defining the computer system architecture view.

6.4 Heuristics

There are many factors to be considered in distributed system design. We need some heuristics on which to

125

base provisional decisions that can then be evaluated and modified if necessary. The main point is to have simple rules, even if some of the time they lead to less than optimal solutions, although we hope that what they lead to will be acceptable most of the time.

If the heuristics produce reasonable results in typical situations, it is usually more effective to spend time checking and testing out a trial design than to spend time trying to make a final decision.

6.4.1 Single coordinated system vs. multiple uncoordinated systems

Consistency requirements usually have to be weighed against the urgency of user need for IT support. Where consistency requirements are stronger this makes a single coordinated system a desirable option. However, uncoordinated systems will be smaller, usually simpler and faster to develop.

If there is a requirement to deliver some functionality quickly to the users, develop a separate, uncoordinated system for it. The uncoordinated systems may later have to be coordinated, which will usually result in higher overall costs than if a single coordinated system had been developed.

6.4.2 Distribution of data

Partitioning the data model

First the data model can be partitioned by a set of standard heuristics to a first-cut design and then we decide on replication according to robustness and performance considerations.

The intention is to produce a data model, which is as self-contained as possible, for each type of location. We shall develop distinct conceptual processing models for the data model of each location type.

Modelling a distributed business system, we expect to find entities in the data model that correspond to physical locations. This assumption is justified by the need to store geographical information like address, telephone number etc pertinent to each location.

The general progression of the first-cut partitioning rules is as follows:

- include location entities into data model

- identify allowable locations for non location entities

- assign an entity to a location if its master has been assigned to this location (this results in horizontal distribution of the entities)

- decide upon horizontal or vertical partitioning in the case of conflicts. Vertical distribution is indicated on the data model by showing aspects as separate entities connected by one to one relations.

Specific versions of these first-cut rules are provided in the method specific extensions in Part 2.

Distribution scenarios for data

At first, assume the most distributed system - ie that most of the data a business location needs will be held at that location. Use both horizontal and vertical partitioning; for example, in EU-Rent:

- partition car vertically into service depot and branch 'aspects'

- partition each car aspect horizontally to allocate instances to branches and service depots.

Then create options for comparison on performance and costs by clustering data at fewer locations. High-throughput business locations may be good candidates for data clustering. For example in EU-Rent city branches may act as cluster locations for neighbouring local agencies.

If it is allowed as an option, define a centralised option to use for comparison. If not, define a 'most clustered' option, with external processes at workstations and data at a minimum number of data storage locations.

Replication of data	At first assume no replication, then trade off performance against robustness, consistency and cost. Options include:

- access data remotely

- move data to where it is most used; for example, in EU-Rent, move car data between branches as ownership of car is transferred between branches. (Consider whether history should move with its primary entities)

- replicate data. For example, in EU-Rent, replicate car data at branches as ownership of car is transferred between branches. (Consider whether the history should also be replicated).

Once replication is decided - do first-cut internal design within location. |
| Centrally-maintained reference data | Some types of data are updated centrally, but are used as read-only data in many locations; for example, in EU-Rent, car group information (description, rental price) is maintained by head office and used by all branches.

Initially, assume that there will be local copies of such data; this increases robustness and performance. Then consider the trade-offs for local storage cost and broadcast of updates from the central location. |
| Low-usage data | Consider whether to recreate low-usage data rather than maintain it. Suppose EU-Rent customers were in four groups, say:

- 10% high usage

- 20% infrequent repeaters

- 1% suspended

- the rest effectively one-offs (less than once per year) - do we want to maintain these? |

Chapter 6
Decisions specific to distributed systems

This is not just a matter of performance, but also of data currency.

If we decide not to maintain all instances of customer, how can we recognise the ones we want to keep? We may have to set up a real world activity to encourage the members of the target group to identify themselves. For example, in EU-Rent we could offer customers special status - fast service when their personal details are in the computer system. This needs some kind of a threshold, such as a 'passport' (a card given to a new customer which is stamped each time they make a rental). The customer would be advised to 'Collect 3 stamps within a year and become a privileged customer.'

This kind of filter may be based on status, although there may be a marketing tie-in, such as discounts, upgrades or free days, to encourage repeat business.

We also need to define conditions for removal or archive of data.

Identifiers	When identifiers have to be issued by the system, avoid the bottleneck of a single 'key-issuer' component for the whole system. It would affect both robustness and performance.
	If there is no real-world universal identifier (car registration number, manufacturer's serial number, driving licence number or social security number) we can use the location identifier as the qualifier for independent entities - but if the entity's location can change, don't regard the location identifier as meaningful. It is simply a mechanism to ensure uniqueness.
	Use hierarchical keys for dependent entities; they can be used only for fixed relationships.
Identification of real-world entities	How can we recognise the same real-world entity, such as customer, in different places? It is easy in EU-Rent - we need to see a driver's licence, and driver identifiers are unique within issuing country. This is not completely reliable - if a person moves long-term to

another country he may be required to obtain a driving licence for that country - but probably good enough for EU-Rent's practical purposes. A customer with two driving licences will be treated as two different customers. It is not so easy if we are renting hotel rooms, or selling airline tickets (at least for domestic flights). We might ask 'Have you used our service before? Where and when was that?'.

Is unique identification of real-world entities just a trade-off, or is there some legislation or strong business rule that makes it mandatory? For example, in the Social Security system, itinerants claim benefit a day at a time, but should not be able to claim day-benefit from more than one social security office per day.

It may not be politically acceptable to ask for social security numbers, for example, unless there is a legislative reason for doing so.

Is it possible to capture identification characteristics, not directly needed by the application - credit card numbers, bank account numbers, passport number? Privacy legislation may restrict whether this can be done.

If we don't have guaranteed unique identifiers, we should provide facilities for administrators to match entity instances on identifier characteristics. and merge duplicates.

6.4.3 Distribution of processes

External design

Generally, the external design will be at least as distributed as the data, ie it is unlikely that there will be more locations that store data than locations that deliver the external design on workstations.

Initially, allocate the external processes needed by users at each business location to workstations at that location.

Then consider whether full functionality can be cost-justified for the locations with a low volume of IT activity. If not, consider providing simpler workstations or dumb terminals at low-volume locations, and locating the user-interface servers at some clustering location. A clustering location would normally be either:

- the dp-location where the data for the local site is stored

or

- some intermediate dp-location served by the data storage location.

It does not have to be a business location.

Conceptual model

If data that serves the external design is stored locally with the workstations, process servers will also be placed there.

If the required data is stored remotely from the external design, the initial allocation of process servers to locations will depend on the preferred technical architecture. Different technical architectures might be used for different design options. The start points would be:

- RDA-oriented architecture: store process servers at business locations, invoke them locally from the external design and use remote data access to stored data

- RPC-oriented architecture: store process servers with their data and invoke them with remote procedure calls from the external design.

Robustness is equivalent for these options. It is dependent on the communication between external design and stored data, and is hardly affected by which end of the line the process servers are stored; RDA software is more mature than RPC software and may be a little more reliable.

The decisions on where to locate process servers will be based mainly on cost and performance. Consider placing process servers at intermediate dp-locations, between the workstations and the data storage locations, trading off:

- the processing power needed to run the servers

- the number of process server computers needed to serve the workstations

- the transmission load on the network

- the cost of the configurations needed to deliver the required performance.

Program-data interface

The program-data interface works at two levels:

- the data location level: this preserves data location transparency for the process servers. It knows where (and under what DBMS) instance data is stored. It would normally be located with the process server, but may need to access some remote facility (such as a central database index) to determine data location

- the database access level: this could be placed with the process server or the data.

6.5 Guidelines for mapping conceptual processes to service architectures

In the most-distributed option, business location, data processing location and data storage location are the same physical location for most processing.

If data has to be separated from business locations, three approaches are:

- put conceptual schema processes at business locations with the functions that invoke them, and use remote database access and distributed commit. This is a useful approach if the data used is spread across different locations. It supports high consistency but may not be as robust as is required - a process cannot succeed if any of the locations it needs data from is off-line

- put conceptual schema processes with their data and have remote procedure calls from the functions at business locations. This is a useful approach if all or most of the data needed by a conceptual process is at one location. It can provide higher performance than the first option and may be more robust - it is dependent on only one communication link

- partition conceptual schema processes with subprocesses located with the data they use, and use remote procedure calls within the conceptual process. This may be a useful approach if the data used is spread across different locations.

Conceptual processes can be tightly-coordinated, but it is possible to run them more loosely. For example, if no data has to be returned from a remote procedure call, then if the called location is off-line, it is possible to suppress the call at the calling location (or not to fail the process when the connection is not successful). Then the remote procedure can be applied as a local process at the called location:

- by shipping it to the called location when it is back on-line

- by letting the called location know informally, by phone or EMail.

However, most of today's technology provides much better support for remote database access than for remote procedure calls. If we want to use remote procedure calls we should expect to have to write some of the middleware ourselves.

There are many variants on the broad options given above:

- even if a process at a dp-location has most of the data it needs there, it may need some instances stored at other locations. The options are to use remote access or to replicate the data

- there may be a constraint to use a shared server (eg for corporate data), with no application processes there - RDA must be used.

One possibility for low-volume business locations is to consider EMail communication for a kind of crude transaction shipping system. The low-volume location (eg EU-Rent hotel or garage branch) needs only data entry and result printing facilities. The transactions are actually run at some clustered location (eg EU-Rent city branch). The advantages are simplicity of design and reliability of EMail networks. The disadvantage is turn-around time.

Confirm design assumptions	We need to build instrumentation into the system to collect data to confirm design assumptions about remote usage or movement of data. This will assist with the tuning of the system after delivery.

Part 2:

Tailored versions of BOS Engineering Method and SSADM

7 BOS Engineering Method extensions

7.1 Introduction

This chapter describes how the generic guidance on developing distributed information systems, described in Part 1, can be used to extend *BOS Engineering Method* and its graphical modelling language, *GRAPES*.

7.1.1 Structure of remainder of this chapter

This chapter:

- describes the development of the BOS Engineering Method (Section 7.1)

- lists related guidance (Section 7.2)

- maps the common decision points, described in Chapter 6, to the BOS Engineering Method (Section 7.3)

- maps the distribution concepts, defined in Chapter 4, to the BOS Engineering Method (Section 7.4)

- lists the modelling tasks when using the BOS Engineering Method specific to the design of distributed systems (Section 7.5)

- describes the extensions to GRAPES (Section 7.6).

7.1.2 Background to BOS Engineering Method

Version 1 of the BOS Engineering Method was developed in parallel with this volume. The major results have already been taken into account in the BOS Engineering Method reference manual. Therefore this volume concentrates on mapping the terminology and decision points to the BOS Engineering Method. Additionally it illustrates the work products in GRAPES with examples taken from EU-Rent.

The three companies Bull, Olivetti and Siemens Nixdorf are engaged in a joint initiative (BOS) for the development of trans-European information systems. As the technical centre of this initiative, the European Methodology and System Center (EMSC) took over the definition of the necessary concepts. The EMSC's working group on methodology analysed the requirements and opportunities for a common information systems engineering method and has subsequently developed a harmonised method based on the methods of the three companies.

As DOMINO/GRAPES from Siemens Nixdorf, OMEGA (a Merise variant) from Bull, and MOiS from Olivetti were found to have a lot in common - similar development processes, similar approaches to system modelling and no contradictory differences; the approach encouraged the definition of the BOS Engineering Method as a highly compatible method. In this context, outstanding features of individual methods - eg the emphasis on communication aspects provided by GRAPES or the emphasis on systemic aspects in OMEGA - did not hamper harmonisation, but improved the power of the common method.

The BOS Engineering Method is advocated by EMSC for the development of trans-European information systems. A special strength is its ability to develop systems with large numbers of components and wide geographical distribution.

The BOS Engineering Method uses the modelling language GRAPES for representing the relevant concepts. During the study for the EU-Rent example it turned out that GRAPES has to be extended to capture all the distribution concepts of the BOS Engineering Method. The European Modelling Language project has been started to enhance the interoperability of various methodologies in the European Union, and enhancements to GRAPES which resulted from the preparation of this volume are being input to the project. GRAPES will develop and migrate towards the European Modelling Language

7.2 Related Guidance

This chapter is based on (but has also influenced the definition of) BOS Engineering Method (Version 1). The relevant related guidance is:

- *BOS Engineering Method reference manual V.1*
- *Representation of work products*
- *GRAPES - Language Description*

Chapter 7
BOS Engineering Method extensions

- *GRAPES BM - Language Description*
- *GRAPES OO - Sprachdefinition.*

Full references may be found in the Bibliography.

7.3 Mapping of common decision points

Figure 7.1 gives the mapping from the decision points introduced in Chapter 6 to the development phases of BOS Engineering Method.

General Decision Point	**BOS Engineering Method Phase** (Related System Model Levels are italicised)
Agree the basis of an IS project in an application area	(Pre-project &) Preliminary Study
Agree the information system requirements	Information System Requirements Specification
Agree the information system architecture	Draft Data Processing Requirements Specification
Agree the information system specification	Information System Specification
Agree the IT system architecture and the user/machine interfaces	Data processing System Specification (1) *Technical Context Model* *Technical Architecture Model*
Agree the specification of the computer system and manual procedures	Data processing System Specification (2) *Technical Details Model*
Agree the information system adaptation	Implementation

Figure 7.1. Mapping of generic decision points to development phases of BOS Engineering Method

7.4	Representation of distribution concepts	This section first gives a mapping of the general distribution concepts introduced in Chapter 4 to the terms used in BOS Engineering Method. Then it defines those work products which are used to describe these concepts. For a complete description of the representation of work products see *Representation of work products*.
7.4.1	Mapping of Terminology	Figure 7.2 maps the distribution concepts of Chapter 4 to the corresponding terms in BOS Engineering Method and lists the work products where the terms are described.

Distribution Concepts (see Chapter 4)	BOS Engineering Method Term[1]	Represented in work product
Actor	Actor	Geographical Business Structure
Actor Role	Role	Organisational Business Structure
Actor Role on Workstation	–	Workstation Type Definition
Actor Type	–	Geographical Business Structure (if required)
Association	Relationship	Global Data Model, Location Data View
Business Location Instance	Business Location Instance	Geographical Business Structure (if required)
Business Location Type	Business Location Type	Geographical Business Structure
Commit Unit	Commit Unit	Procedure Definitions
Commit Unit Trigger	Event	Procedure Definitions
Data Server	–	Geographical DP-structure, Local Database Schemes
DP-Input Message	DP-Input Message	Interaction Structure Definitions
DP-Output Message	DP-Output Message	Interaction Structure Definitions
DP-Location Instance	DP system	Geographical DP-Structure
DP-Location Type	(DP system)	Geographical DP-Structure

Chapter 7
BOS Engineering Method extensions

Distribution Concepts (see Chapter 4)	BOS Engineering Method Term[1]	Represented in work product
Input to Method	–	Interaction Structure Definition *(of a procedure that uses that method)*
Location Instance	–	Geographical business structure, Geographical DP-structure definition
Manual Activity	(Procedure)	Procedure Definitions
Message Channel	Communication Request	Geographical DP-Structure
Message in Dialogue	DP-input/DP-output message	Interaction Structure Definitions
Method	Method	Interaction Structure Definitions
Method Dependency	–	Information Resource Definitions
Method Implementation	–	Information Resource Module Definition
Method Invocation	–	Information Resource Definitions
Method Invocation Implementation	–	Communication Module Definition
Object Class	Information Resource	Information Resource Definitions
Object Class Partition	Local Data Entity	Local Database Schema
Output by Method	–	Interaction Structure Definition *(of a procedure that uses that method)*
Procedure Implementation	–	Interaction Structure, Application Module Definition
Procedure Used in Role	–	Organisational Business Structure
Procedure/Function	Procedure	Procedure Definitions
Process Server	–	Implementation Assignment
Record Population Partition	–	Local Database Schemes
Record Type	Record Type	Local Database Schemes

Distribution Concepts (see Chapter 4)	BOS Engineering Method Term[1]	Represented in work product
Record Type Storage Capability	–	Local Database Schemes
Role at Location Type	–	Geographical Business Structure
Role Played		Geographical Business Structure
User-interface Server		Implementation Assignment, Workstation Type Definitions
Validation/Formatting implementation	–	Dialogue Module Definition
Validation/Formatting Process	–	Procedure Definitions, Message Definitions
Workstation	Workstation	Workstation Type Definitions, Geographical Business Structure
Workstation Requirements	Workstation Type	Organisational Business Structure

[1] A '__' means that although there is no explicit correspondence between the concept and a BOS Engineering Method term, the concept is used implicitly within the method. Terms in parentheses are either specialisations or generalisations of the concept.

Figure 7.2: Mapping of distribution concepts to BOS Engineering Method terms

7.4.2 Examples of the Work Products

In this chapter we use the EU-Rent example to illustrate work products that describe facets of distribution.

Organisational Business Structure

The organisational hierarchy shows the decomposition into organisational units, the relevant roles and the procedures carried out by them. See Figure 7.3.

Chapter 7
BOS Engineering Method extensions

Organisational Unit	Roles	Procedures
Financial Department	Invoice Management	register payment control payment
Rental Department	Reservation Management	make reservation cancel reservation register new customer delete customer change customer
	Rental Management	prepare check-out check-out check-in prepare invoice register payment control car return register car return register car damage
	Car Management	make car ready control car register car for service
	Service Agent	cleaning of car etc
Management Department	Branch Management	assign cars to reservations produce list of cars initiate transport cancel transport register car pick-up register car arrival investigate car

Figure 7.3: Organisational Business Structure

Geographical Business Structure (on business location type level)

In its draft state, the Geographical Business Structure describes location types rather than instances. It documents the business locations (differentiated by activity levels) and the roles associated with them. The workstation requirements are also documented. See figure 7.4.

Business Location Type	Associated Roles	Workstation Requirements
Head Office	Fleet Management Location Management	5 Terminals, 3 Printers, etc
Airport Branch	Branch Management Reservation Management Rental Management Invoice Management Car Management Service Agent	...
City Branch	Branch Management Reservation Management Rental Management Invoice Management Car Management	...
Local Agency	Branch Management Reservation Management Rental Management Invoice Management	...
Depot	Depot Management Car Maintenance	...

Figure 7.4: Geographical Business Structure (on business location type level)

Geographical Business Structure (on instance level)
: The geographical business structure can be completed to show the actual geographical distribution of the business locations, the actors working there and the workstations installed.

Remark: Typically this table will not be compiled into a specific work product, because it changes quite frequently. Rather it contains a reference to existing documentation within an organisation.

Organisational Interaction Definition
: A location interaction diagram shows the interaction between the identified business location types, ie it shows their synchronisation in order to achieve a business transaction. See Figure 7.5. There may be several Location Interaction Diagrams corresponding to different business transactions. Business location types

may appear several times if a business transaction spreads over more than one location instance.

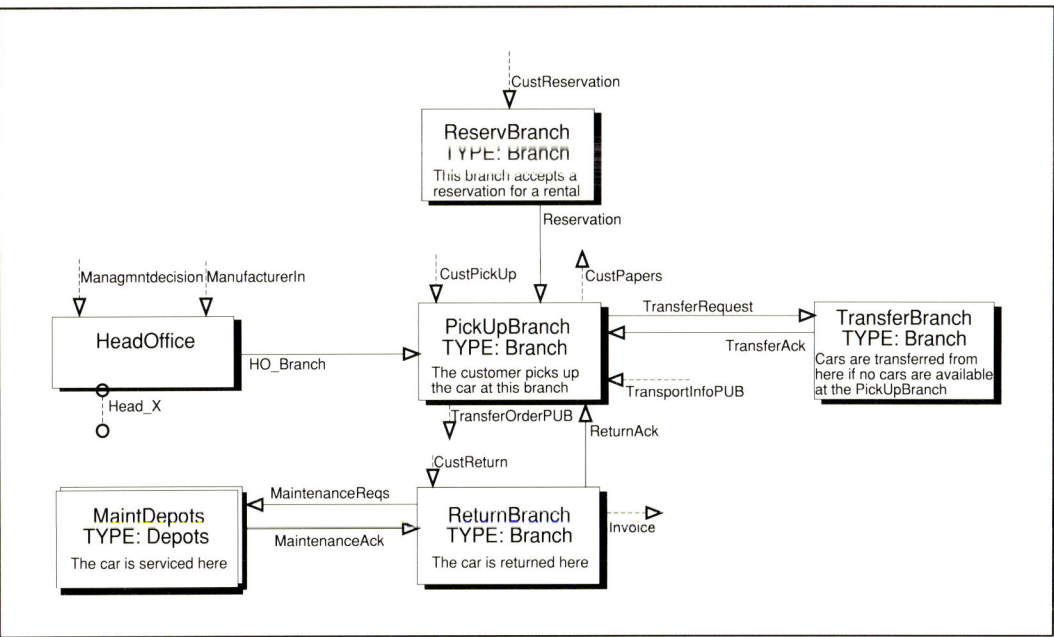

Figure 7.5: Location interaction diagram

Geographical DP-Structure

The Geographical DP-Structure identifies the data-processing systems and the business locations (or workstations) served by these data-processing locations. Additionally it documents the logical and physical communication channels between dp-locations. See Figure 7.6.

DP-System	Business locations served
Germany South, München Airport	München Airport München Balanstraße etc
Germany North, Frankfurt	Hamburg Hafenstraße etc
Great Britain, London	Oxford Branch Ullapool Branch etc

Figure 7.6: Geographical DP-Structure

Location Data View   The location data view shows the data needed at a business location type to execute the assigned procedures. It is a subset of the Global Data Model together with restrictions defining the entities which may be accessed. See Figure 7.7.

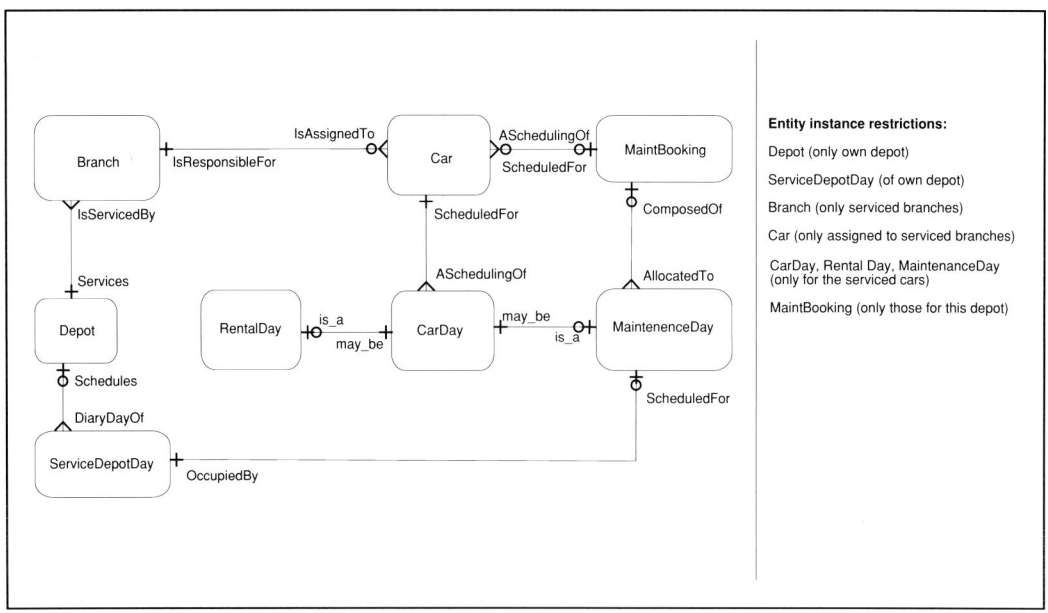

Figure 7.7: Location Data View of a Depot

Chapter 7
BOS Engineering Method extensions

Local Database Schema
: The Local Database Schema defines the records stored on a data server at a data-processing location type. See Figures 7.8 and 7.9.

Figure 7.8: Record Storage Capabilities of a Service Depot

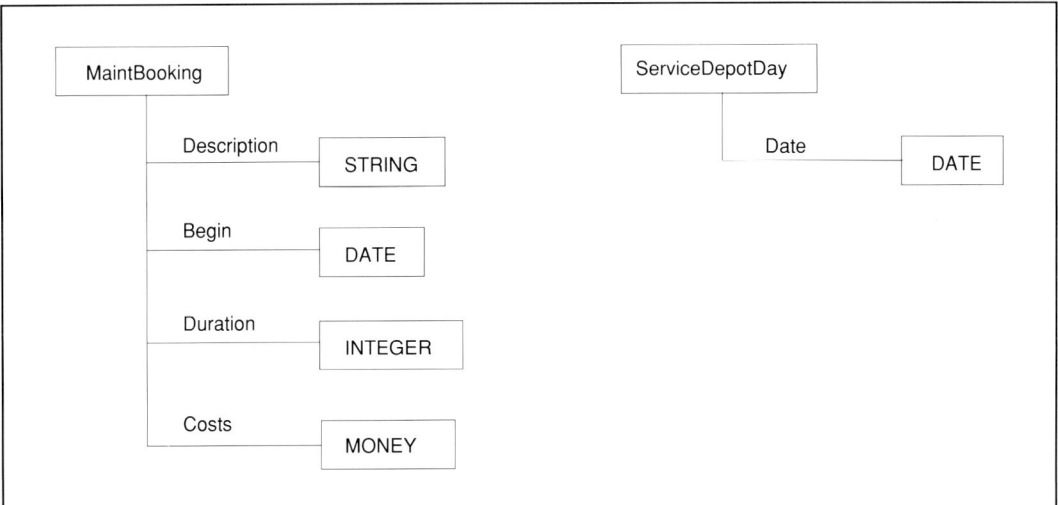

Figure 7.9: Record Structure of data stored at a Service Depot

7.5 Method specific heuristics and rules

In this section we list those modelling tasks specific to the design of distributed systems. For more details see the *BOS Engineering Method reference manual*. In particular this section covers:

- definition of geographic business structure (Section 7.5.1)

- definition of organisational interactions (Section 7.5.2)

- definition of location data views (Section 7.5.3)

- robustness analysis and design for procedures (Section 7.5.4)

- identification of DP systems and their locations (Section 7.5.5)

- distribution of information resources and data (Section 7.5.6)

- location assignment to procedure implementations (Section 7.5.7)

- location assignment to method implementations (Section 7.5.8)

- implementing internal messages by data and data access (Section 7.5.9)

- specification of internal communication protocols (Section 7.5.10).

Each modelling task is described in terms of its input and output work products and the approach to the task. Where appropriate examples or rules for ensuring consistency with other work products are given.

Input or output work products that act purely as additional sources of information are optional and are shown in square brackets. In contexts where only some of the concepts in a work product are of interest, the concepts of interest are listed in round brackets.

7.5.1 Definition of Geographical Business Structure

Input Work Product:
- Organisational Business Structure.

Output Work Product:
- Geographical Business Structure.

Chapter 7
BOS Engineering Method extensions

Approach	In this modelling task business locations and the actors working there are examined. The Business locations of a company may be listed in extensive branch office catalogues. Business location types are identified according to the roles performed in business locations. Business locations of the same location type typically communicate with the same external partners (types).
	In addition the activity level of each business location type is specified. The activity level describes the number of actors working in a business location type, the number of roles executed in parallel and the number of events processed in a time period. Business location types might be classified into business location subtypes according to the activity levels of business locations of the same business location type.
	The national languages to be supported are also defined for each business location (type).
Consistency rules	The roles identified in the organisational business structure have to be taken into account. Each role has to be assigned to at least one location type.

7.5.2 Definition of Organisational Interactions

Input Work Products:	• Procedure Definitions
	• Geographical Business Structure
	• Organisational Business Structure.
Output Work Products:	• Organisational Interaction Definition (Business Locations [Types], External Partner)
	• Organisational Interaction Definition (Organisational Units)
	• Organisational Interaction Definition (Roles).

Approach

The organisational interaction description may encompass different types of interaction descriptions, between:

- roles

- procedures at different business locations (business location types) and external partners

- organisational units

- business locations (business location types) and external partners.

Thus the organisational interaction structure shows the geographical or organisational distribution of procedures and their communication.

Interaction between roles

To model interaction between roles, the roles and their communication needs are examined.

Interaction between procedures at different business locations

The communication between procedures executed at different business locations (types) is described. It can be identified by analysing the roles assigned to the business location type and procedures assigned to the roles.

Interaction between organisational units
Each organisational unit is assigned several roles. Thus the interaction between organisational units can be derived from their roles and the interaction between the roles.

Interaction between business location types and with external partners

The business location types are defined according to the roles that are performed there. Thus the interaction between them can be derived from the interaction structure between roles. In addition the communication between the business location types and the external partners is described by examining the external input/output messages and assigning them to the business location types which receive/send them.

7.5.3 Definition of Location Data Views

Input Work Products:
- Geographical Business Structure
- Organisational Business Structure
- Procedure Definitions
- Information Resource Definition.

Output Work Product:
- Location Data Views (for each business location/business location type).

Approach

Dependent on the distribution of the information system and the distribution of data that is involved, the data view for each business location or business location type is developed. The location data view describes the data that has to be available at a business location/business location type.

For each business location/business location type it must be determined:

- what data is accessed (either enquired on or updated)
- via which access paths
- how often the data is accessed
- how many data entities are needed.

The set of accessed entity types and the access mode (enquiry or update) are identified as follows.

The analysis is performed top down from the definition of the business location types (business location), by roles (actors and their assigned roles) and their assigned procedures, to the methods called by the procedures.

The entity types and relationships enquired on or updated by these methods are noted together with their access mode. If only a certain subset of the entities of an entity type is accessed and this subset is (mostly) disjoint from the subset of entities accessed at other locations, this should be noted. An example of this would be if a local branch only accessed customer entities associated with that branch).

The frequency of data access via the different modes is estimated. The enquiry and update frequency is determined by estimating the execution frequency of each procedure. Typically only a subset of the procedures produce the most access traffic and are therefore important in estimating the access frequencies via the different modes.

The global data of the whole information system is constrained vertically into a subset of all data entity types. If an actor only accesses a subset of the entities of a certain type (for example if a business location is only responsible for the customers managed in that local area), the subset may also be horizontally constrained.

Thus the data that must be available at each geographical business location can be derived.

7.5.4 Robustness Analysis and Design for Procedures

Input Work Products:

- Procedure Definitions

- [Interaction Structure Definitions]

- [Batch Step Definition]

- [Access Path Definitions (via DP system boundaries)]

- [Implementation Assignment].

Output Work Products:	• [Procedure Definitions (for degraded service)]
	• [Interaction Structure Definitions]
	• [Batch Step Definition]
	• [Local Database Schemes].
Approach	The purpose of this modelling task is the analysis of robustness requirements and the design of degraded procedures in case of communication failures.

The main question to be answered is:

- What should happen if a procedure cannot access certain data stored at a remote location?

If the availability of data is absolutely necessary, then the modelling task 'Distribution of Information Resources and Data' should be revisited. Otherwise a degraded service for a procedure has to be designed.

Sometimes it is possible to handle the procedure manually, ie to take manual notes on prepared forms for the time being and to carry out the procedure on-line later.

On-line solutions are possible, if the DP system that serves the business location is still running. The procedure may be split into an on-line part and a batch part that is carried out when communication is available again.

If new data entities need to be created, the data can be stored on-line in local storage and transferred by a batch step to the remote DP system when communication is available again. Eg, customer data is stored locally, and included in the database later.

For reading and updating of data entities, store all relevant data needed to carry out the batch part of the procedure locally. The batch part carries out the real business procedure.

In both cases the effects on the business have to be considered carefully. Since each procedure corresponds to a real world action, conflicts may arise with business rules.

Example

A company may hold a credit limit for each customer, that is queried every time an order from a customer is processed. If this credit limit is exceeded the order is rejected (or delayed).

If the DP-system where this credit limit is held is not reachable, the order may be processed even though the credit limit is exceeded.

7.5.5 Identification of DP Systems and their Locations

Input Work Products:
- Geographical Business Structure
- Procedure Definitions
- Location Data Views
- Organisational Interaction Definition
- [Implementation Assignment].

Output Work Product:
- Geographical DP Structure.

Approach

The design of the physical DP structure must be done very carefully, because it strongly influences the operational costs of the distributed DP system.

Where DP systems with enough spare capacity are already installed, they might also be considered for executing the application packages.

A set of options for DP structures must be analysed according to costs, available technology, robustness and

Chapter 7
BOS Engineering Method extensions

privacy considerations, etc. Typically there are two extreme alternatives:

- design a centralised system. All business locations are connected to this central system.

- design a maximally distributed system. All business locations have one (or eventually several) DP systems. Processing capability and data storage is locally available.

Other options can be constructed by starting from the maximally distributed system and clustering geographically or logically neighbouring sites into one DP system.

Clusters are designed to reduce hardware, software and communication costs.

7.5.6 Distribution of Information Resources and Data

Input Work Products:	• [Information Resource Definitions]
	• Procedure Definitions
	• Location Data Views
	• [Access Path Definitions]
	• Global Data Model
	• Geographical Business Structure.
Output Work Product:	• Local Database Schemes
Approach	The aim of this modelling task is to define the storage location of the data of an information resource. It uses a decision table that allows a first-cut assignment of (the data of) the information resources to DP systems. For

155

fine-tuning a more precise analysis of local and remote data access is needed.

The decision to store an information resource at a particular storage location is guided by the following criteria:

- ownership

- volumes

- remote access frequency

- robustness.

Ownership: 'Which data entities belong naturally (or legally) to a business location and thus to the DP system supporting it?' One way to determine the ownership from the global data model is as follows:

1. Determine the entity types that coincide with business location types

2. All entity types that are in a direct many to one relationship to a business location type are candidates for being 'owned' by this business location. For example, all cars are owned by a local branch.

3. Step 2 can be iterated for indirect many to one relationships. For example, car days associated to a car has an indirect many to one relationship to branch.

4. Steps 2 and 3 may result in conflicts where the same entities are owned by several business locations and ownership is not unique. For example, a rental has a pick-up and a return branch.

There may also be entity types that are not in a direct or indirect many to one relationship with a business location entity type. Both cases might be resolved by finding a business location that has a significantly greater access frequency than the others. If not this results by default in global ownership.

Ownership is assigned at the information resource instance level. Thus ownership partitions an information resource into subclasses, that are stored at different DP systems.

Ownership is used to identify a storage DP system candidate. In the following, 'local' means the location that has the ownership.

Volumes: 'What storage capacity is needed to store the data encapsulated in an information resource?'

- *high:* The required storage capacity is significant with respect to available storage capacity or overall required storage capacity.

- *low:* The required storage capacity is negligible with respect to available storage capacity or overall required storage capacity.

Remote access frequency: 'How often is an information resource read, or updated (created, deleted) by remote DP systems?'

This can also be derived from the location data views of the supported business locations. This criterion should be documented as one of:

- *low access*: this information resource is only occasionally accessed remotely (compared to local accesses from the 'owner').

- *high read only*: this information resource is often remotely read but rarely updated.

- *high update*: this information resource is often read and/or updated remotely.

Robustness: 'Can processing at a remote DP system continue, if the access to the information resource is not available?'

- *required*: Certain important processing cannot continue if access to this entity fails.

- *not required*: The main processing can be carried out (at least in a degraded manner) independently of this data.

Depending on the results, one of the following storage concepts will be most suitable:

- *local*. Store the information resource partition locally. This is normally used if the ownership can be clearly identified and robustness considerations at other DP systems are of minor importance.

- *central*. Store the information resource centrally. This is normally used if the ownership is not clear and the data is updated by many DP systems.

- *repl*. Replicate the same information resource at all DP systems. This is normally used if the storage volumes and update rates are low or high availability of data is required.

- *cache*. Store the information resource centrally but also cache instances locally. This means that the information resource is stored centrally, but each access makes a local copy of the information resource instance. Subsequent read accesses at the same DP system are then available locally. Special mechanisms must be provided to handle updates to the data and to avoid unlimited growth of cache volumes.

The final row in the decision table in Figures 7.10a and 7.10b gives a recommendation for storage concepts.

Ownership	local	local	local	local	local	--	--
Volumes	--	low	high	high	low	--	high
Remote Access Frequency	low	high read only	high read only	high read only	high read only	high update	high update
Robustness	--	not req'd	not req'd	required	required	not req'd	required
Storage concept	local	repl.	local/ cache	cache/ repl.	repl.	central	cache

Figure 7.10a: Decision table for storage concepts - part 1

Ownership	global	global	global	global	global	global
Volumes	low	low	high	high	high	high
Remote Access Frequency	low/ high read only	high update	low	low	high read only	high read only
Robustness	--	required	not req'd	required	not req'd	required
Storage Concept	repl.	repl.	central	cache/ repl.	cache	cache/ repl.

Figure 7.10b: Decision table for storage concepts - part 2

If high availability of data is needed, further considerations have to be made to improve the availability of the network and the computer equipment.

7.5.7 Location Assignment to Procedure Implementations

Input work products:
- Procedure Definitions
- [Interaction Structure Definitions]
- [Batch Step Definitions]
- Geographical DP Structure

	• [Local Database Schemes]
	• [HW/SW Configuration].
Output Work Product:	• Implementation Assignment (for procedures).
Approach	First-cut assignment: The automated parts of the procedures (interaction structures and batch steps) are implemented on that DP system serving the business location where the batch step is triggered and the interaction structure is used. Where parts of the procedure produce output messages at another business location supported by another DP system, this part of the procedure may be implemented at that DP system.

This ensures that the procedure is available even if the communication with other DP systems fails and service has to be carried out in a degraded manner.

The first-cut assignment may be reviewed, if the technology available for communication is known. For example, if distributed commit management is not available, or only available in a restricted form it may be necessary to implement commit units on DP systems where the manipulated data is located. |

7.5.8 Location Assignment to Method Implementations

Input Work Products:	• Information Resource Definitions
	• Local Database Schemes
	• [Batch Step Definitions].
Output Work Product:	• Implementation Assignment (for methods).

Chapter 7
BOS Engineering Method extensions

Approach

First-cut rules for the allocation (or assignment) of method implementations:

1 If the system software supports remote procedure calls, implement methods where the data is located.

2 If the system software only supports remote database access, implement methods where the calling procedures are located.

The decision should also be guided by the following considerations.

If data location transparency is required but not provided by the database technology, it should be implemented by the methods. The methods map data requests internally to the appropriate DP system locations. The methods are implemented where they are invoked.

7.5.9 Implementing Internal Messages by Data and Data Access

Input Work Products:
- Internal Message Definitions
- Procedure Definitions
- [Interaction Structure Definitions]
- [Batch Step Definitions]
- [Local Database Schemes].

Output Products:
- [Global Data Model]
- [Information Resource Definitions]
- [Procedure Definitions]
- [Internal Message Definitions]

- [Interaction Structure Definitions]
- [Batch Step Definitions]
- [Local Database Schemes].

Approach

If the selected system software does not support the paradigm of message passing the internal messages must be replaced by information stored in a permanent database. The creation of a data entity is then equivalent to the sending of a message. The looking up and perhaps updating of the data entity is equivalent to receiving and responding to a message.

The Data Catalogue is updated.

Example

If a rented car is returned to another branch, the pick-up branch must be informed that the car has been returned. (The branch manager of the pick-up branch must carry out special procedures if the car is not returned by the time agreed at pick-up).

The return of a car is modelled by an internal message sent from the return branch to the pick-up branch. If the underlying technical architecture does not support the exchange of messages, the sending of a message indicating the car has been returned can be simulated by adding a field to the rental entity which shows the current state of the rental (eg 'booked', 'picked-up', 'returned', 'payment received' or 'closed'). Methods must be defined to update this state field. The branch manager or an automated procedure must still check for non-returned cars.

Remarks

(1) Modelling the cooperation between components via messages allows complex synchronisations of messages which start a procedure to be specified simply. To specify the same using data states is considerably more complex.

For example, an invoice should be printed automatically after both the mileage of a returned car is reported and the validity of the credit card is checked. Both messages must arrive before printing can start. The sequence of arrival is irrelevant. The respective state description is now more complex and is one of:

```
(no mileage, no credit card check)
(mileage, no credit card check)
(no mileage, credit card check)
(mileage, credit card check)
```

In this example, the state descriptions can be recorded in null-values of the respective records holding mileage and credit card information, but nevertheless the handling and description at state level is quite complicated.

(2) Monitoring complex state changes in a system may require the specification and implementation of demons that react if the database is in a certain state. However the implementation of demons in a distributed environment is at least very inefficient and may even be impossible.

7.5.10 Specification of Internal Communication Protocols

Input Work Products:
- Procedure Definitions
- Geographical DP Structure
- Hardware/Software Configuration
- Implementation Assignment.

Output Work Product:
- DP System Interaction (internal communication).

Approach

The implementation assignments are analysed according to their requests for communication with other DP systems inside the information system. These communication requests can be for example:

- remote procedure calls

- remote database accesses
- file or message transfers.

An estimation of average and maximum throughput rate, and the required maximum response time for each communication type is given for each DP system. See Figure 7.11.

Communication request	Communication protocol	Throughput average (bytes per day)	Throughput maximum (bytes per second)	Maximum response time (seconds)
Customer look-up and Booking look-up	Remote database access via X.25 WAN	3000 * 200	4 * 200	5
Return message	X.400 via X.25 WAN	10 * 200	---	---

Figure 7.11: Specification of internal communication protocols

In general, only those communication requests producing the biggest loads on the network need to be analysed.

If several physical communication links to different DP systems are available, the estimation of communication requests has to be split up according to the physical links.

For the communication requests an appropriate physical communication structure (such as star shaped with a central node in the middle, hierarchically organised or a fully connected network) has to be defined.

Thus each physical communication link is specified by:

- the source DP system
- the target DP system (for a dedicated line)
- the type of connection link (either dedicated or dial-up)
- the maximum throughput rate (eg 9600 Baud)
- the protocol layers used (eg X.25, TCP-IP, X.400).

Chapter 7
BOS Engineering Method extensions

Consistency Rules	Each DP system must be able to communicate with the DP systems it needs to access.
	The throughput of each physical link must be bigger than the sum of required maximum rates of throughput rates of the communication requests flowing over that line.

7.6 Extensions to GRAPES

This section discusses deficiencies of GRAPES detected when doing the case study. Some short-term work arounds are proposed and solutions to overcome the deficiencies are sketched. In the following we assume familiarity with the basic concepts of GRAPES.

7.6.1 Data Views

GRAPES allows designers to define databases specified by ER-diagrams. It is not possible to define sub-views (ie a reduced set of entity types and relationship types) on to such a database.

Short term work-around: Use ER-diagrams to specify the sub view (but no explicit association with the viewed database is possible).

Possible solution: Allow data stores on a lower level to be associated with data stores on a higher level. The consistency condition is that the ER-diagram on the lower level is a sub-view of the corresponding ER-diagram on the higher level.

7.6.2 Too many objects in diagrams for physical distribution

One of the big strengths of GRAPES is its facility to animate and simulate a complex system.

But big distributed systems may consist of large numbers of business locations cooperating with each other. Animation within GRAPES is insufficiently powerful at present to draw a communication diagram that shows the interaction of say 100 instances. Simulation needs a precise specification of the instances and their interaction in order to estimate throughput rates and other quantitative factors.

165

Short term work-around: Specify only a small number of business locations and show their interaction (for example by using a location interaction diagram). These diagrams can be used for animation.

Possible solution: Typically the business locations can be classified into a small number of business location types. Extend GRAPES by mechanisms to specify arrays of objects. These extensions should also include facilities for dynamic addressing.

8 BOS Engineering Method applied to EU-Rent

8.1 Introduction

This chapter shows how BOS Engineering Method, as extended in Chapter 7, can be used to develop a distributed system. It does this by applying the method to the development of the EU-Rent case study. The chapter is divided into the following sections:

- Business Context Model (Section 8.2)
- Business Service Model (Section 8.3)
- Business Organisation Model (Section 8.4)
- Technical Distribution Scenarios (Section 8.5).

8.2 Business Context Model

The business context model describes the external partners of the information system and how they interact with it without regard to the internals of the information system.

8.2.1 Context Definition

The external partners of the EU-Rent information system are customers, who request rentals, transport companies, who transport cars from one branch to another for EU-Rent, and manufacturers, who sell cars and take back old cars from EU-Rent.

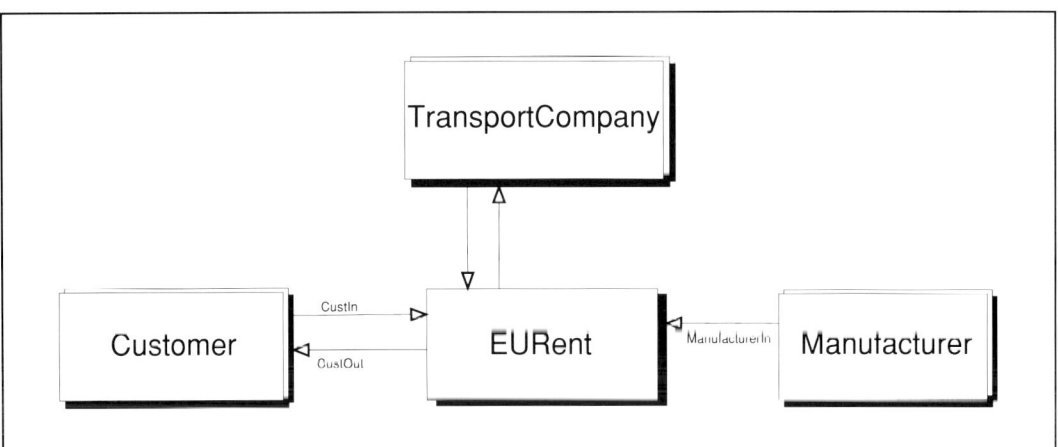

Figure 8.1: Communication Diagram showing the interaction of external partners with EU-Rent

Figure 8.1 shows the external partners and how they interact with EU-Rent. The detail of the interactions is described in interface tables which show the messages going in and out. For each message its data type and frequencies are given (frequencies per week for the whole system, ie total of all business locations). See Figures 8.2 to 8.5.

Name	Data Type	Description	Frequency		
			time unit	avg.	max.
ReservRequest	ReservRequestDT	A customer makes a reservation before picking up the rented car. Reservation and PickUpBranch may be different locations.	week	400,000	
CarPickUpWORes	CarPickUpDT	A customer rents a car without any Reservation. They may rent a car if there is one to rent at the branch or be sent to a nearby branch.	week	20,000	
CarPickUpWithRes	ReservationID	The arrival of the customer starts the process of delivering a reserved car.	week	360,000	
ReservCancel	ReservCancelDT	A customer may cancel a reservation before picking up the car.	week	40,000	
CarReturn	RentalID	This signal means that the car has been returned to the return branch.	week	380,000	
Payment	PaymentDT	A rental ends with the payment for the car rental.	week	380,000	

*Figure 8.2: Messages sent from customer to EU-Rent (IT **CustIn**)*

Name	Data Type	Description	Frequency.		
			time unit	avg.	max.
ReservAcknow	ReservationAckDT	An accepted reservation is acknowledged to the customer immediately by phone or by letter.	week	398,000	
ReservDenial	DenialDT	A rental may be denied in the case of overbooking, black listing, etc.	week	2,000	
Invoice	InvoiceDT	After the car has been returned, an invoice is sent or handed over to the customer.	week	380,000	
CarKeysPapers	SIGNAL	When the car rental contract is signed car keys and papers are handed over to the customer.	week	380,000	

*Figure 8.3: Messages sent from EU-Rent to customer (IT **CustOut**)*

Name	Data Type	Description	Frequency.		
			time unit	avg.	max.
TransportOrder	TransportOrderDT	The order for a car transfer is sent to a car transport company.	week	7,010	

*Figure 8.4: Messages sent from EU-Rent to transport company (IT **TransportOrder**)*

Name	Data Type	Description	Frequency		
			time unit	avg	max
TransportOrder	CarTransferID	This message is sent when a transport loads the cars.	week	7,000	
TransportCancel	CarTransferID	This message is sent, if a transport is cancelled.	week	10	
TransCarDelivery	CarTransferID	This message is sent when a transport delivers its cars.	week	7,000	

*Figure 8.5: Messages sent from transport company to EU-Rent (IT **TransportInfo**)*

8.2.2 EU-Rent Business Transactions (Trigger/result schema)

EU-Rent Business Transactions include:

- **CarRental** (Renting of cars)

- **CapacityPlanning&Transfer** (The car capacity for the next day is planned and any necessary car transfers from nearby branches are organised)

- **OpenBranch** (Opening a new branch)

- **CloseBranch** (Closing a branch)

- **MaintainCar** (Regular maintenance and repair of cars).

In this case study only the car rental business transaction (**CarRental**) is described in detail.

CarRental encompasses making a reservation, booking, check-out, check-in and invoicing.

The trigger/result schema (see Figure 8.6) defines the combination of events that triggers the business transactions (or business sub-transactions) and the output messages delivered as a result of the business transaction. The triggers and results are the messages defined in the interface tables (see Figures 8.2 to 8.5), eg the trigger **ReservRequest** (in Figure 8.6) is a message in the interface table **CustIn** (see Figure 8.2).

Chapter 8
BOS Engineering Method applied to EU-Rent

Trigger	Business transaction/procedures	Result
ReservRequest ReservCancel	**CarRental** Reservation	ReservAcknow ReservDenial
CarPickUpWithRes CarPickUpWORes	Check-out	CarKeysPapers
CarReturn	Check-in	Invoice
Payment	Control Payment	

*Figure 8.6: Trigger/Result Schema for the business transaction **CarRental***

Overview of CarRental

In the following, the procedures of **CarRental** are described informally.

Reservation:
When a customer makes a reservation (**ReservRequest**) they get (by phone or by letter) an acknowledgement (**ReservAcknow**) or a denial (**ReservDenial**) immediately. In general reservations are acknowledged. They may be denied, for example, if a customer is on the blacklist or has bad credit card status. Customers can cancel reservations (**ReservCancel**).

Check-out:
Cars can either be picked up with an advanced reservation (**CarPickUpWithRes**) or by walk-in customers (**CarPickUpWORes**). In the latter case the rental can be denied, if the required car is not available at the branch. The customer receives the car, keys, paper and booking contract (**CarKeysPapers**) when he picks up the car.

Check-in:
When a car is returned (**CarReturn**), the car mileage and fuel are checked, and the invoice prepared.

Control Payment:
The payment of the invoice is registered.

Information Systems Engineering Library
Distributed Systems Application Development

8.2.3 External Message Definitions

The syntax and semantics of the data items of the input and output messages are defined.

Figure 8.7 shows a part of the data catalogue with some of the data type definitions used in the interface tables in Figures 8.2 and 8.3.

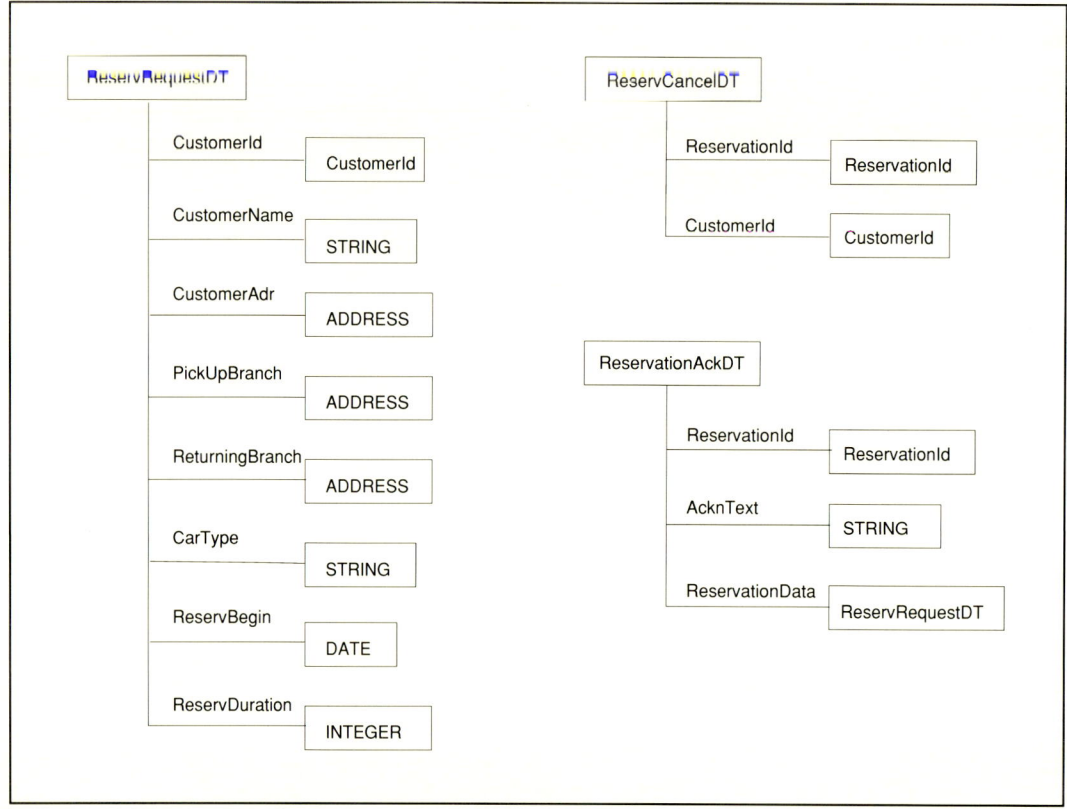

Figure 8.7: Data type definitions for external messages

8.3 Business Service Model

The business service model defines the behaviour and information processed in an enterprise. This is done by the examination of the business transactions and the definition of the global data model together with the information resources.

8.3.1 Business Transaction Definitions

Here only the business transaction **CarRental** is described. Business transaction are defined in a task CD's that show their subtasks, and the relationships between subtasks and to tasks of external partners. Tasks are connected by events that are produced by one task and trigger the following tasks.

The main subtasks of **CarRental** are **Reservation, Rental of Car** and **Control Payment**. The task **Reservation** is triggered by the request for a reservation from the customer. The booking data is transmitted to the task **Rental of Car** that takes place when the customer picks up the car. The task **Rental of Car** decomposes into the subtasks **pick-up** and **return of a car**; these details are described on the next level of refinement. Finally in the task **Control Payment** the receipt of customer payment is monitored and registered. All events shown in this diagram are complex events, that are refined together with the tasks on the next level of detail (see Figures 8.8 to 8.11).

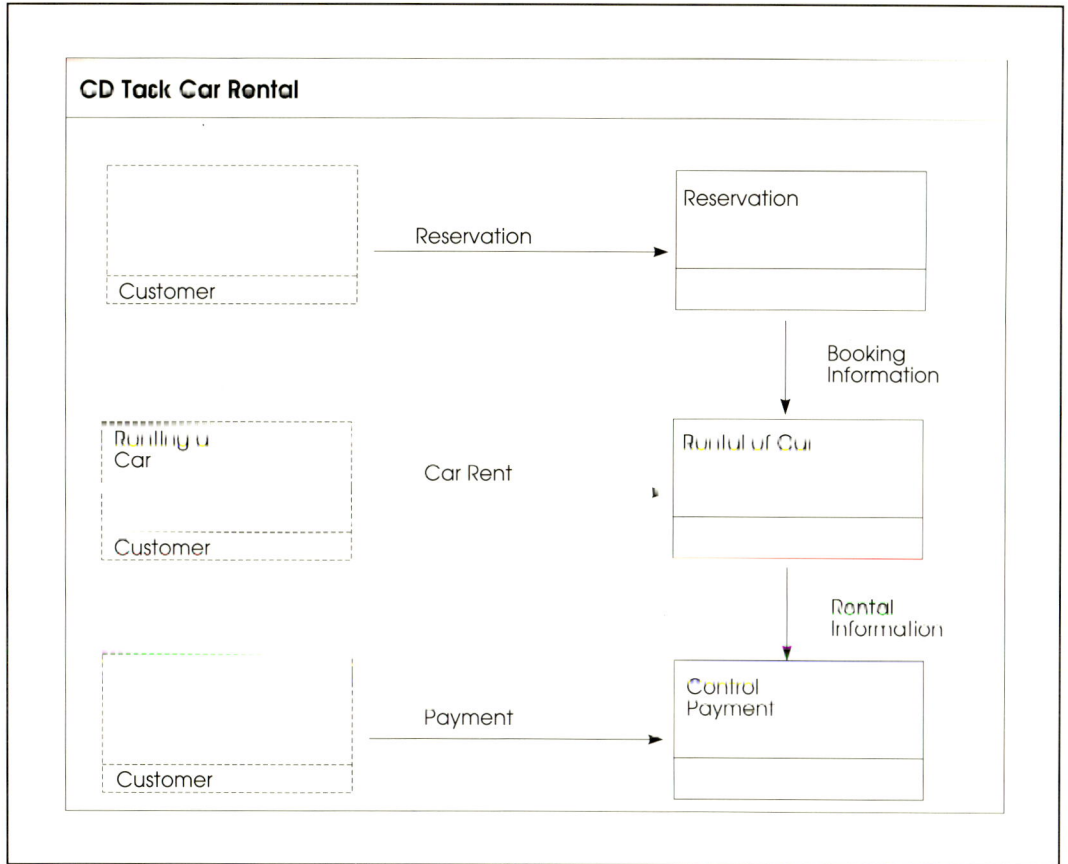

*Figure 8.8: Task CD for the business transaction **Car Rental***

The elementary tasks correspond to procedures. The procedures are described in more detail in the Business Organisation Model, in Section 8.4.

The subtask **Reservation** consists of the elementary subtask **MakeReservation** assigned to the role Reservation Management. Figure 8.19 gives an overview of the roles of EU-Rent and their assigned elementary tasks (procedures). The event **Reservation** represented in Figure 8.8 is refined into the events **Reservation Request**, **Reservation Denial** and **Reservation Acknowledgement** in Figure 8.9

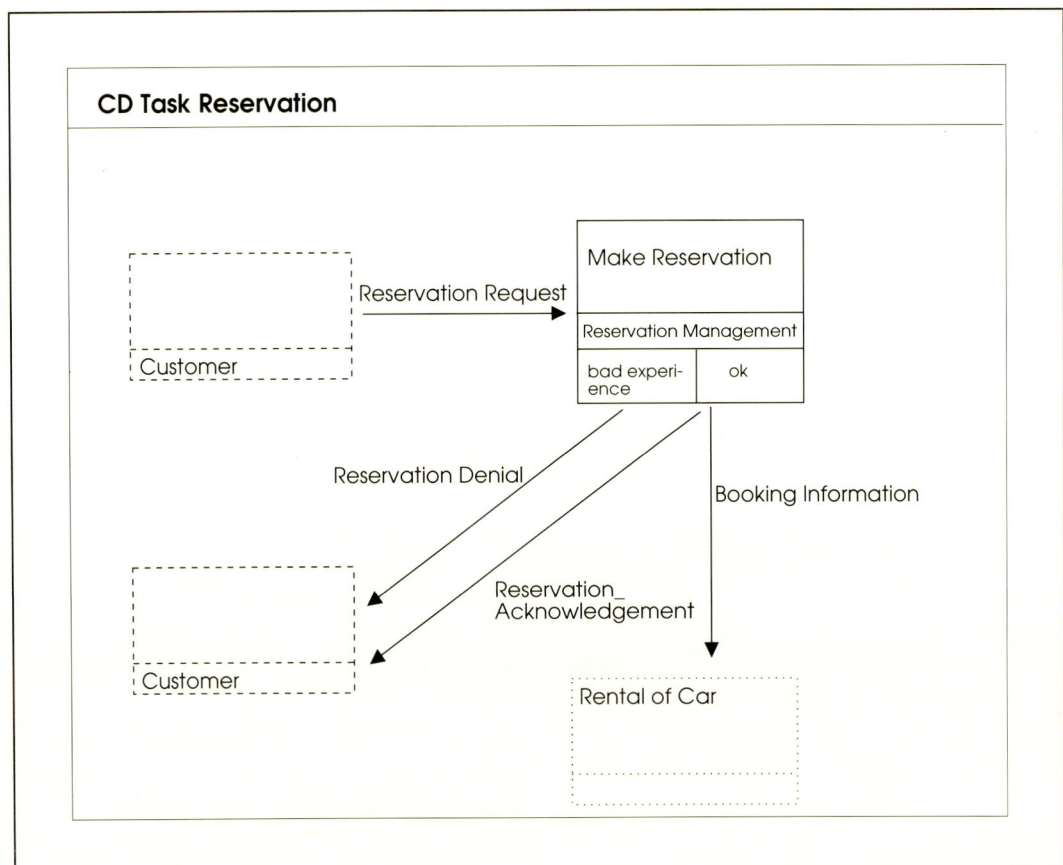

Figure 8.9: Task CD for the subtask *Reservation*

Chapter 8
BOS Engineering Method applied to EU-Rent

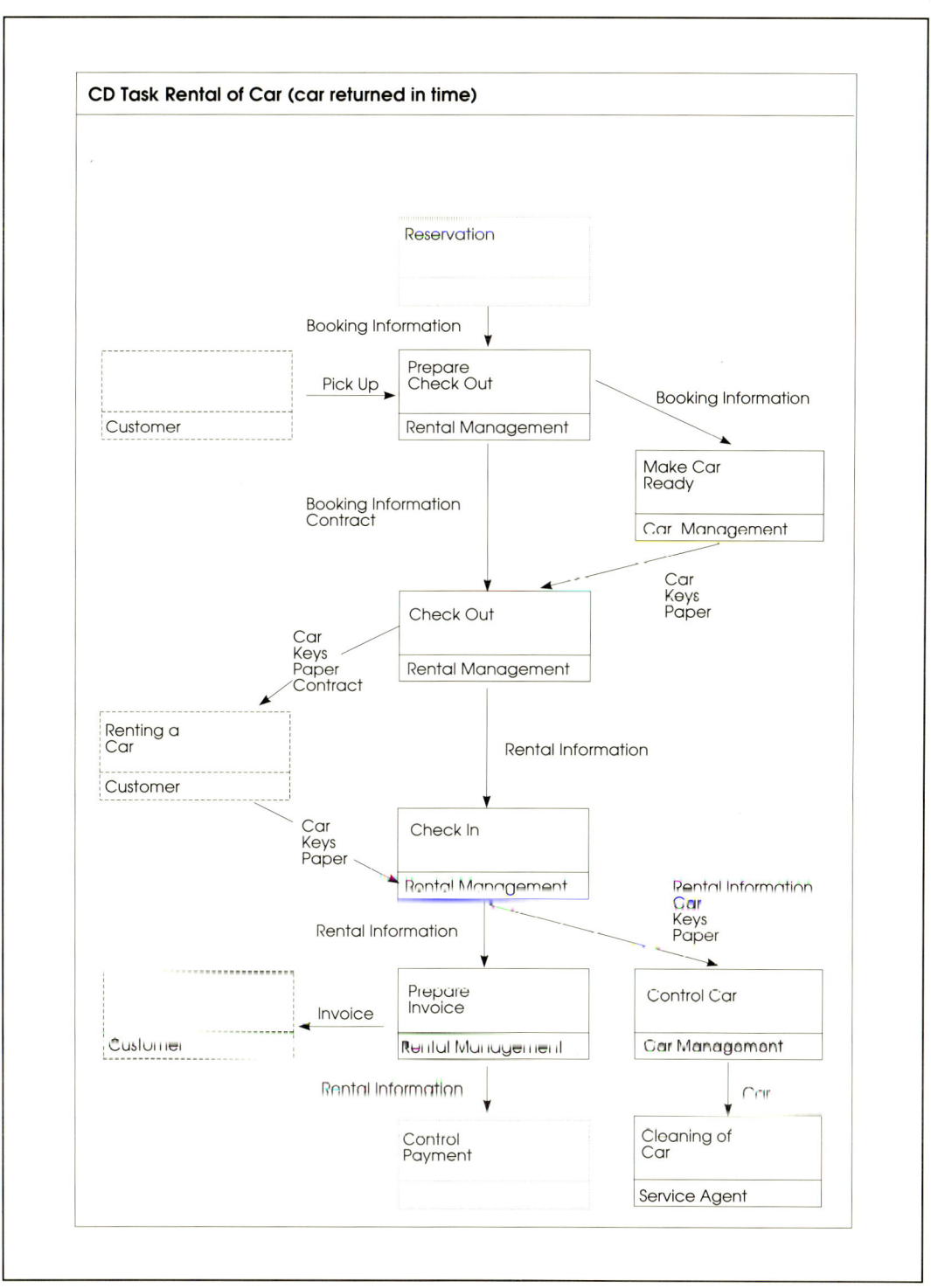

Figure 8.10: Task CD for the subtask **Rental of Car**

The subtask **Rental of Car (car returned in time)** is more complex and consists of several subtasks: **Prepare Check-out, Make Car Ready, Check-out, Check-in, Prepare Invoice, Control Car** and **Cleaning of Car**. See Figures 8.10 and 8.11. These tasks are performed by several different roles such as **Rental Management** or **Car Management**.

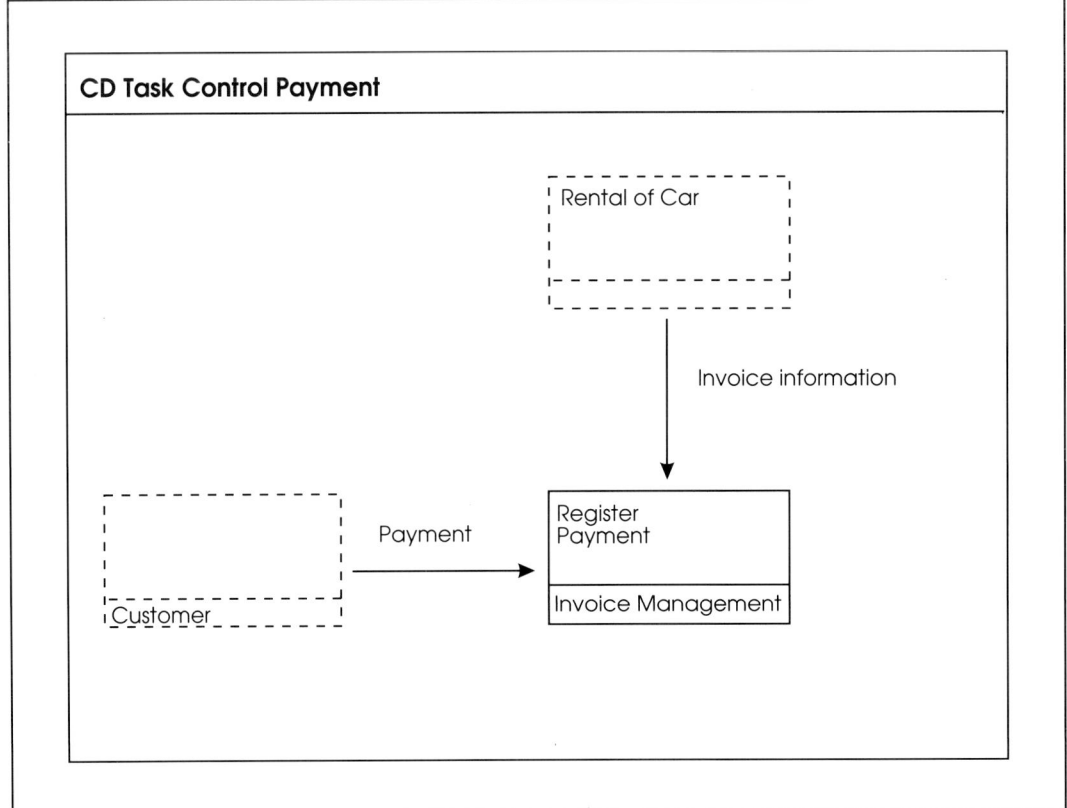

*Figure 8.11: Task CD for the subtask **Control Payment***

Chapter 8
BOS Engineering Method applied to EU-Rent

8.3.2 Global Data Model   The Entity Relationship Diagram in Figure 8.12 shows the entity and relationship types of the business area under consideration.

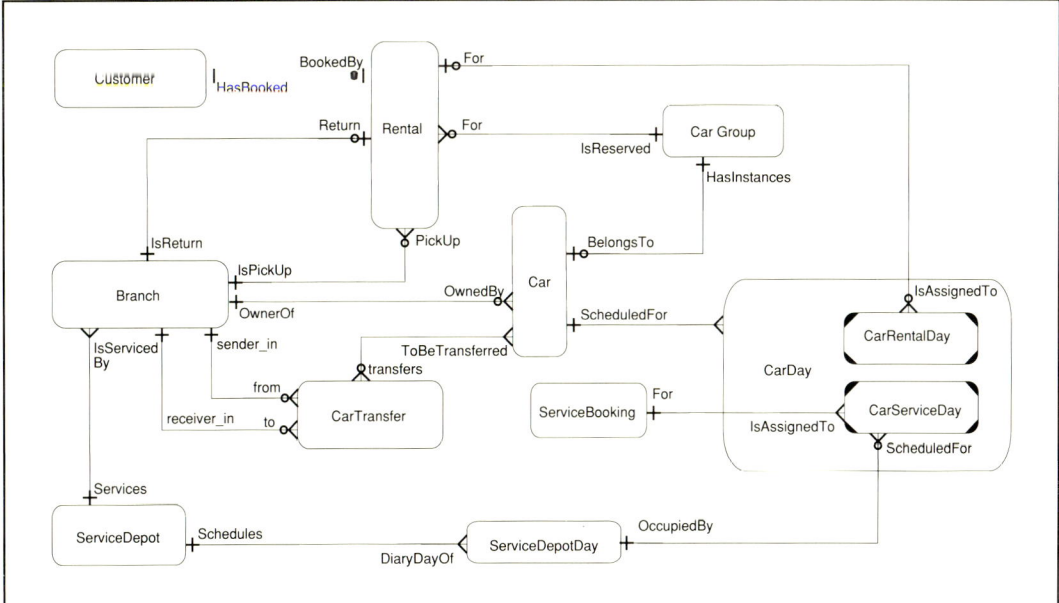

Figure 8.12: Global Data Model of EU-Rent

The following entities are explained explicitly here:

Service Booking:
All information about a service for a car is stored in service booking, eg date, duration, costs.

Car Day:
A day in a car's life.

Car Rental Day/
Car Service Day:
A car day may be either a car rental day, ie the car is rented on that day, or a car service day, ie the car is booked for service at a service depot on that day.

Service Depot Day:
The service depot has a calendar that shows for each day which cars are to be serviced. A service depot day is one day in that calendar.

The attributes of the entities are defined in Figure 8.13.

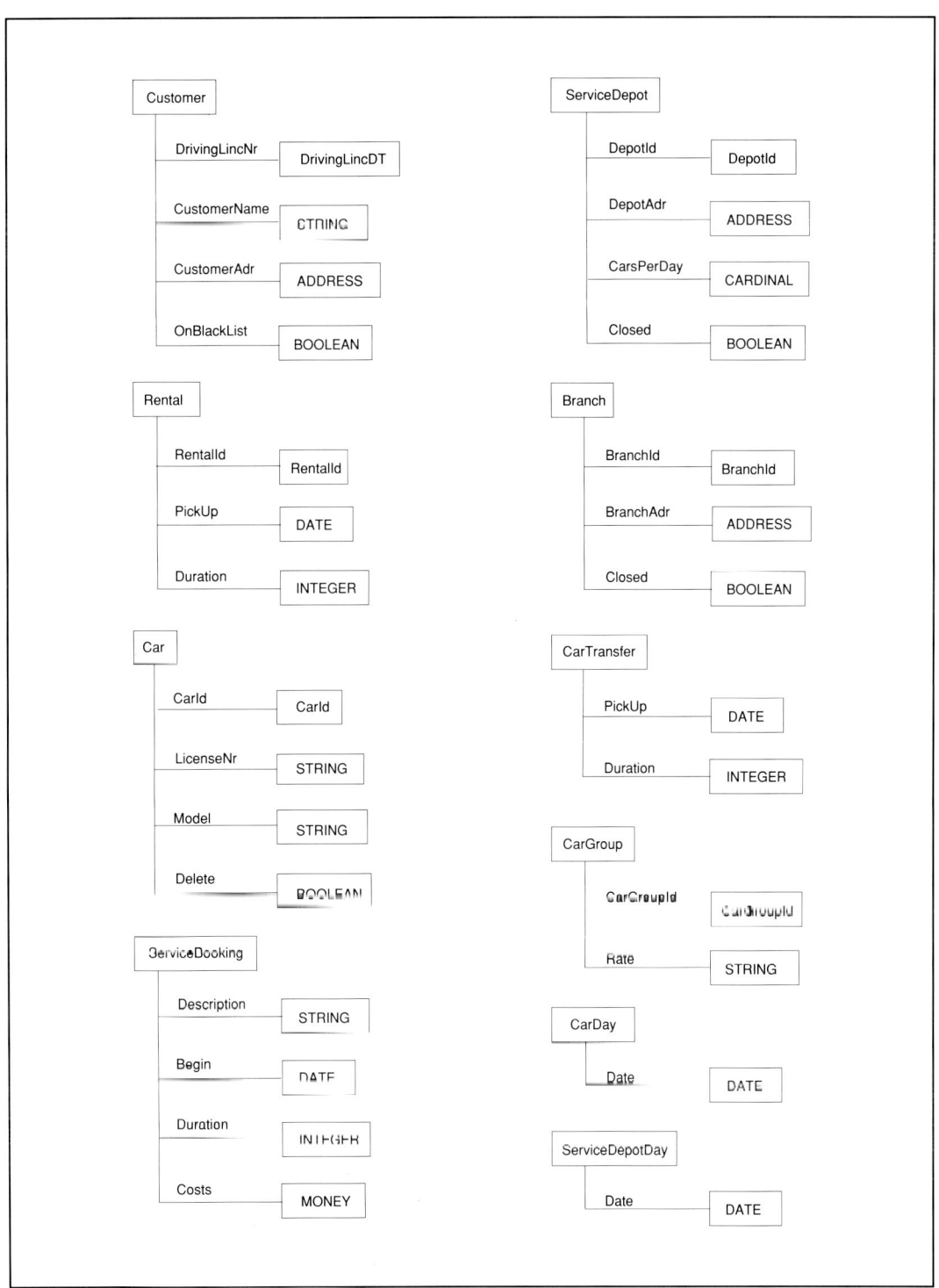

Figure 8.13: Attributes of global data model entities

8.3.3 Information Resource Definitions   The information resources of EU-Rent, the assigned entities and some of their methods are listed in Figure 8.14.

Information Resources - Methods

Information Resource	Entities	Methods
Rental	Rental	reservations to be served assign car to reservation insert reservation cancel reservation register return register pick-up check rentals read rental data prepare contract prepare invoice
Car	Car Car Day Car Rental Day Car Service Day	book car for rental book car for service register new car cancel rental days cancel service days
Car Group	Car Group	–
Customer	Customer	–
Branch	Branch	–
Car Transfer	Car Transfer	–
Service Booking	Service Booking	–
Service Depot	Service Depot Service Depot Day	–

Figure 8.14: Information Resource overview

Only the information resources **Rental** and **Car** are described in more detail in this case study.

Information Resource Rental

The data view of the information resource **Rental** (see Figure 8.15) shows all the entities and relationships that are affected by the methods of the information resource. The outlines of entities that are the responsibility of this information resource are shown in bold. (In Figure 8.15 only **Rental** is emboldened.)

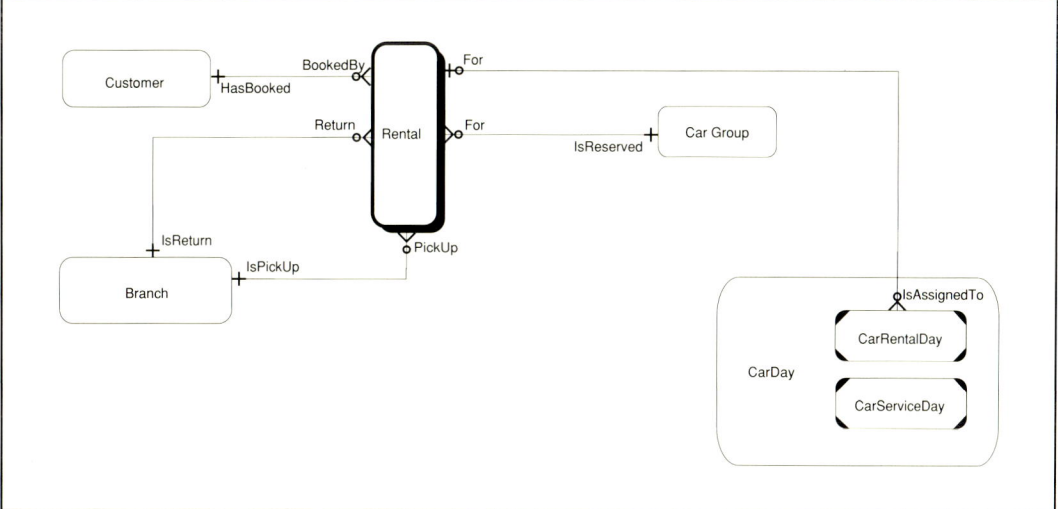

*Figure 8.15: Data View for Information Resource **Rental***

	Date: Wed Feb 16 15:36:41 1994

CLASS

Rental

Comment:

    Entities: Rental

Methods

  ReservationBeServed
    (* Produce list of reservations for the next day that have no car assigned for branch (BranchId)*)

BranchId	:	BranchID	=

    --> ReservationListDT

  AssignCarToReservation
    (* Assign available car from branch (BranchId) to the reservation*)

BranchId	:	BranchID	=

    -->

  InsertReservation

Reservation	:	ReservationRequestDT	=

    --> RentalId

  CancelReservation

RentalId	:	RentalID	=

    -->

  RegisterPickUp
    (* Register pick up of car *)

RentalId	:	RentalID	=

    -->

  RegisterPickUp
    (* Register return of car *)

RentalId	:	RentalID	=

    -->

Model: EurcthInformationResources   Name: Rental   Type: CLT
Parent: */CLT Reservation

Figure 8.16: Class template for Information Resource **Rental**

The class template of **Rental** (see Figure 8.16) shows the methods and their interfaces (parameters) for the Information Resource **Rental**. For example, the method **ReservationsBeServed**, with the input parameter **BranchId**, produces a list of unserved reservations for a particular branch.

Information Resource Car

The information resource Car is responsible for the entities Car, Car Day, CarRentalDay and CarServiceDay as shown in the data view of the information resource Car in Figure 8.17.

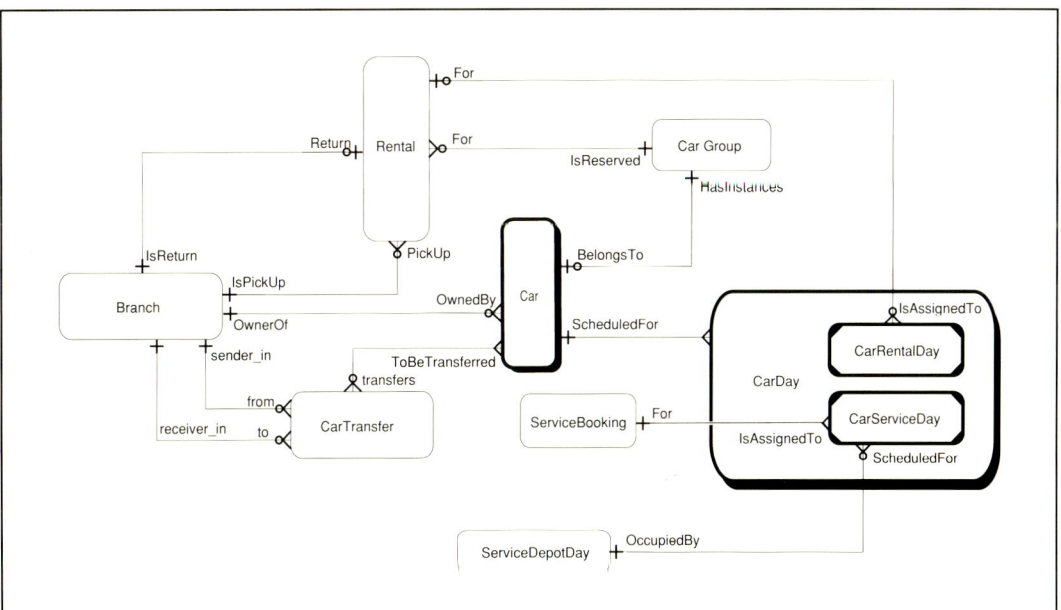

*Figure 8.17: Data View for Information Resource **Car***

The class template of Car is shown in Figure 8.18.

Title			Date: Wed Feb 16 15:15:13 1994

CLASS

Car

Comment:

Entities: Car
    Car Day
    Car Rental day
    Car Service Day

Methods

BookCarForRental
    (* Car (CarId) is booked for a rental *)

CarId	:	CarID	=
RentalBegin	:	Date	=
RentalDuration	:	INTEGER	=

    --> BOOLEAN (* Car is booked *)

BookCarForService
    (* Car (CarId) is booked for a service *)

CarId	:	CarID	=
ServiceBegin	:	Date	=
ServiceDuration	:	INTEGER	=

    --> BOOLEAN (* Car is booked *)

CancelRentalDays
    (* The reservation of the car for the rental (RentalId) is cancelled *)

| RentalId | : | RentalId | = |

    -->

CancelServiceDays
    (* The service booking for a car is cancelled *)

| ServiceBookingId | : | ServiceBID | = |

    -->

RegisterNewCar

| LicenceNr | : | STRING | = |
| Model | : | STRING | = |

    --> CarId

DeleteCar

| CarId | : | CarID | = |

    -->

:

Model: EurentInformationResources   Name: Car   Type: CLT
Parent: MDIV InformationResources

*Figure 8.18: Class Template for Information Resource **Car***

8.4 Business Organisation Model

8.4.1 Organisational Business Structure

Figure 8.19 shows the organisational units of EU-Rent, their roles and the procedures assigned to the roles.

Organisational Unit	Roles	Procedures
Financial Department	Invoice Management	register payment control payment
Rental Department	Reservation Management	make reservation cancel reservation register new customer delete customer change customer etc
	Rental Management	prepare check-out check-out check-in prepare invoice register payment control car return register car return register car damage etc
	Car Management	make car ready control car register car for maintenance etc
	Service Agent	cleaning of car etc
Management Department	Branch Management	assign cars to reservations produce list of cars initiate transport cancel transport register car pick-up register car arrival investigate car etc

Figure 8.19: Organisational Business Structure of EU-Rent

8.4.2 Procedure Definitions

In this case study only the procedure **MakeReservation** is defined in detail. This procedure is assigned to the role **Reservation Management** and is part of the business transaction **Car Rental** (subtask **Reservation**).

Procedures use methods of the information resources to manipulate the data entities. Procedures communicate by the exchange of messages, these may be external messages to external partners (eg **ReservDenial** in Figure 8.20) or internal messages to other procedures.

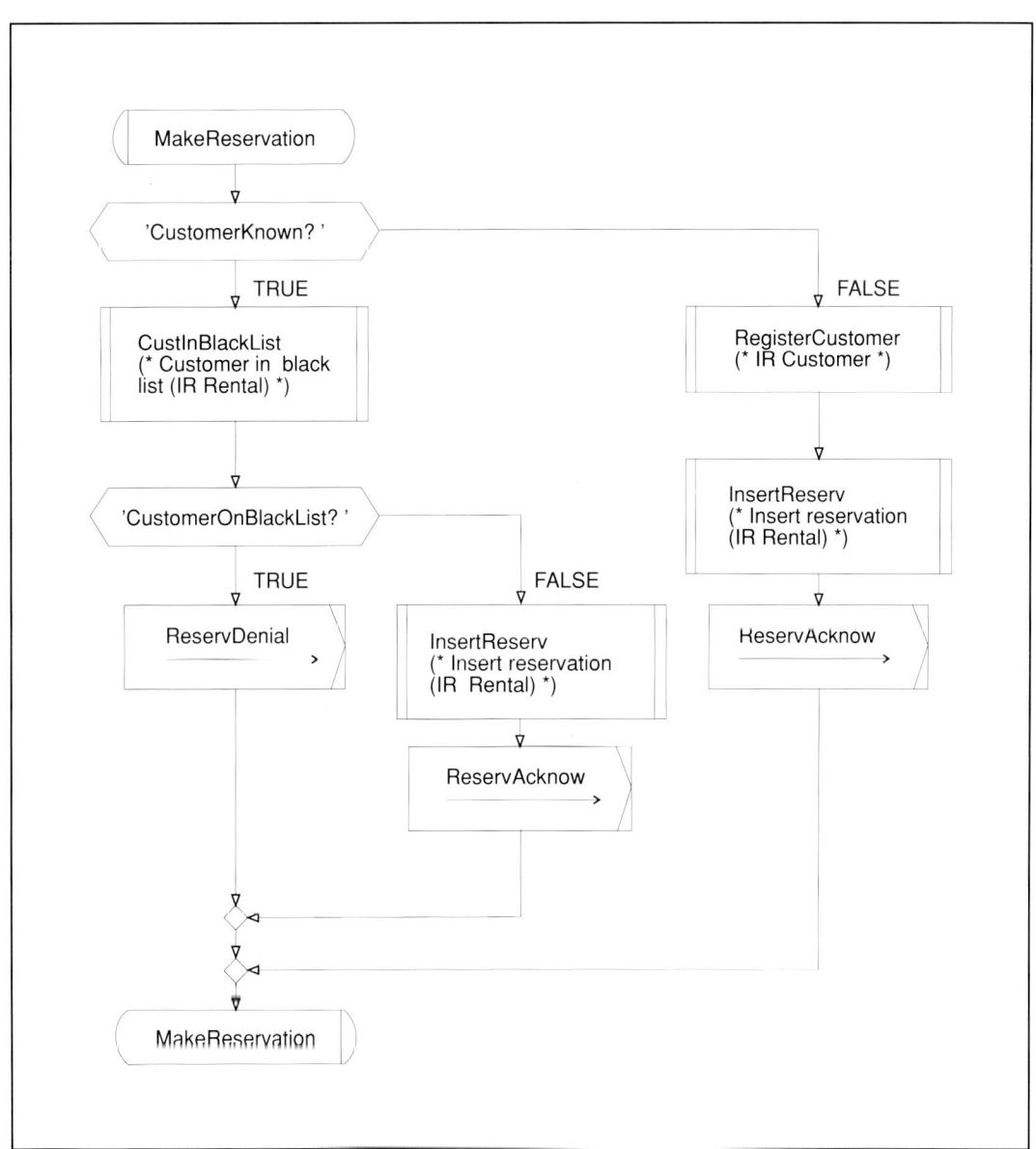

Figure 8.20: *Process diagram for the procedure* **MakeReservation**

8.4.3 Internal Message Definitions

Figure 8.21 shows how the roles interact with each other during the business transactions **Rental** and **CapacityPlanning&Transfer**. All internal messages between the roles and most of the external messages they produce are shown. The internal messages are defined in Figure 8.22.

The roles concerned with these business transactions are **Reservation Management**, **Branch Management**, **Rental Management**, **Car Management** and **Service Agent**. As the reservation, pick-up and the return of car may take place at different locations, the actors executing these roles have to communicate via internal messages. Figure 8.21 shows this maximum distribution. Therefore the roles occur several times. The location for each is given in brackets (eg Rental Management (PickUp Branch)).

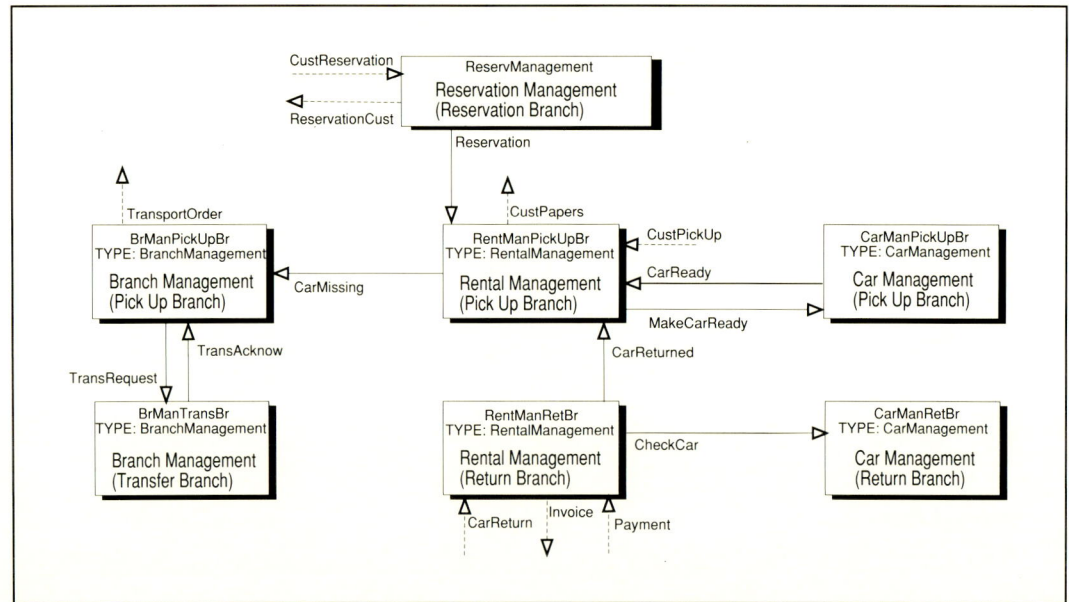

Figure 8.21: Communication diagram for the roles supported at branches

Name	Data Type	Description	Frequency.		
			time unit	avg.	max.
Reservation	ReservRequestID	A reservation for another pick-up branch is transferred to this branch	week	100	
MakeCarReady	CarID	Car management are requested to make a car ready for pick-up	week	380	
CarReady	SIGNAL	Rental management is informed that the car is ready for pick-up	week	380	
CheckCar	CarID	Car management are requested to check for a returned car	week	380	
CarReturned	RentalID	The pick-up branch is informed that the car has been returned at the return branch	week	6	
CarMissing	RentalID	The branch management is informed that the car has not been returned in time	week	6	
TransRequest	DeliverCarListDT	The branch manager asks another branch manager for additional available cars	week	7	
TransAcknow	DeliverCarListDT	The branch manager of the transfer branch sends the cars together with a transfer list to the receiving branch	week	7	

Figure 8.22: Internal message definition

8.4.4 Geographical Business Structure

Figure 8.23 shows the business location types and the EU-Rent roles assigned to them.

Business Location Types	Roles
Head Office	Fleet Management Location Management
Branch	Branch Management Reservation Management Rental Management Invoice Management Car Management Service Agent
Depot	Depot Management Car Maintainer

Figure 8.23: EU-Rent Business Location Types

Branch location types are refined according to different activity levels into:

- airport branch
- city branch
- local agency

8.4.5 Location Data Views

The Location Data Views describe data views for business location types, ie those entities which are accessed by roles at the business location types.

Figures 8.24 to 8.26 show Location Data Views of branch, service depot and head office respectively.

Chapter 8
BOS Engineering Method applied to EU-Rent

Location Data View
of branch

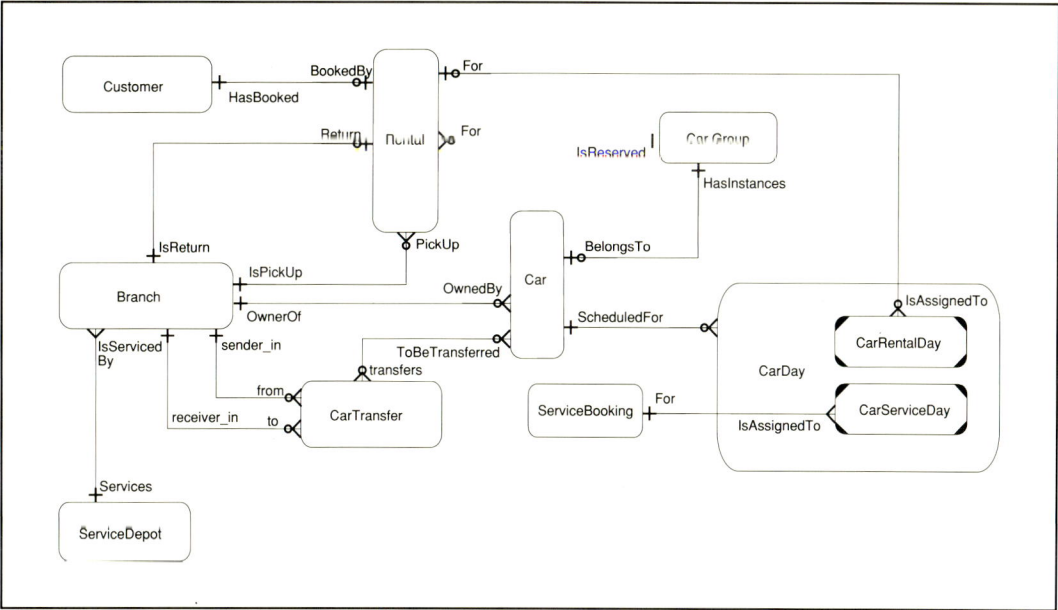

Figure 8.24: Location Data View of branch

Location Data View
of service depot

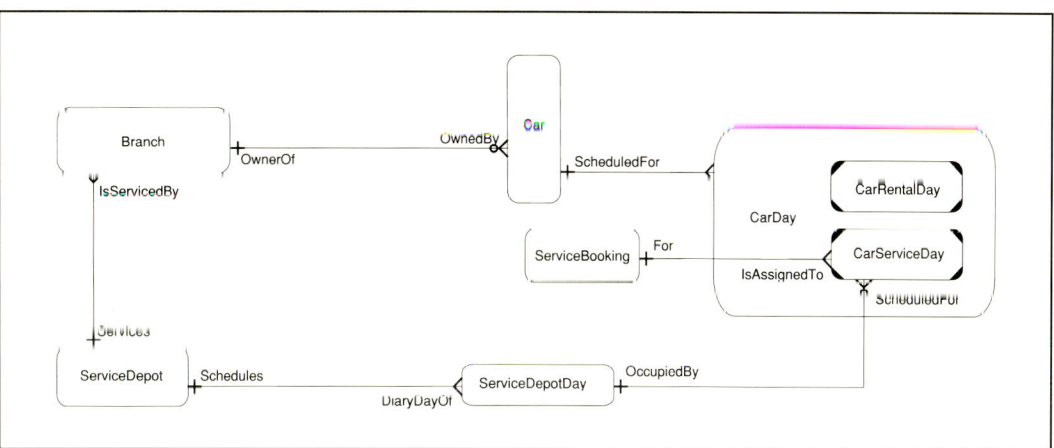

Figure 8.25: Location Data View of service depot

Location Data View
of head office

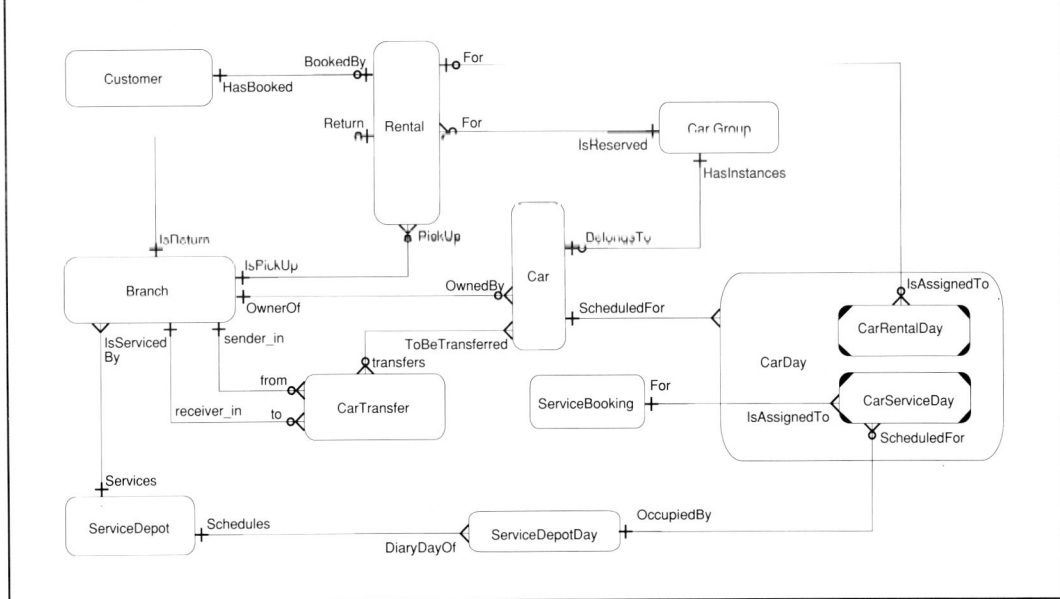

Figure 8.26: Location Data View of head office

8.4.6 Organisational Interaction Definitions

Figure 8.27 shows the interaction between the business location types at different locations. The business location type branch is used several times as the reservation, pick-up and return of a car may take place at different locations. The roles executing these activities therefore coordinate each other, ie they communicate by the exchange of messages.

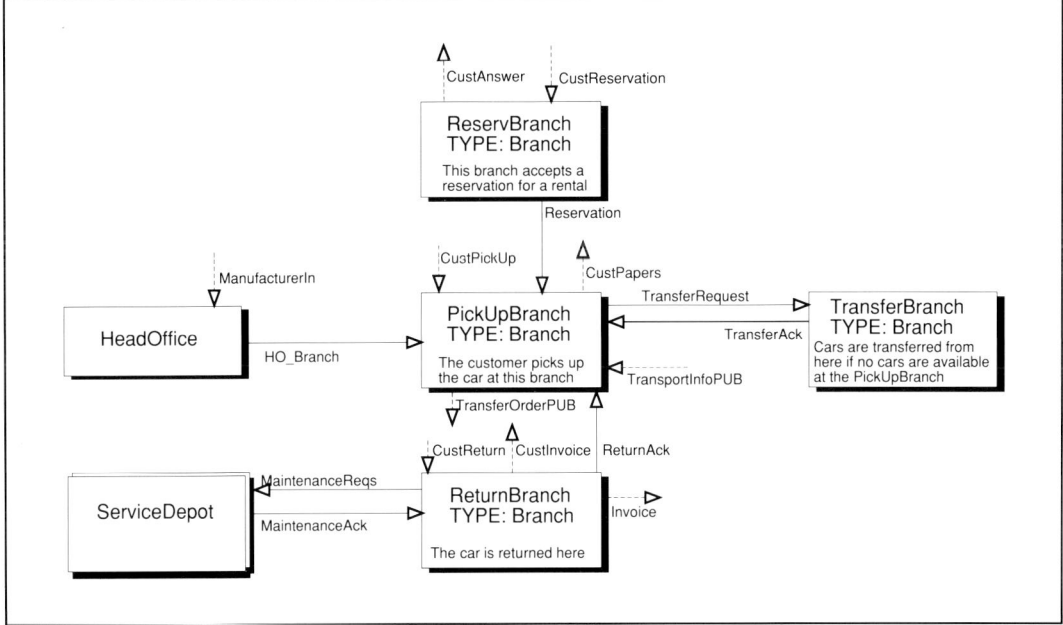

Figure 8.27: Interaction between business location types

8.5 Technical Distribution Scenarios

8.5.1 General remarks

EU-Rent is subject to a variety of technical distribution scenarios. In the following we describe three different degrees of distribution:

- *central system.* A central database server and workstations connected on-line via a wide area network

- *fully distributed system.* Each EU-Rent Branch holds its own data and does processing locally if possible

- *clustered system.* A set of 20 cluster servers each one serving the branches of a certain region. Together the cluster servers host a distributed database.

For the last two systems we analyse the required data volumes and number of communication requests more thoroughly.

For this analysis we assume the trigger frequencies shown in Figure 8.28 for procedures at branches, depots and head office. A number n, in the table, for procedure P at location type L means 'procedure P is invoked on average n times a week at location L'. A zero entry means less than 0.5 occurrences of the procedure at that location type per week. An empty entry means there are no occurrences of the procedure at this location type.

Role	Procedure	Occurrences per week		
		Branch (1000)	Depot (400)	Head Office
Fleet Management	register new cars			2
	write off cars			2
Location Management	open new branch			0
	open new service depot			0
	delete outdated customers			1
Branch Management	assign cars to reservations	7		
	produce list of cars needed	7		
	initiate transport	7		
	cancel transport	0		
	register car pick-up	7		
	register car arrival	7		
Reservation Management	register new customers	40		
	change customer	1		
	make reservation (*)	400		
	cancel reservation	40		
Rental Management	check-out (*)	380		
	check-in (*)	380		
	control car return	6		
	register car return (*)	380		

Role	Procedure	Occurrences per week		
		Branch (1000)	Depot (400)	Head Office
	register car damage	10		
	investigate car	6		
	prepare invoice (*)	380		
Invoice Management	register payment (*)	300		80000
Control Payment				7
Car Management	make car ready	380		
	control car	380		
	register car for maintenance	8		20
Service Agent	cleaning of car	380		

Figure 8.28: Trigger frequencies for procedures

The procedures marked with an asterix (*) obviously produce the most load in the system. These are the procedures comprising the business transaction *car rental*.

The estimates of loads and throughputs given later in this chapter are based on the trigger frequencies of procedures in Figure 8.28.

8.4.1 Centralised System

General Description   There is a central database server for EU Rent at head office, and intelligent terminals (PCs) in each branch and each depot. See Figure 8.29. The branches are connected to the central database server via modem lines.

All persistent data is stored on the central database server. For the processing we have two slightly different alternatives:

    a external processing is done locally at branches and depots. Conceptual and internal processing is carried out on the central database server. Branches and depots are equipped only with user-interface servers and coordinate with the central system via remote processing (rp) protocols which invoke database transactions on the central system.

b all processing is carried out locally at branches and depots. Branches and depots access the central database using commit management via remote database access (rda) mechanisms. This necessitates that they are equipped with a dp-system that can act as both a workstation and a process server.

In both cases the computers at branches and depots are either working on-line, or are connected for every request to the central dp-system.

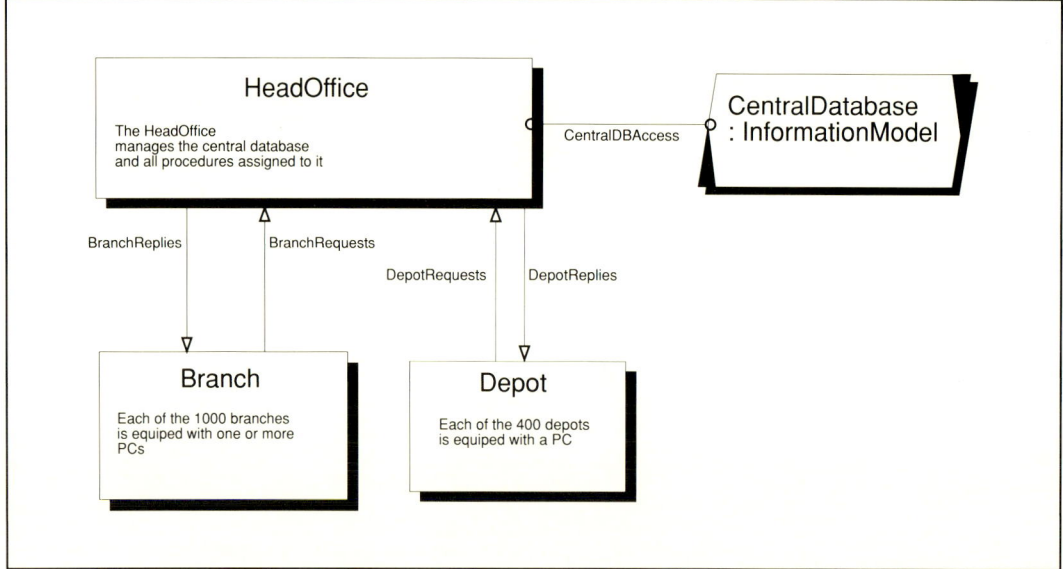

Figure 8.29: Structure of the centralised option for the EU-Rent IT system

Since this scenario is not very interesting from the point of view of distribution, this option is not discussed in further detail.

8.4.2 Fully Distributed System

This scenario assumes that every location at which a procedure can be triggered (here branch, service depot and head office) has processing and data storage capabilities. This leads to the hardware structure shown in Figure 8.30:

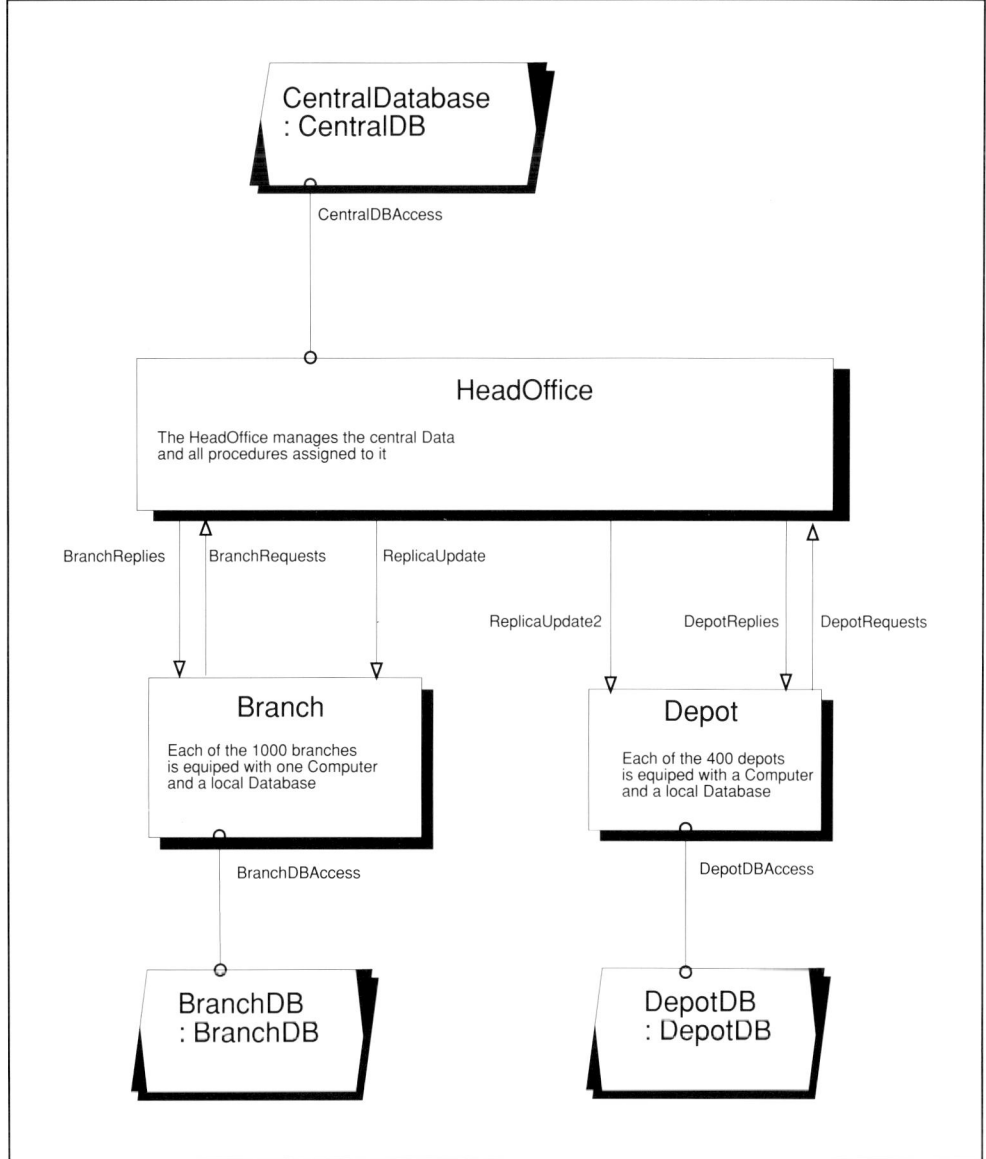

Figure 8.30: Structure of the fully distributed option for the EU-Rent IT system

Processing should be carried out at locations where triggers cause input to the system. Data should be stored at locations where most accesses and updates occur.

The table in Figure 8.31 identifies the locations at which procedures are implemented. Procedures can be triggered from different location types.

Procedure	Implementation Location		
	Branch	Depot	Head Office
register new cars			X
write off cars			X
open new branch			X
open new service depot			X
delete outdated customers			X
assign cars to reservations	X		
produce list of cars needed	X		
initiate transport	X		
cancel transport	X		
register car pick-up	X		
register car arrival	X		
register new customers	X		
change customer	X		
make reservation	X		
cancel reservation	X		
check-out	X		
check-in	X		
control car return	X		
register car return	X		
register car damage	X		

Chapter 8
BOS Engineering Method applied to EU-Rent

Procedure	Implementation Location		
	Branch	Depot	Head Office
investigate car	X		
prepare invoice	X		
register payment	X		X
control payment	X		
make car ready	X		
control car	X		
register car for maintenance	X	X	
cleaning of car	X		

Figure 8.31: Assignment of procedure implementations to location types

In order to define the storage location of each data entity the following properties must be analysed for each data entity type:

- ownership
- volumes
- remote access frequency
- robustness.

Ownership: 'Which data entities naturally (or legally) belong to a business location and thus to the DP system supporting it?'

For example, a branch has the 'responsibility' for both the cars in its car park and those picked up at the branch, but not yet returned. Thus at any instant a car is 'owned' by exactly one branch.

Volumes: 'What storage capacity is needed to store the data entities?'

high: Required storage capacity is significant with respect to available storage capacity or the overall storage requirement.

199

low: Required storage capacity is negligible with respect to available storage capacity or the overall storage requirement.

For example, the complete sets of customer and rental data records require very high storage capacities. Car group data only needs a low storage capacity.

Remote access frequency: 'How often is an entity read, updated, created or deleted by remote DP systems?'

The remote access frequency can be derived from the location data views of the supported business locations and should be documented as one of the following:

low access: the data entity is only occasionally accessed remotely (compared to the number of local accesses from the 'owner').

high read only: the data entity is often read remotely but rarely updated.

high update: the data entity is often read or updated remotely.

For example, the car data is updated only occasionally from other locations. The car group data is very frequently accessed by branches, but always read only. The customer data is updated often from various branches.

Robustness: 'Can processing at a remote DP system continue, if data entity is not accessible?'

required: Certain important processing cannot continue if access to the data entity fails.

not required: The main processing can be carried out (at least in a degraded manner) independently of this data.

For example, the access to all data concerning customers, rentals, cars, car days and branches is required to continue the rental business. Access to maintenance and service depot data is not essential for robustness

Chapter 8
BOS Engineering Method applied to EU-Rent

There are four different types of storage concepts to be considered for each entity type:

- Store individual data entity partitions locally *(local)*. This is normally used if the ownership can be identified clearly and robustness considerations at other DP systems are of minor importance.

  Car data, for example, is stored at branches.

- Store the data entities centrally *(central)*. This is normally used where ownership is unclear and the data is updated by many DP systems.

  For example, customer data used in rental business typically cannot be assigned to a specific 'home' branch, because near home customers usually use their own cars. Thus customer data is subject to be stored centrally or will be cached (see below).

- Replicate data entities to all DP systems *(repl.)* that access those data entities. This is normally used if the storage volumes and update rates are low or if high availability of data is required.

  For example, car group data can be replicated to each branch.

- Store the data entities centrally but also cache instances locally *(cache)*. This means that the entity is stored centrally, but each access makes a local copy of the instance. Subsequent read accesses at the same DP system are then available locally. Special mechanisms must be provided to handle updates to the cached data and to avoid unlimited growth of cache volumes.

  For example, customer data is stored in a central database. When creating a new rental, customer data is transferred to the local branch and kept there until the car has been returned and the rental paid for.

Using the decision table in Figures 7.10a and 7.10b the first-cut storage concepts in Figure 8.32 can be derived:

201

Entity Type	Ownership	Volume	Remote access frequency	Robustness	Storage concept
Customer	global	high	high update	required	cache
Rental	local (pick-up branch)	high	low	required	local (at pick-up branch)
Car	local (owner branch)	high	low	required	local (at owner branch)
CarGroup	global	low	high read only	required	replicated
Branch	global	low	high read only	required	replicated
ServiceDepot	global	low	high read only	not required	replicated
ServiceBooking	local (concerned depot)	low	low	not required	local (at concerned service depot)
CarTransfer	local (receiving branch)	low	low	not required	local (at receiving branch)
CarDay	local (via scheduled car)	high	low	required	local (at owner branch)
CarRentalDay	local (via rental to pick-up branch)	high	low	required	local (at pick-up branch)
CarServiceDay	local (to service depot)	low	low	not required	local (at service depot)
ServiceDepotDay	local (to service depot)	low	low	not required	local (at service depot)

Figure 8.32: First-cut storage concepts for entities

Description of DP Locations

Three types of DP location can be identified:

- head office
- branch

- service depot.

Head Office

The Central Database holds the master copies for the data that is replicated in the individual branches and depots. See Figure 8.33.

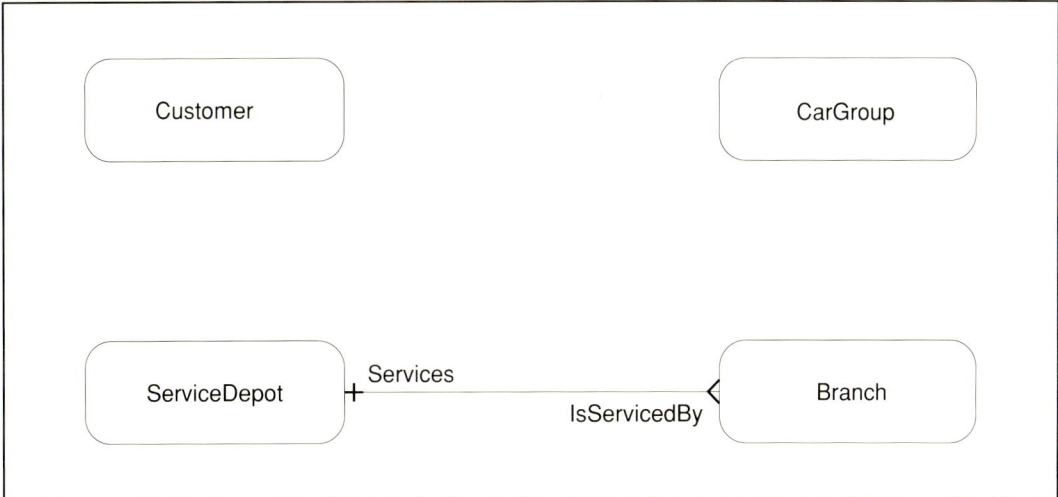

Figure 8.33: Data held in the central database at Head Office

Branch

The local database at each branch holds the data shown in Figure 8.34.

Remark: The customer data is looked-up centrally and cached locally at each branch when accepting a reservation or booking. Customer data is kept as long as a rental for this customer at this pick-up branch is open. Changes to customer data are done both locally and on the central database ('write-through'). This may lead to inconsistencies when a customer has open reservations at different pick-up branches.

Service Depot

The database at each depot holds the data shown in Figure 8.35.

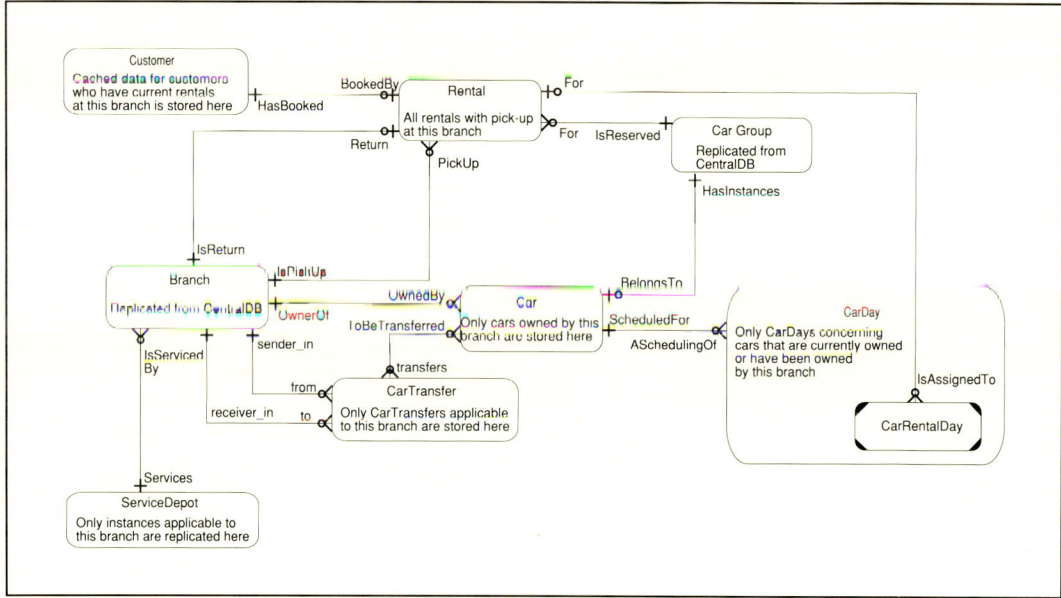

Figure 8.34: Data held in the branch databases

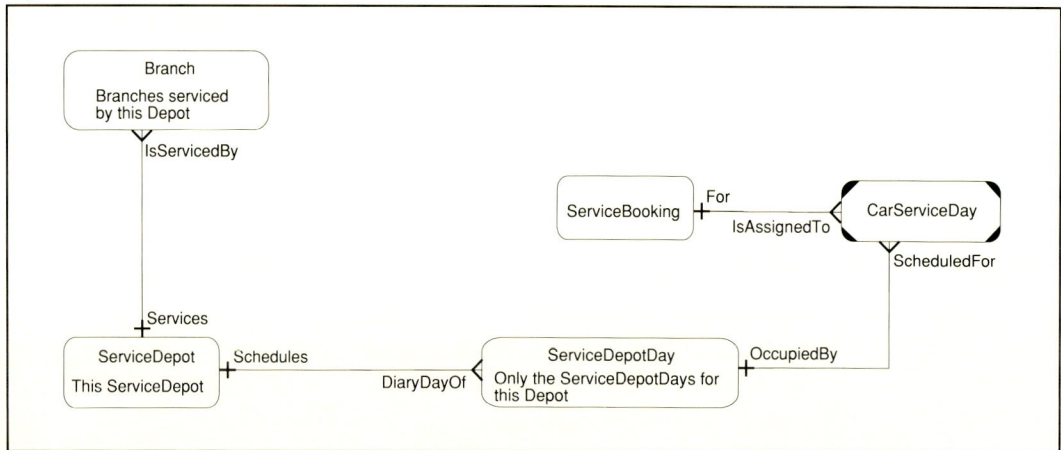

Figure 8.35: Data held in the depot databases

Robustness analysis

The system that requires most robustness is the branch dp-system, because it carries out most of the operational business.

How is the execution of a procedure degraded, if a branch is disconnected from the network? For the analysis in Figure 8.36 we consider a network breakdown time of 5 minutes to 5 hours.

Procedure	Robustness Considerations (no entry means: uncritical)
assign cars to reservations	must be postponed or done manually
produce list of cars needed	
initiate transport	must be postponed or done manually
cancel transport	
register car pick-up	
register car arrival	may be critical because car data cannot be transferred, manual back-up needed.
register new customers	critical (*)
change customer	critical (*)
make reservation	critical if reservation branch is not pick-up branch. Customer status (blacklist) cannot be checked. Reservation data must be forwarded by telephone.
cancel reservation	critical if reservation branch is not pick-up branch. Reservation data must be forwarded by telephone.
check-out	
check-in	critical: Car Return Notification cannot be forwarded to pick-up branch. Car ownership cannot be transferred.
control car return	
register car return	
register car damage	
investigate car	
prepare invoice	critical if return branch is not pick up branch: Rental data for invoicing is not accessible. Manual back up needed.
register payment	
register car for maintenance	uncritical for a break-down time of up to 5 hours.

Figure 8.36: Robustness analysis of procedures

The most critical procedures are marked with an asterisk. The criticality of these procedures can be reduced, if the write-through to the central database can be delayed and known customers inserted manually into the local database and matched with the central database when the network is up again.

Volumes and data transfers

We concentrate here on volumes and data transfers between branches and between branches and head office. To estimate the throughput of the system, the branches are classified as follows:

- *branches in major airports*: There are 100 such airport branches. They stay open 16 hours per day, 7 days per week. Business is spread uniformly across the day

- *branches in major cities*: There are 200 such city branches. They stay open 11 hours per day, 6 days per week. Nearly all pick-ups take place between 8 a.m. and 11 a.m. Nearly all returns take place between 4 p.m. and 7 p.m. Reservations are spread evenly over the day

- *branches in local agencies* such as hotels and garages: There are 700 such local agencies. Their transactions follow the same usage pattern as major city branches.

Volumes per branch

Critical Volumes are Cars, CarDays, Customers, and Rentals. See Figure 8.37. Rentals are kept on-line in the database for one year. To estimate the size of the local customer data cache we estimate that customer data has to be kept cached for the rentals of one week.

Chapter 8
BOS Engineering Method applied to EU-Rent

Data Entity	Overall (1000)	Local Agency (700)	City Branch (200)	Airport Branch (100)
Car	200,000	129	300	500
Rental	20,000,000	8,500	35,250	70,000
CarDay	100,000,000	42,000	176,250	350,000
Customer	5,000,000	163	678	1,346

Figure 8.37: Critical data volumes at branches for a fully distributed system

Data Transfers per branch

Car-Rentals are classified as walk-in rentals and rentals with advanced reservations:

- 80% of all rentals are rentals with advanced reservations; of these:

    - 30% are booked at the pick-up branch

    - 70% are booked at another branch.

- 10% of the rentals with a reservation are cancelled or the customer doesn't show up ('no-shows')

- 20% of all rentals are walk-in rentals without advanced reservations

- 50% of all rentals are returned to the pick up branch and 50% are returned to another branch.

We have simplified the analysis by assuming that these numbers are the same for airport branches, city branches and local agencies.

Figure 8.38 gives the throughput analysis of a branch computer system during one peak hour.

	Activity	Airport Branch	City Branch	Local Agency
A	Average number of rentals per hour	12.00	8.70	2.10
B	Number of rentals during peak hours	24.00	16.00	4.00
C	Accepted reservations (80% of A + 10% of 'no-shows')	10.56	7.65	1.85
D	Local reservations (Look up customer in central database) (30% of C)	3.17	2.30	0.56
E	Reservations for other branches (Look-up customer in central database, forward details to pick-up branch) (70% of C)	7.39	5.35	1.29
F	Peak-hour pick-ups (100% of B)	24.00	16.00	4.00
G	Peak-hour pick-ups with reservation (80% of F)	19.20	12.80	3.20
H	Peak-hour walk-in pick-ups (Look-up customer in central database) (20% of F)	4.80	3.20	0.80
I	Peak-hour returns (100% of F)	24.00	16.00	4.00
J	Peak-hour returns (to same branch) (50% of I)	12.00	8.00	2.00
K	Peak-hour Returns (to another branch) (Return notification to pick-up branch) (50% of I)	12.00	8.00	2.00
L	Peak hour transactions (C + F + I)	58.56	39.65	9.85
M	Accesses to central database (D + E + H)	15.36	10.85	2.65
N	Accesses to other branches (E + K)	19.39	13.35	3.29
O	Sum of remote accesses (incoming and outgoing) (M + 2 * N)	54.14	37.55	9.23

Figure 8.38: Analysis of peak-hour throughput for rentals

The computer system in each branch must be capable of supporting the number of transactions (line L) and the number of remote branches accesses to the local branch's database (line O).

The branch communication facilities (modems, X.25 lines etc) must have the capacity to handle accesses to and from other branches (with some spare capacity for additional transactions)

8.4.3 Clustered system

This scenario refines the previous one. The major problem with the previous scenario is the cost of furnishing every branch and depot with a computer system capable of commit management and local database management.

In order to reduce costs, processing is centralised into a set of 20 cluster DP-systems each serving all the branches and depots in a certain region.

This leads to the hardware structure shown in Figure 8.39.

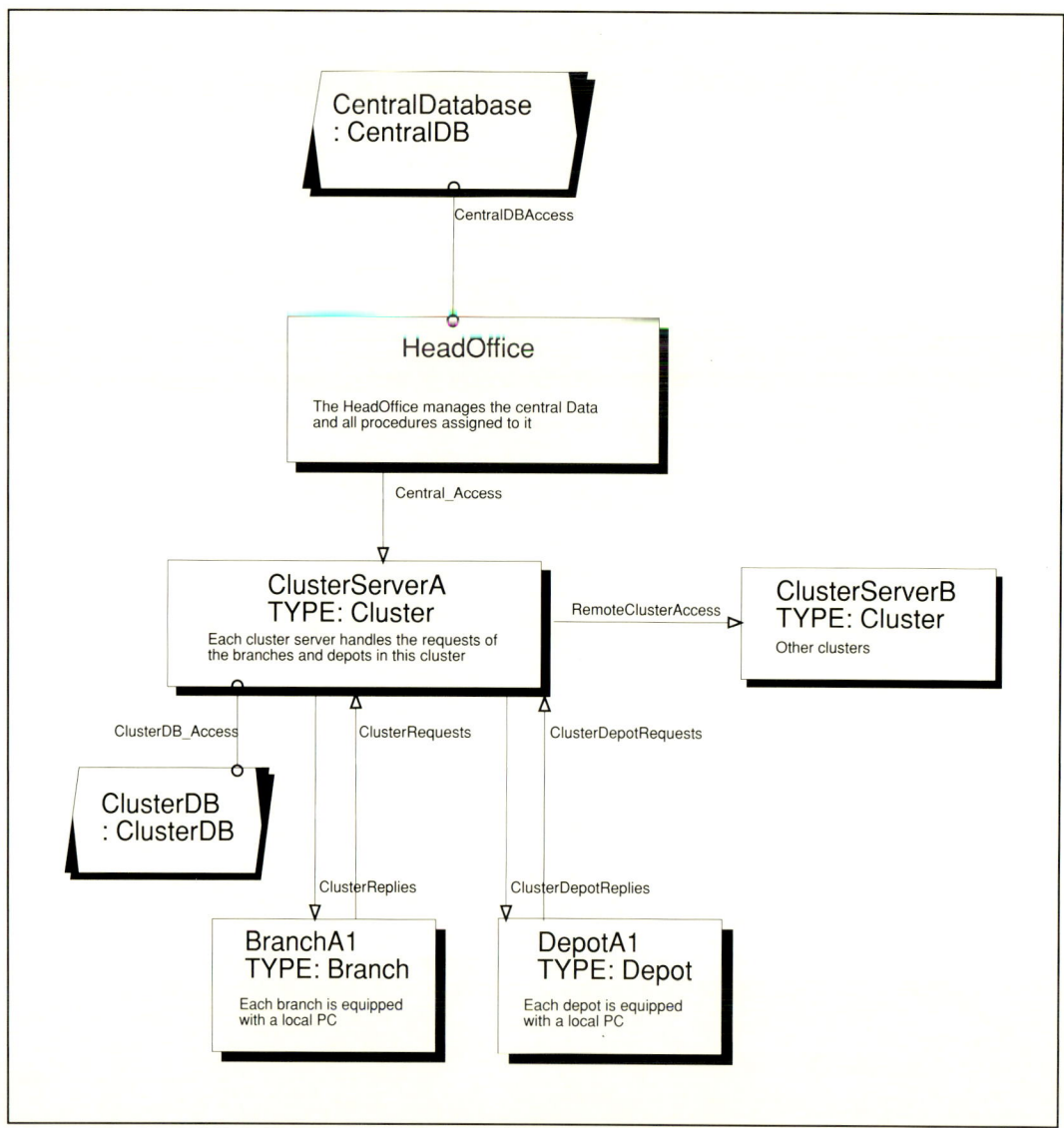

Figure 8.39: Structure of the clustered option for the EU-Rent IT system

Description of DP-Locations and Workstation Locations

This option is derived from the fully distributed option as follows:

The locations of procedures are the same as in the fully distributed option.

The storage locations are derived by amalgamating the data stored at depots and branches in the fully distributed option into one database at a cluster server.

Branches and Depots

Branches and Depots are equipped with PCs that implement the user-interface server. The PCs are connected either on-line or on demand to a cluster server.

Head Office

Head office is equipped with a dp-system that provides distributed commit handling, local database access and remote access to the databases at cluster servers.

The central database holds master copies of the data shown in Figure 8.40 (as in the fully distributed scenario). This data is replicated to the cluster servers.

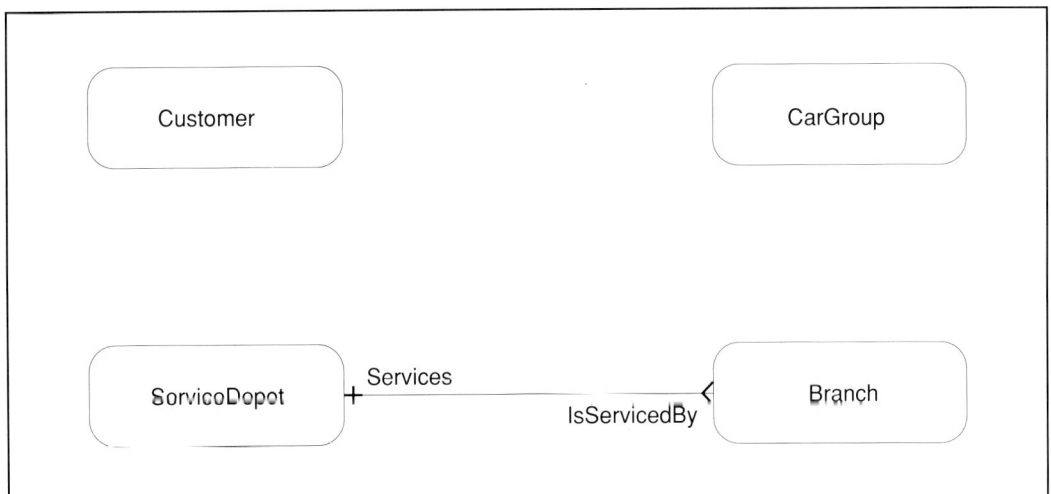

Figure 8.40: Data held in Head Office database under clustered option

Cluster server

The cluster server database holds the sum of the data that was stored previously in branches' and depots' local databases. As a simplification customers are not cached, but replicated to all clusters. See Figure 8.41.

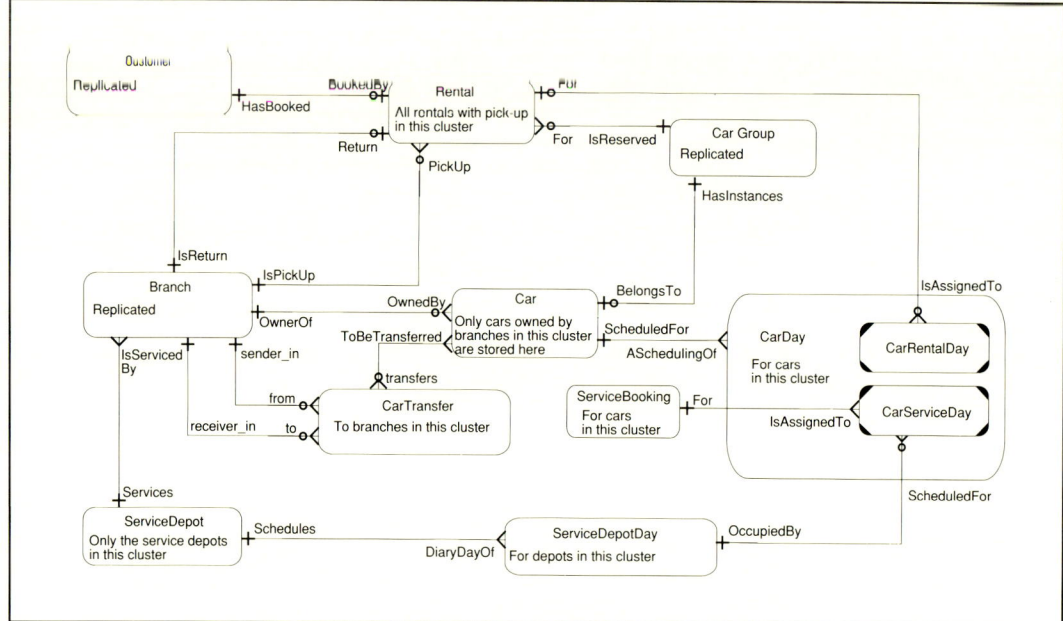

Figure 8.41: Data held in database at a cluster server

Remark: Customers do not usually rent cars at their home locations. Therefore it is not reasonable to assign a default storage location to customer data.

Robustness analysis

The communication network carries two risks:

- if the connection between the branch / depot and the cluster server breaks down, no automated processing is possible: complete manual back-up procedures are needed

- if the connection between two cluster servers or between a cluster server and the head office breaks down, car data transfer and changes to customer data are not possible: Mechanisms for postponing

Chapter 8
BOS Engineering Method applied to EU-Rent

updates for replicated data and car data transfer are necessary.

Volumes and data transfers

We concentrate here on volumes and data transfers at cluster servers. We assume that all clusters share approximately the same load. A cluster server serves approximately 5 airport branches, 10 city branches, and 35 local agencies.

Critical Volumes are Cars, CarDays, Customer, and Rentals. See Figure 8.42. We assume that on average Rentals last for 5 CarDays. Rentals are kept on-line in the database for one year.

Data Entity	Overall (1000)	Cluster Server (20)	Head Office
Car	200,000	10,000	0
Rental	20,000,000	1,000,000	0
CarDay	100,000,000	5,000,000	0
Customer	5,000,000	5,000,000	5,000,000

Figure 8.42: Critical data volumes for clustered option

<u>Data Transfers per Cluster Server</u>

Car-Rentals are classified as walk-in rentals and rentals with advanced reservations.

- 80% of the rentals are rentals with advanced reservations; of these:

  - 70% are booked inside the pick-up cluster

  - 30% are booked inside another cluster

- 10% of the rentals with reservations are cancelled or the customer doesn't show up ('no-shows')

- 20% of all rentals are walk-in rentals without advanced reservations

- 80% of all rentals are returned to a branch in the same cluster as the pick-up branch, 20% are returned to another cluster

- 20% of all rentals require updates to customer data (either because the customer is new or their details have changed).

Figure 8.43 gives the throughput analysis of a branch computer system during one peak hour (based on the assumption that a cluster server serves 5 airport branches, 10 city branches, and 35 local agencies).

	Activity	Cluster Server
A	Average number of rentals per hour	220.5
B	Number of rentals during peak hours	420
C	Accepted reservations (80% of A + 10% no-shows)	194.04
D	Local reservations (70% of C)	135.83
E	Reservations for other clusters (forward to pick-up cluster) (30% of C)	58.21
F	Peak-hour pick-ups (100% of B)	420
G	Peak-hour pick-ups with reservation (80% of F)	336
H	Peak-hour walk-in pick-ups (20% of F)	84
I	Peak-hour returns (100% of F)	420
J	Peak-hour returns (to branch in pick-up cluster) (80% of I)	336
K	Peak-hour returns (to a branch in another cluster) (Return notification to pick-up cluster and car data transfer) (20% of I)	84

	Activity	Cluster Server
L	Peak hour transactions (C + F + I)	1034.04
M	Accesses to other clusters (Rental and car data transfer and customer replicates update at 20 locations) (E + K + 20 * 20% of (C + H))	1254.37
N	Update accesses from other clusters (E + K)	142.21
O	Sum of remote accesses (incoming and outgoing) (M + N)	340.03

Figure 8.43: Peak-hour throughput analysis for Rentals

Each cluster server must be capable to support the number of transactions in line L.

The branch communication facilities (modems, X.25 lines, etc) must have the capacity to handle the incoming and outgoing accesses to and from other branches (line O).

9 SSADM extensions

9.1 Introduction

This chapter describes how the generic guidance on developing distributed systems, described in Part 1, can be used to extend SSADM version 4.

Structure of this chapter

Section 9.1 describes the background to SSADM and how this volume fits within the context of SSADM.

Section 9.2 describes SSADM and other CCTA guidance related to this volume.

Section 9.3 describes the SSADM modules and stages; how the common decision points described in Chapter 6 can be mapped on to the SSADM stages and how the distribution concepts defined in Chapter 4 map to SSADM terminology.

Section 9.4 summarises the changes to SSADM and explains the changes to the SSADM structural model and products.

Section 9.5 explains the changes affecting SSADM techniques.

Section 9.6 introduces additional SSADM techniques.

Section 9.7 describes those services (see Chapter 5) which are required to support conventional and object-oriented implementations of requirements, specified with SSADM products.

9.1.1 Background to SSADM

The late 1970s and early 1980s saw the development of a number of proprietary analysis and design methodologies that provided:

- a development framework of stages and steps from which projects could be planned

- defined end products by which progress can be measured and controlled

- techniques to help the analyst with the analysis and design of part or all of a system.

In 1980 CCTA, the UK Government Centre for Information Systems, surveyed the methodologies available in the market, with the intention of selecting one to be recommended for use in government departments. Eventually CCTA decided to commission the development of a new methodology that incorporated widely-used techniques, but within a more general and flexible framework. This became the Structured Systems Analysis and Design Method (SSADM).

Version 1 of SSADM was released in 1981. Although developed initially for use within UK government departments SSADM successfully addressed many of the system development problems that also existed in the private sector. The method has therefore been widely adopted outside UK government, encouraged by CCTA's making it available free of any license fee.

Since its launch, SSADM has been under continuous improvement and extension; Version 2 was released in 1984 and Version 3 in 1987. Since 1988 SSADM has been under the control of the SSADM Design Authority Board, chaired by CCTA and including representatives of the International SSADM User Group (ISUG), British Computer Society, Computer Services Association, Information Systems Examination Board and British Standards Institute.

Version 4, the current version of SSADM, was launched in May 1990. SSADM is a product-oriented specification of what practitioners need to do to undertake systems analysis and design for a single IT project. It starts with a Project Initiation Document that identifies a proposed information system. It finishes when the information system has been specified in terms appropriate to the chosen implementation environment. 'Core' SSADM (contained in the *SSADM V4 Reference Manuals*) is supplemented by a number of Information Systems Engineering (ISE) Library volumes, which give guidance on how to tailor SSADM in a variety of contexts.

Chapter 9
SSADM extensions

9.1.2 CCTA programme of guidance on IS engineering

CCTA is developing the Information Systems Engineering Library as a source of advice and guidance on ISE issues. Within the ISE Library, CCTA is developing guidance on the development of information systems at two levels.

At the more detailed level individual volumes, such as this one, extend SSADM to address specific technical areas. Bodies other than CCTA, such as specialist sub-groups of the International SSADM User Group, may also develop ISE Library Volumes. The *ISE Library Volume Customising SSADM* describes the rationale for SSADM and provides guidance for those considering tailoring SSADM.

At the higher level, the ISE Library provides guidance on ISE issues independently of SSADM.

9.1.3 Related areas of development

Some other volumes under development within the ISE Library have concepts in common with this volume; principally:

- *Application Partitioning and Integration with SSADM* which shows how SSADM can be used to integrate separately-developed applications. There are three reasons for this approach: to develop related applications in parallel and then plug them together for implementation, to implement related applications at different times, to implement related applications in different places.

- *Reuse in SSADM using OO*. The approach in the present volume for the distribution of database update and enquiry processes uses the same concepts as the approach in *Reuse in SSADM using OO* for object-oriented database design with SSADM.

9.2 Related guidance

The following publications contain guidance related to that contained in Chapters 9 and 10:

- *SSADM V4 Reference Manuals*

219

- Quits and Resumes on Entity Life Histories: *A Comparison of Alternative Approaches*, ISUG

- The 'rationale' in *ISE Library Volume: Customising SSADM*

- *ISE Library Volume: Application Partitioning and Integration with SSADM*

- *ISE Library Volume: Reuse in SSADM using OO.*

For further information on the provision of cooperation services and architectures described in Chapter 5 refer to:

- the GOSIP (UK Government Open Systems Interconnection Profiles) subprofile on Open Distributed Transaction Processing which is designed for use during the planning and procurement of transaction processing hardware and software.

- *Electronic Data Interchange in Government: The Business Opportunities*, Information Management Library.

For full references to these publications and details of availability please see the bibliography.

9.3 Mapping of distributed systems guidance to SSADM

9.3.1 SSADM Modules and Stages

SSADM consists of five modules, with defined inputs and outputs for each module. See the bottom row of Figure 9.1.

Chapter 9
SSADM extensions

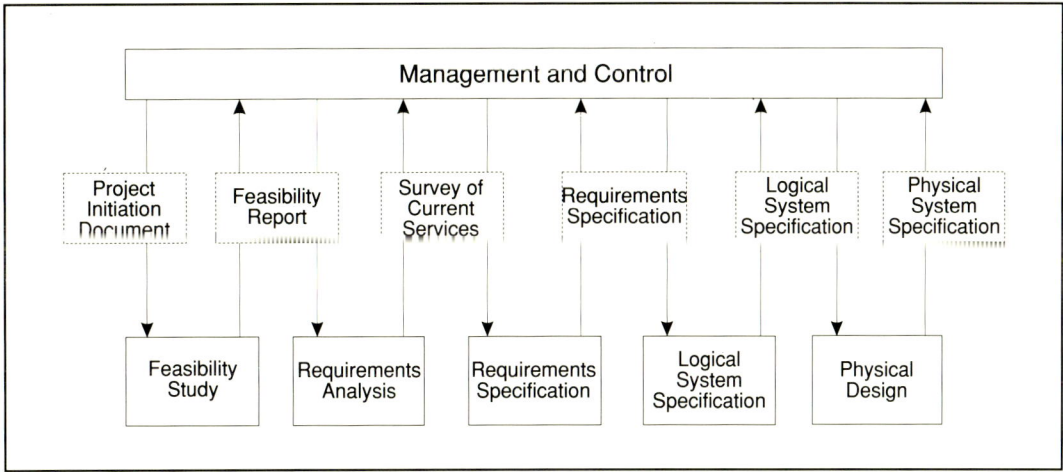

Figure 9.1: SSADM modules with inputs and outputs

Modules 2 - 5 constitute the SSADM Full Study; they break down into six stages. See Figures 9.2 and 9.3.

Modules	Stages	
Requirements Analysis	1 Investigation of Current Environment	} in } sequence
	2 Business System Options	}
Requirements Specification	3 Definition of Requirements	
Logical System Specification	4 Technical System Options	} in } parallel
	5 Logical Design	}
Physical Design	6 Physical Design	

Figure 9.2: The modules and stages of the SSADM Full Study

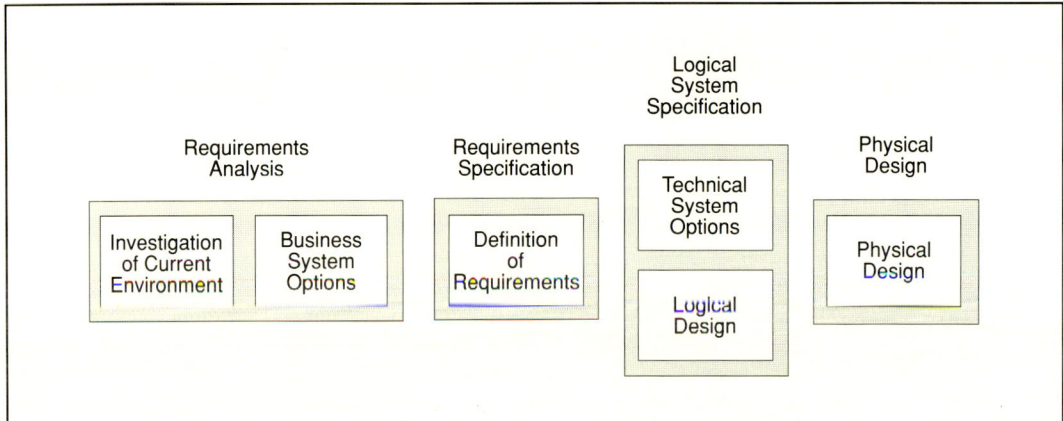

Figure 9.3: SSADM modules and stages

9.3.2 Mapping of common decision points

Figure 9.4 describes the mapping from the decision points described in Part 1 to the modules and stages of SSADM.

Generic decision points	**SSADM Modules/Stages**
Agree the basis of an IS project in an application area	Feasibility Study
Agree the information system requirements	Requirements Analysis
Agree the information system architecture	Business System Options
Agree the information system specification	Requirements Specification
Agree the computer system architecture and the user/machine interfaces	Logical Design
Agree the specification of the computer system and manual procedures	Physical Design
Agree the information system adaptation	Implementation (outside SSADM scope)

Figure 9.4: Mapping of generic decision points to SSADM modules and stages

Chapter 9
SSADM extensions

9.3.3 Representation of distribution concepts in the work products

Figure 9.5 describes the mapping of the general distribution concepts defined in Chapter 4 to SSADM terminology, and indicates where the terms are described in SSADM products. Distribution concepts outside the scope of SSADM have no entries; those within the scope but for which no SSADM equivalent exists have brief comments in italics. For a complete description of SSADM products see SSADM V4 Reference Manuals. Throughout Chapters 9 and 10 the term 'commit unit' is used synonymously with the SSADM term 'success unit'.

Distribution concept	SSADM term	Described in (SSADM product)
Actor	User (instance)	*Individual users not described*
Actor Role	User Role	User Catalogue or User Roles
Actor Role on workstation	*no specific term*	Menu for User Role or User Role/Function Matrix
Actor Type	User (type)	User Catalogue
Association	Relationship	LDM, Relationship Description
Business Location Instance	*no specific term*	*Individual locations not described*
Business Location Type	*no specific term*	*Modelled as entity type on LDM*
Commit Unit	Event Enquiry	Effect Correspondence Diagram Enquiry Access Path
Commit Unit Trigger	Event Data System-recognised Event Enquiry Trigger	Update Process Model Update Process Model Enquiry Process Model
Data Processing Location Instance	*no specific term*	*Individual locations not described*
Data Processing Location Type	*no specific term*	*May be modelled as entity type on LDM*

Distribution concept	SSADM term	Described in (SSADM product)
DP Input Message	Input structure	Function Definition
DP Output Message	Output structure	Function Definition
Input to Method	Effect Data	Derived from event data
Location Instance	no specific term	Individual locations not described
Manual Activity	User Procedure	User Manuals
Message Channel	no specific term	
Message in Dialogue	External Data Flow	I/O Structure I/O Structure Description
Method	Effect	Entity Life History Effect Correspondence Diagram
	EAP entity access	Enquiry Access Path
Method Dependency	ECD correspondence EAP correspondence	Effect Correspondence Diagram Enquiry Access Path
Method Implementation	no specific term	
Method Invocation	no specific term	Effect Correspondence Diagram Enquiry Access Path
Method Invocation Implementation	no specific term	
Object Class	Entity Aspect	LDM, Entity Description
Object Class Partition	no specific term	
Object Population Representation	no specific term	
Output by Method	no specific term	

Distribution concept	SSADM term	Described in (SSADM product)
Procedure Implementation	*no specific term*	
Procedure used in Role	Entry in User Role /Function Matrix	
Procedure/Function	Function	
Record Population Partition	*no specific term*	
Record Type	Database Record	
Record Type Storage Capability	*no specific term*	
Role at Location Type	*no specific term*	
Role Played	*no specific term*	
Validation/Formatting Implementation	Input module Output module	Physical Process Specification
Validation/Formatting Process	Input Process Output Process	Specific Function Model
Workstation	*no specific term*	
Workstation Requirements	*no specific term*	

Figure 9.5: Mapping of distribution concepts to SSADM terms

9.4 Changes to modelling steps and techniques

9.4.1 Summary of changes to SSADM

Only one structural change is needed to SSADM as defined in the Version 4 Reference Manuals. Stage 2, Selection of Business Options, is handled in two parts:

- selection of business option for functional scope - agree which non-mandatory requirements are to be satisfied

- selection of distribution option for chosen business option.

This avoids creation of a large number of options. However, there may be some rework and modification of the functional scope after distribution options have been created, costed and their impact on users evaluated.

There are some changes of detail to products. Most of these stem from the effects of classifying SSADM products in the 3-schema Specification Architecture described in Part 1 and relating the 3-schema Specification Architecture to distributed locations. See Figure 9.6

SSADM products	schema	server type	location type
functions, dialogues	external design	user interface server	business
LDM, ECDs, EAPs	conceptual model	process server	data processing
PDI, database	internal design	data server	data processing

Figure 9.6: Relationships between SSADM products, 3-schema Specification Architecture, server types and location types

(Note that 'location types' are components of functional design, not necessarily separate physical locations. However, we should be able to move functional components around the physical geography with minimal impact.)

An important new concept is introduced. An entity that is shared between locations is divided into 'aspects' (as described in Part 1); each aspect is a view of a more widely-defined entity. This partitioning of data (and initial allocation of database update and enquiry processes) is done from the Logical Data Model. For Entity-Event Modelling and process design, aspects are treated as if they were separate entities.

Techniques are clearly recognisable as the standard SSADM V4 techniques. Most changes are minor, to accommodate entity aspects and to comply with the 3-schema Specification Architecture.

Three new techniques are introduced:

- Robustness Analysis: this is carried out on distribution options to identify what business activity can be supported if locations are cut off from the rest of the system

- First-cut Distribution Design: this is based on the first-cut data design technique in SSADM V4, and aims for the most distributed design option. Further design options are created by clustering data at fewer locations

- Communications Mapping: this summarises the types and volumes of communication between locations in the distributed design.

9.4.2 Changes to the SSADM Structural Model & Products

Feasibility Study

No structural change of the Feasibility Module is needed. Some changes are needed to the detail of steps, with a possibility of more work being needed to define options.

010: Prepare for Feasibility Study

The Project Initiation Document should provide an overview of the geography of the organisation (and indicate where the analyst can find out about the detail), and must state why there is a requirement for distribution. Justification for such a requirement may be based on:

- non-functional requirements (eg continuity of service, local ownership of data)

- cost

- stability of design (eg ability to add locations without affecting performance).

The Project Initiation Document must also state whether a centralised solution is an acceptable option.

020: Define the Problem	The Requirements Catalogue is extended to include requirements for:

- robustness - what must locations be able to do if they are cut off?

- consistency - to what extent are locations allowed to be temporarily inconsistent?

If there is a current distributed system, the Data Flow Model may need to show the same types of component in different locations:

- communication between different instances of the same DFD process

- use of different instances of the same type of data store

- communication with different instances of the same type of user.

Some extensions of DFD notation are needed - see 'Changes to Techniques' in Section 9.5.3.

030: Select Feasibility Options	The feasibility study options must focus on getting the functional scope as tightly-defined as possible. Distribution options can be examined only in fairly broad terms, unless substantially more resource is put into the feasibility study than is normally the case. The procedure described later in this section for Business System Options could then be used.
040: Assemble Feasibility Report	The procedure is unchanged. The Feasibility Report must address distribution requirements in addition to the contents defined in the SSADM V4 Reference Manuals.

Chapter 9
SSADM extensions

Stage 1: Investigation of Current Environment	No structural change of stage 1 is needed. Some changes are needed to the detail of steps.
Step 110: Establish Analysis Framework	As for Feasibility Study, project input documentation should describe the geography of the organisation and must say why there is a requirement for distribution, which may be based on: • non-functional requirements (eg continuity of service, local ownership of data) • cost • stability of design (eg ability to add locations without affecting performance). The project initiation document must also state whether a centralised solution is an acceptable option. Planned project activities, end-product definitions and plans for involvement of users must all take account of distribution issues.
Step 120: Investigate and Define Requirements	Requirements must address needs for robustness and consistency, and constraints on distribution must be identified. Types of business location must be defined, and cross referenced to requirements. A requirement may serve more than one type of business location. See 'Requirements Definition' in Section 9.5.1.
Step 130: Investigate Current Processing	The procedure is unchanged. If there is a current distributed system, the Data Flow Model may need to show the same types of component used in different locations; some extensions of DFD notation are needed. See 'Data Flow Modelling' in Section 9.5.3.

Step 140: Investigate Current Data	Unchanged. The LDM is developed as a single model for the entire system (not as separate LDMs for each type of location).
Step 150: Derive Logical View of Current Services	The procedure includes an additional technique, event identification (see under 'Entity Access Matrix' in bullets which follow), and some of the guidelines for development of DFM and LDM are different:

- Data Flow Model

    The DFM is directed at the external design. It is not concerned with where data is stored; there is no location information on data stores (although this is sometimes needed for DFMs of current distributed systems).

    The logical DFM is built from the bottom up, around user roles (this is one of three possibilities recommended in the *SSADM V4 Reference Manuals*).

    User roles are defined at business locations. If the same user role occurs at more than one type of business location, a separate low-level DFD is drawn for it (see 'maintenance organiser' in the EU-Rent case study). The DFM is then organised around business location types in the required system. Each type of business location can be shown as a subset of the low-level DFDs that describes the functionality that will support it in the required system.

    Every process needed by a business location is assumed to be invocable from a workstation at that location; there is no location role shown on DFD processes (this is sometimes needed for DFMs of current distributed systems).

    Communication, via DFD processes, between different instances of the same user role at different locations may have to be shown on the DFDs. Roles for external entities may be indicated.

Chapter 9
SSADM extensions

- Logical Data Model

    The procedure for validating the LDM is extended a little. As each process is used to validate the LDM:

    - a list of attributes is built up for each entity type (ask 'What attributes are needed in this entity to support this process?')

    - enquiry rows in the Entity Access Matrix (see step 150) are created

    See also Section 9.5.2.

- Entity Access Matrix

    The Entity Access Matrix is an extension of the idea of the entity-event matrix; it includes access to entities for enquiries as well as updates.

    Once the attributes and relationships in the LDM are known, the LDM can be analysed to determine the events essential to keep the database up-to-date. See 'Creating the Entity Access Matrix', in Section 9.5.5; this describes a technique for event identification without the requirement to build ELHs. Enquiries will have already been included in the matrix during validation of the LDM.

Step 160. Assemble Investigation Results	Unchanged.
Alternative approach for building logical DFDs	If the new external design is likely to be radically different from that of the current system (or if no current system exists), the Entity Access Matrix would support an alternative approach for creating logical DFDs for the required system:

  - events and queries in the Entity Access Matrix can be mapped on to user roles (Who provides the input? Who uses the output?)

231

- functions can be built bottom-up by grouping together events and queries for the same user role, serving a common purpose and invocable in immediate sequence

- logical DFDs can be built bottom-up by grouping functions for the same user role.

Stage 2: Business System Options

In order to deal with distribution issues, business system options have to be developed in greater detail than in Core SSADM V4. There is potentially a problem with the number of options offered to the project board. If there were, say, three options for functional scope, each of which could be distributed in two or three ways, the number of options would be impracticably large.

A two-part procedure is proposed:

- selection of business option, concerned with functional requirements not supported in current systems - how mandatory requirements will fit with current services, what combinations of non-mandatory requirements will be offered as options

- selection of distribution option, concerned with how the agreed business option can be distributed across the business and data processing locations. This is addressed in two additional steps in stage 2, as shown in Figure 9.7.

Chapter 9
SSADM extensions

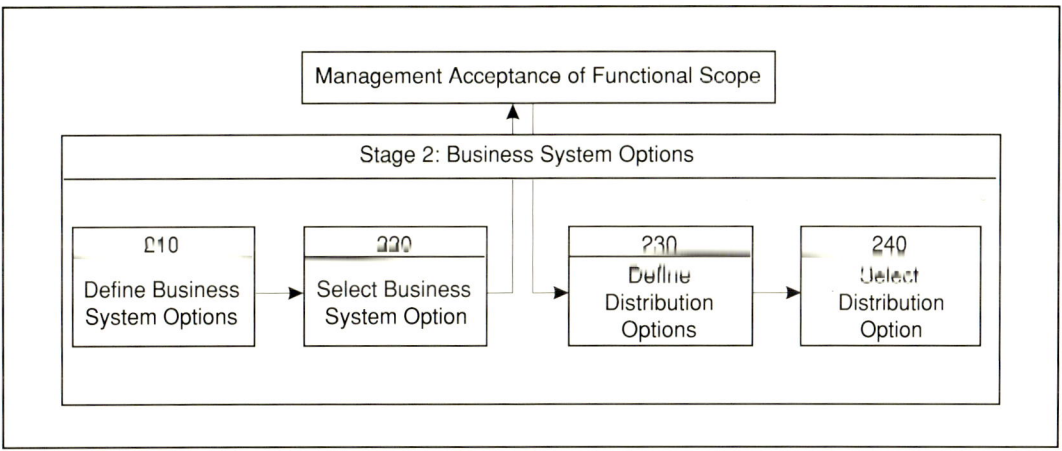

Figure 9.7: Business System Options with additional steps

Although the steps are shown as a sequence, in practice there is likely to be some iteration between the options for functional requirements and the distribution options.

Step 210: Define Business System Options

The procedure in this step is not changed, but the products are a little different:

- level-2 logical DFDs are organised (in step 150) around user roles in business location types. In this step, functional requirements in the different options are explored and presented by business location type, on modified versions of these level-2 DFDs (rather than on the level-1 DFD as recommended in the *SSADM V4 Reference Manuals*)

- cost-benefit analyses for options can be only partially developed.

Step 220: Select Business System Option

The procedure in this step is not changed. However, the option selected here may be modified after cost-benefit analysis of the distribution options.

Distribution Options

The major concepts in distribution are:

- functions (external design) are available at business locations that need to use them

233

- update and enquiry processes (conceptual model) are available at data processing locations and are invoked by functions

- the database (internal design) is stored at data processing locations and accessed by update and enquiry processes

- distribution is based on partitioning the LDM and deciding:

  - where to store data

  - where to store event and enquiry processes:

    .. at business locations, with the functions that invoke them
    .. at data processing locations, with the data they use
    .. distributed across several types of data processing location
    .. split between data processing and business locations

  - whether to replicate data

  - how to manage history of entities that move from location to location

  - the trade-off between robustness and temporary inconsistency.

This means that a fairly detailed LDM is needed. Some of the work normally done in step 320 of SSADM V4, Develop the Required Data Model, has to be done in step 230 to develop the distribution options.

Step 230: Define Distribution Options

The procedure is:

- define the outputs needed to support each new functional requirement in the selected business option; validate the LDM to ensure that the functions can be delivered; define LDM attributes

- analyse the LDM's attributes and relationships to identify events; extend the Entity Access Matrix (see 'Creating the Entity Access Matrix', in Section 9.5.5)

- identify the user role that supplies the input for each type of event; map functions to event and enquiry processes (additional input functions may have to be defined to accommodate some events)

- add volumes to the Entity Access Matrix; for each event/enquiry indicate (using the function/event/enquiry mapping) which types of business location may invoke it

- use the first-cut distribution rules (see 'New Techniques', in Section 9.6.2) to produce a 'most distributed' trial design

- create a centralised design for comparison, if permitted; if not, create a 'most clustered' design

- apply clustering guidelines (as suggested in Chapter 6) to create a partially-clustered design.

For each design:

- identify the communication between types of location, and state whether it is to be loosely-coordinated (allowing temporary inconsistencies between locations under defined conditions) or tightly-coordinated (completely consistent across all affected locations). There is likely to be a mixture of both types in any given system

- carry out a robustness analysis for each type of business location:

    - what can a location do if it is cut off from the communications network?

    - what can a location not do if it is cut off?

    - what can other locations not do if a location is cut off?

- identify the inconsistencies that are allowed to occur between data at different locations, and the timescales within which they will be corrected

- estimate costs.

Step 240: Select Distribution Option	This step is similar to step 220, Select Business Option. When costs of the distribution options have been estimated, the option selected in step 220 may have to be reviewed and modified.
Stage 3: Requirements Specification	There is no need for structural change to Requirements Specification. The main change is that some of the work done in this stage in Core SSADM has already been done in defining distribution options in stage 2.
Step 310: Define Required System Processing	No change is needed to the procedure in this step; production of the required DFDs is slightly simplified: - level-2 DFDs have been partly developed in creation of options - DFDs are already organised by user role within business location type - new functional requirements have been mapped to events and enquiries - their scope, input and output should be fairly well-understood.
Step 320: Develop Required Data Model	Much of the work described for this step in the *SSADM V4 Reference Manuals* has been done at Step 220, Define Distribution Options. What is now needed is a separately-drawn LDM for each type of data processing location. Where an entity type is used in more than one type of location, it is split into aspects (as described in Part 1). Some attributes may be replicated in more than one aspect. See Section 9.5.5.

Step 330: Derive System Functions	No change is needed to the procedure in this step. Identification of functions is simplified - DFDs are organised as groups of functions serving user roles.
Step 340: Enhance Required Data Model	No change is needed to the procedure in this step, although there are two minor changes to the Relational Data Analysis technique, concerned with keys and entity aspects. See Section 9.5.4.
Step 350: Develop Specification Prototypes	Unchanged.
Step 360: Develop Processing Specification	No change is needed to the procedure in this step. Simple Entity Life Histories are easier to develop, since the Entity Access Matrix has been produced in stage 2. There are some changes to the Entity Life History analysis technique to deal with: • entity aspects • disciplined quits (now Part of Core SSADM; but not in the V4 Reference Manuals; described in *Quits and Resumes on Entity Life Histories*; note that the approach described in this volume also works with 'undisciplined quits') • optimised states (optional, but recommended) • rules (optional, but recommended). See 'Changes to SSADM Techniques', Section 9.5.5.
Step 370: Confirm System Objectives	Unchanged.
Step 380: Assemble Requirements Specification	Unchanged.

Stage 4: Technical
System Options

Step 410: Define
Technical Options

The procedure is generally the same as in the *SSADM V4 Reference Manuals*, but the creation of options has to take account of the distributed processing architecture that will best support requirements (see Section 9.7, 'Mapping from specific requirements to services').

Generally:

- consolidated Update and Enquiry Process Models (as in SSADM V4), with remote database access and distributed commit, support high consistency but may not be as robust as is required - a process cannot succeed if any of the locations it needs data from is off-line

- partitioned processes with remote procedure calls can support more robust operation. They can be run as tightly-coordinated procedures, but it is possible to run them more loosely.

For example, in EU-Rent, when head office notifies branches of a new rental price for a car group, some branches may be off-line. When head office detects this it could, since no data is required in response, suppress the calls to off-line branches and simply call on-line branches. Then the price update could be applied locally to the branches that were off-line:

- by shipping it to them when they are back on-line

- by letting them know informally, by phone or EMail.

However, most of today's technology provides much better support for remote database access than for remote procedure calls. If we want to use remote procedure calls we should expect to have to write some of the middleware ourselves.

Chapter 9
SSADM extensions

Step 420: Select Technical System Options	The procedure is unchanged. The selection procedure has to take account of the capability of the technology chosen to support distributed requirements, especially: • remote database access • remote procedure calls • data location transparency • process location transparency • data replication transparency.
Stage 5: Logical Design	No structural change is needed for this stage.
Step 510: Design User Dialogues	Unchanged.
Step 520: Define Update Processing	The procedure is unchanged, but the technique for defining update processing is extended to cover: • developing a consolidated UPM (as in the *SSADM V4 Reference Manuals*); the PDI will manage remote database access where needed • partitioning the ECD by location, and developing local UPMs; correspondence between locations will be managed by remote procedure calls. See Section 9.5.7. • Object-oriented implementation, where each ECD node is defined as a separate method. See 'Object-oriented Implementation of the Conceptual Schema', Section 9.7. The approach(es) taken will depend on the technology selected in stage 4.
Step 530: Define Enquiry Processing	The same options exist for enquiry processes as for update processes.

Step 540: Assemble Logical Design	Unchanged.
Stage 6: Physical Design	The scope of this volume does not extend to the detail of physical design, but an overview of the approach is provided.
	Physical design in SSADM V4 is more general than stages 1 to 5. It provides guidance on how to specify the physical design method, rather than being the specific physical design method.
	Feedback from projects using the approach in this volume with a range of distributed technology will be essential before the development of detailed guidance for distributed physical design could be contemplated.
Step 610: Prepare for Physical Design	The procedure is similar to that in the *SSADM V4 Reference Manuals*; the classification system for database storage and performance needs to be extended to include distributed aspects. The table of services in Section 5.4 provides a useful starting point, but further product-specific information will be needed.
	In this step, timing forms (or spreadsheets) are developed for the selected DBMS. In a distributed system there may be more than one DBMS, and some transactions may be spread across them. Timing forms for distributed transactions should include communication across the network.
Step 620: Create Physical Data Design	The procedure for First-cut Data Design is generally as described in the *SSADM V4 Reference Manuals*; the first-cut rules differ slightly to take account of multiple aspects of the same entity types. A First-cut Data Design will be needed for each type of data storage location (as partitioned in the selected distribution option).
	Assume that aspects will be implemented locally (eg Customer-rentals will be replicated at every branch where a particular customer is active). Map aspects on to distinct database tables or record types. Ensure that

aspects of the same entity have a common external identifier (such as Customer Number) that can be used to select an entity instance consistently across all its aspects.

Step 630: Create Function Component Implementation Map	Creation of the Function Component Implementation Map should be in one way slightly easier than in Core SSADM. The separation of concerns imposed by the 3-schema Specification Architecture means that common components at the level of event, enquiry, I/O structure and format should be clearly visible.

However, replicated processes and the possibility that some database processes may be partitioned across several locations makes it more difficult to provide general guidance on creating the FCIM, especially on use of common components, although it is often clear what is needed in specific situations. More feedback from practice is needed. |
| Step 640: Optimise Physical Data Design | The general idea of physical design is as in the *SSADM V4 Reference Manuals*, but there are more design issues to be considered. In particular, minimising the volume of messages passed between sites may be important, since communication between sites is usually both slow and expensive.

Additional possibilities for performance trade-offs include:

- replicate data locally
- move local aspects to more clustered locations
- batch messages to reduce communication overheads between sites
- reduce consistency:
  - to increase robustness
  - to allow batch communication between sites. |

Step 650: Complete Function Specification	There is only one significant difference from the *SSADM V4 Reference Manuals*. The function, as represented in the external design, needs to invoke process servers for the events and enquiries it uses. In many cases a function will access process servers at only one data processing location. In some systems some functions will be able to access more than one data processing location; such functions need to know which processes they may invoke from where.
	Where the distribution of processing in the network is fairly static there should be no major problems; the function simply has to be extended with criteria for what process servers to use, and under what conditions. If distribution of processing is dynamic, it would be possible to construct a 'function to UPM/EPM interface' (analogous to the PDI), but this is rare in practice.
	In some client/server and object-based architectures these process server invocations will be in the event manager (the upper structure of the UPM or EPM) called by the function rather than in the external design.
Step 660: Consolidate Process Data Interface	There are some additional requirements of the PDI in a distributed system:

- there may be a requirement to hide data location (and possibly data replication) from conceptual model processes, inside the PDI

- if, during optimisation, aspects of the same entity are mapped on to a single physical table or record type, the PDI may need to take account of access to the same database record by more than one update or enquiry process

- where a record instance may be hit by more than one message for the same event, the PDI may have to manage selective locking, so that other events and enquiries are locked out but multiple messages for the same event are allowed in. The system will have to allocate identifiers for event and enquiry instances, which will be passed to the PDI with each call.

Step 670: Assemble   Unchanged
Physical Design

9.5 Changes to current   The following SSADM techniques require modification:
SSADM techniques

- Requirements Definition (Section 9.5.1)
- Logical Data Modelling (Section 9.5.2)
- Data Flow Modelling (Section 9.5.3)
- Relational Data Analysis (Section 9.5.4)
- Entity Life History Analysis (Section 9.5.5)
- Effect Correspondence Diagram (Section 9.5.6)
- Update Process Models (Section 9.5.7)
- Enquiry Process Models (Section 9.5.8)
- Internal Design (Section 9.5.9).

9.5.1 Requirements   Requirements definition has to be extended to address:
Definition

- what is required from the distributed system (not mutually exclusive):

    - non-functional requirements (eg continuity of service, local ownership of data)

    - minimising cost

    - stability of design (eg ability to add locations without affecting performance)

- robustness - what each type of business location is required to be able to do if it is cut off from other business locations

- consistency - what parts of the system are allowed to be loosely-coordinated (ie may be temporarily inconsistent)? Within what timescales must they be made consistent?

- constraints on distribution, eg architectural standards, compatibility with already-installed technology, procurement policy, existing data processing locations, requirement to share data with other systems.

9.5.1 Logical Data Modelling

There are two significant changes to the use of the LDM:

Validation

When Business System Options are developed, the LDM needs to be specified in sufficient detail to support event identification, so that some analysis of distributed processing can be carried out (see 'Creating the Entity Access Matrix' in Section 9.5.5).

We can achieve this by extending the technique for validating the LDM against processing requirements. There are three changes to validation of the LDM:

- when the LDM is validated with processing requirements (especially enquiries), define attributes informally. As each entity is visited, ask 'What attributes would be needed to provide the required output?'

- for each Business System Option, define the required access to the LDM for each functional requirement and extend the attribute lists for the entities

- for each enquiry, complete a row of the Entity Access Matrix.

Entity Aspects

Substructures of the LDM have to be mapped to types of data processing location. We need a technique for splitting entity types that are needed in more than one type of data processing location. We can split LDM entities into aspects. For example, see Figure 9.8.

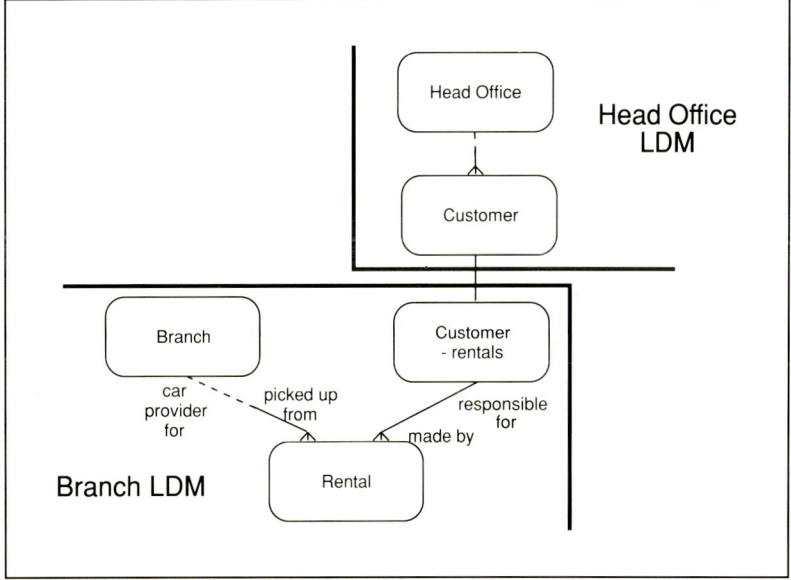

Figure 9.8: Partitioned LDM showing base and dependent aspects for Customer

The aspect is a modelling concept. The two aspects of customer do not have to be implemented separately, but 'rental behaviour' and 'head office behaviour' are modelled separately so that, when comparing design options, it is easy to see the differences between:

- implementing the rental aspect once at head office, with remote access from branches

- replicating the rental aspect of customer at each branch where the customer is active.

The message traffic in the network is determined by which relationship is cut for distribution.

This approach is also used in *ISE Library Volume: Application Partitioning and Integration with SSADM* to split shared entities across applications that will be implemented at different times, even if they are implemented at the same location. In *ISE Library Volume: Reuse in SSADM using OO*, 'aspect' corresponds to stored object - ie the behaviour of a real-world entity type may be modelled over several object classes, which may be stored in different locations.

Entity aspects can also be used to model parallel lives in Entity-Event Modelling. See Section 9.5.5.

9.5.2 Data Flow Modelling

Extension of notation

For representation of a current distributed system, the notation for DFDs is extended to show roles of external entities, process locations and data stores. Role names are given in square brackets (a convention similar to that for entity roles in entity-event modelling). See Figure 9.9.

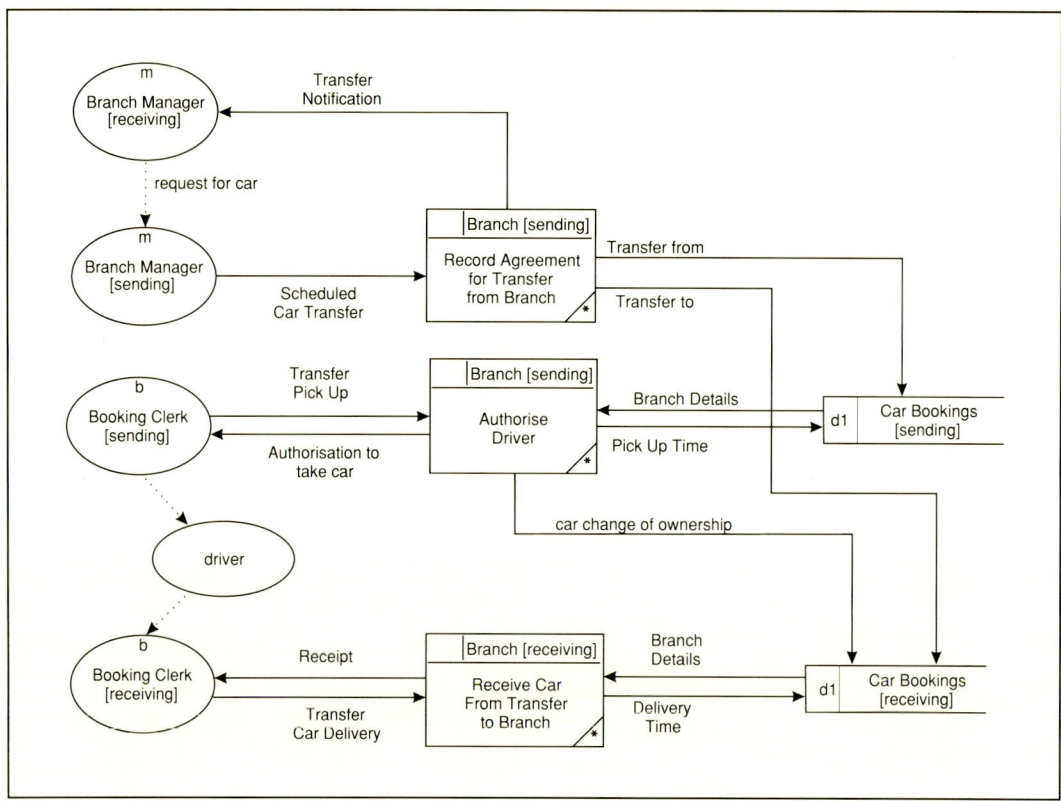

Figure 9.9: *DFD showing instances of the same external entities and data store types at different locations*

Logical and Required DFDs show only the external design

For Required System DFDs and functions derived from them, only the external entity roles need be distinguished. In the external design we assume:

- functions are to be available 'from the workstation'

- data location transparency: the data in the data stores is available in the system - the external design doesn't need to know where.

There is no reason to show process location role or data store role on the DFDs.

9.5.3 Relational Data Analysis

There are two minor changes to Relational Data Analysis.

System-generated Keys

For some entities mechanisms are needed within the system to generate keys for new instances. We should avoid the bottleneck of having a single key-issuing algorithm at a single location.

Two possibilities are:

- to concatenate the location identifier with a 'next key' generator at each location. The important point for Relational Data Analysis is that: if the entity can move to other locations, this is not a hierarchical key - the location id is not meaningful, it is simply a way of ensuring uniqueness

- to use hierarchical keys. When a 'next key' is needed, 'last key issued' can be obtained by checking other details of the relevant master. In a distributed system this might involve enquiries across the network. A way of avoiding this is to add a 'last key issued' attribute to the master.

Aspects

When an entity is split, one aspect is defined as the 'base' aspect, modelling basic existence of the entity, others are dependent aspects. Usually the base aspect is the one highest up the corporate hierarchy - at head office in the example in Figure 9.8.

In Relational Data Analysis, each aspect of an entity can be treated as a separate TNF relation, except that:

- some attributes may occur in more than one aspect: for example, customer name and address might be required in both the head office and branch aspects of customer. This is consistent with an aspect's being a view of some more widely-defined entity

- all aspects of the same entity should have the same key. However, some CASE tools automatically consolidate entities with the same key (or do not permit more than one entity definition with the same key). To get round this, it may be necessary to add an attribute to the key, indicating aspect type.

9.5.4 Entity Life History Analysis

Recommended Changes to ELH Analysis

There are two significant changes to the method for development of Entity Life Histories - building an Entity Access Matrix before developing ELHs, and modelling of entity aspects.

The Entity Access Matrix

In the 3-schema Specification Architecture described in Part 1, an essential characteristic of the conceptual schema is that, once it is known what information support has to be provided, the content of the LDM and the means of keeping it up to date are defined by a process of discovery.

We can use this concept in step 230 to identify the events needed to update the LDM (ie before the required system DFDs are developed) and develop a matrix of required access to the LDM. We need to know about events, and from which types of location they originate, in order to develop distribution options. This change has two effects:

- events are identified from the LDM, and then reconciled with DFD inputs and outputs, rather than being identified from the DFDs (although in practice a mixture of the two approaches will probably be used)

- at step 360, Develop Processing Specification, simple ELHs are built faster and more easily, using the Entity Access Matrix.

Chapter 9
SSADM extensions

Creating the Entity Access Matrix   The Entity Access Matrix is an extension of the idea of the entity/event matrix, including access of entities by enquiries as well as updating by events. A suggested format is shown in Figure 9.10.

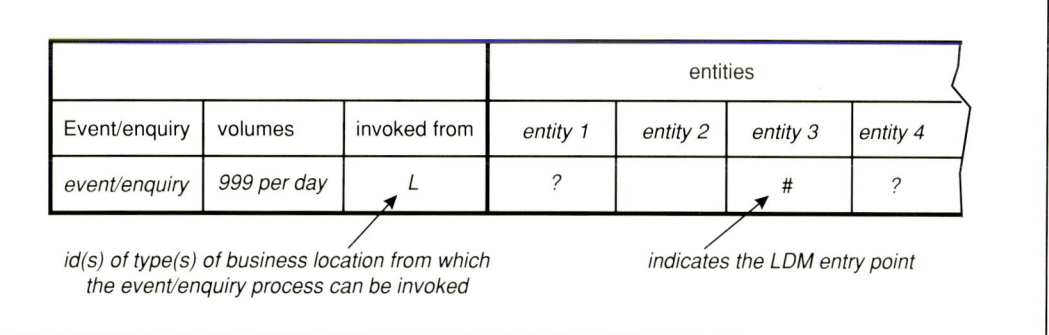

Figure 9.10: Suggested format for the Entity Access Matrix

It is useful to set up the matrix on a tool such as a spreadsheet, that allows restructuring by row and column.

Enquiry Access   As the LDM is validated against enquiries:

- create a row in the matrix for each enquiry and mark each entity accessed

- identify the attributes needed for each entity to support the enquiry and add them to the entity definition

- add the business location(s) from which the enquiry can be invoked, and the volumes.

Take these actions both in validating the current LDM and when including functional requirements in Business System Options. It may be necessary to create supplementary, BSO-specific tables if different BSOs include different subsets of functional requirements.

Event Identification   If we have a Logical Data Model whose attributes are defined, we can analyse it to identify the changes that

249

are needed to keep the database up-to-date. From the changes that need to be modelled we can look for the business events that cause them, and fill the events in the matrix. Many of the events will be identifiable on the DFDs.

Examine every entity in the LDM for events in the following categories:

- **Birth** Each entity type must have its own distinct type of birth event, unless:

    - it is a detail entity of a master entity which is invalid without any details (the birth of the master will also be the birth event of one or more details)

    - it is a master entity which is born at the same time as its first detail entity.

- **Death** There are two kinds of death event - the 'update death', after which the entity may not be updated any more, and the 'history death', after which it may be deleted. For some entity types the same event fulfils both purposes.

    An entity type will have its own distinct type of update death, unless:

    - it is dead as soon as it is born (common in an entity at the bottom of a data model)

    - it shares the death event of one of its masters.

- **State-Changing Event(s) & Date Event(s)** A state-change event changes the state of an entity. It usually 'freezes' or 'thaws' the entity in some way. (In fact, it is usually an aspect of the entity that is frozen or thawed, rather than the whole entity - see Section 9.5.2 on 'Entity Aspects').

    To 'freeze' an entity (aspect) is to move it into a state where some types of event are no longer permitted to affect it. To 'thaw' it is to move it into a state where the events are again permitted.

Look out for date events which have a state-changing effect.

- **Relationships with Masters** Identify events which cause an entity's relationship with each of its masters to be tied, cut or swapped. These will depend on the kind of relationship. See Figure 9.11.

Type of relationship	Operation	Event that triggers operation
fixed, mandatory	tie	must be the birth of this entity
fixed, optional	tie	may be the birth of this entity may be 'delayed master notification'
changeable, mandatory	tie	must be the birth of this entity
	*swap	specific swap event death of master (entity switched to another master)
changeable, optional	tie	may be the birth of this entity
	cut	may be the death of this entity may be specific cut event
	*swap	may be specific swap event

Figure 9.11: Events that cause entity relationships to be tied, cut or swapped

* Where 'swap' events are identified, mark the master in the matrix. Two instances of the master are involved - they may be stored at different locations.

- **Relationships with Details** Identify events which cause masters to gain or lose a detail. They are the events that cause details to be cut, tied and swapped. See Figure 9.12.

Type of relationship	Operation	Event that triggers operation
fixed (mandatory from detail's view)	gain?	must be the birth event of the detail entity
fixed (optional from detail's view)	gain?	may be birth event of the detail entity 'delayed master notification'?
changeable	gain? lose?	any tie or swap event of the detail entity any cut or swap event of the detail entity

Figure 9.12: Events that cause a master entity to gain or lose a detail

- **Non-Key Attributes** Identify the events which cause attributes (other than primary and foreign keys) to be updated. See Figure 9.13.

Type of attribute	Operation	Event which triggers operation
fixed attributes	store	birth of this entity 'late notification' event?
changeable attribute	store update	likely to be the birth of this entity likely to be a simple, distinct, event
optional attribute	set null?	may be birth of this entity may be event that removes this entity from criteria for selection on this attribute

Figure 9.13: Events that cause non-key attributes to be updated

Entering Events into the Matrix

For each event identified:

- complete a row in the matrix, with volumes
- identify the entry point to the LDM - which entity type will be identified by the input for the event.

Reconcile Events with Functions

The IT system will automatically recognise many time-based events, such as dates and specified points in the processing schedule (eg end of working day, start of financial year). All other types of event should be recognisable as DFD inputs from external entities, although some events are likely to be at a lower level of detail than the DFDs. All DFD inputs should be represented as events. Identify any omissions and rectify them.

Define a mapping between functions and events/enquiries. An event or enquiry may be invoked by more than one function.

Functions are invoked from business locations. Define a code for each business location type. Using the function/event/enquiry mapping, use these codes to identify the entry point to each event and enquiry in the matrix - thus showing which business location(s) invoke each event and enquiry.

Entity aspects

The technique for partitioning the LDM between locations is to split shared entities into aspects. When an entity is split, one aspect is defined as the 'basic' aspect, modelling basic existence of the entity, others are dependent aspects. See customer and customer rentals in Figure 9.14.

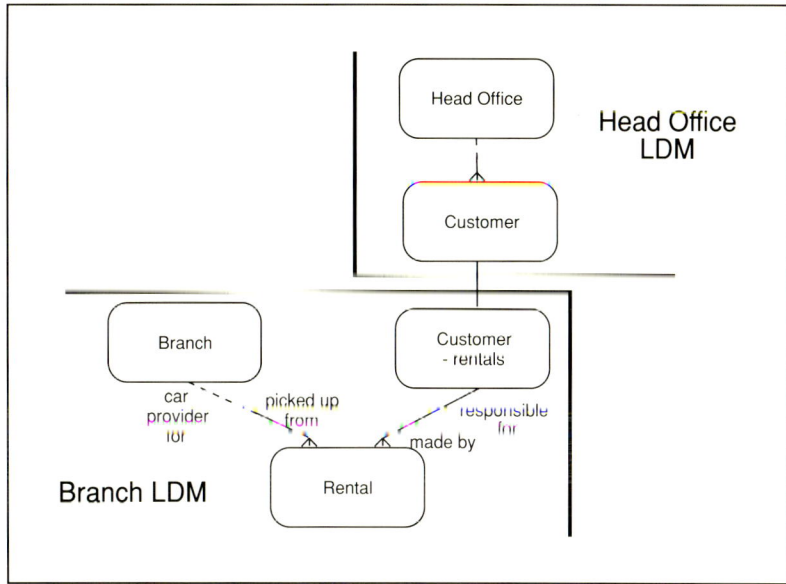

Figure 9.14: Base and dependent aspects of customer

Usually the base aspect is the one highest up the corporate hierarchy - at head office in the example.

When developing ELHs for aspects:

- develop an ELH for the base aspect, as for any independent entity

- develop an ELH for each dependent aspect as if it were a separate entity in one-to-one correspondence with the base aspect, with two exceptions:

    - no cut/tie, gain/loss operations are needed

    - the subordinate aspect can exist only while the base aspect exists; its birth and death are constrained by the birth and death of the base aspect.

Note that for aspects in different locations, some attributes may be replicated. Operations will be needed to update them in each aspect ELH.

ELHs for Aspects

Customer base aspect The customer base aspect is concerned with maintaining the customer's existence in EU-Rent (or in EU-Corporation if car rental, airline and hotel systems are to be integrated) and maintaining reference data. See Figure 9.15.

Chapter 9
SSADM extensions

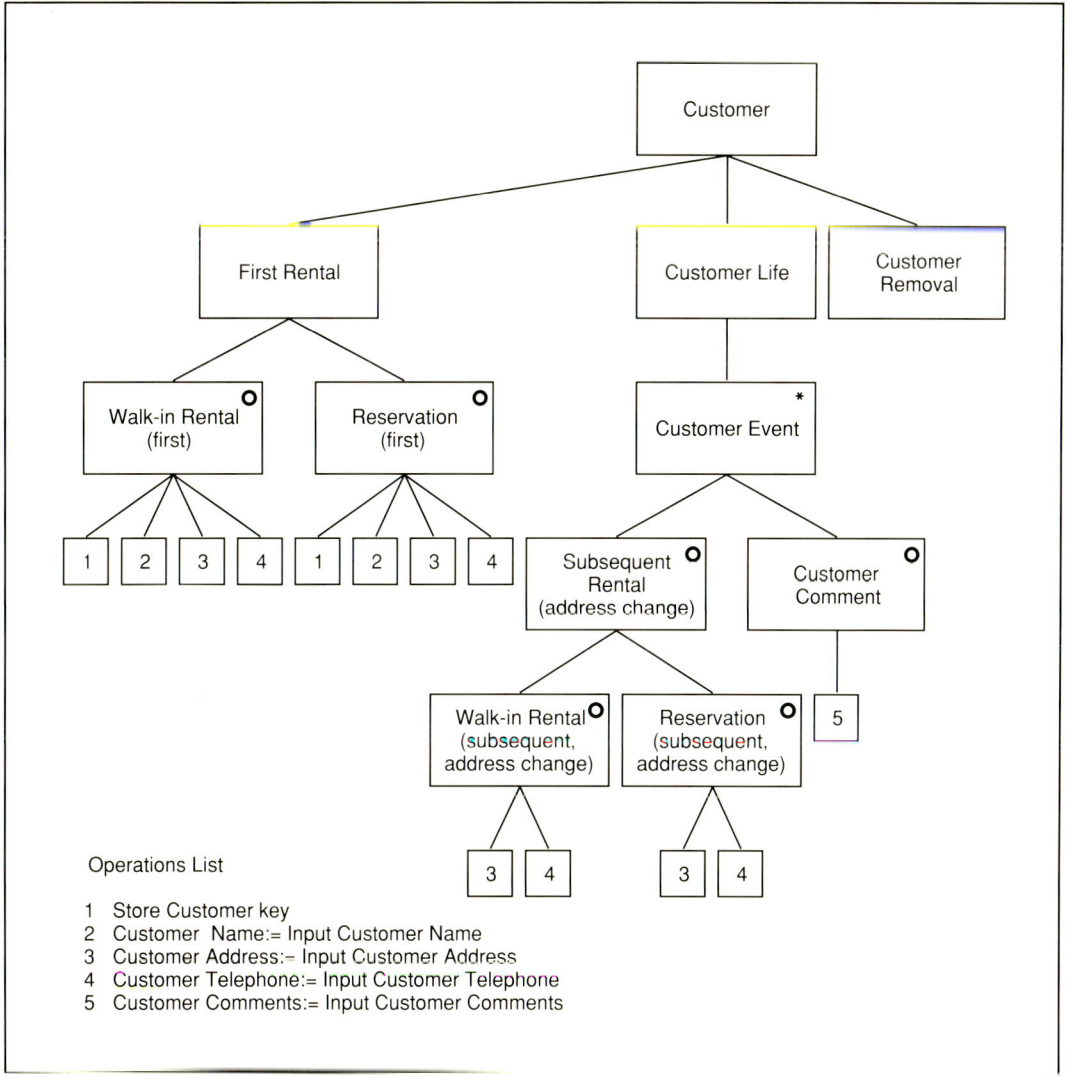

Figure 9.15: ELH for customer base aspect

Rentals aspect of customer - behaviour at branches The rentals aspect of customer is concerned with customer behaviour at branches - ie with managing rentals, subject to customer status. See Figure 9.16.

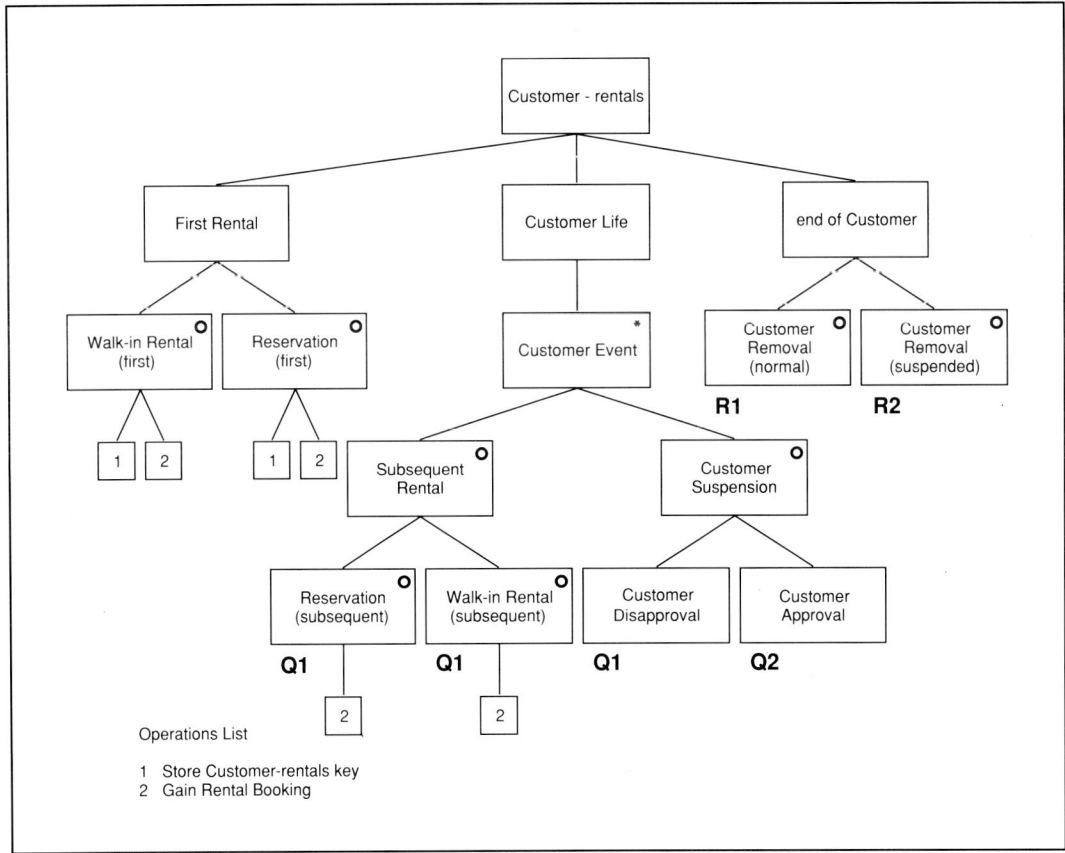

Figure 9.16: ELH for rental aspect of customer

Although customer disapproval and approval decisions are made at head office, the events have to be included in this aspect. They define a restriction on behaviour at branch.

Suggested Changes to ELH Analysis

Four further changes to ELH development are suggested, but they are not essential. The method will work without them but they would simplify some parts of it. They deal with:

- state optimisation

- parallel lives modelled as separate aspects

- rules

Chapter 9
SSADM extensions

- subtypes.

State optimisation

In many ELHs, some events simply change the entity's state. Some entity states are equivalent, as described below. If equivalent states were optimised to a single value there would be no need for the write back operation when the entity was set to an output state equivalent to its input state. This would generally result in a useful saving of database updates in SSADM-developed systems. It would have extra benefits in a distributed system if the write were to be done over the network, requiring remote access and a two-phase commit.

We may reduce the number of states required in an ELH in two steps:

1 Unify the states of effects that end options under a selection

In SSADM V4, each event in an ELH is given a distinct state value as in Figure 9.17.

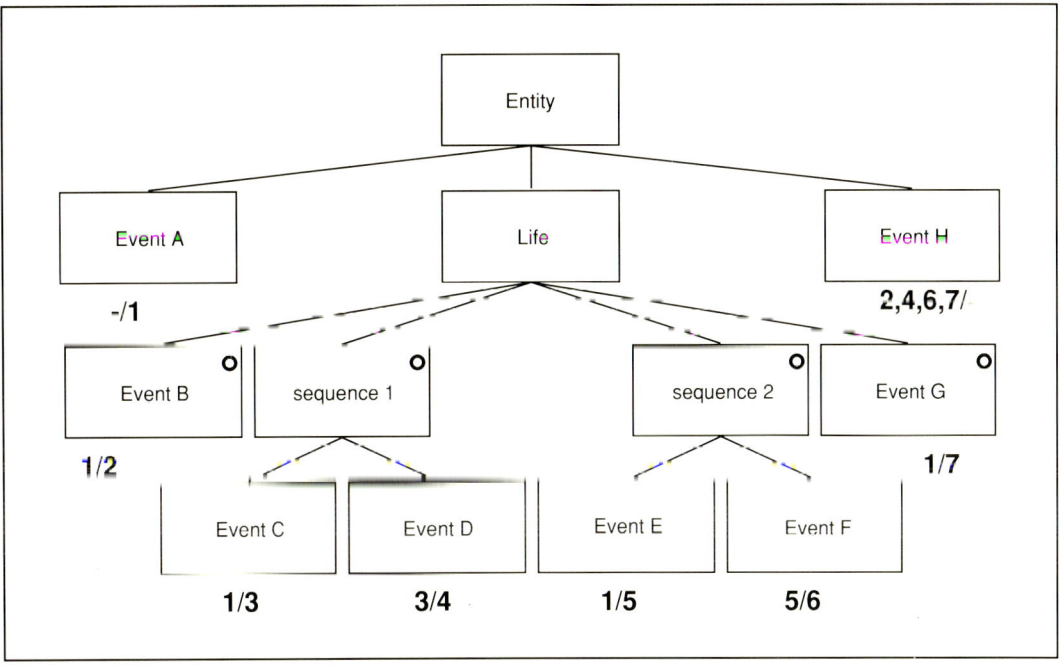

Figure 9.17: ELH with unoptimised states ending selections

257

In Figure 9.17, states 2, 4, 6 & 7 all mean 'Entity is in a valid state for event H to occur'. They are equivalent, and can be optimised to the same value as in Figure 9.18.

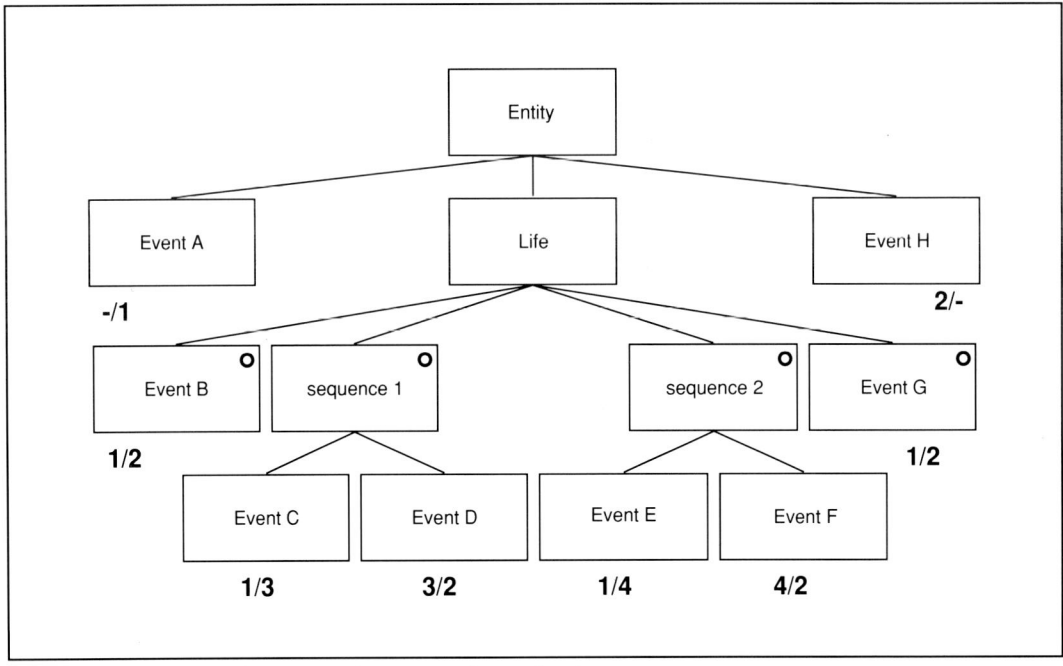

Figure 9.18: ELH with optimised states ending selections

Note what was state 5 in Figure 9.17 has been renumbered as state 4 in Figure 9.18.

2 Unify the state before an iteration with that after the iterated component. In Figure 9.19 the iteration could be null, so state 1 means 'Either event Y or event Z could happen next'.

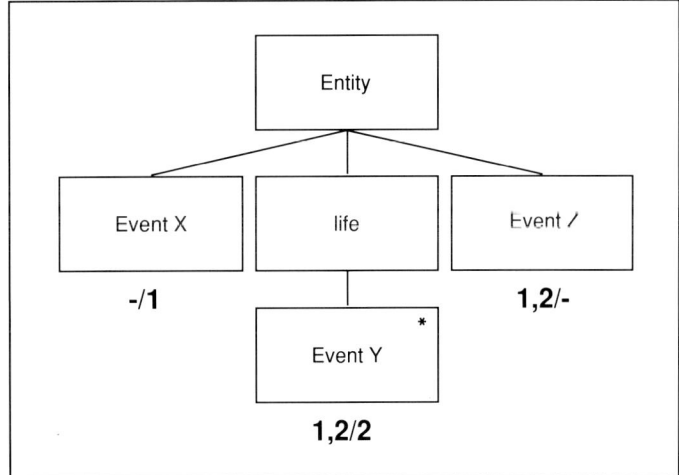

Figure 9.19: ELH with unoptimised states before and after iteration

Similarly, state 2 means 'Either event Y or event Z could happen next'. States 1 and 2 can be optimised to the same value as in Figure 9.20.

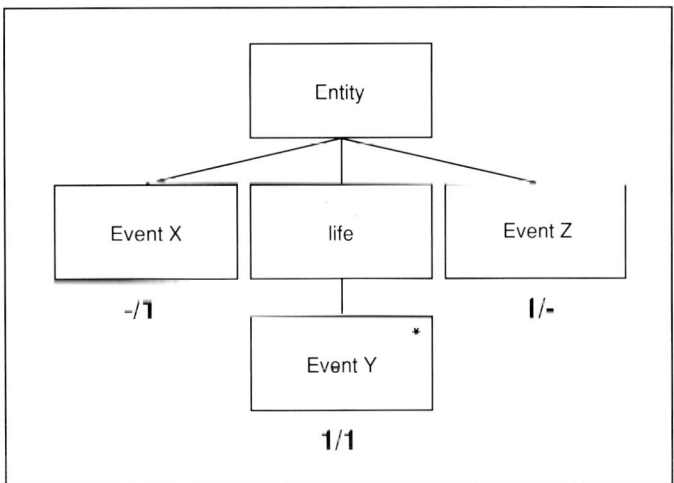

Figure 9.20: ELH with states before and after iteration optimised

The iteration rule and the selection rule can generally be combined. To illustrate this imagine an iteration of the mid-life of the ELH in Figure 9.18. After the iteration rule has also been applied, the ELH would appear as in Figure 9.21.

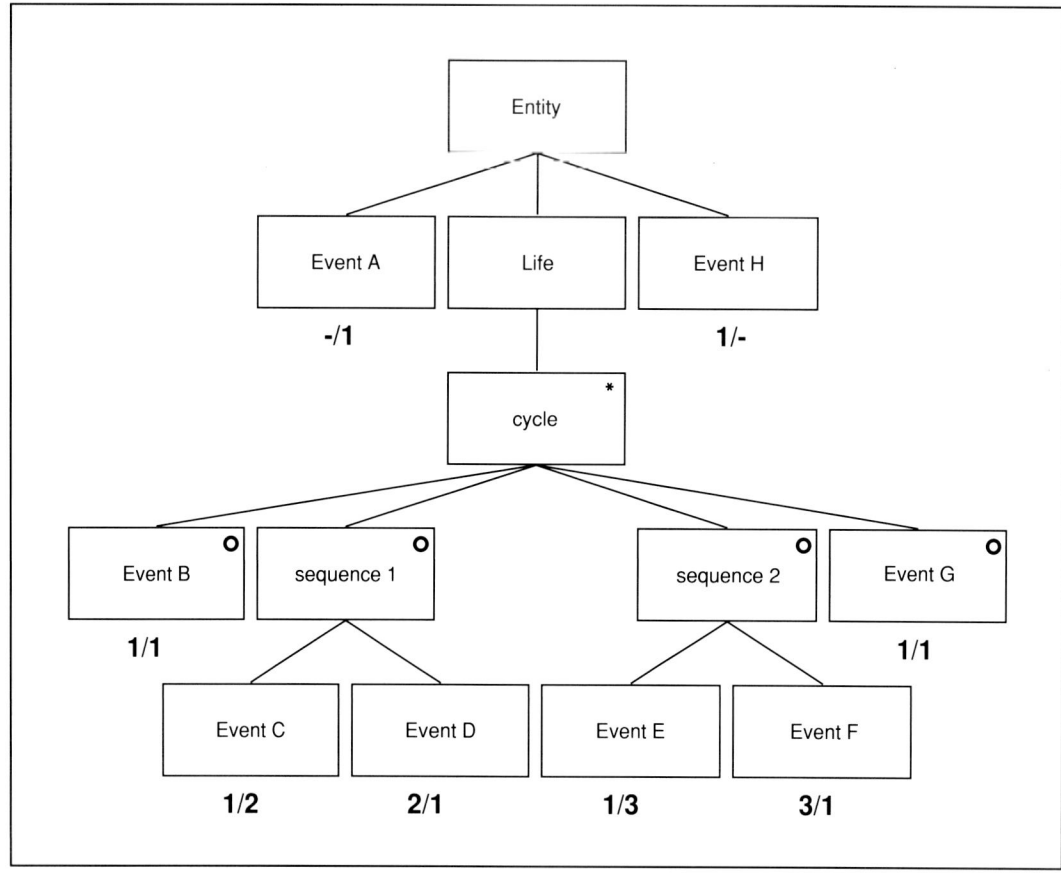

Figure 9.21: ELH with optimised states after application of both rules

Exception to the rules for state optimisation There is one exception to the preceding rules. When the options of a selection end in iterations, the exit states cannot be optimised to the same value. For example, see Figure 9.22.

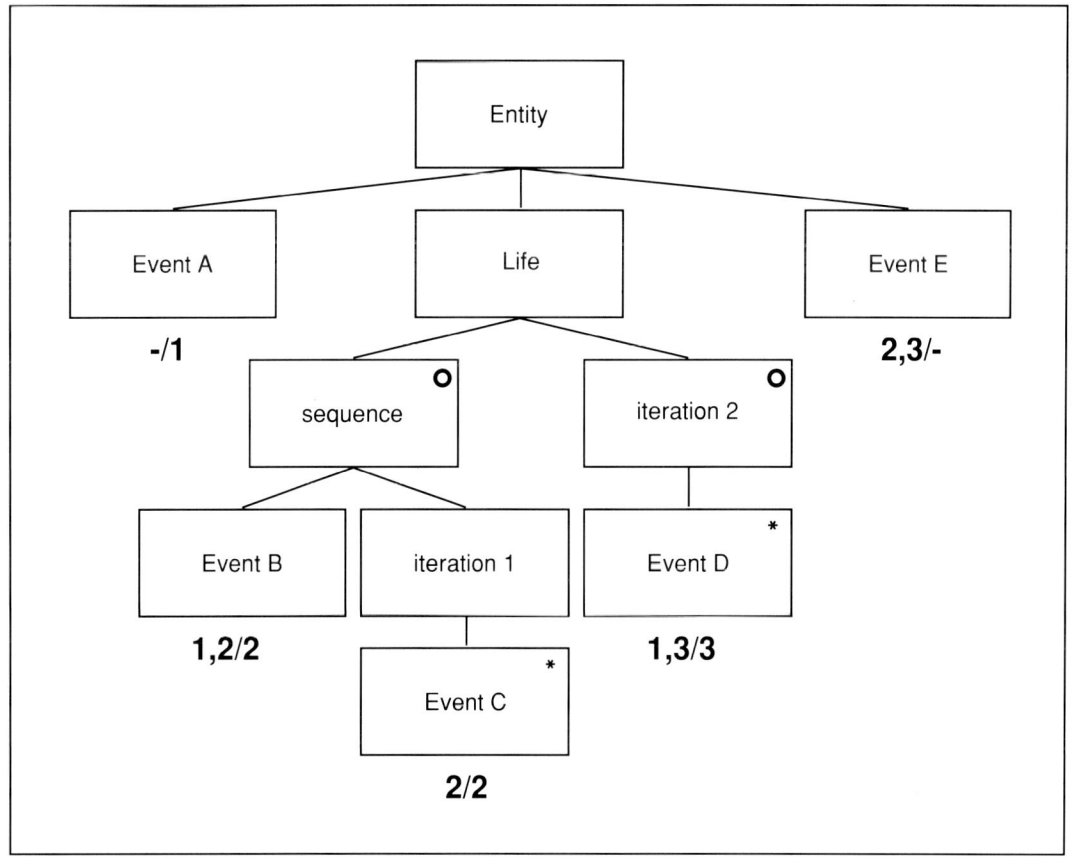

Figure 9.22: Iterations ending selections are the exception whose states cannot be optimised

State values determine the events that may validly precede other events. Figure 9.23 gives the valid sequences of events for the ELH in Figure 9.22.

Event	May be followed by any one of:				
Event A	Event B		Event D	Event E	
Event B		Event C		Event E	
Event C		Event C		Event E	
Event D			Event D	Event E	
Event E					none

Figure 9.23: Valid successor events for the events in Figure 9.22.

The 'may be followed by' possibilities are the same for event B and event C; we can optimise their exit states to the same value (this follows the guideline 'unify the state before an iteration with that after the iterated component').

But if we optimised the exit states for event C and event D to the same value (using the guideline 'unify the states of events which end options under a selection'), it would imply that event B, event C or event D could all be followed by the same types of event. For example, it would permit an iterated mixture of events of type C and type D. The 'may be followed by' rules would be broken.

Parallel lives modelled as separate aspects

When a project LDM has been divided into subsystem LDMs, any entity (including a partitioned aspect) may have asynchronous cycles in its behaviour. In entity-event modelling terms, it has parallel lives. Entity aspects provide a consistent way of handing partial views of entities, including parallel lives of entities within projects. Four reasons for using separate aspects rather than the SSADM V4 parallel life notation are:

- a parallel life may be a subordinate aspect of the entity in a different location from that of its base aspect

- states can be optimised (see preceding discussion); the rules for state optimisation in parallel lives are not simple

- some types of entity birth and entity death cannot be easily modelled in the parallel life notation

- it is consistent with the approach in *Reuse in SSADM using OO*, where entity aspect corresponds to stored object.

For example, EU-Rent may want to run promotions offering special prices, bonus days, etc to selected customers. If a customer were allowed to be in only one promotion at a time there would be an iterated sequence, 'join promotion - leave promotion' requiring a parallel life.

Rather than develop a single ELH for customer, with parallel lives, we could separate the customer into two aspects, as in Figure 9.24. This would allow the promotions behaviour of customer to be modelled separately from the rental application. It could then be implemented on the same server, or located separately (eg on a separate promotions database), or delivered later.

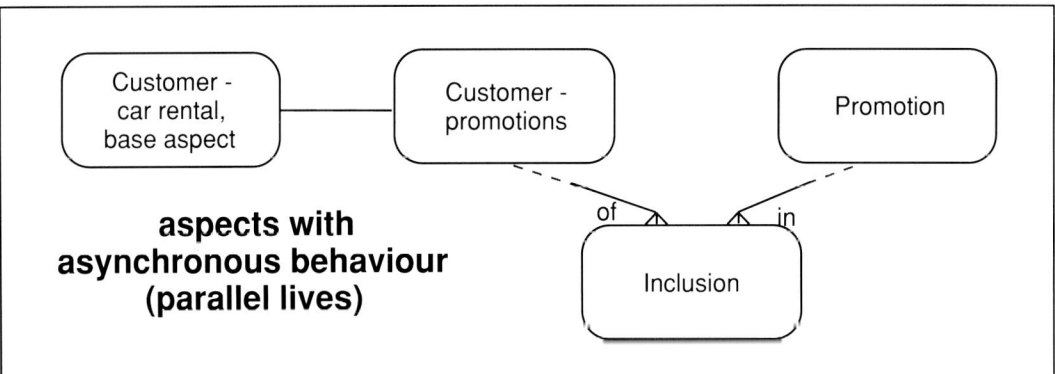

Figure 9.24: Aspects with parallel lives

The ELH for the customer-promotions aspect is like the 'parallel leg' (as in SSADM V4), set between the customer birth and death events. See Figure 9.25.

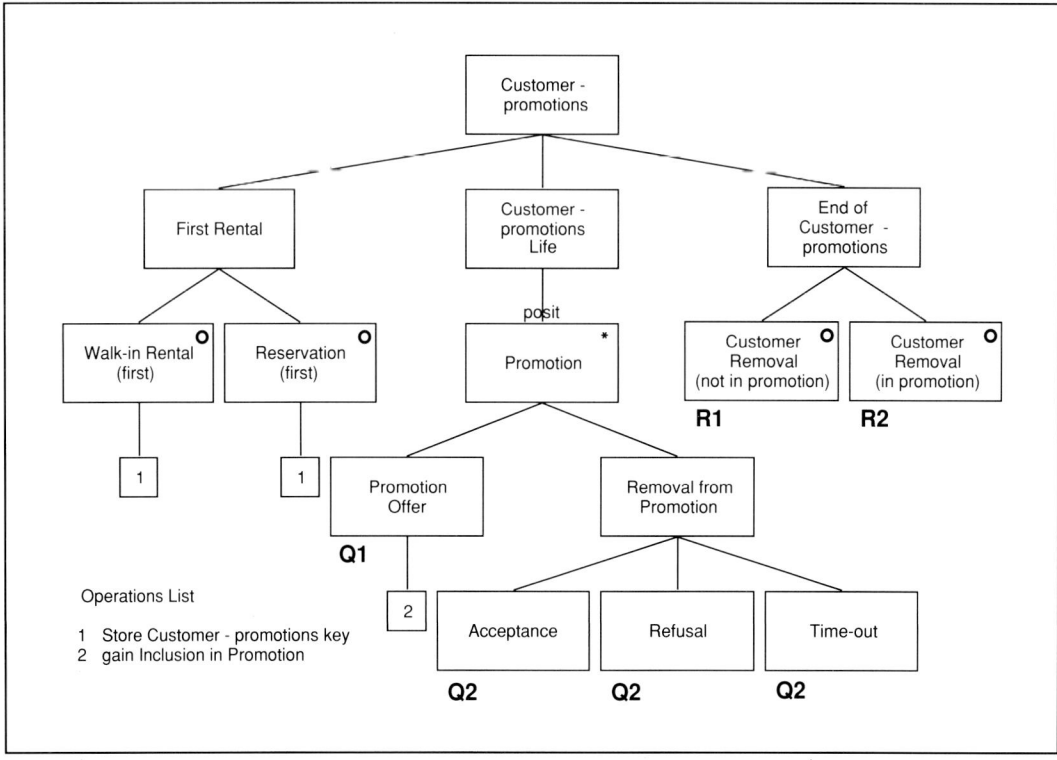

Figure 9.25: ELH for customer-promotions aspect

Note that the ELH examples in this volume conform to the 'disciplined quit' convention, where a quit may occur instead of the marked event, rather than after it (as in the *SSADM V4 Reference Manuals*).

Rules

Business rules that need to be implemented in a system fall within a spectrum of inevitability. The extremes of the spectrum are:

- Laws of Nature

  Some rules are verities - 'they can't not be'. For example:

- we can't rent a car unless there is a customer to rent it

- we can't rent a car that has been written off or sold.

- Policies

    Some rules are just arbitrary policy decisions. Some policies are so strong that they can be regarded as laws of nature for the organisation. For example:

    - once we have taken a decision to close a branch, we won't allow any cars to be bought by it or transferred to it

    Some policies may be changeable. For example:

    - a car must be physically present in a branch before a branch manager can arrange to transfer it. This could change in the future to allow a branch manager to arrange to transfer a car that is expected back from rental or service.

The more business rules we incorporate into ELHs, the more complex they become. If we have built policies into ELHs and they change, then the ELHs, ECDs and the programs that implement them have to be changed.

A way of keeping the design more stable under this kind of change is to build the 'laws of nature' and strong policies into ELHs, and handle changeable policies by rules. A rule is an acceptance condition for an event, supported by an enquiry; for example, checking that a car is actually at the branch before accepting a transfer schedule event.

The alternative to this is to model current location of car as a life in parallel with scheduling of car. The ELH in Figure 9.26 constrains scheduling of transfer not to happen when a car is on rental, on service or scheduled for another transfer.

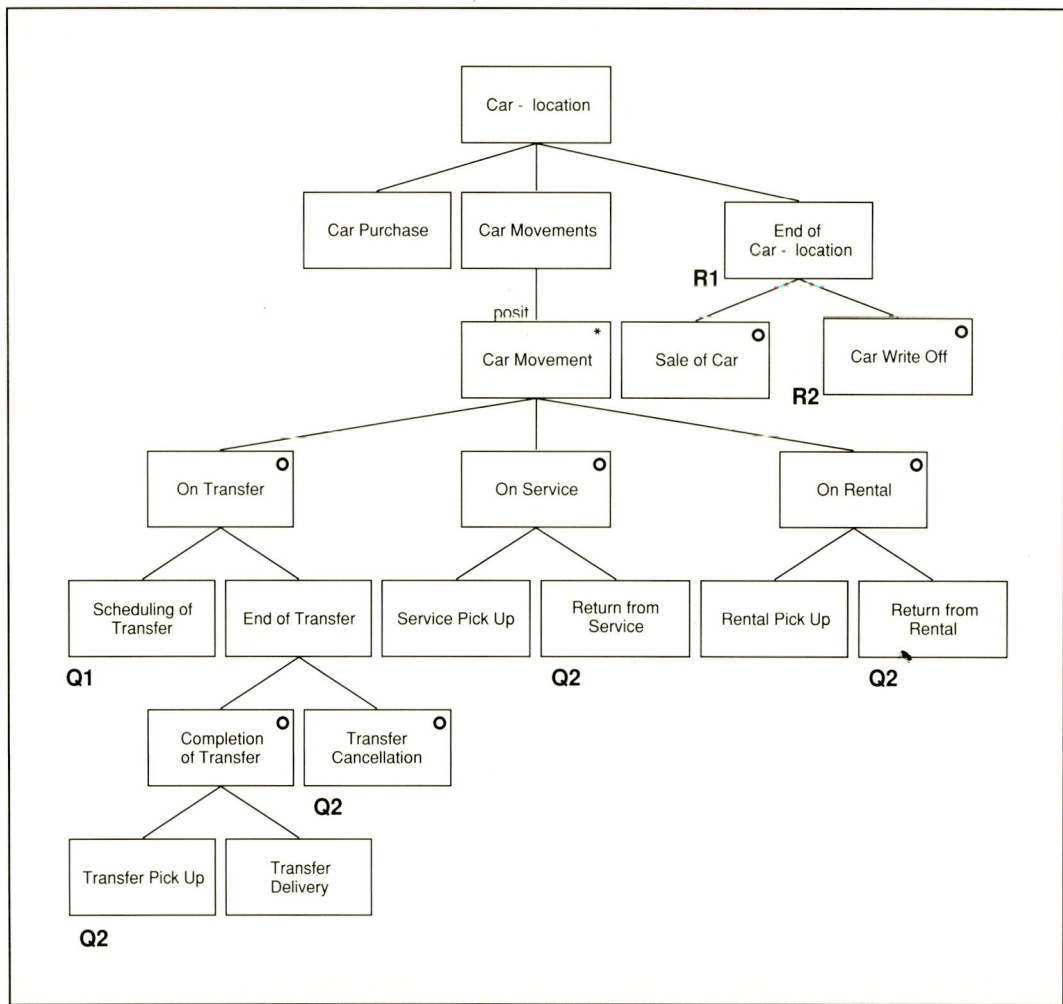

Figure 9.26: ELH constraining scheduling of transfer

Note that the ELH in Figure 9.26 uses the 'disciplined quit' convention, where a quit is taken instead of the event (rather than after the event) it appears under. If the event under which the resume appears is applicable, then the entity takes the state after that event, otherwise the entity moves to the state after the event under which the quit occurred.

Subtypes

All relevant aspects of an entity exist in parallel; entity aspects have separate ELHs. Subtypes are mutually exclusive. ELHs for subtypes of an entity can be drawn as a high-level selection in a single ELH. Attributes and relationships of the supertype are updated 'through the subtypes'. For example, in the ELH for car booking in Figure 9.27, booking start date and booking end date (attributes of the supertype) are updated by operations in Walk-in Rental, Rental Booking, Service Booking and Transfer Booking.

Overall, this approach gives simpler ELHs for super and subtypes. In physical design, if the supertype is implemented as a table or record type separate from the subtypes, it will have to be read as well as the subtype; this should be hidden in the PDI.

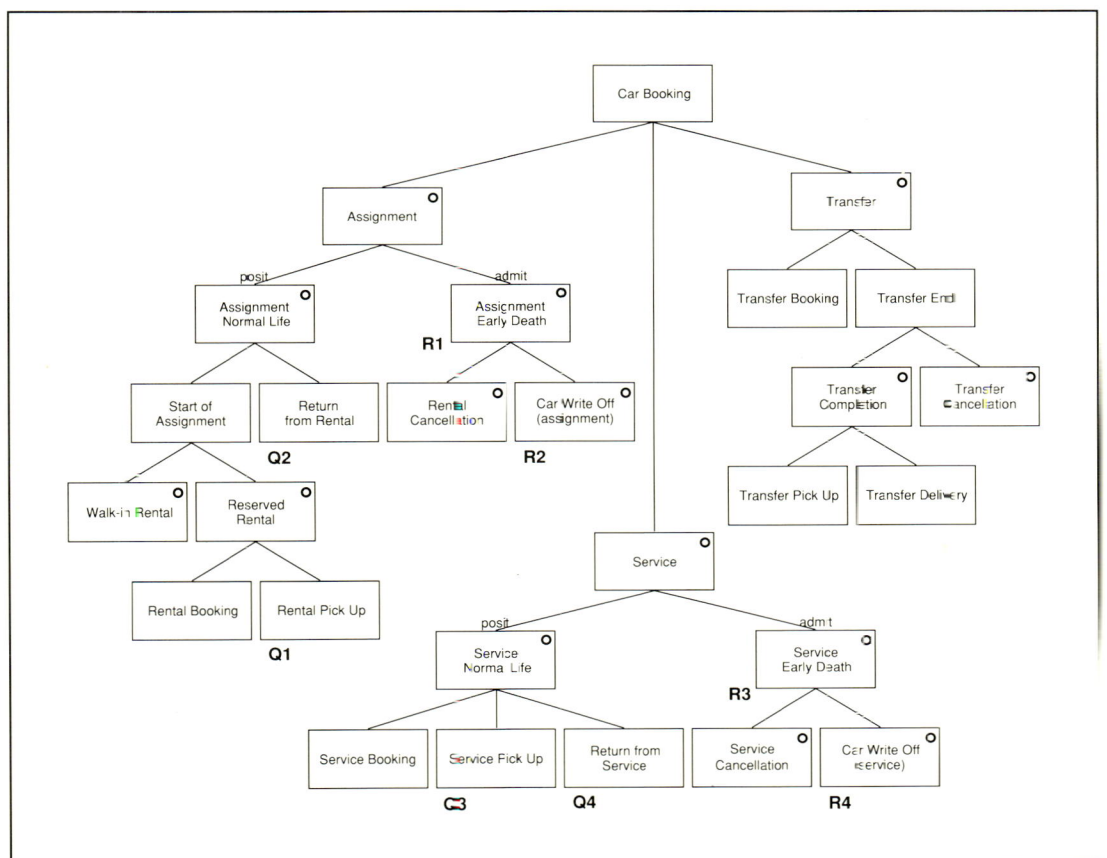

Figure 9.27: ELH for subtypes of car booking drawn as a high level selection in a single ELH

Note that the ELH in Figure 9.27 also uses the 'disciplined quit' convention.

9.5.6 Effect Correspondence Diagrams

The technique for creating Effect Correspondence Diagrams is unchanged, except that each entity aspect affected by an event is drawn as if it were a separate entity type as in Figure 9.28.

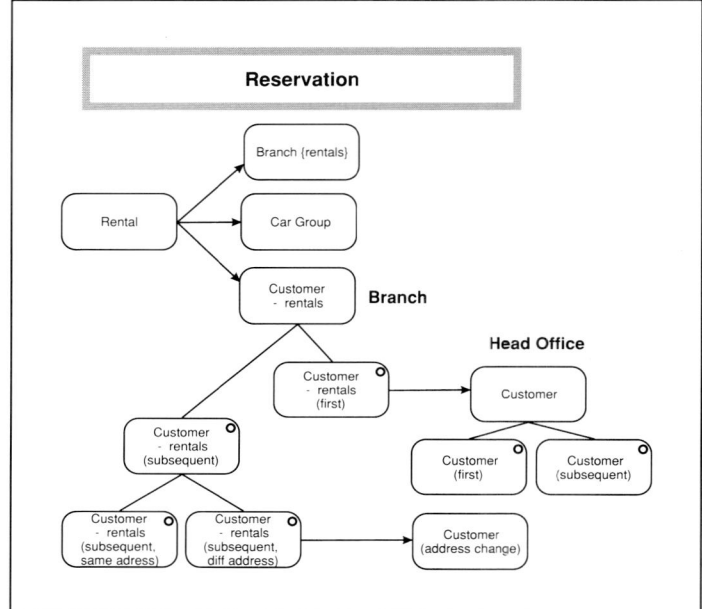

Figure 9.28: ECD for reservation with customer aspects drawn as if they are separate entity types

The ECD in Figure 9.28 indicates the difference between a customer's first becoming active at a branch, and first being known to EU-Rent at head office.

A minor change in notation is to use 'directional correspondences' to indicate the direction of traversal of the LDM(s). This is not essential, but makes it easier to see the requirement for message passing when producing process models.

Chapter 9
SSADM extensions

9.5.7 Update Process Models

There are three approaches for creating update process models. One is to create UPMs exactly as in SSADM V4 (treating aspects as separate entities) and have the PDI issue local and remote database calls, as appropriate, for accesses to the LDM.

A second is to treat each entity aspect as a separate object class and specify an object-oriented implementation. See 'Object-oriented Implementation of the Conceptual Schema' in Section 9.7.

The third approach is to create local process models for each location. For example, the ECD in Figure 9.28 can be partitioned into branch processing and head office processing as in Figure 9.29.

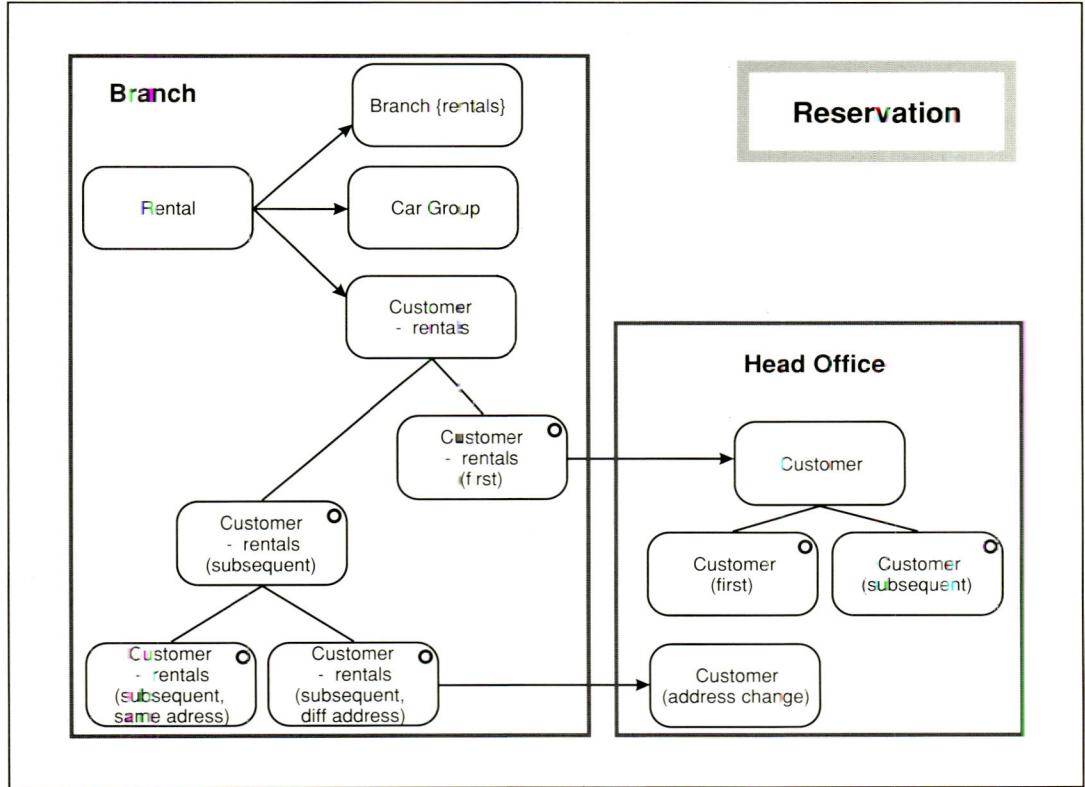

Figure 9.29 ECD for reservation partitioned into branch and head office processing

Within a partition, the technique for creating Update Process Models is as in the *SSADM V4 Reference Manuals*, with one addition: where there is correspondence between entity aspects at different locations (two occur in Figure 9.29), operations are needed for:

- a remote procedure call

- event failure if the remote procedure returns a failure message.

Figure 9.30 shows a partially completed UPM for reservation.

Chapter 9
SSADM extensions

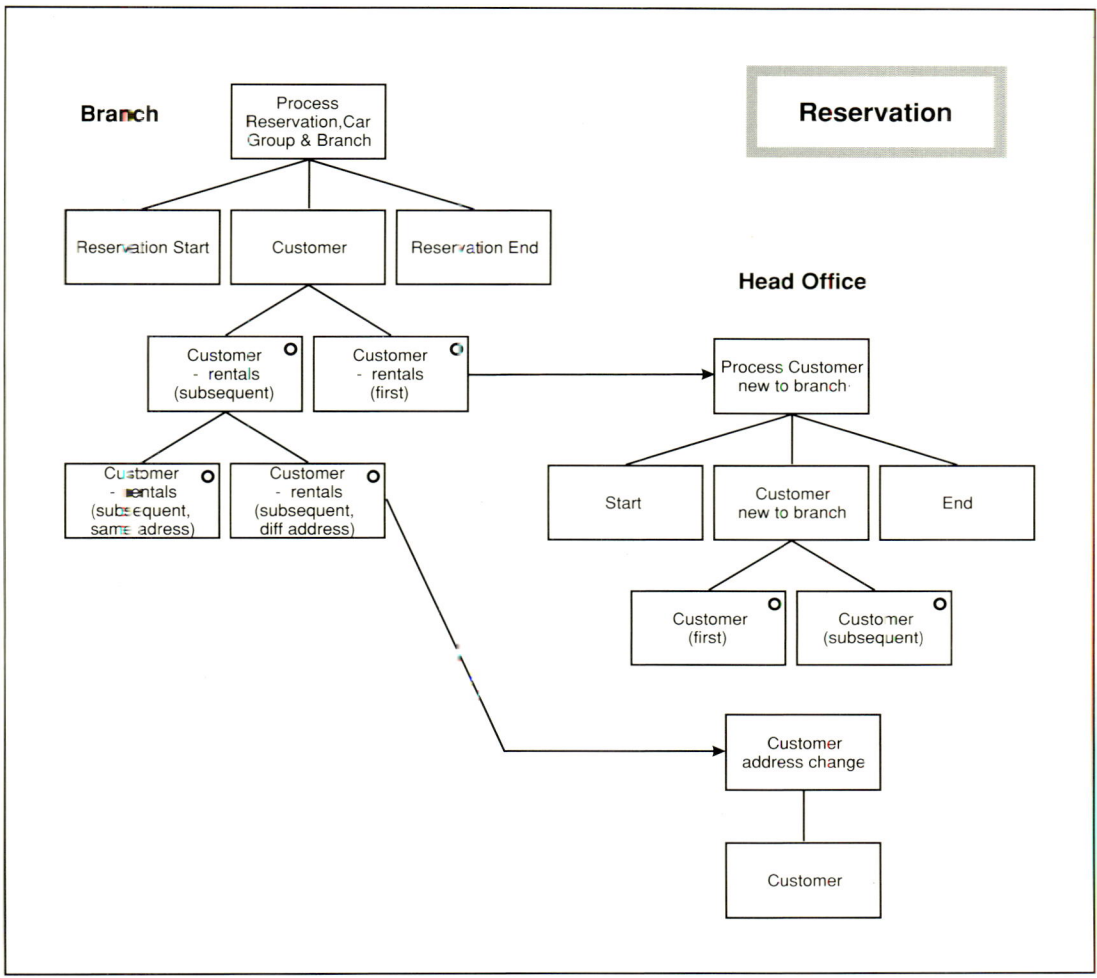

Figure 9.3C: Partially complete UPM for reservation with arrows denoting need for remote procedure call and event failure operations

9.5.8 Enquiry Process Models

The technique for developing Enquiry Process Models is very similar to that for Update Process Models, working from the Enquiry Access Path.

9.5.9 Entity aspects and internal design

In EU-Rent, the base aspect of customer belongs naturally at head office - it is the system-wide recognition that a person is a customer of EU-Rent at at least one branch. If we included events from hotel and air travel activities it would be the corporate recognition of a customer.

271

However, customer names and addresses are required at branches, eg for printing on contracts, to contact the customer if a car is overdue for return. We might consider replicating this aspect at branches where the customer is active.

The customer-rentals aspect could be implemented:

- at head office, as a single database, accessed remotely by branches. This would provide maximum consistency of customer data and minimum data storage for customers. Against this, communication costs would be high, performance might be unacceptably slow, and robustness would be low - no customer processing could be done if head office were off the network

- partitioned across branches without replication of customer, so that each customer instance is allocated to a 'home' branch, accessed remotely by other branches. This would also provide maximum consistency of customer data and low data storage for customers. If most customers dealt mainly with their home branches, then compared with the head office option, communication costs would be reduced, performance and robustness would be increased. However, this option assumes that it is possible to assign a 'home' branch to a customer. The branch nearest their home address is probably not a good one, since most people who rent cars do so when they are away from home - we need the one where they do most business. There is also the requirement to relocate data if a customer can be swapped to a different 'home' branch

- partitioned across branches with replication of customer, so that customer-rentals is maintained for each branch at which the customer is active; each instance of customer-rentals will own its local rentals. This supports maximum robustness of customer processing - a branch can process customers whether or not it can communicate with head office and other branches - but increases the storage for customer data, and carries an overhead for updating customer approval/disapproval status in multiple locations. There is also the risk that if a branch is operating in isolation, or if head office is cut off, a disapproved customer might be allowed rentals.

The conceptual model does not deal with issues of robustness and performance such as those mentioned above. They are dealt with in physical design. Effect Correspondence Diagrams (ECDs) and Update Process Models (UPMs) may contain operations for communication between different aspects of the same entity, but do not include operations for managing consistency of multiple copies of data.

Data location and data replication should be managed within the Process-Data Interface, and be transparent to the application code developed from the ECDs and UPMs.

9.6 Additional SSADM techniques

The following techniques have to be added to SSADM:

- Robustness Analysis (Section 9.6.1)
- First-cut Distribution Design (Section 9.6.2)
- Produce Communication Map (Section 9.6.3).

9.6.1 Robustness Analysis

Robustness analysis is carried out for each distribution option. It is done initially from the Entity Access Matrix produced in stages 1 and 2. It is then confirmed for the selected option after EAPs and ECDs have been produced in stage 3.

The procedure is to examine the data that is local to each type of business location and list:

- what an instance of the location could do if it were cut off from the communications network
- what an instance of the location could not do if it were cut off from the communications network
- what other locations could not do if an instance of this location type were cut off both for:

- other instances of this location type

- other location types

If some processes may be loosely coordinated, look for acceptable workarounds:

- applying part of a transaction locally and storing the rest of it until communication is re-established. There may be backout problems if part of the transaction does not work.

- designing locally-input transactions to handle local processing, and informing other locations by phone or EMail.

9.6.2 First-cut Distribution Design

(See case study in Chapter 10 for detailed example.)

The first-cut distribution design is produced in step 230 and aims for the most distributed option. The first-cut design provides a self-contained data model for each type of business location. Entity types shared between business location types are split into aspects. In physical design, databases at different locations can be designed to be loosely- or tightly-coordinated.

1 Add business location types to the LDM, and add relationships between business locations. Add the central data processing location (as used in the centralised option), if it is not also a business location.

Draw one-to-many relationships from the central data processing location to entities at the top of the LDM (i.e those which have no LDM masters).

2 Treat each business location type (and the central DP location) as a geographical root and define a hierarchical structure under it (analogous to the first-cut design in SSADM V4).

Use the least-dependent-occurrence rule to place entity types that are in more than one hierarchy. When a shared entity has been placed in one hierarchy, split each of its other masters into two aspects, one in its own hierarchy and the other with the shared detail.

3 Review the placement of shared details to take account of significant differences in volume of use. Use the Entity Access Matrix for guidance.

4 Identify the required behaviour of aspects of shared entities, and the volume of communication between them.

5 Decide an approach for placement of instances of 'subordinate' aspects, taking account of:

- disjoint partitioning

- replication

- movement of data between locations

6 Decide the placement of history of movable entities.

7 Draw the data model for each location; include reference data on related locations if needed for output.

8 Summarise the communication between locations:

- coordination of aspects

- movable entities

- multiple relationships between master and detail.

9.6.3 Produce Communication Map

The communication map (see Figure 9.31) provides a summary of the communication between data processing locations and is produced to support distribution options (see step 8 of the first-cut distribution rules).

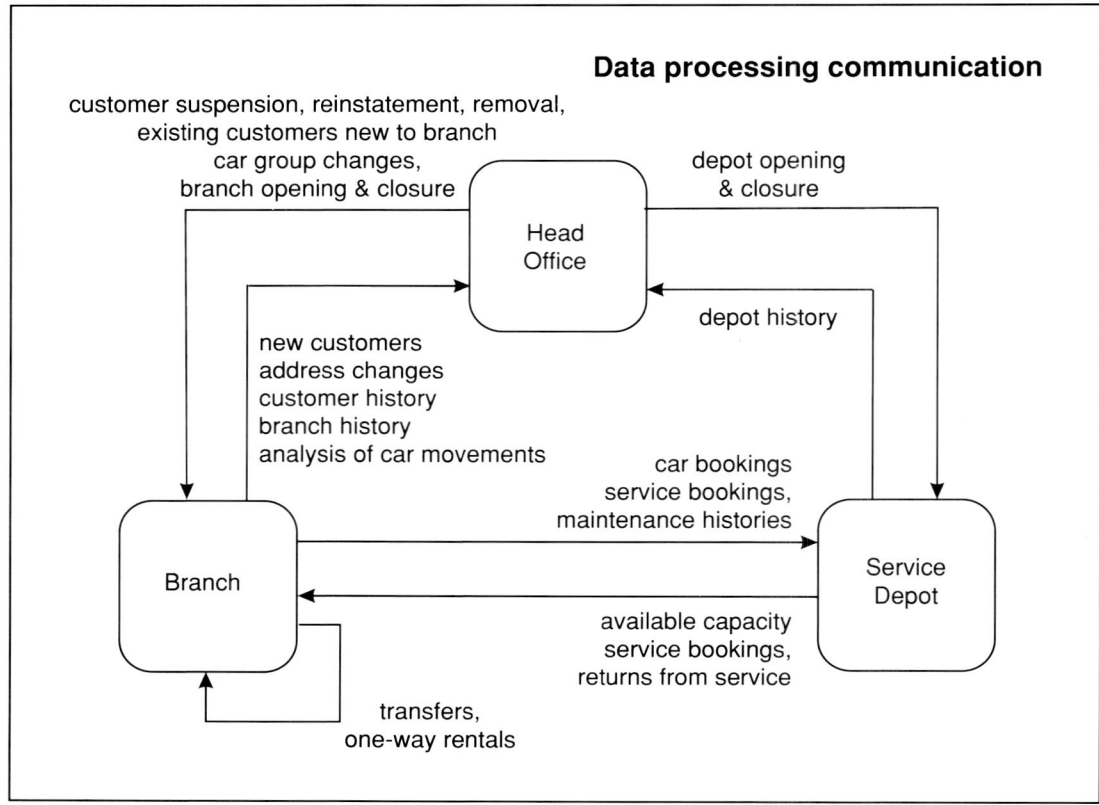

Figure 9.31: Communication Map summarising communication between data processing locations

The Communication Map is developed from the Entity Access Matrix built in step 230, Develop Distribution Options, and confirmed and extended after update and enquiry processes have been developed in stage 5.

The Communication Map is supported by a table of volumetric data. See Figure 9.32.

The table of volumetric data is one of the summaries used to estimate traffic across the network, and hence, the cost and performance of the network. The other summaries used to estimate traffic across the network are:

- summary of messages between business locations and data processing locations (ie invocations of events and enquiries by functions, and the responses) where they are different locations. For example, in EU-Rent option 3 (see Chapter 10), city branches act as data processing locations for hotel and garage branches

- summary of messages between data processing locations and data storage locations (ie PDI calls) where they are different locations. For example, in EU-Rent option 3, all customer data is at head office.

From	To	Approx. message size	No per week	
Head Office	Branch			
	Customer disapproval	10	50	x 4
	Customer approval	10	50	x 4
	Customer removal	10	5,000	x 4
	Reservation (new customer)	150	5,000	
	Reservation (existing customer, new to branch)	150	1,000	
Branch	Head Office			
	Customer history	500	100	x 4
	Reservation (new to branch)	30	6,000	
	Inactive Customers	16	20	x 1,000
Branch	Branch			
	Reservation (change of address)	150	2,000	
	Transfer Pick-up	40	900	
	Reservation (different branch)	50	40,000	
	Rental Cancellation (different branch)	18	4,000	
	Walk-in Rental (different branch)	50	2,000	
	Transfer booking	20	1,000	
	Transfer cancellation	20	100	

From	To	Approx. message size	No per week
Service Depot	Branch Available Capacity Service Booking Service Cancellation Return from service	200 30 20 40	8,000 8,000 1,000 14,000
Branch	Service Depot Car Bookings Service Booking Service Cancellation Car Maintenance History	200 30 20 400	8,000 8,000 1,000 14,000
Notes: • It is assumed that the typical customer is active at 4 branches • Insignificant volumes (branch and depot opening & closing, creation and removal of car groups, change of rental rates) have not been documented.			

Figure 9.32: Communication Map - volumes table

9.7 Mapping from specific requirements to services

Conventional programming of UPMs/EPMs implies RDA

Each UPM reads and writes data from and to databases which may be local or remote. This means that *remote read/write services* are required. For the same reasons as those identified for object-oriented implementation (see next sub-section), a *location transparency service* and a *distributed commit service* are required.

Object-oriented implementation of ECDs/EAPs implies object-oriented distributed transaction processing	Database update and enquiry processes may be implemented in an object-oriented architecture, as described in Chapter 5. Each ECD or EAP method invocation is most naturally implemented by a *remote procedure call* service. Because the distribution selected may not be the 'natural' one, but may be chosen to minimise costs and/or simplify support, the distribution may change during the lifetime of the system. This means that a *location transparency service* is required.

ECDs represent commit units. This means that a *distributed commit service* is required. |
Hybrid implementation may be required to support business location functionality implemented on data processing location databases	The ECDs could be cut up by business location. Each ECD fragment could then be collapsed into a UPM-like structure. The UPM fragments would communicate with each other using a *remote procedure call service*. Each UPM fragment would access its own data using *remote read/write services*. For the same reasons as those identified earlier, a *location transparency service* and a *distributed commit service* are required.
Function to EAP/ECD/UPM/EPM is via object-oriented distributed transaction processing messages, or local procedure calls	If the I/O code in a function is on the same machine as the required conceptual processing a local procedure call is required, otherwise a *remote procedure call service* is required. Alternatively, *message services* can be used.
Object-oriented implementation of the Conceptual Schema	Given a suitable object-oriented programming environment, the methods can be extracted from the entity behaviour models and their bodies can be extended to include the subsidiary method invocations defined by the effect correspondence diagrams. They can then be implemented directly. For example, the effect correspondence diagram in Figure 9.33 may be extended to show the methods for invoking other objects, as illustrated in Figure 9.34.

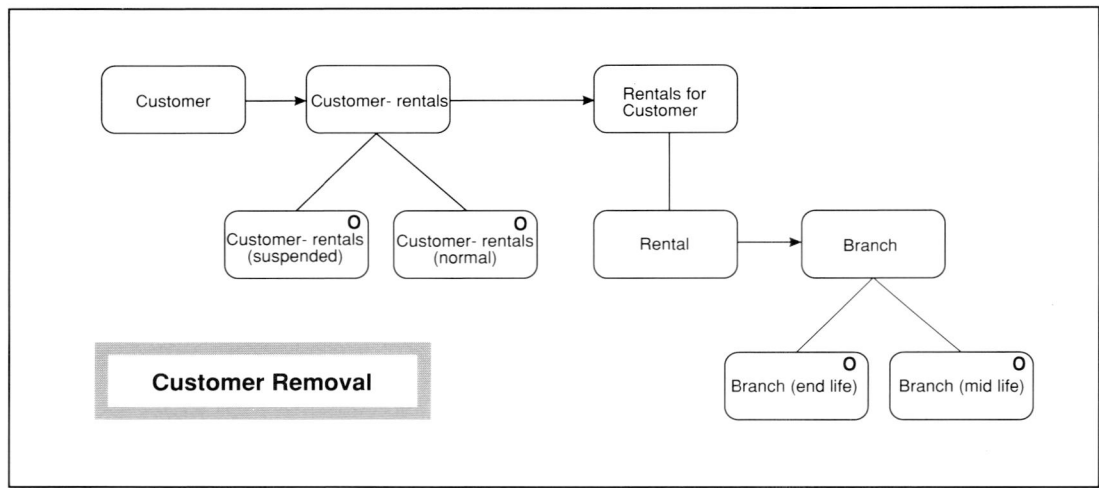

Figure 9.33: ECD for customer removal

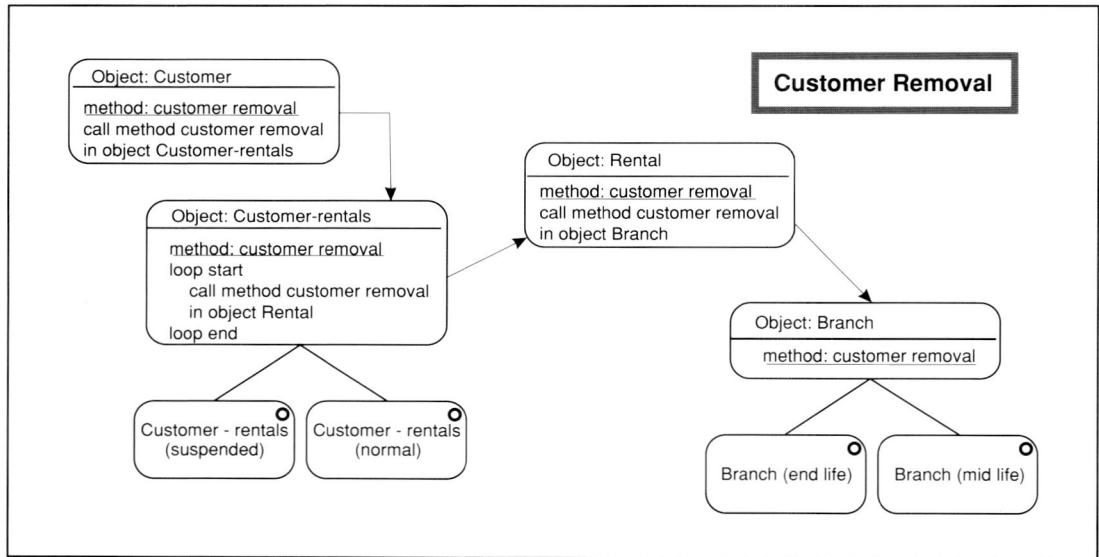

Figure 9.34: ECD for customer removal showing method invocation of other objects

Only the calling code has been shown in Figure 9.34. The rest of each method body has been omitted. Note how the iteration of detail invocations is placed in the method of the master entity.

Roll-back of commit units

What if the OO environment does not deal with automatic roll-back of failed commit units? What if the customer has an outstanding balance to pay? What if the method in the first rental succeeds, but the one in the next rental fails? What we need is to extend the communication protocol, with something like a two-phase commit. We can do this by allowing the original invocation methods to return replies, and extending the object definitions to include these as in Figure 9.35.

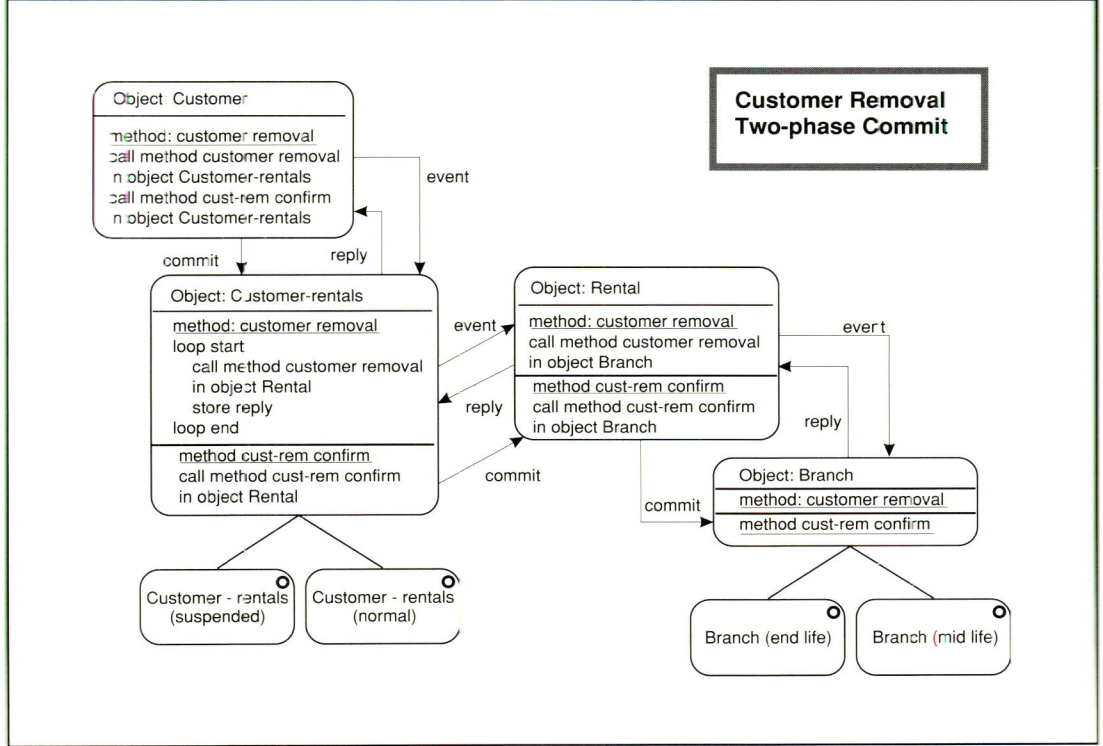

Figure 9.35: ECD for customer removal extended to show calls and replies for two-phase commit

Once again, only the calling code has been shown and the rest of each method body has been omitted.

Collation of information

What if the objects need to exchange information before they can process an event? Examples of this in practical information systems are few and far between, however the two-phase commit solution still works, as long as:

- the event is fanned out through all the objects

- these objects return local data with their replies, and

- there is a single entity (called the 'home entity') which can collate all the replies, decide whether the event succeeds or fails, and initiate the commit phase by sending out the results of its computation.

In the customer removal example the customer entity is the home entity.

Multiple hits on an entity instance

There is the possibility that an instance of an entity type which is accessed as the master of an iterated detail, may be hit more than once by the same event. For example, one branch may be hit by many rentals when a customer is removed.

In the simple two-phase commit model we have built so far, when the branch is hit by the second rental it will be locked for the first rental. The situation is then:

- the event cannot be committed (and the branch unlocked for the second rental) until customer has invoked the 'cust-rem confirm' method

- customer cannot invoke the 'cust-rem confirm' method until it gets an 'OK' reply from customer-rentals

- customer-rentals cannot reply 'OK' until all its rentals have replied 'OK'

- the second rental for the branch is locked out; the method invocation will time out, and it will reply 'not OK' to customer-rentals

- customer-rentals will reply 'not OK' to customer and the whole event will fail.

There are three ways to deal with this extra complexity:

- **sort out messages when they get to the object.** Add code into the method of the object, to distinguish the first hit of an event from any second or subsequent hit of the same event (so that processing such as locking can be done on the first

invocation only) and to detect the last commit
message (so processing such as unlocking can be
done on the last invocation only)

- **add an event manager to sort out and pass
  different messages.** We can introduce some kind of
  event manager program which keeps a track of
  which entities have already been invoked with an
  event in the first phase, and when each is invoked
  for the last time with a commit message in the
  second phase

- **move the database processing message into the
  event manager program.** This is really the
  conventional programming solution, as follows.

Conventional programming implementation

In the absence of an OO environment, or where it is more convenient to implement in a conventional programming or application generation environment, the method invocation groups defined by the Effect Correspondence Diagrams can be turned into subroutines which can be called by each other or by a scheduler such as a TP monitor.

For example, consider the following Effect Correspondence Diagram in Figure 9.36.

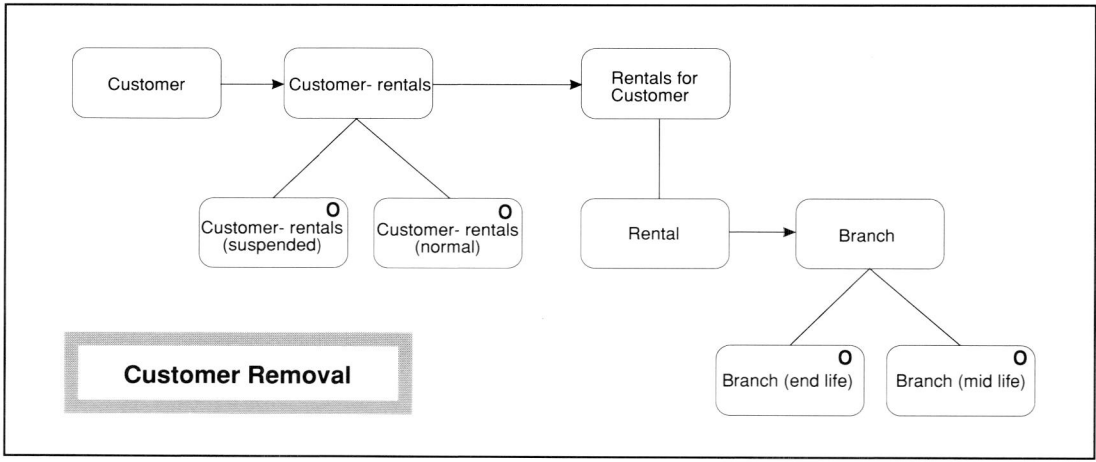

Figure 9.36: ECD for customer removal

In SSADM V4 this ECD can be collapsed into an Update Process Model via the intermediate structure in Figure 9.37 which abstracts from the message passing nature of the correspondences, giving the collapsed structure shown in Figure 9.38.

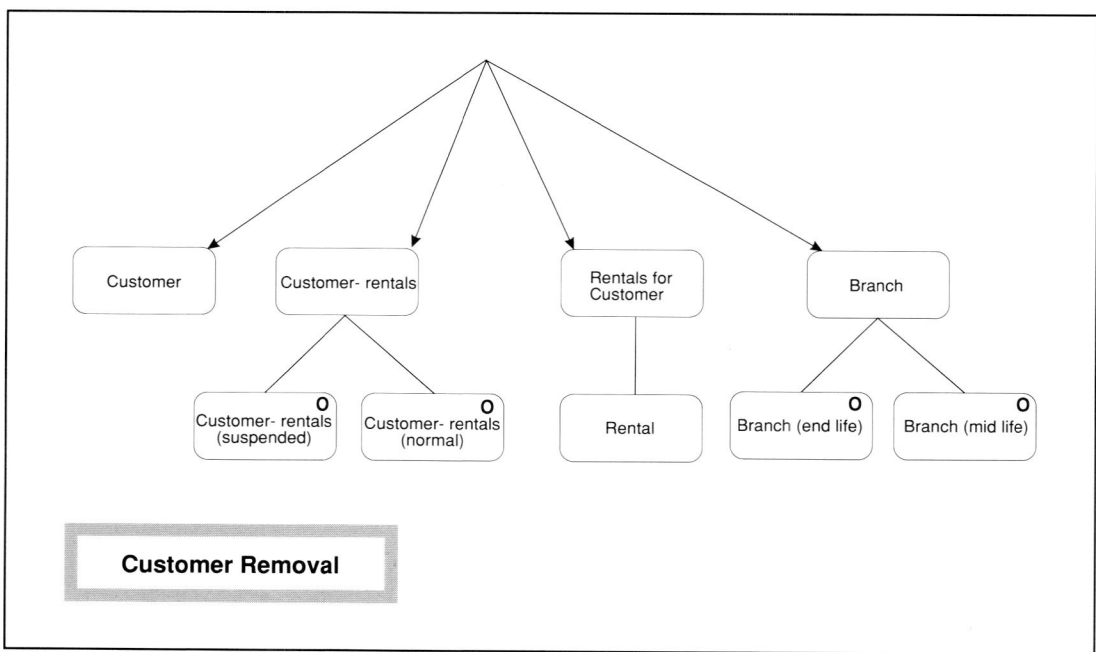

Figure 9.37: Intermediate structure for customer removal

Chapter 9
SSADM extensions

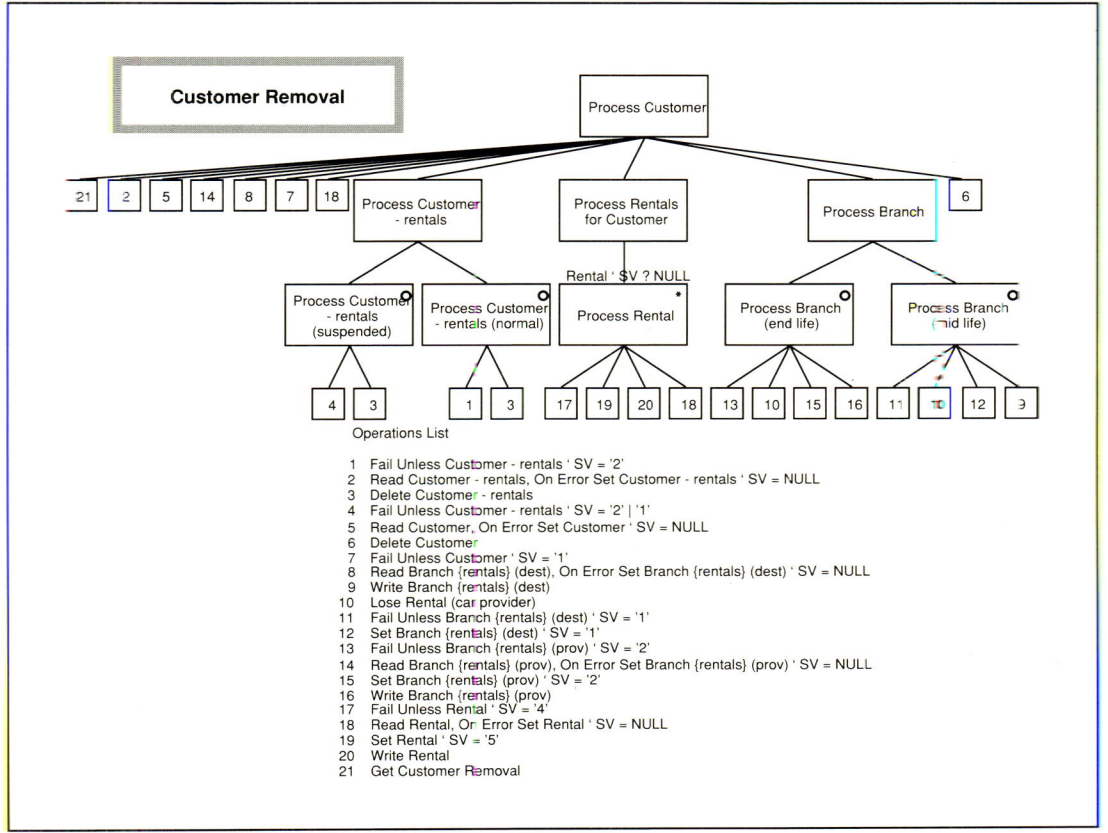

Figure 9.38: *Update Process Model for Customer Removal*

On transferring the operations from the original method bodies, adding database manipulation operations, adding invocations of groups of methods being implemented as other self-contained subroutines, and adding iteration conditions, we get an 'executable' program.

10 SSADM extensions applied to EU-Rent

10.1 Introduction

This chapter shows how SSADM, as extended in Chapter 9, can be used for the analysis and design of a distributed system by applying it to the EU-Rent case study.

Structure of remainder of this chapter

The remainder of this chapter is divided into the following sections:

- current system (Section 10.2)
- preparation for design options (Section 10.3)
- centralised option (Section 10.4)
- distribution options (Section 10.5)
- option sizing and costing (Section 10.6).

10.2 Current System

We devote a significant amount of space to describing the current system and its problems because it stores processing and data at different locations. It turns out that the difficulties noted in describing this system also occur in describing the required system.

Purposes of this section:

- to describe the current system in more detail than in Section 2.2, using DFDs and associated text
- to highlight nine problems of the current system, leading to requirements for the new system.

Note: In SSADM, Data Flow Diagrams have a 'location' attribute for each process. It has been suggested that this can be used to map processes to locations in a distributed system. This section also indicates a number of difficulties with this suggestion.

10.2.1 Top level DFD

The workings of the current system are summarised in the following DFDs and associated text. In the course of this section we illustrate nine problems of the current system, and some difficulties in using DFDs to show processes at different locations.

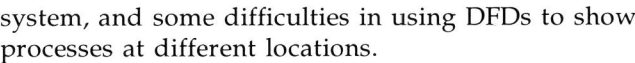

Figure 10.1: Top level DFD for EU-Rent

Note: the 'Maintenance Organiser' shown on the top level DFD in Figure 10.1 is later decomposed into two different external entities - branch manager and depot manager - either of whom may input a maintenance booking cancellation. Not every DFD methodology, or DFD builder, uses the notion of decomposing external entities in this way.

<u>Difficulty 1: One DFD high-level process may involve processing at several locations.</u>

It is impossible to allocate a location to a DFD process which at some lower level is decomposed into processes occurring at different locations.

For example it turns out that the function 'arrange car maintenance' on the top-level DFD contains processes in both branch and service depot.

This is a minor point so long as we are not tempted into dividing the process into distinct DFDs, by location. This would separate the most tightly bound and 'cohesive' processes in the whole system (eg simultaneous booking of a maintenance job at the branch and at the depot).

Current System Problem 1: double bookings.

A car may be at various times, booked for rental, booked for maintenance, and scheduled for transfer to another branch. The problem is that clerical procedures are not always followed properly, and double bookings do sometimes occur. It is very important not to disappoint customers who have booked a rental in advance, and almost as important not to waste time in the service depots.

10.2.2 Distributed data and processing nodes in the current system

The key business information is recorded in several places.

Cars are classified into car groups. All cars in a group are of equivalent specification and have the same rental price.

Each of the 1000 branches maintains a **car bookings** file, organised by car group, in which the planned usage of cars is scheduled and historical usage is recorded, and a **reservations** file, in which advance reservations are recorded.

Each of the 400 service depots maintains a **service diary**, in which the planned maintenance of cars is scheduled and historical maintenance is recorded. It shows the cars booked in for maintenance on each day, and thereby enables the service depot to control the amount of scheduled work.

Current System Problem 2: non-coordination of distributed data.

There are two occasions when it is common for discrepancies to arise between distributed data stores. First, when a branch manager books a car for maintenance in the car bookings file, this is not always reflected correctly in the service depot's service diary.

Second when a branch manager schedules a car for transfer to another branch, the car 'ownership' (recorded in the car bookings file) is not always successfully transferred. At any given time the car may be logged in the car bookings file at both branches, or at neither.

10.2.3 DFD process 1: Manage car pool

The car bookings file contains details of the cars currently 'owned' by the branch. A car entry is added to the car bookings file when a car is acquired by a branch and deleted when the car is disposed of.

When cars are transferred, two different branch managers are involved. In Figure 10.2 the extended notation for DFD external entities shows different roles for branch manager.

Chapter 10
SSADM extensions applied to EU-Rent

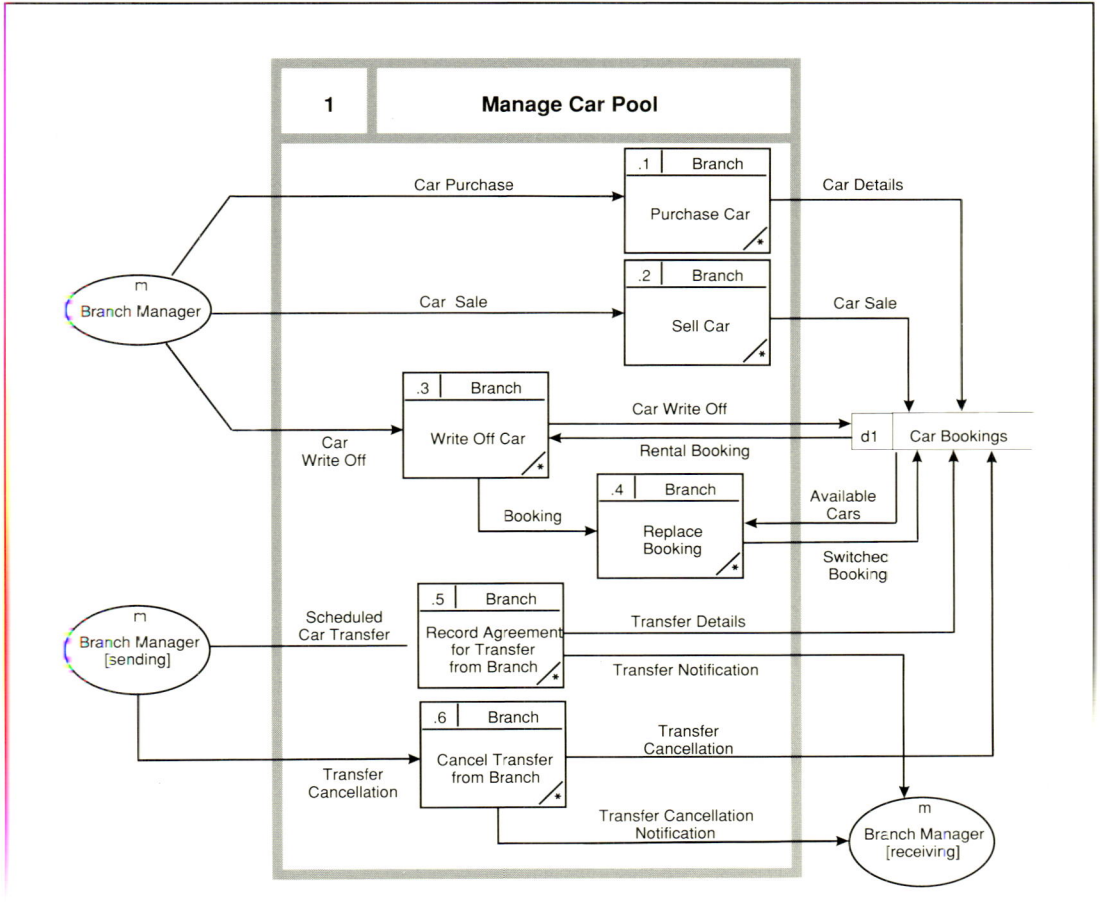

Figure 10.2: DFD process 1 - Manage car pool

A branch manager may add a car to the pool at the branch by purchasing it (the money comes from head office), or by arranging for one to be transferred from another branch.

A branch manager may reduce the car pool by selling a car, or scheduling its transfer to another branch, as long as the car is located at the branch at that time and is not booked for rental or maintenance on the following day.

A car may be written off at any time, if authorised by the branch manager. If a written-off car is booked for rental the following day another car must be booked to replace it. (The procedures for checking reports of cars written off while out on rental, or being transferred, are outside the scope of the system.).

Cars tend to accumulate at some branches (Calais for example, fills up with cars hired by people whose own car has broken down on holiday). From time to time a branch manager will telephone around other branches, seeking to gain or lose a few cars.

When branch managers have reached an agreement over the telephone, the manager of the 'sending' branch will schedule each car transfer in the car bookings file, and request a driver to transfer it to the 'receiving' branch. A transfer may be cancelled at any time until the car is picked up. The pick-up represents confirmation of the scheduled transfer.

Current System Problem 3: finding where to transfer cars to/from.

It is difficult for branch managers to know which branches have too many or too few cars.

10.2.4 DFD process 2: Control car movements

Drivers are hired to pick up cars from the branch for maintenance or transfer to other branches, and return them after maintenance. See Figure 10.3. The pick-up of a car represents confirmation of the scheduled maintenance or transfer.

When a car is picked up for maintenance, the time is noted in the car bookings file and the driver is given an authorisation. When a car is returned from maintenance, the time is noted in the car bookings file and the driver is given a receipt.

When a car is picked up for transfer, the time is noted in the car bookings file and the driver is given an authorisation. In terms of ownership, this event represents the loss of the car from the sending branch, and the transfer of the ownership to the receiving branch; the receiving branch is notified by telephone that the car has been picked up. When the car is delivered, the time is noted in the car bookings file and the driver is given a receipt.

Chapter 10
SSADM extensions applied to EU-Rent

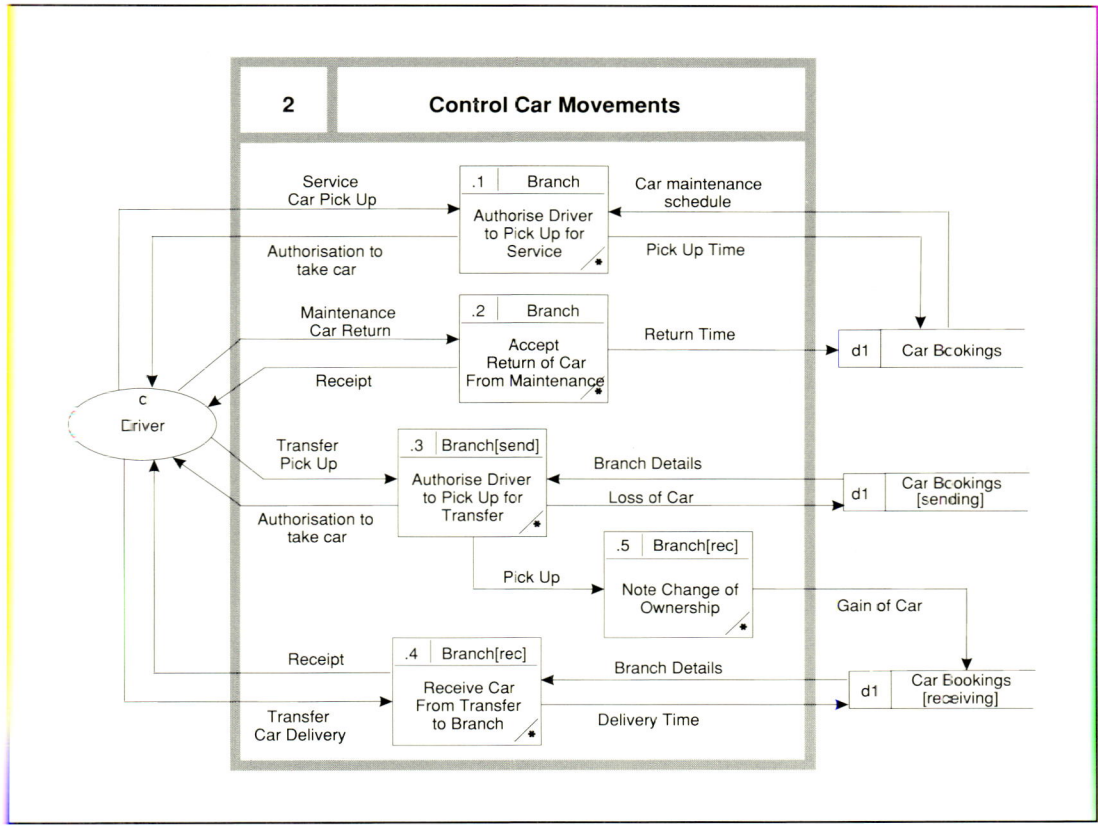

Figure 10.3: DFD process 2 - Control car movements

The extended notation for DFD locations and data stores indicates that two branches and their car bookings files are involved in a car transfer. The data flow pick-up between processes 2.3 and 2.5 in Figure 10.3 is a telephone call or fax between the two branches.

10.2.5 DFD process 3: Process car rental

Advance reservations are recorded by car group. Then, about a day before start of rental, booking clerks book specific cars to fill reservations. See Figure 10.4.

293

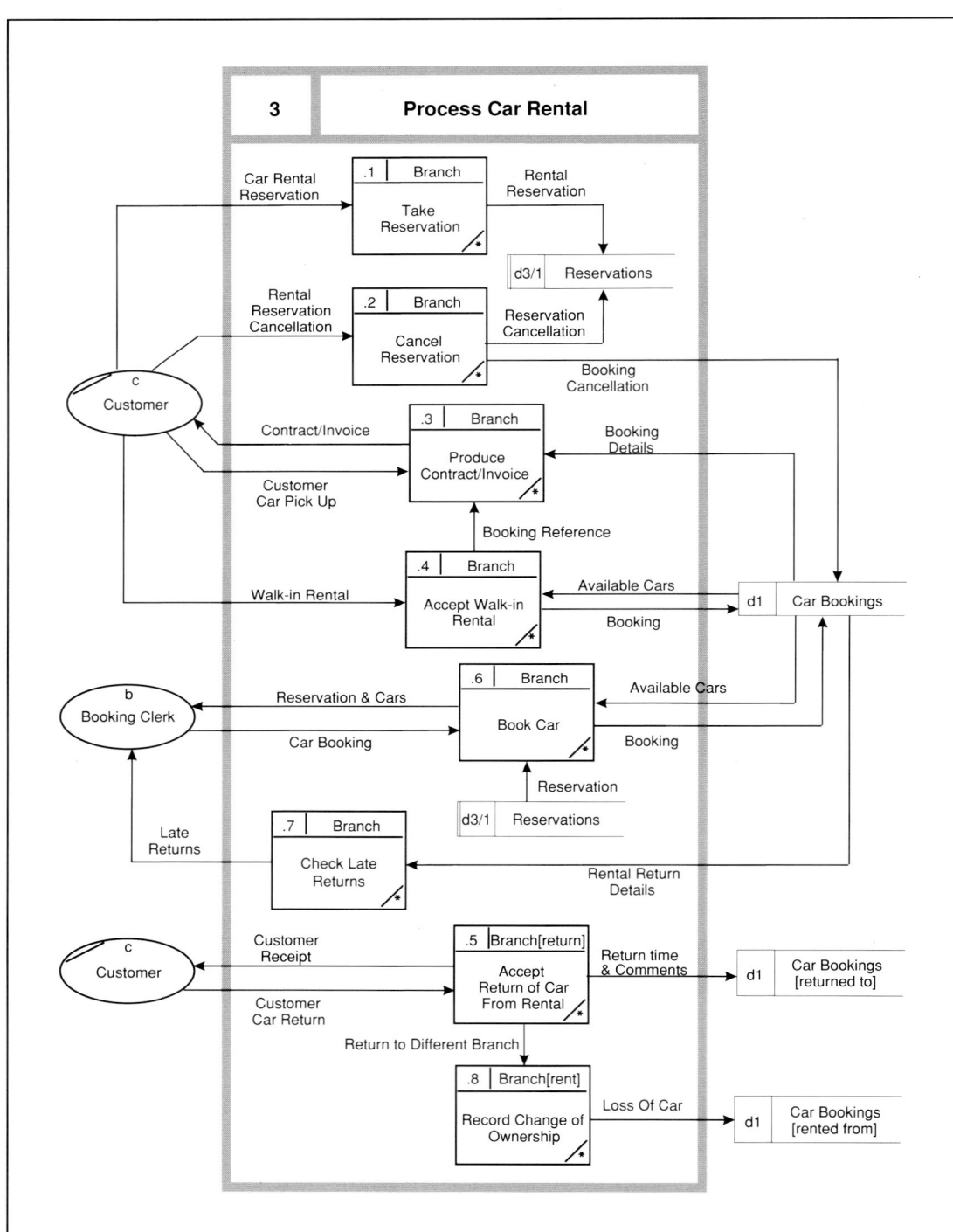

Figure 10.4: DFD Process 3 - Process car rental

The branch manager must ensure that there are sufficient cars in each group to meet his reservation commitments each day. He may have to phone other branches and arrange transfers. In extremis a customer may be given a car in a group other than the one he reserved.

Advance reservations are recorded in the **reservations** file showing a reference, customer details, start of required rental and number of days of rental. Each day, booking clerks look through the rentals due to start on the following day, look in the car bookings file for the group and book a specific car for each reservation.

To book a car the procedure is:

- find, in the car bookings file, a car of the requested group that is available for the duration of the rental (ie that is not booked for service within the rental period, and does not have 'to be transferred' status)

- create a booking for it in the car bookings file. The reservation reference and customer name are copied into the booking, customer details (driving licence, credit card number, contact telephone number etc) are recorded and a 'booked-day' is created for the assigned car for each day of the rental.

Rental reservations may be cancelled at any time until the car is picked up. The pick-up represents confirmation of the reservation. If a reservation is cancelled after a car has been booked, the car is released (by deleting the booked days from the car bookings file).

When a car is picked up for rental, the time is noted in the car bookings file and a contract/invoice is printed, with a copy for the customer to take away. When a car is returned from rental, the time is noted in the car bookings file, the customer pays and is given a receipt. If the car is returned to a different branch, ownership of the car is transferred to that branch; the branch from which the car was rented is notified by telephone.

A customer may walk in and request an immediate rental. If a suitable car is available a booking is made in the car bookings file and a contract/invoice is produced as for an advance reservation.

Booking clerks may reject a rental reservation. Reasons to reject would normally be based on past experience of the customer, such as late returns, bounced cheques, damage to car.

Current System Problem 4: checking of bad risks.

Any comments about customers are noted in the reservations file at the end of the rental; this may require creation of a dummy reservation to record comments for a walk-in rental or one-way rental. There is no uniform way of identifying customers in the reservations file, which makes it difficult to track the history of any given customer.

Current System Problem 5: identification of customers.

There is in any case the problem of identifying customers. Booking clerks cannot be relied upon to remember everyone, and they do not know which customers have previously rented from other branches.

Current System Problem 6: rented cars returned to a different branch.

When a rented car is returned to a different branch, the branch that rented it sometimes doesn't get to hear of this. On the day the car is due to be returned, a booking clerk may book it for rental on the following day.

10.2.6 Check Late Returns

To check that a car has been returned, the procedure is that every day one of the booking clerks looks through the car bookings file and makes a list of rentals due to end the day before, but for which no return has been noted.

Where a return has not been noted, the booking clerk first checks the compound to see if the car is there, and with other clerks to see if they forgot to note its return. If not then the clerk calls whatever telephone number the customer has supplied. If there is no answer, the clerk must ring around all the other branches to discover if the car has been returned there instead.

Current System Problem 7: checking late returns.

It is clear that the above is a tedious and time consuming task, which ought to be resolved by providing automatic notification of a car returned to a different branch, and enabling automatic search for where a car has been returned to.

10.27 DFD process 4: Arrange car maintenance

A branch manager may book a car in for service at the service depot, as long as the car is free and the service depot has capacity for that day. See Figure 10.5. The branch manager talks with the manager of the service depot, and between them they find a date when the car is not booked for rental, and the service depot has time available to do the work. In theory, the process 'take booking for maintenance' is done at the same time by both a branch manager and a depot manager.

A branch manager **or** a depot manager may cancel a maintenance booking at any time until the car is picked up. This process requires coordination between the relevant branch manager and the depot manager, to ensure the service diary and the car bookings file are in step.

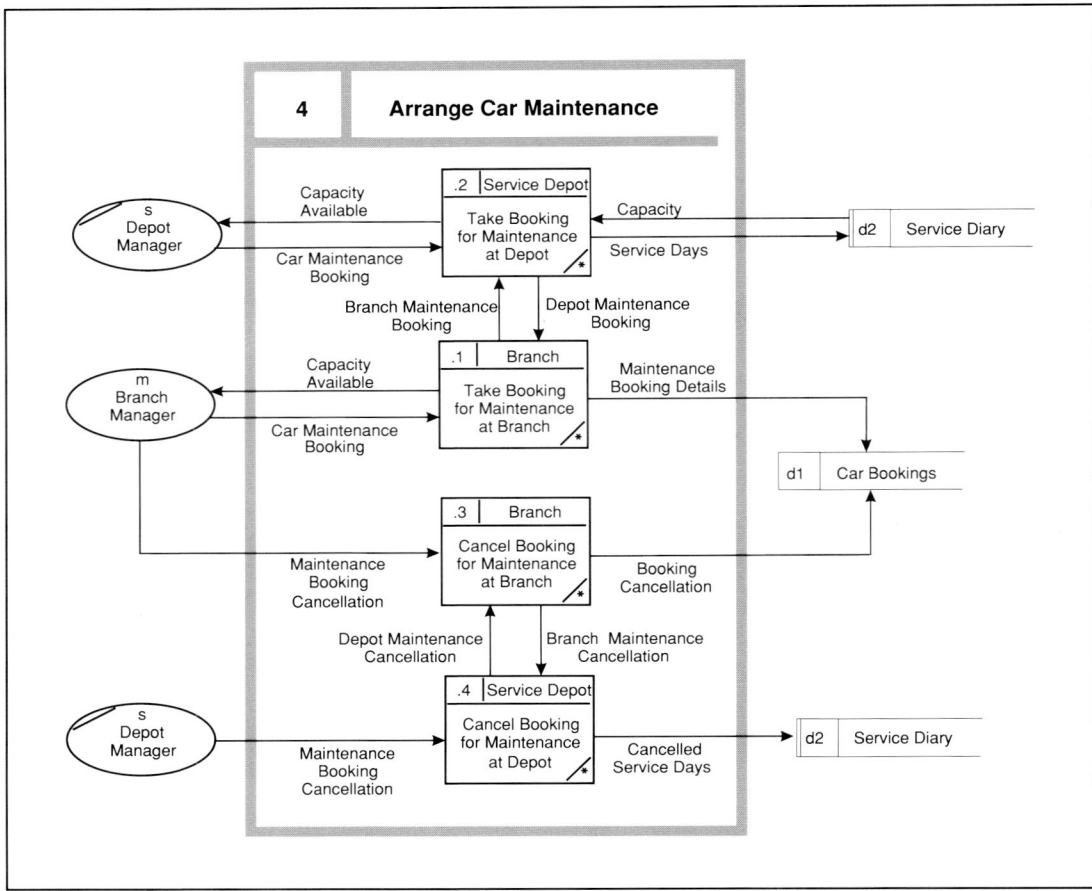

Figure 10.5: DFD Process 4 - Arrange car maintenance

It turns out that the DFD in Figure 10.5 contains processes in both branch and service depot. One temptation we should avoid is to divide it into distinct DFDs, by location, - this would separate the most tightly bound and 'cohesive' processes in the whole system (eg simultaneous booking of a maintenance job at the branch and at the depot).

Issue to be resolved for current DFDs - synchronisation of processes in different locations

It is difficult to know how to show, in current DFDs, the informal coordination of processes in different locations. How much inter-process communication should be shown, if any? Do data flows show only the passage of data items, or do they show:

- questions such as:

  - 'this car needs servicing; I have these dates available, are they OK with you?'

- decisions such as:

  - 'let's go ahead and book it in both the service diary and the car bookings file for those days'.

It seems too informal to show such communications only as dotted arrows between the external entities, since they are within scope of what is to be automated in the required system.

Current System Problem 8: overload of service depot.

In the current system, not all maintenance bookings are properly recorded in the service diary, meaning that over-booking may occur.

10.2.8 One more problem

Current System Problem 9: analysing the movement of cars.

After a car has been moved between branches (by transfer or one-way rental), its record is deleted from the car bookings file of the sending branch and a new record is created in the car bookings file of the receiving branch. Thus, there is no history of which branches a car has been owned by. It is difficult to analyse how often transfers take place, which branches experience 'losses' and 'gains' of cars most often, and so on.

10.3 Preparation for Design Options

The preparation for design options is dealt with in the following sub-sections:

- requirements (Section 10.3.1)

- logical system description (Section 10.3.2)

- distributed locations (Section 10.3.3)

- conceptual processes (Section 10.3.4)

- correspondences between functions and events/enquiries (Section 10.3.5)

- meeting requirements (Section 10.3.6)

- summary of design options (Section 10.3.7).

10.3.1 Requirements

Several different design options may be offered to the user; it is not clear that a single requirements list will always suffice. However, what we have done in the case study is develop one requirements list, and then show later how each design option measures up to the list of requirements.

In fact most of the requirements are met by all of the design options, especially those requirements of the new system which may be phrased directly in terms of supporting and improving upon the current system operation.

However, where a system is to be distributed there are two general requirements which may be added on top of these, robustness and consistency. Perhaps the major difference between the design options will be the degree to which these two general requirements are met. It is important to include robustness and consistency in the requirements list.

Robustness

When the network is down in a centralised system, then users at any location can do no work. But the robustness of a distributed system is a far more complicated issue, since some processing may be possible.

Having partitioned data between locations, at each location there are two kinds of process:

- intra-location processes, requiring data only at that location

- inter-location processes, requiring data at other locations.

An extra consideration for users therefore, when being presented with design options, is how much of the processing which they are responsible for can be carried out when the network is down and only intra-location processes are possible.

Consistency

In a centralised system, where the database is in one place, it is (in SSADM) self-evident that the database should be maintained so that data in it passes all consistency or integrity checks.

In a distributed system, this is not so self-evident. There is the possibility that designers may design processes which cause the data in different locations to get out of step.

It needs to be stated whether consistency is to be maintained at all times. If not, it needs to be stated what data inconsistencies are allowed, and what (potentially considerable) additional processes have to be designed to re-align inconsistent data.

The requirements list	The new system should not only support the current system operation, but improve on it by meeting these requirements.

Requirement 1: Robustness

To maximise the work possible at each branch and each service depot when the telephone network is down (each design option needs to state what can and cannot be done at a location when the network is down).

Requirement 2: Consistency of Data

To prevent any discrepancy between records located in different data stores.

Requirement 3: Prevention of double bookings

To ensure that double-booking never takes place.

Requirement 4: Finding where to transfer cars to/from

To inform branch managers of which branches have too many or too few cars.

Requirement 5: Checking of bad risks

To set up a record of customers and their rentals which can easily be inspected when looking for comments about bad experiences.

Requirement 6: Identification of customers

To set up a system for identifying customers as certainly and as swiftly as possible.

Requirement 7: Rented cars returned to a different branch (1)

When a car is returned by a customer to a different branch from where it was rented, to transfer ownership automatically and immediately to the new branch.

Requirement 8: Rented cars returned to a different branch (2)

When a car is returned by a customer to a different branch from where it was rented, inform the branch from which the car was rented. If there are any maintenance bookings for the car, inform the new owner branch of them; if the service depot that serves the new owner branch is different from the service depot for the old branch, cancel the bookings.

Requirement 9: Prevention of overload of service depot

To ensure that a service depot never accepts more bookings than it can handle.

Requirement 10: Analysis of transfers by customers

To provide analyses of how often transfers take place as a result of rentals returned to a different branch, which branches experience 'losses' and 'gains' of cars most often, and so on.

Requirement 11: Printed outputs

Chapter 10
SSADM extensions applied to EU-Rent

The system should take over the printing of outputs as far as possible, notably the contract/invoice, and receipts for drivers and customers.

10.3.2 Logical System Description

Of the logical system description we provide the LDS (Figure 10.6), the top level logical DFD (Figure 10.7) and five of the lower-level DFDs (Figures 10.8 to 10.12).

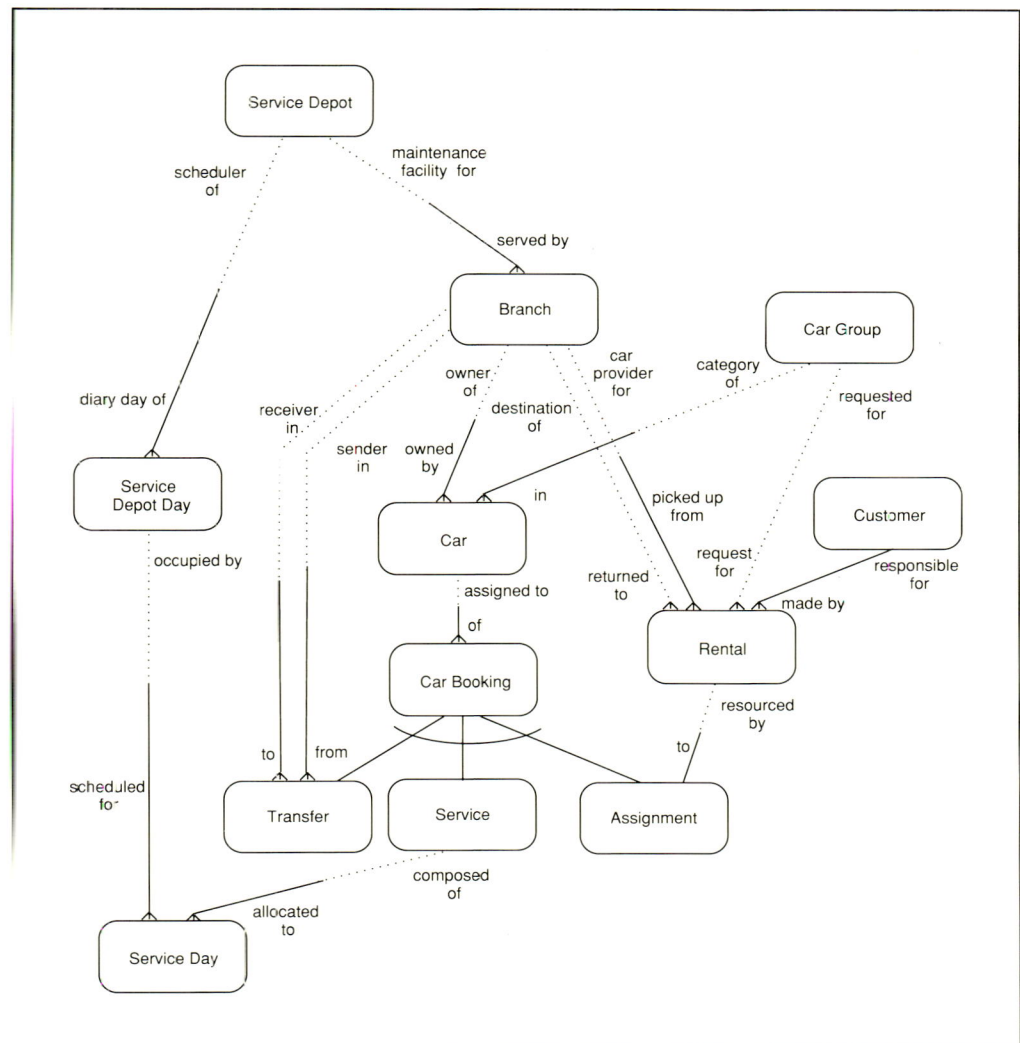

Figure 10.6: Logical Data Structure

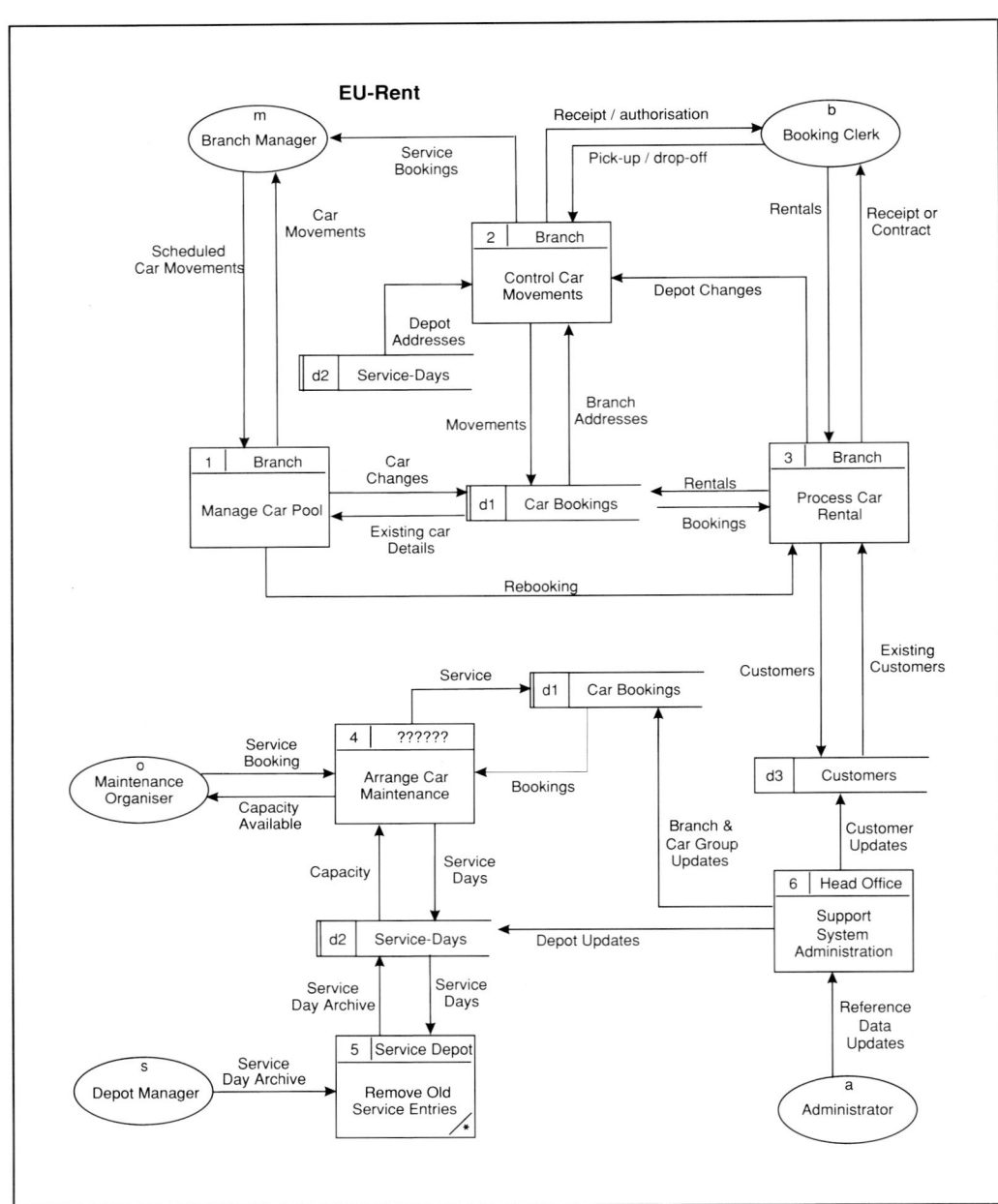

Figure 10.7: Top-level Logical DFD

Chapter 10
SSADM extensions applied to EU-Rent

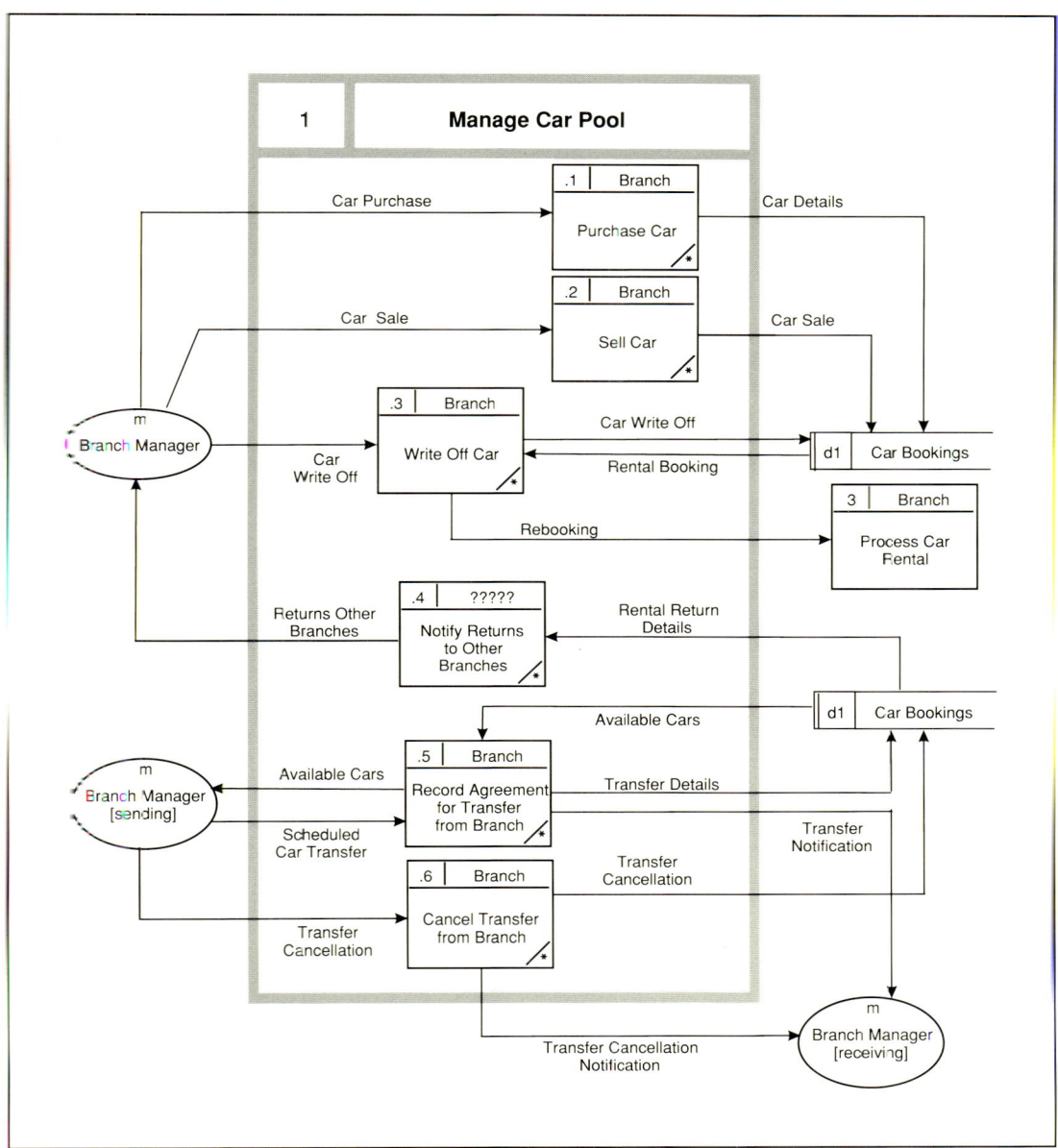

Figure 10.8: *Logical DFD Process 1 - Manage car pool*

Since we assume data location transparency, there is no requirement to distinguish car bookings data stores at different locations.

Information Systems Engineering Library
Distributed Systems: Application Development

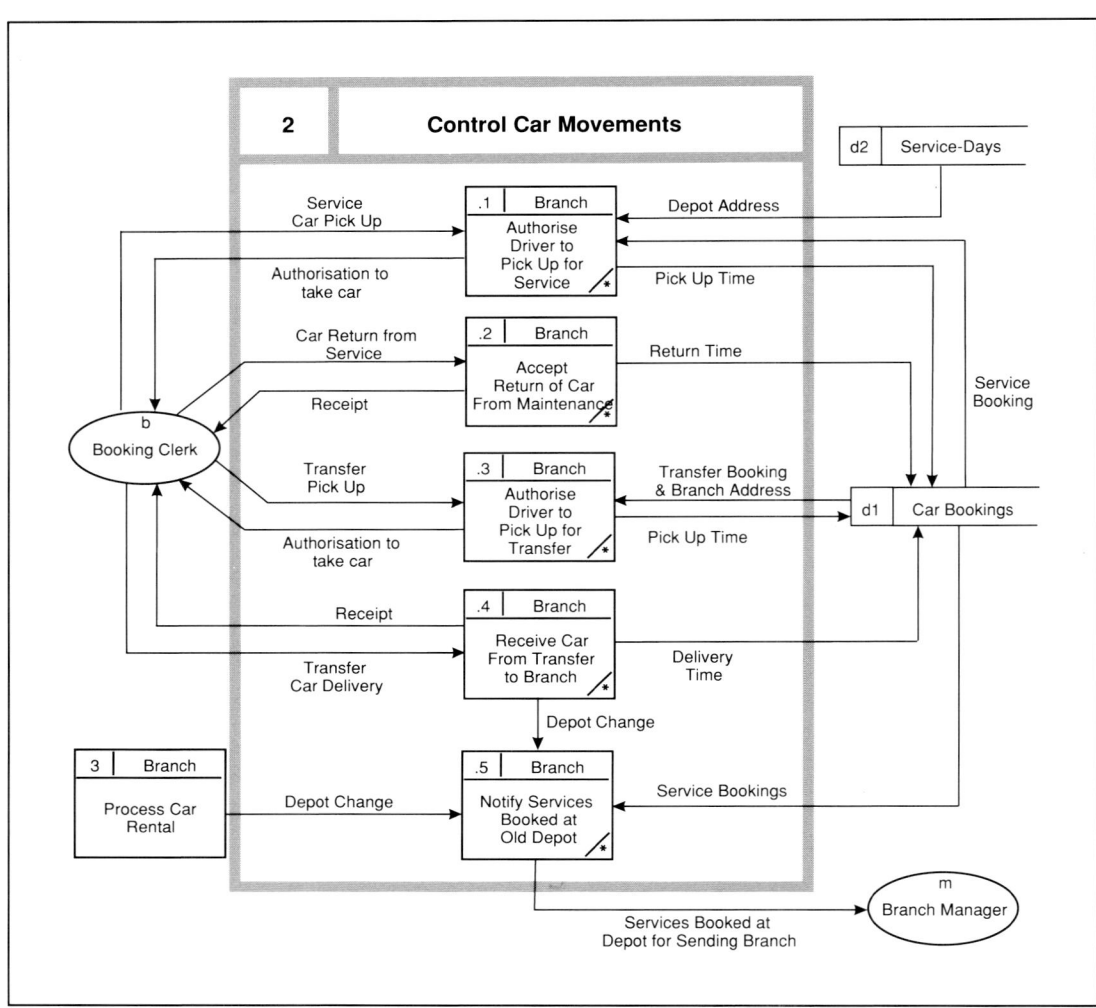

Figure 10.9: Logical DFD Process 2 - Control car movements

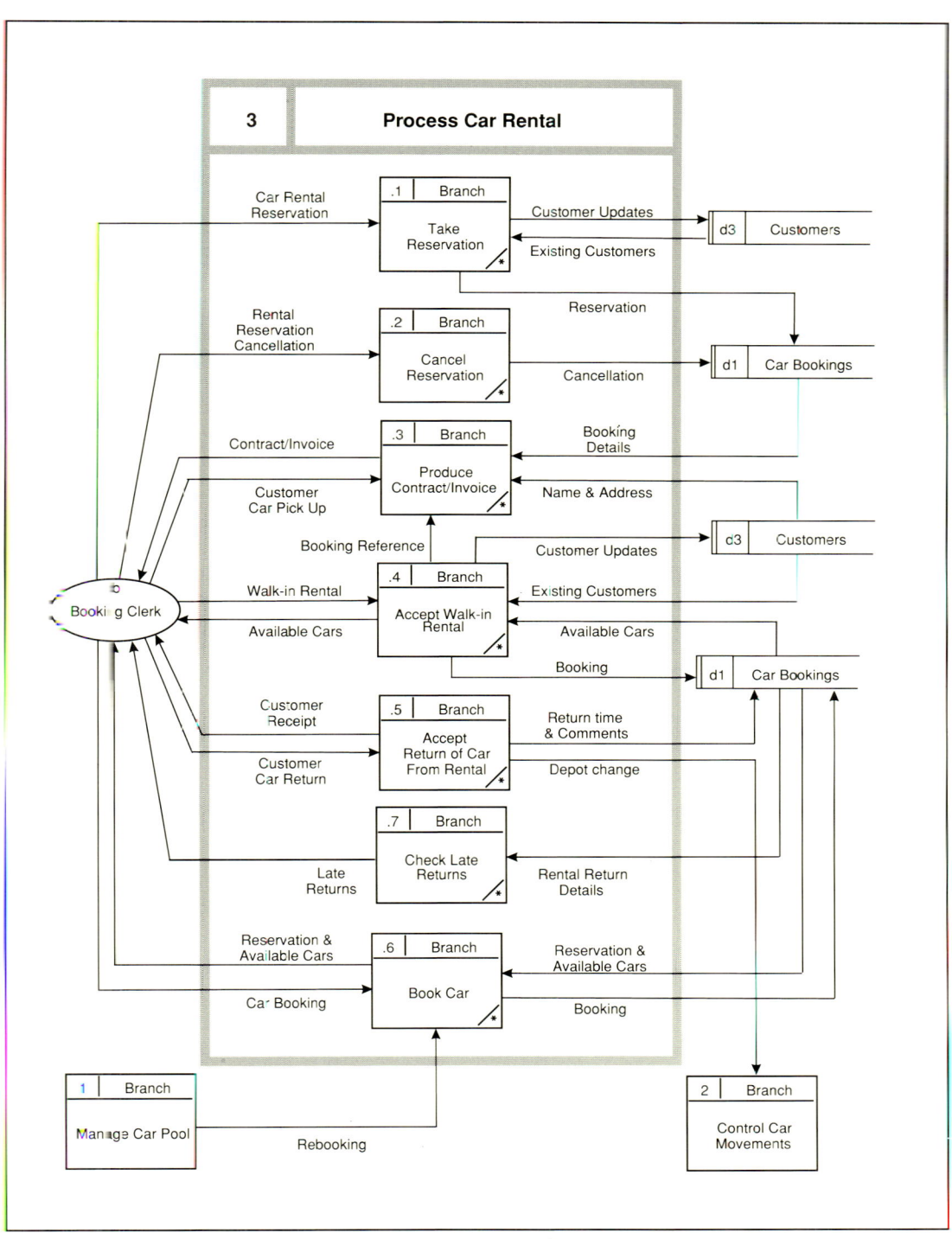

Figure 10.10: Logical DFD Process 3 - Process car rental

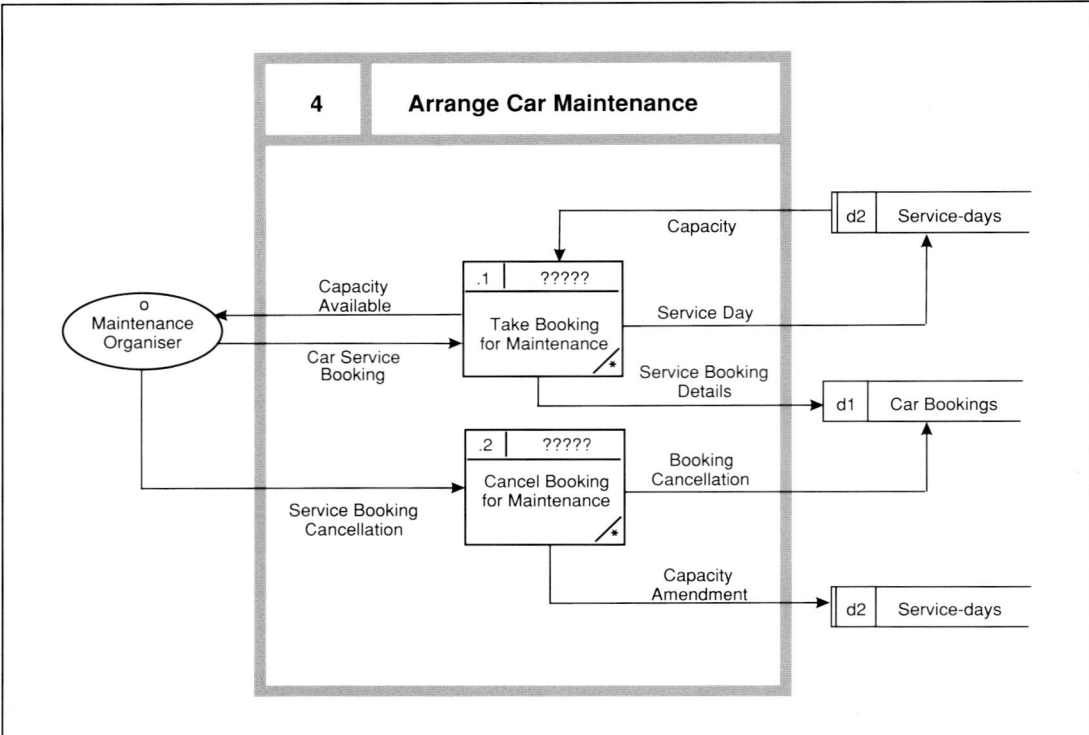

Figure 10.11: Logical DFD Process 4 - Arrange car maintenance

The lower-level DFDs in Figures 10.8 -10.12 have been organised to show the processes by user role. This is one of several strategies suggested in SSADM V4, and probably the best, since it helps in the definition of the user role/function matrix, menus and dialogues.

The role of maintenance organiser is undertaken by both service depot manager and branch manager, so the functions incorporated in the DFD in Figure 10.11 would be triggered from service depots and branches.

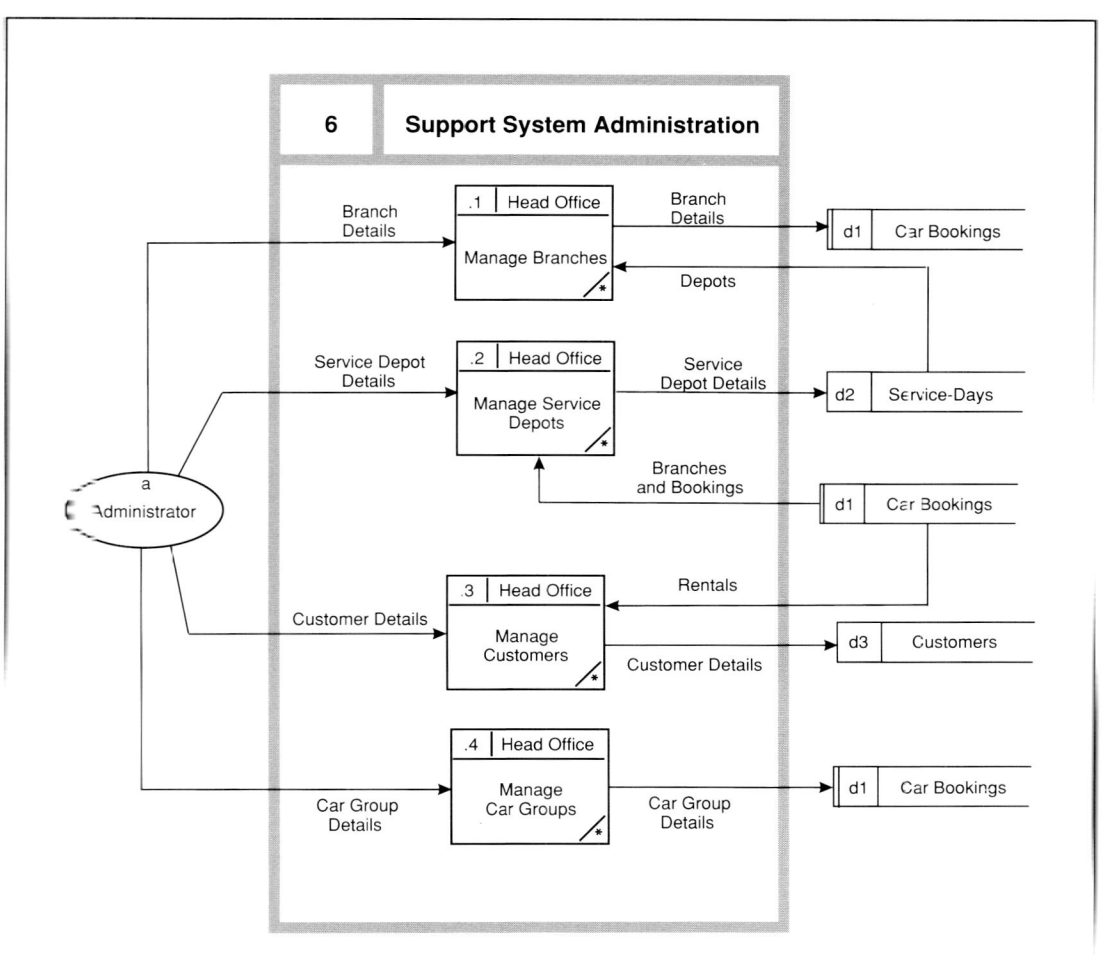

Figure 10.12: Logical DFD Process 6 - Support system administration

10.3.3 Distributed Locations

Business Location Types

There are three business location types in EU-Rent:

Head Office:-	1 instance
Service Depot:-	400 instances
Branch Office:-	1000 instances.

Business locations are locations from which functions (processes in the external design) may be triggered, and to which system-initiated outputs are delivered.

Data Location Types

Data Processing Location Types

Data processing locations are locations from which events and enquiries (processes in the conceptual model) may be triggered. A conceptual process may invoke conceptual processes at other data processing locations.

Data Storage Location Types

Data storage locations are locations at which databases (data in the internal design) are held.

Data Processing & Storage

In most cases (using current database technology), conceptual model processes will be held at the same locations as (most of) the data they use. Some data may be shared, so that conceptual processes may use data stored at other data processing locations.

Business Locations and Data Processing Locations

Design options are developed within the spectrum bounded by:

- centralised data processing: there is one location with a single database and all conceptual processes - workstations have only external processes and working data storage

- full local distribution: conceptual model processes invoked by functions (and the data they use) are held at the business locations - each business location is also a data processing location and a data storage location.

Between the two extremes, data processing and data storage locations are separated from business locations. One possibility is that data and conceptual processes are clustered at high-throughput business locations, each serving a number of low-throughput business locations as well as its own workstations (this might be called the 'regional centre' approach). Another is that conceptual processes are held at workstations and data is stored elsewhere (remote database access). A third is that conceptual processes and data are stored together, but not necessarily at workstations (one of the possible client/server approaches). For a full discussion of these points see Chapter 6.

Function/Business Location Type Matrix

The Function/Business Location Type Matrix in Figure 10.13 summarises the triggering of functions. It enables us to identify functions which dominate the system in terms of volume.

What does an entry in the matrix mean?

Assuming that an entry means that function X may, at some time, be triggered from location type Y, we have entered volumetric information, showing how often the function occurs per week at one instance of the location type. All figures are averages rounded to the nearest whole number, so 0 means less than one per two weeks.

Function	Average Weekly Occurrence at Business Location Type		
	Branch (1,000)	Service Depot (400)	Head Office (1)
Analysis of car movements			1
Book car	400		
Branch history			20
Car group maintenance			0
Cancel booking for maintenance	1	2	
Cancel reservation	40		
Cancel transfer	1		
Car maintenance history		16	
Cars returned to other branches	6		
Check late returns	6		
Customer history			100
* Customer pick-up	380		
Maintenance schedule		6	
Manage branches			10
Manage car groups			1
Manage customers			5,500
Manage service depots			10
Purchase car	2		
Record agreement for transfer	1		
Service pick-up	14		
Transfer delivery	1		
Transfer pick-up	1		
Remove old service entries		5	
* Return from rental	380		
Return from service	14		
Sell car	2		
Take booking for maintenance	8	20	
* Take reservation	400		
Walk-in rental	20		
Write off car	0		

* Volumes of these three functions dominate the throughput. Design options are prepared with this in mind.

Figure 10.13: Function/Business Location Type Matrix

Although 'Book car' also has high numbers, it is carried out as a single function for each branch, in which, at the end of each day, all the reservations for the following day are matched against the cars available. EU-Rent requires that it be done this way to reflect its business practice:

- at close of business each day, branch managers have to ensure that there are cars physically available to meet their commitment for the following day. The practice is to leave it as late in the day as possible to take account of car returns and walk-in rentals during the day

- reservations for the highest-cost car groups are allocated first; then any left-over cars in higher groups may be used for upgrades if there are insufficient cars to meet demand in lower-cost groups.

'Book car' does not have the same impact on performance as the functions marked with asterisks, which all have to be processed individually.

10.4 Conceptual Processes

Conceptual processes are of two types - events and enquiries.

Enquiries and Reports needed to support business activities

The LDM is validated (and most of its attributes defined) by checking that it can deliver the outputs needed to support business activities. Those needed to meet EU-Rent requirements are given in Figure 10.14.

Output Required	Description of Business Activity
To support branch:	
Available cars	to see what cars are available to fill reservations that have not been assigned cars automatically (eg offer a different car group) and for walk-in rentals
	to see whether cars are available to fill other branches' requests for transfers (this can be used by a branch manager to enquire about cars at other branches - see requirement 4)
Bookings for car	to ensure that there are no double bookings for car
Branch rentals for day	to identify what cars are needed for the following day's rentals - provides input to assignment of cars to reservations
Capacity available	to see what dates are available for service bookings
Late returns for branch	to prompt the booking clerk to contact the customer and find out why the car has not been returned
Returns from other branches	to let the branch manager know which cars have been lost from his branch, by being returned to other branches
Scheduled maintenance	when a car is transferred, if there are service bookings for the car and the new branch is served by a different service depot, to let the branch manager know that he must cancel the service bookings and arrange equivalent bookings at the new service depot.
To support service depot:	
Bookings for car	see under branch
Capacity available	see under branch
Car maintenance history	for reference when car is being serviced

Output Required	Description of Business Activity
Maintenance schedule	services scheduled for the immediate future (coming week, month etc) to support planning of work at depot.
To support head office:	
Analysis of car movements	Analysis of movement (and change of ownership) of cars by transfers and by rental returns to branches other than the renting branch - currently just monitoring the situation, but it may lead to additional business rules in the future
Branch history	Analysis of rentals and gains & losses of cars - input to decisions on whether to keep branch open, change staff levels, etc
Car group usage	Analysis of rentals and maintenance costs of car group - input to decisions on rental rates to charge, how many cars to buy in each group
Customer history	Input to decisions on whether to suspend, reinstate or remove customer

Figure 10.14: Enquiries and reports needed to support business activities

Relationships and Attributes in the EU-Rent LDM

To identify events we can analyse the attributes and relationships in the LDM (see Figure 10.15), and identify what changes are needed. Many of the events required will be recognisable as data flows on the DFDs. For a full discussion of event identification see Section 9.5.5.

Entity	Relationships with masters	Non-key Attributes
Branch	Service Depot	Branch Address √ Branch Cars
Car	√ Branch (owned by) √ Car Group	Purchase Date
Car Booking	Car	Booking Start Date Booking End Date Pick-up Time Return Time
Assignment subtype Service subtype	Rental	√ Service Description Service Hours Parts Cost
Transfer subtype	Branch (from) Branch (to)	
Car Group		Car Group Description √ Car Group Rental Rate
Customer		Customer Name √ Customer Address √ Customer Telephone No √ Comments about Customer √ Date of Last Rental
Rental	Customer o Car Group Branch (picked up from) o Branch (returned to)	Rental Start Date Rental End Date Cancellation Time Reason for Cancellation
Service Day	Car Booking Service Depot Day	
Service Depot		Service Depot Address √ Capacity

Entity	Relationships with masters	Non-key Attributes
Service Depot Day	Service Depot	Capacity √ Booked in Number
Key: √ changeable relationship or attribute o optional relationship		

Figure 10.15: Changeable LDM attributes and relationships used for event identification

Business Rules enforced by entity states

In addition to the changeable attributes and relationships, we need to identify any restrictions on entities - business rules of the form 'when an entity is in this state, these kinds of changes are not permitted'. See Figure 10.16.

Rule	Entities affected	Events
A customer may (by decision of EU-Rent management) be suspended. During suspension, no rentals are allowed for the customer.	Customer	Customer Disapproval
Suspension may be removed. Rentals are allowed again.	Customer	Customer Approval
After the decision has been taken to close a branch, no further cars may be bought by that branch or transferred to it, although the branch cannot be removed until all its cars have been written off, sold, or transferred elsewhere.	Branch	Decision to Close Branch
The workload for a service depot day can be changed (by adding or cancelling service days) at any time up to the service date - the date of the service depot day.	Service Depot Day Service Day	Service Date

Figure 10.16: Event identification from restrictions on entities

EU-Rent Entity Access Matrix (entities/events & enquiries)

We produce Entity Access Matrices to identify those entities accessed as a result of each event (see Figure 10.17) and those entities accessed during enquiries or the compilation of reports (see Figure 10.18).

Chapter 10
SSADM extensions applied to EU-Rent

- ➡ entry point to LDM
- ✓ updated by event/accessed in enquiry
- ✶ more than one role for different instances of entity type

Events \ Entities	Branch	Car	Assignment	Service	Transfer	Car Group	Customer	Rental	Service Day	Service Depot	Service Depot Day
Branch Cars	➡	✓									
Branch Opening	➡									✓	
Branch Removal	➡									✓	
Car Purchase	✓	➡				✓					
Car Sale	✓	➡		✓	✓	✓			✓		✓
Car Write Off	✓	➡	✓	✓	✓	✓			✓	✓	✓
Customer Approval							➡				
Customer Comment							➡				
Customer Disapproval							➡				
Customer Removal							➡				
Decision to Close Branch	➡										
Group Withdrawl		✓				✶					
Rate Change						➡					
Rental Booking		✓	✓			✓		➡			
Rental Cancellation	✓	✓	✓			✓		➡			
Rental Pick Up			✓				✓	➡			
Reservation	✓						✓	✓	➡		
Return from Rental	✶	✓	✓					➡			
Return from Service				➡							
Service Booking		✓		➡					✓		✓
Service Cancellation		✓		➡					✓		✓
Service Date									✓		➡
Service Depot Closure										➡	
Service Depot Capacity Change										➡	
Service Depot Day Archive			✓						✓	➡	
Service Depot Opening										➡	
Service Pick Up				➡							
Specification of Group						➡					
Transfer Booking	✶	✓			➡						
Transfer Cancellation	✶	✓			➡						
Transfer Delivery	✓				➡						
Transfer Pick Up	✶	✓			➡						
Walk-in Rental	✓	✓	➡					✓			

Figure 10.17: Entity Access Matrix showing the entities updated as a result of each event

- ⊷ entry point to LDM
- ✓ updated by event/accessed in enquiry
- ✽ more than one role for different instances of entity type

Enquiries & Reports	Branch	Car	Assignment	Service	Transfer	Car Group	Customer	Rental	Service Day	Service Depot	Service Depot Day
Available Cars	⊷	✓	✓	✓	✓	✓					
Analysis of Car Movements	⊷						✓		✓		
Branch History	⊷						✓		✓		
Bookings for Car		⊷	✓	✓	✓						
Branch Rentals for Day	⊷						✓	✓			
Capacity Available										✓	⊷
Car Group Usage		✓	✓	✓		⊷					
Car Maintenance History		⊷		✓				✓			
Customer History	✓						⊷	✓			
Late Returns for Branch	⊷	✓	✓				✓	✓			
Maintenance Schedule				✓					✓	⊷	✓
Returns Other Branches	⊷	✓	✓				✓	✓			
Scheduled Maintenance	✓	⊷		✓						✓	

Figure 10.18: Entity Access Matrix showing entities accessed for enquiries and reports

10.3.5 Correspondence Between Functions and Events/Enquiries

Function (external design)	Event/Enquiry (conceptual model)
Initiated at Branch	
Serving Branch Manager	
Cancel Transfer	Transfer Cancellation
Cars Returned to Other Branches	Returns Other Branches
Purchase Car	Car Purchase
Record Agreement for Transfer	Available Cars Transfer Booking
Sell Car	Car Sale
Write Off Car	Car Write Off Available Cars Rental Booking
Serving Booking Clerk	
Book Car	Available Cars Rental Booking
Cancel Reservation	Rental Cancellation
Customer Pick-up	Rental Pick-up
Check Late Returns	Late Returns for Branch
Return from Rental	Rental Return Scheduled Maintenance
Return from Service	Service Return
Service Pick-up	Service Pick-up
Take Reservation	Reservation
Transfer Delivery	Transfer Delivery Scheduled Maintenance

Function (external design)	Event/Enquiry (conceptual model)
Transfer Pick-up Walk-In Rental	Transfer Pick-up Available Cars Walk-In Rental
Initiated at Service Depot Car Maintenance History Maintenance Schedule Remove Old Service Entries	Car Maintenance History Maintenance Schedule Service Day Archive
Initiated at Branch and Service Depot Cancel Booking for Maintenance Take Booking for Maintenance	Service Cancellation Bookings for Car Capacity Available Service Booking
Initiated at Head Office Analysis of Car Movements Manage Branches Manage Car Groups Manage Customers	Analysis of Car Movements Branch Opening Branch History Branch Cars Decision to Close Branch Branch Removal Specification of Group Rate Change Car Group Usage Group Withdrawal Customer History Customer Disapproval Customer Approval Customer Comment Customer Removal

Function (external design)	Event/Enquiry (conceptual model)
Manage Service Depots	Depot Opening Depot Closure

Figure 10.19: Correspondences between functions and event/enquiries

10.3.5 Meeting Requirements

Robustness

Requirement 1, to maximise the work possible at each branch and each service depot when the telephone network is down. The way this requirement is met cannot be determined from the logical design; how well it is satisfied varies between the design options.

Consistency of data

Requirement 2, to prevent discrepancies between records located in different data stores, will be met by designing a data model which integrates all the system data, and implementing it using a database management system capable of:

- guaranteeing referential integrity

- detecting and preventing deadlock

- rolling-back commit units.

(These features must be provided whether the database is distributed or not.)

Some compromises in meeting this requirement may be needed for the distributed options.

Prevention of double bookings

Requirement 3, to ensure that double-booking never takes place, is met by the entity type car booking, with the restriction that car bookings cannot overlap.

Knowing where to transfer cars to/from

Requirement 4, to inform a branch manager of which branches have too many or too few cars, is met by assigning to each branch an 'ideal' number of cars in the entity type branch, and providing an enquiry function based on this data.

Checking of bad risks

Requirement 5, to set up a record of customers and their rentals which can easily be inspected when looking for comments about bad experiences, is met by the entity types customer and rental booking.

Identification of customers

Requirement 6, to set up a system for identifying customers as certainly and as swiftly as possible, is met by using a person's driving licence number for this purpose, in the entity type customer. This means that customers will no longer be seen as belonging to any specific branch, but will be considered on a company-wide basis.

Rental cars returned to a different branch

Requirement 7, when a car is returned by a customer to a different branch from where it was rented, to transfer ownership automatically, is met by automating the synchronous update of data for the two branches.

Requirement 8, when a car is returned by a customer to a different branch from where it was rented:

- inform the branch from which the car was rented - this is met by reporting the update that meets requirement 7

- if there are any maintenance bookings for the car, inform the new owner branch of them - this can be determined by enquiring on the maintenance bookings for the car.

- if the service depot that serves the new owner branch is different from the service depot for the old branch, cancel the maintenance bookings and arrange equivalent bookings at the service depot for the new branch - this can be met by enquiring on the service depots for the rental branch and return branch used in the update for requirement 7.

The branch manager at the new branch has to initiate the maintenance cancellation and rebooking.

Prevention of overload of Service Depot

Requirement 9, to ensure that a service depot never accepts more bookings than it can handle, is met by automating the synchronous update of the two entity types 'Service Days' and 'Service Depot Days'

Analysis of transfers by customers

Requirement 10, to provide analyses of how often transfers take place as a result of rentals returned to a different branch, which branches experience 'losses' and 'gains' of cars most often, is met by providing an analysis by branch of rentals (where rental branch and return branch are different) and transfers.

10.3.7 Summary of Design Options

Three options have been considered, though not costed. They are summarised here and detailed in the next four sections.

Option 1: Centralised option

Meets requirements 2 through 11.
Does not meet requirement 1.

Option 2: Fully Distributed Option

Meets all requirements.

Option 3: Partially Clustered Option

Meets all requirements. Compared to Option 2 it is:

- lower on cost of equipment

- higher on communications cost

- less robust (ie does not meet requirement 10 as well as Option 2).

10.4 Option 1 - Centralised Option

The purpose of this section is:

- to develop the case study for the centralised option, using the SSADM techniques of LDM, DFDs and entity-event modelling.

This option meets all requirements apart from requirement 1.

10.4.1 LDM

The database structure in Figure 10.20 is based directly on the LDM in the logical system description, but the data is held centrally at head office and is not distributed at all.

While this option does not meet the requirement for robustness, it meets all the other requirements and is useful for comparison purposes.

Chapter 10
SSADM extensions applied to EU-Rent

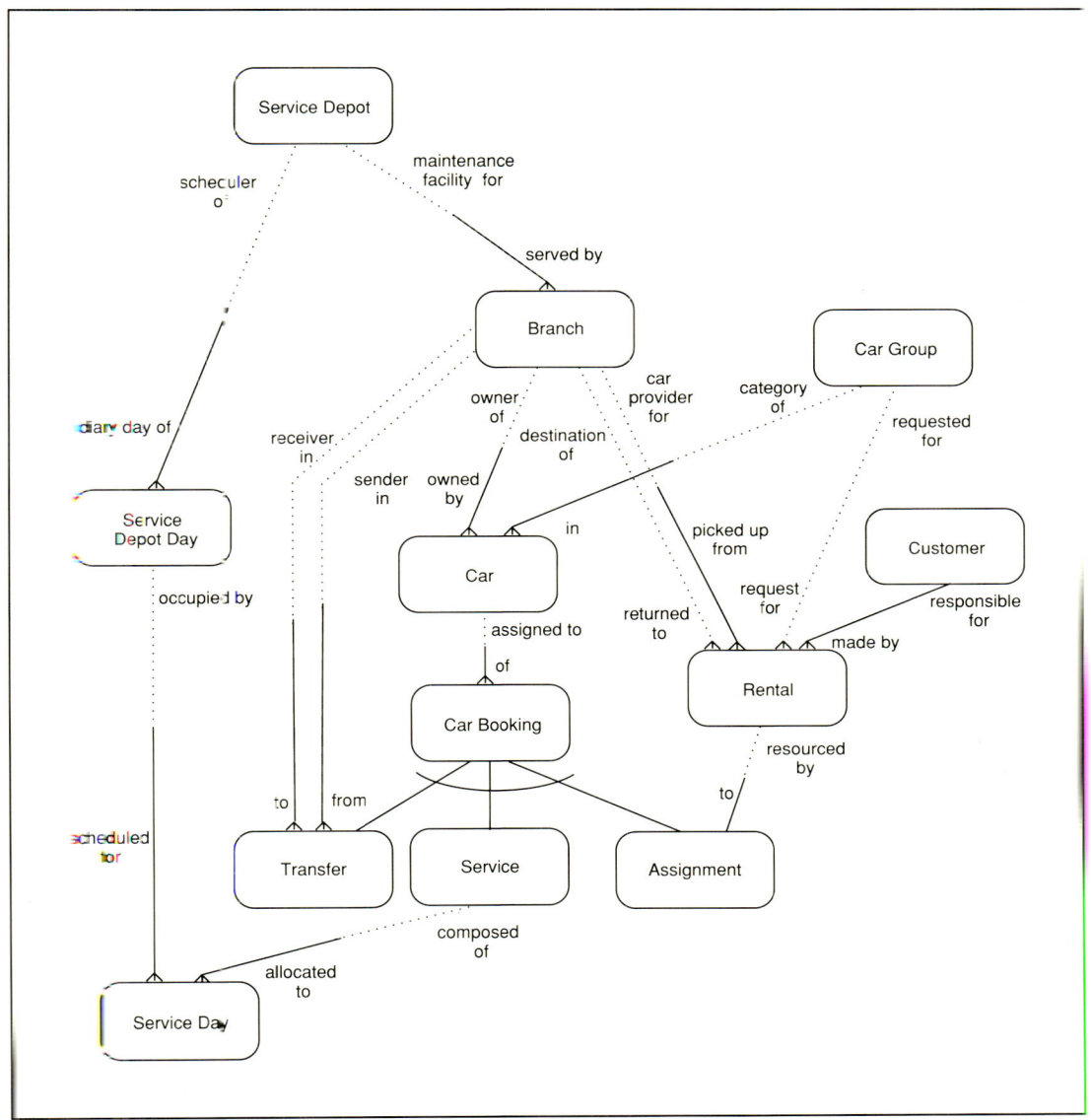

Figure 10.20: Logical Data Structure for centralised option

10.4.2 DFDs

DFDs are as in the logical system description (see Figures 10.7 - 10.12). Only the Top-level Logical DFD is shown here in Figure 10.21.

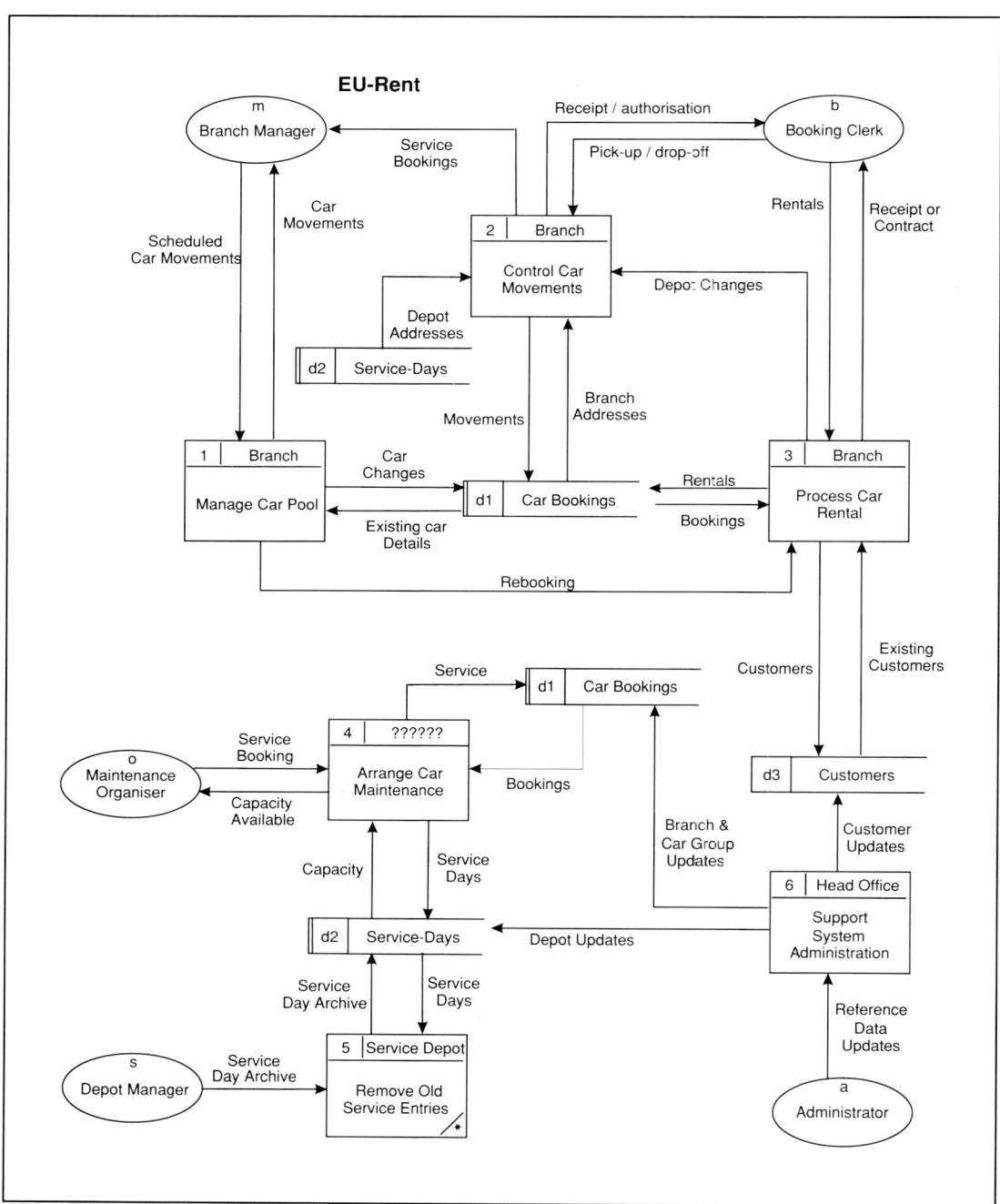

Figure 10.21: Top-level Logical DFD for centralised option

Lower-level DFDs (see Figures 10.8 -10.12 in the logical system description), on-demand queries and reports are mapped on to business location types and define the functions available at each:

Head Office

   6 Support System Administration

   Analysis of Car Movements
   Branch History
   Car Group Usage
   Customer History

Service Depot

   4 Arrange Car Maintenance
   5 Remove Old Service Entries

   Bookings for Car
   Capacity Available
   Car Maintenance History
   Maintenance Schedule

Branch

   1 Manage Car Pool
   2 Control Car Movements
   3 Process Car Rental
   4 Arrange Car Maintenance

   Available Cars (also required from one branch on other branches' data)
   Bookings for Car
   Branch Rentals for Day
   Capacity Available
   Scheduled Maintenance

10.4.3 LDM / Data Store Correspondences

These are shown in Figures 10.22 to 10.24.

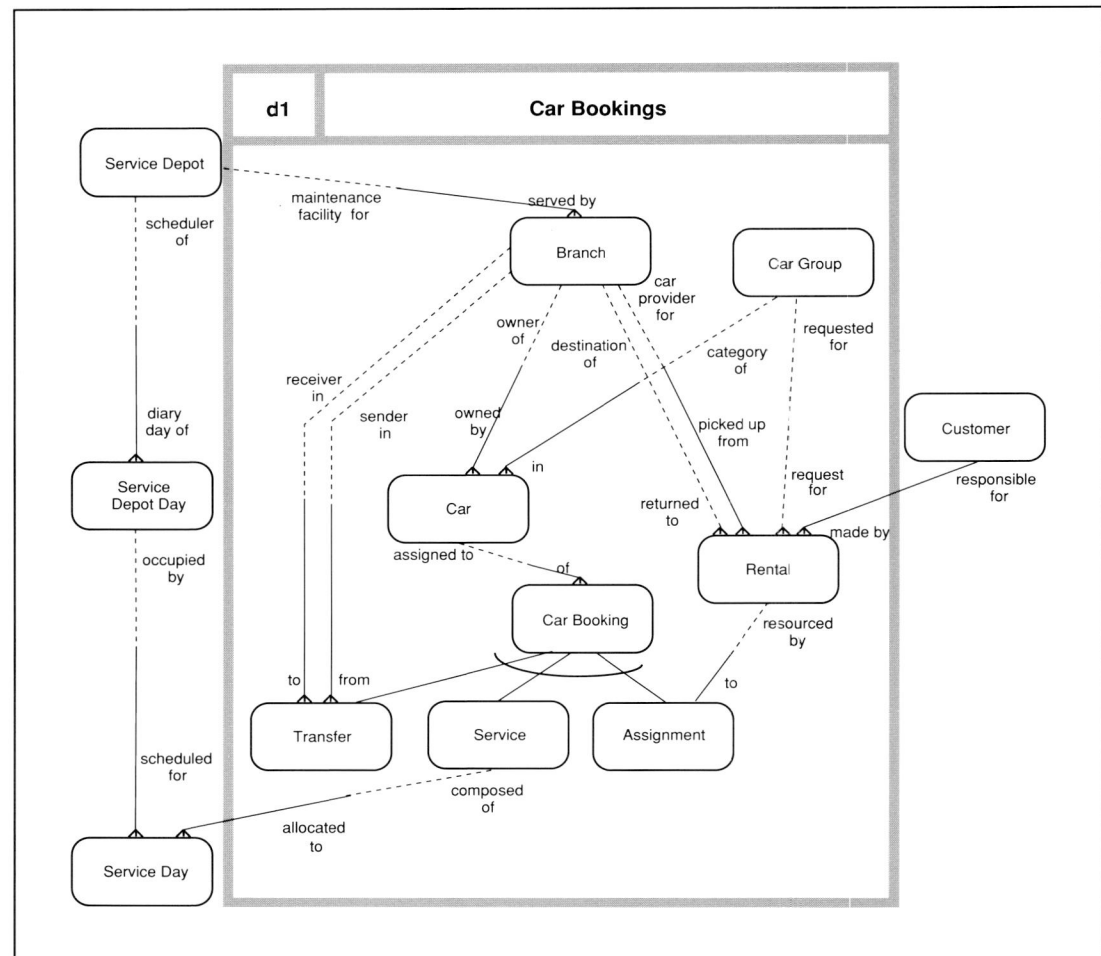

Figure 10.22: LDM / Data Store correspondence for car bookings

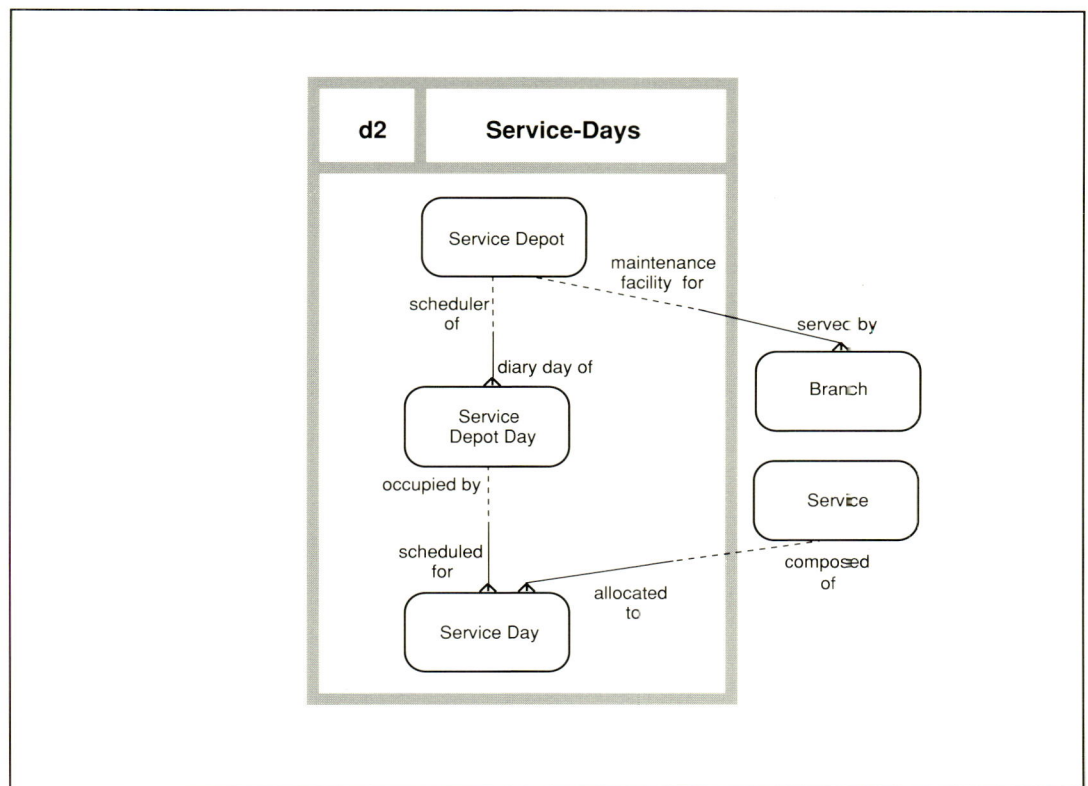

Figure 10.23: LDM / Data Store correspondence for service-days

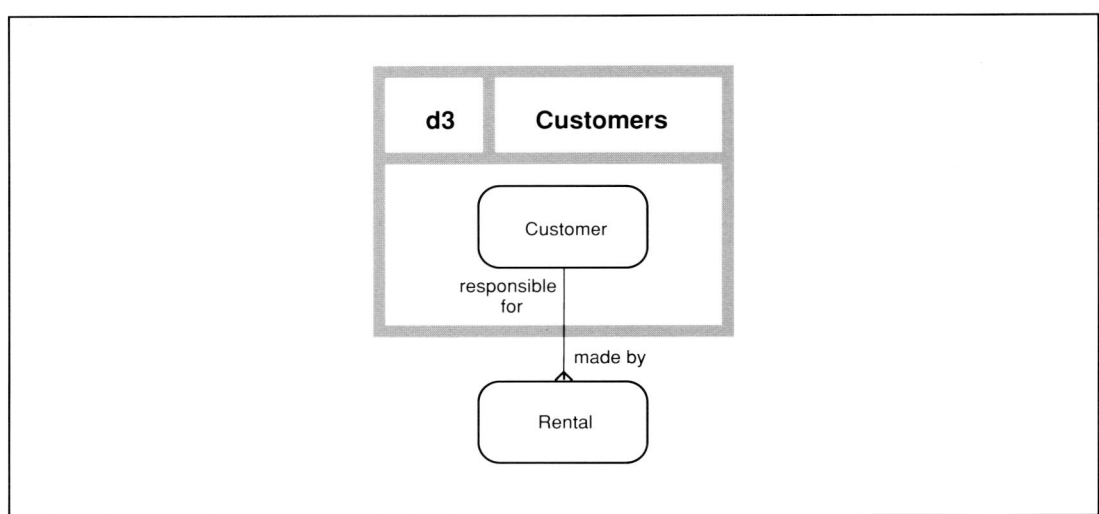

Figure 10.24 LDM / Data Store correspondence for customers

Option 1: Robustness Analysis

Since the day-to-day business of updating this database is entirely done at service depots and branches, this option completely fails to meet requirement 1 for robustness. If the network is down, branches and service depots cannot continue working, other than informally.

A second trouble with this option is the time and expense caused by service depots and branches having to use the communications network to head office for every transaction involving a customer.

It is clear that distributing the database (see later options) will reduce the communications traffic, and increase the robustness of the system.

10.5 Distributed Options

The distributed options are discussed in Sections 10.5 to 10.7. The purpose of these three sections is to:

- present two distributed design options

- develop the case study for each option, using the SSADM techniques of LDM, DFDs and entity-event identification.

10.5.1 Business Locations and External Design Processes

A major activity in developing design options is trying to minimise the overheads of remote data access. However, this should not be visible in the external design - we assume data location transparency for external design processes.

This means that the functions available to each business location type (and the DFDs used to present them to users) are generally the same in the centralised option and in each distributed option. There may be exceptions if we decide to offer reduced functionality in order to achieve the required level of robustness, performance or cost.

10.5.2 Requirements for access to data

We can extend the Entity Access Matrices in Figures 10.17 and 10.18 to show volumes (these are numbers of events and enquiries, not numbers of accesses to entity instances) as in Figures 10.25 and 10.26. From the function/event and enquiry mapping we can also indicate the business location of the function that triggers the event/enquiry process (H - Head Office, D - Service Depot, B - Branch).

Events	Weekly volume	invoked from	Branch	Car	Assignment	Service	Transfer	Car Group	Customer	Rental	Service Day	Service Depot	Service Depot Day
Branch Cars	200	H	→	✓									
Branch Opening	1	H	→									✓	
Branch Removal	1	H	→									✓	
Car Purchase	2,000	B	✓	→				✓					
Car Sale	1,800	B	✓	→		✓	✓	✓			✓		✓
Car Write Off	200	B	✓	→	✓	✓	✓	✓			✓	✓	✓
Customer Approval	50	H							→				
Customer Comment	200	H							→				
Customer Disapproval	50	H							→				
Customer Removal	5,000	H							→				
Decision to Close Branch	1	H	→										
Group Withdrawl	0	H			✓			★					
Rate Change	0	H							→				
Rental Booking	380,000	B			✓	✓		✓	→				
Rental Cancellation	40,000	B	✓	✓	✓			✓	→				
Rental Pick Up	380,000	B				✓				✓	→		
Reservation	400,000	B	✓					✓	✓	→			
Return from Rental	380,000	B		★	✓	✓				→			
Return from Service	14,000	B				→							
Service Booking	16,000	B,D			✓	→					✓		✓
Service Cancellation	2,000	B,D			✓	→					✓		✓
Service Date	2,000	D									✓	→	
Service Depot Closure	0	H										→	
Service Depot Capacity Change	10	H										→	
Service Depot Day Archive	2,000	D				✓						✓	→
Service Depot Opening	0	H										→	
Service Pick Up	14,000	B				→							
Specification of Group	0	H						→					
Transfer Booking	1,000	B	★	✓			→						
Transfer Cancellation	100	B	★	✓			→						
Transfer Delivery	900	B	✓				→						
Transfer Pick Up	900	B	★	✓			→						
Walk-in Rental	20,000	B	✓	✓	→					✓			

Figure 10.25: Entity Access Matrix for entity updates showing weekly volumes of events

Figure 10.26

Enquiries and Reports	Weekly volume	invoked from	Branch	Car	Assignment	Service	Transfer	Car Group	Customer	Rental	Service Day	Service Depot	Service Depot Day
Available Cars	60,000	B	⇢	✓	✓	✓	✓	✓					
Analysis of Car Movements	1	H	⇢					✓			✓		
Branch History	10	H	⇢					✓			✓		
Bookings for Car	15,000	B,D		⇢	✓	✓	✓						
Branch Rentals for Day	7,000	B	⇢						✓	✓			
Capacity Available	15,000	B,D											✓ ⇢
Car Group Usage	1	H		✓	✓	✓		⇢					
Car Maintenance History	14,000	D		⇢				✓				✓	
Customer History	100	H	✓						⇢	✓			
Late Returns for Branch	5,000	B	⇢	✓	✓					✓	✓		
Maintenance Schedule	2,000	D						✓				✓	⇢ ✓
Returns Other Branches	7,000	B	⇢	✓	✓					✓	✓		
Scheduled Maintenance	40,000	B	✓	⇢		✓							✓

Entities grouping: Assignment, Service, Transfer form "Car Booking".

Figure 10.26: Entity Access Matrix for entity accesses showing weekly volumes of enquiries and reports

The functions provided at head office are non-urgent, except for customer approval and disapproval. All but customer removal have very small volumes. Apart from these three, head office functions are largely ignored in design options.

Almost all the functions at branches and service depots are needed for day-to-day operations.

10.6 Option 2 - Fully Distributed Option

10.6.1 First-cut distribution design

The first-cut distribution design aims for the most distributed option, and provides a self-contained data model for each type of business location. Entity types shared between business location types are split into aspects. In physical design, databases at different locations can be designed to be loosely- or tightly-coordinated.

1 Add business location types to the LDM - head office, branch (already present), service depot (already present) - and add relationships between business locations. Also add the central data processing location (as used in the centralised option), if it is not also a business location.

   Draw one-to-many relationships from the central data processing location to entities at the top of the LDM (i.e those which have no LDM masters).

2 Treat each business location type (and the central DP location) as a geographical root and define a hierarchical structure under it (analogous to the first-cut design in SSADM V4).

   Use the least-dependent-occurrence rule to place entity types that are in more than one hierarchy. When a shared entity has been placed in one hierarchy, split each of its other masters into two aspects, one in its own hierarchy and the other with the shared detail.

   For example, in Figure 10.27, car, rental and service day were placed in the branch class hierarchy under their respective masters of branch and service. The other masters, car group, customer and service depot day were then split into two aspects.

3 Review the placement of shared details to take account of significant differences in volume of use. Use the Entity Access Matrix for guidance. See Figure 10.28, with service days placed as it is at service depot because service days are used more often from depots (35,000 events/enquiries per week) than from branches (18,000 events/enquiries per week).

4 Identify the required behaviour of aspects of shared entities, and the volume of communication between them.

5 Decide an approach for the placement of instances of 'subordinate' aspects, taking account of:

- disjoint partitioning

- replication

- movement of data between locations.

6 Decide the placement of history of movable entities.

7 Draw the data model for each location; include reference data on related locations if it is needed for output.

8 Summarise the communication between locations:

- coordination of aspects

- movable entities

- multiple relationships between master and detail.

Steps 4 to 8 will now be described in greater detail.

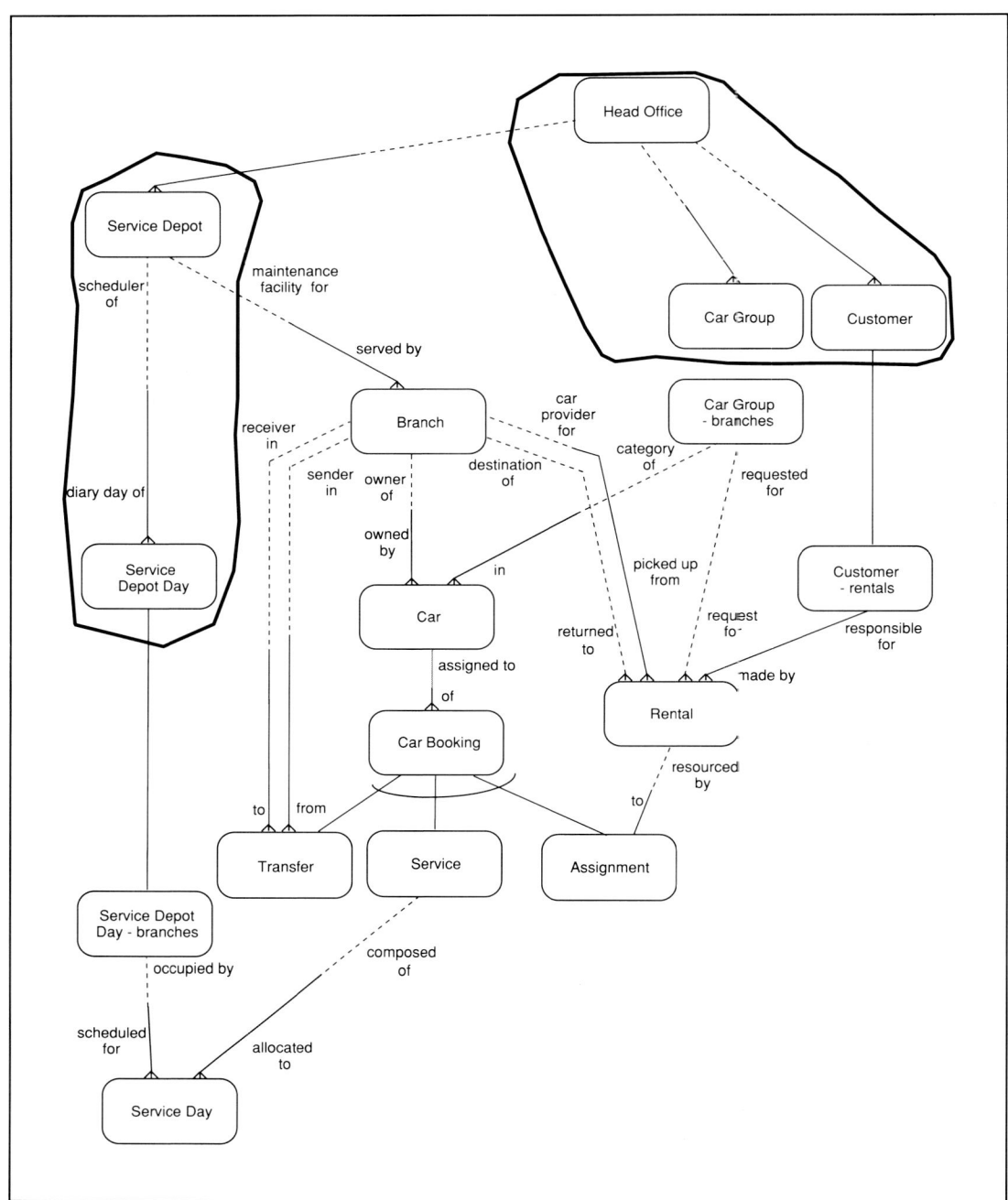

Figure 10.27: First-cut distribution design after step 2 - place shared details in hierarchies and split non-hierarchical masters into aspects

Chapter 10
SSADM extensions applied to EU-Rent

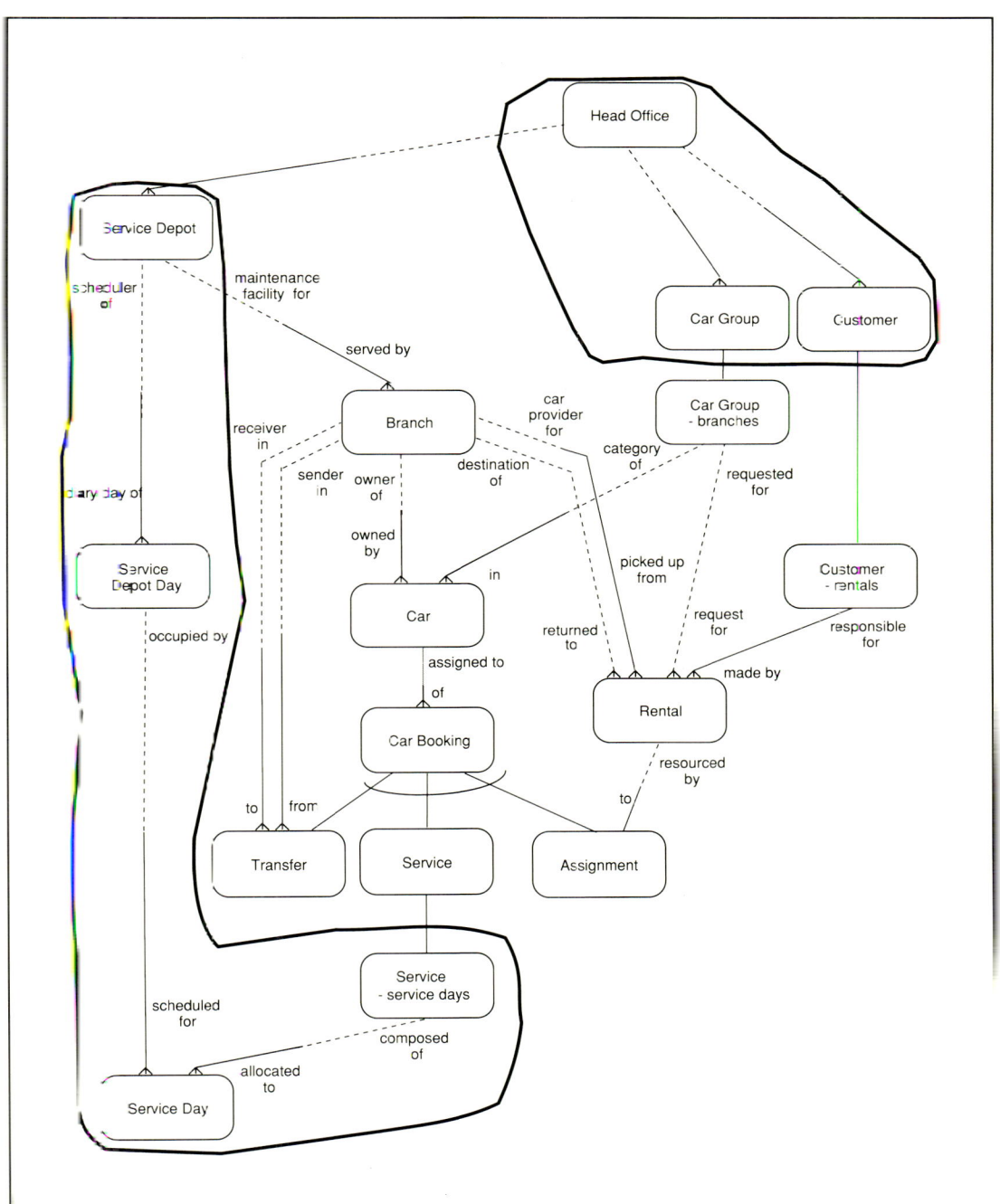

Figure 10.28: Step 3 - Review placement of shared details by volume of use

Step 4 - Behaviour of aspects

There are three split entities:

Car group is split between head office and branch

Car group is used by branches:

- as reference data (group description, rental rate)

- as a category for grouping reservations that have not yet been allocated specific cars.

All changes to car group attributes (insignificant numbers) are made from head office. They can be copied to branch aspects.

Service is split between branch and service depot

At a branch, service is required mainly to ensure that there are no double bookings for a car. Its essential attributes are start and end date.

At a service depot, service is required to plan work. There are two parts to this:

- indicating that a service on a single car spans several service depot days - ie to act as an index by car to service days

- to hold a description of what work is done. A description is input when the service is scheduled. On return from service the time and materials are recorded and the description may be updated.

When service bookings are made from branches (8,000 per week), the description and start and end dates can be sent to service depots to create service days. Each of these is preceded by an enquiry on capacity available.

When service bookings are made from service depots (8,000 per week), start and end dates can be sent to branches to create service bookings. Each of these is preceded by an enquiry on bookings for car.

Customer is split between head office and branch

Customer is used at head office in two ways:

- to disapprove/approve customers in order to prohibit/permit rentals; each disapproval (50 per week) is preceded by an enquiry on customer history

- to remove old, inactive records from the system; this activity (average 5000 customers per week) is preceded by selection of customers that have not been active for more than some specified period and are not suspended (blacklisted customers are not deleted, even if they have not been active). Updates to last rental date are made from branches.

Customer is used at branch in three ways:

- to check status to determine whether rentals are permitted

- to support the business rule that a single customer whose driving licence has been shown to the branch must be responsible for a rental

- to provide reference information for printing name and address on contracts, for billing, for contact over late return of car etc.

Customers are created from branches (5,000 per week).

Status changes and deletion notifications can be copied from the head office aspect to branch aspects. Other attributes required at branches are maintained at branches.

Step 5 - placement of 'subordinate' aspects	Conceptually, a base entity (eg customer) and a subordinate aspect (eg customer-rentals) are in one-to-one correspondence. When a subordinate serves many locations the options for placement are:

- store the subordinate with the base entity (eg store customer-rentals at head office); the locations that it serves (branches) will access it remotely

- store the subordinate at each location that it serves; unless there is a disjoint partition (see under 'service - service days' which follows), this requires replication of the subordinate aspect.

(Note: since aspects are modelled distinctly in the conceptual schema, ie they have distinct ELHs and are separate nodes in ECDs, their physical placement can be changed under physical design control without disturbing the conceptual schema.)

This step deals with concurrently 'live' aspects. History is dealt with at step 6.

Service - service days: placement at service depot

At any given time, a car can be at only one branch, and hence serviced by only one service depot. If a car moves to a branch serviced by a different depot, any scheduled services are cancelled and replacement services are arranged at the new depot.

Each 'live' instance of service-service days can be placed at its car's current depot. No 'live' instance needs to be copied to more than one depot.

This is a disjoint partitioning of the global set of service - service days. Disjoint partitioning is the simplest way to distribute instances across locations. The base aspect and the subordinate aspect are in one-to-one correspondence at the instance level.

Car group - branches: placement at branch

Car groups are used by all service depots - there is not a disjoint partition. The factors to be considered are:

- size: 10 instances

- volume of events by location (use the Entity Access Matrix):

    - head office: less than one per two weeks

    - branch: 800,000+ per week (gains & losses of rentals and cars)

- volume of enquiries by location (use the Entity Access Matrix):

  - head office: 1 per week

  - branches: 67,000 per week

These volumes clearly indicate that the set of car groups should be replicated at every branch and attribute changes broadcast from head office to branches. This is often the case with reference data, code tables, lists of valid values etc.

Customer - rentals: placement at branch

A customer may be concurrently active at several branches - there is not a disjoint partition. Factors to be considered are:

- size: 5,000,000 instances

- volume of events by location (use the Entity Access Matrix):

  - head office: 5,300 per week (5,000 removals)

  - branch: 800,000+ per week (gains of rentals, rental pick-ups)

  - birth at branch - see if base aspect already exists: unknown

- volume of enquiries by location (use the Entity Access Matrix):

  - head office: 100 per week

  - branch: 20,000 per week

These indicate that customer - rentals aspects should be replicated at branches, but further analysis is needed on:

- what proportion of customers are active at more than one branch

- numbers of rentals per customer/branch

- proportion of reservations and rental pick-ups with customer change of address.

Step 6 - history of movable entities

Car

There is a requirement to hold a maintenance history of the car, for enquiry by the depot when maintenance is being carried out. During its life in the system, a car may move between branches (and may be maintained by different depots). The placement options are whether history should be kept:

- spread across the service depots that have serviced the car

- at the branch that currently owns the car. This requires that service data (time, materials, description of work done) are copied into the service base aspect when the service is completed.

There are about 14,000 (35 per depot) maintenance histories per week. This is insignificant in terms of performance. The system is more robust if the required history is at only one location, so we shall take the second option.

Chapter 10
SSADM extensions applied to EU-Rent

Step 7 - data model
for each location.

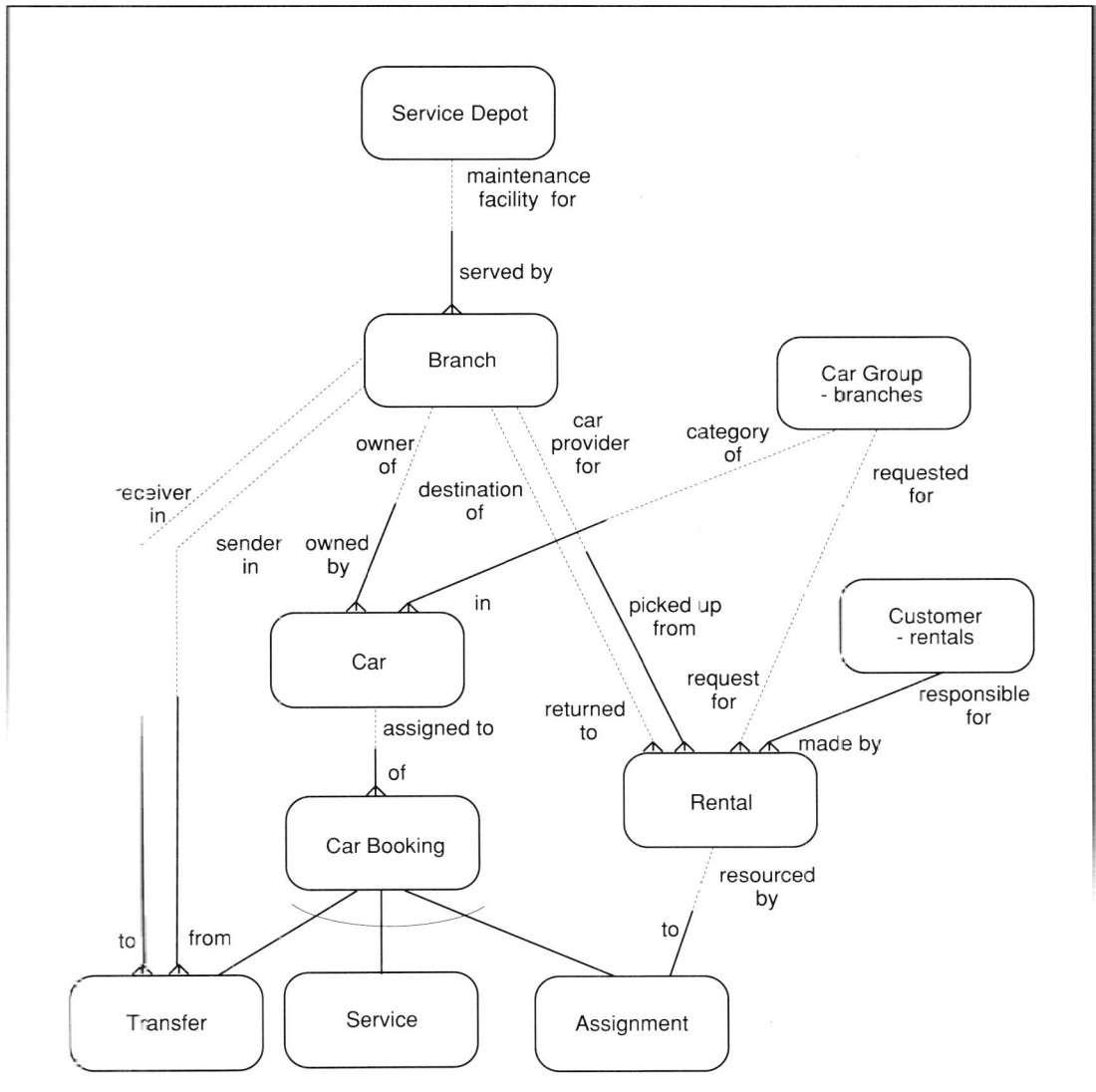

Figure 10.29: *Data model for branch*

Since service depot address is needed for directions issued to drivers for service transfers, the service depot for the branch at which the data model is implemented is included in Figure 10.29. (This is a special case of aspects.)

We could distinguish between the branch at which the data model is implemented and other branches to which cars are to be transferred as in Figure 10.30.

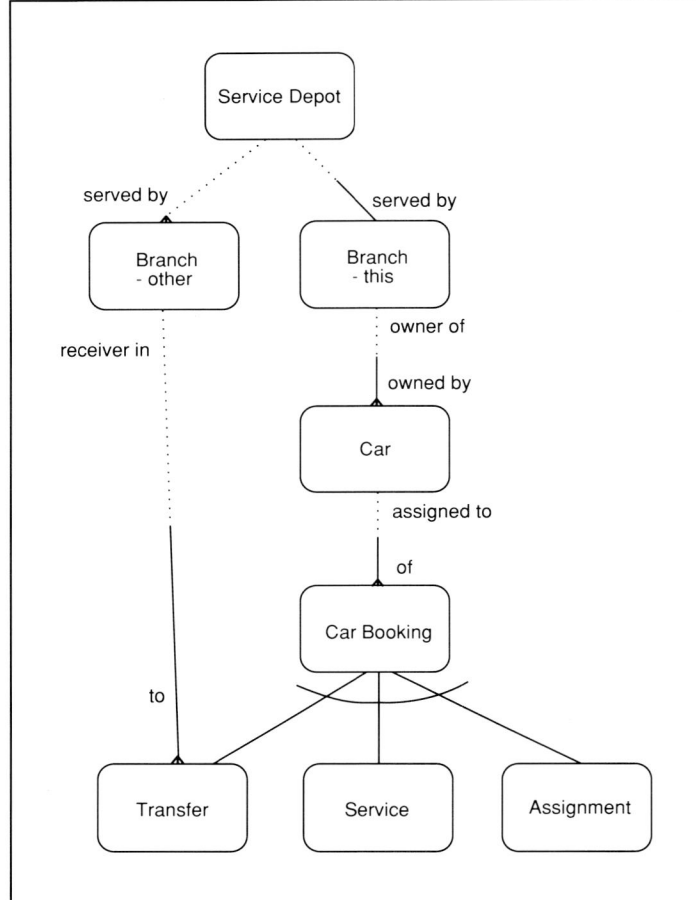

Figure 10.30: LDM with 'Branch' split into 'this' and 'other' aspects

This is another special case of aspects. 'Branch - this' would have all the attributes which 'Branch' previously had; 'Branch - other' would simply have a branch identifier, and an indication of whether it was served by the same depot as 'Branch - this' (we need to know this on arranging a transfer - if a car is transferred to another branch served by the same depot, any future service booking for the car can stand. If 'Branch - other' in a transfer is served by a different depot, any future service booking must be cancelled and a replacement service booking made at the new depot).

We have shown only transfers from 'Branch - this'; these are the transfers that the branch must know about to avoid conflicts with rental assignments and service bookings. Transfers to 'Branch - this' are in other partitions of the LDM, where the sending branches have the role of 'Branch - this'. There is one problem - a branch also needs to know about transfers to it from other branches, to predict how well it can meet future demand. This leads to the need for splitting Transfer into 'to' and 'from' aspects as in Figure 10.31.

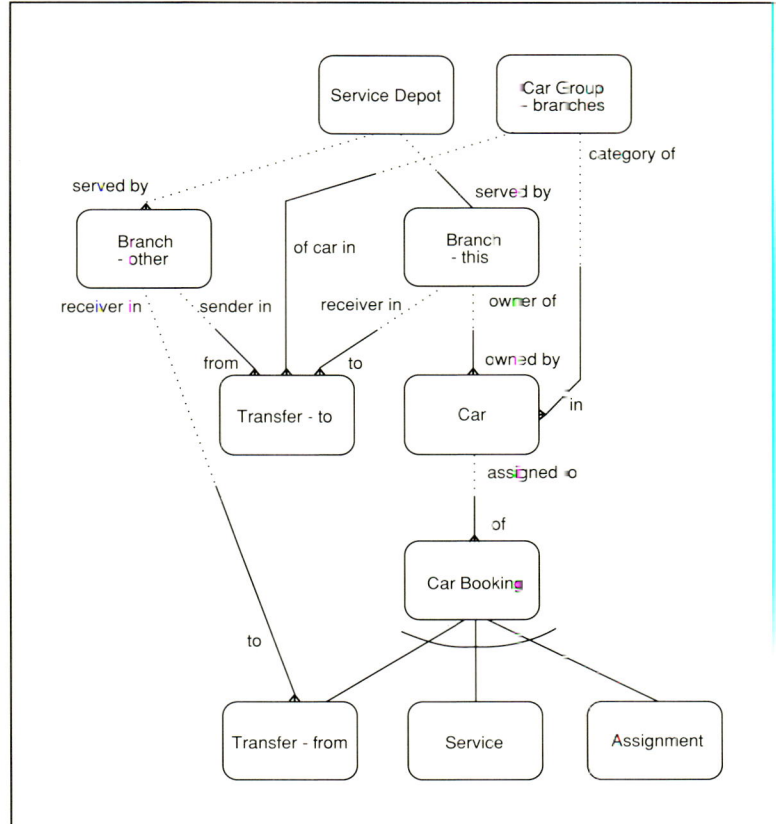

Figure 10.31: LDM with Transfer split into 'to' and 'from' aspects

Note that in physical design:

1. If we choose the 'most distributed' option, then for speed and robustness, we might duplicate branch address in 'Branch - other', and duplicate full transfer details in both aspects of Transfer.

2. This type of splitting into aspects is a design mechanism to specify needs for robustness of IT services at locations. We might actually choose to place 'Branch - other' at the 'Branch - this' location and manage the relationship across the network with no replication of data.

In practice, we might not elaborate the branch LDM in this way - just make design notes on these issues, and work from the more general LDM illustrated in Figure 10.29.

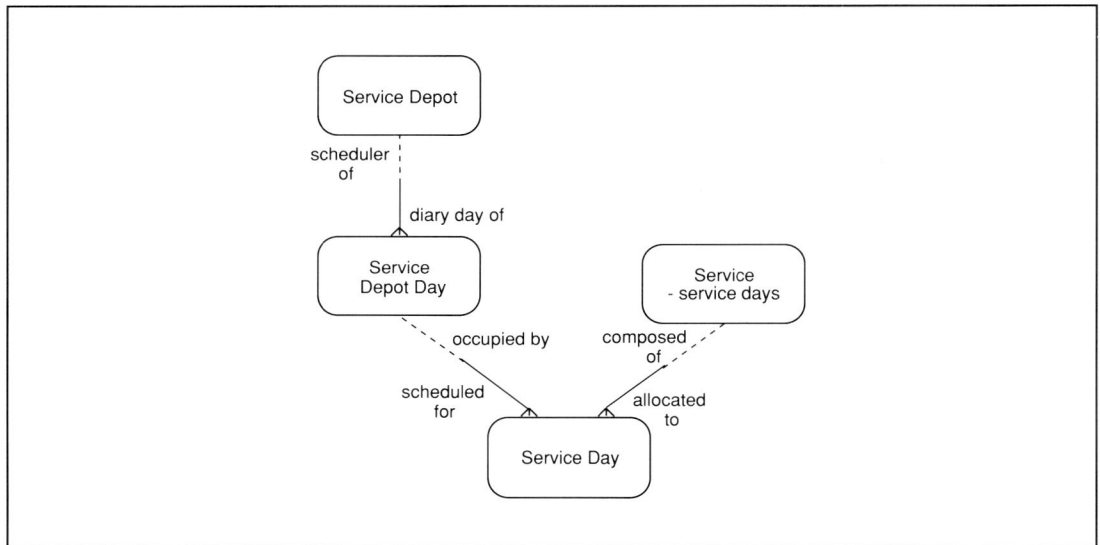

Figure 10.32: Data model for service depot

'One-of-a-kind' entities, like depot in a depot-based data model, are not usually included as entities in LDMs. However, there may be states that control what is allowed to happen to detail entities at the location so depot is included in Figure 10.32 (and head office in Figure 10.33).

In physical design, service depot's state could be implemented as a control record, rather than as a conventional database record. Service depot day's relationship 'must be a diary day of' would then be implemented as 'is in the database at this location'.

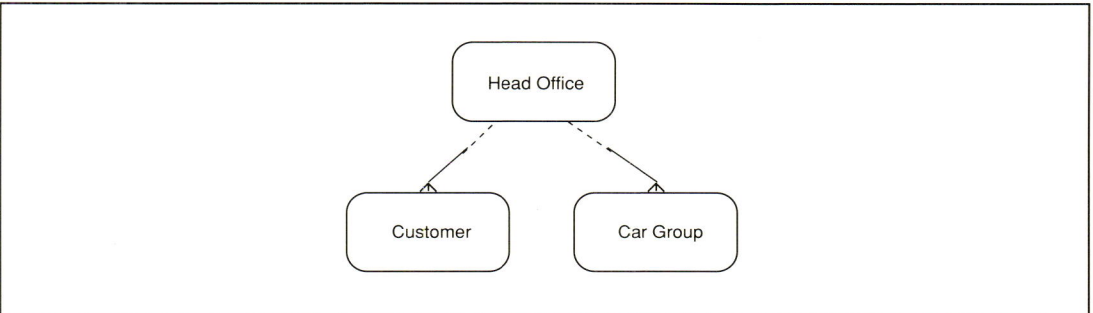

Figure 10.33: Data model for head office

Step 8 - Summarise the communication between location types

Communication Map

In the most distributed option, each business location has its data processing services available locally. The communication map is essentially about communication between data processing locations. For example, see the communication map in Figure 10.34.

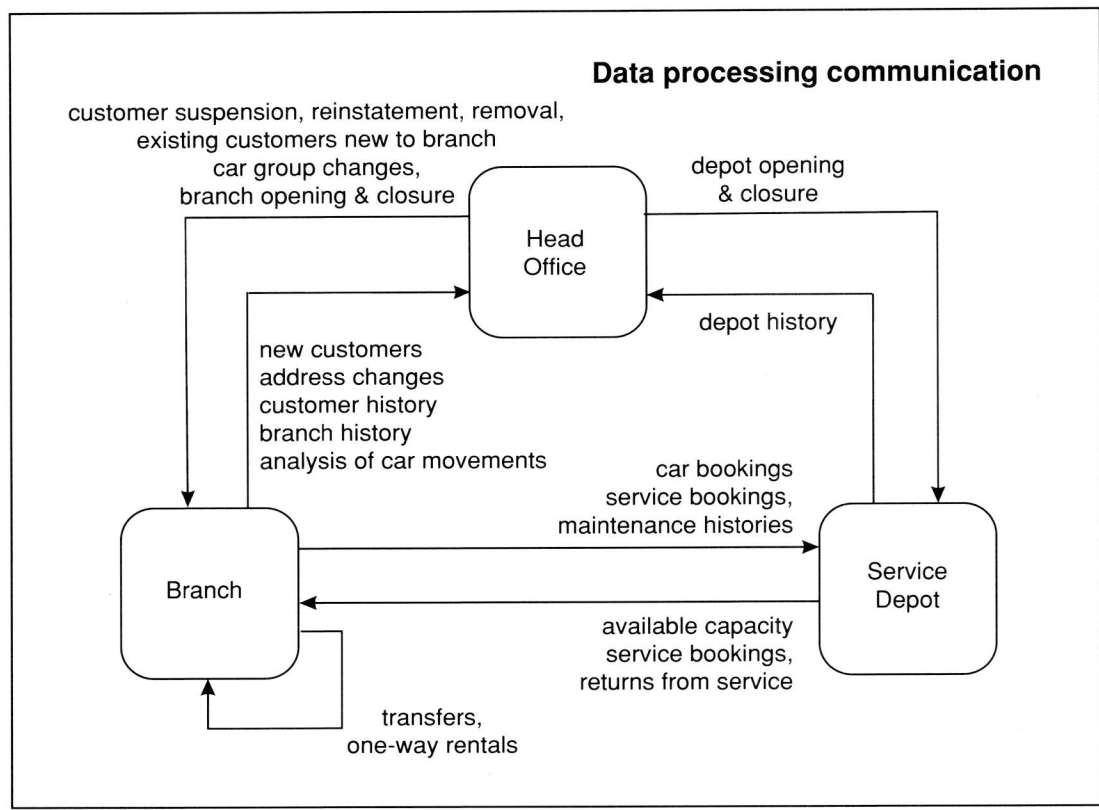

Figure 10.34: Communication between data processing locations

Chapter 10
SSADM extensions applied to EU-Rent

Figures 10.35 to 10.37 give volumes of the communication traffic shown in Figure 10.34.

Aspect	Event/enquiry	No. per week
Customer (copied down to say, 3 branches)	Customer approval Customer disapproval Customer history Customer removal	50 50 1 5,000
Customer - rentals	Reservation (new customer) Reservation (existing customer, new to branch) Reservation (change of address)	5,000 1,000 2,000
Car Group (copied down to 1,000 branches)	Group withdrawal Rate change Specification of Group	< 1 < 1 < 1
Service	Service booking Service cancellation	16,000 2,000
Service - service days	Car Maintenance History Return from service	14,000 14,000

Figure 10.35: Coordination of aspects (events/enquiries that affect both aspects of split entities)

Entity	Event/enquiry	No. per week
Car	Transfer Pick-up	900

Figure 10.36: Movable entities (entities moved from one location to another)

Entity	Event/enquiry	No. per week
Branch	Reservation (different branch) Rental Cancellation (different branch) Walk-In Rental (different branch)	40,000 4,000 2,000
Branch	Transfer booking Transfer cancellation	1,000 100

Figure 10.37: Multiple relationships between master and detail (Creation/swapping/deletion of details that are related to different instances of the same master entity type, where the masters may be in different locations)

10.6.2 Option 2 - Robustness Analysis

We have assumed that the system is loosely-coordinated.

What can head office do if it is cut off?

- Specify new car group
- Withdraw car group
  - but there isn't much point

- Change rental rate
  - but branches will not know - could broadcast on EMail and have a local update

- Suspend a customer
- Reinstate a customer
  - but branches will not know - could telephone the branches and have a local update

- Customer Comment

What can head office not do if it is cut off?

- Analyse car movements by branch
- Open a branch
- Notify branch it is to close
- Remove a branch
- Analyse car group usage
- Obtain customer history
- Remove, say, 1000 customers
  - volumes too big to be practical for EMail broadcast

- Open a service depot
- Close a service depot

What can a service depot not do if head office is cut off?

- Open
- Close

What can a branch not do if head office is cut off?

- Check whether a customer new to it is already known within EU-Rent
  - and whether they are currently suspended
- Know about customer suspension/reinstatement
- Let other branches know of customer change of address
- Hear from other branches of customer change of address

What can a service depot do if it is cut off?

- Schedule maintenance work
  - but cannot obtain maintenance histories for cars
- Remove old service entries

- Cancel maintenance booking
  - but time is still reserved in branch database; could phone or EMail

What can a service depot not do if it is cut off?

- Obtain maintenance history of cars to be serviced

- Take booking for maintenance
  - cannot check if car is available on possible dates
- Know about maintenance bookings cancelled by branch
  - could be informed by phone or EMail
- Copy maintenance history data into branch aspect of service
- Close

What can head office not do if a service depot is cut off?

- Close the depot

What can a branch not do if its service depot is cut off?

- Take booking for maintenance
  - cannot check depot capacity
- Let service depot know about cancelled service bookings

What can a branch do if it is cut off?

- Cancel Transfer
  - but cannot let receiving branch know - could phone or EMail
- Purchase Car
- Sell Car
- Write Off Car

- Take Reservation
- Walk-in Rental
  - for return to this branch, but cannot check if new customer is already known to system, and if so, whether they are suspended
- Cancel Reservation
- Book Car
- Customer Pick-up

- Return from Rental
  - if rental is from this branch
- Transfer Delivery
- Return from Service
- Check Late Returns
  - but will not know about returns to other branches.

What can a branch not do if it is cut off?

- Let other branches know about changes of customer address
- Know about changes of customer address from other branches
- Know about customer suspension/reinstatement
- Know about cars returned to other branches
- Know about transfers from other branches that have been cancelled
- Return from Rental

Chapter 10
SSADM extensions applied to EU-Rent

- if rental is not from this branch (ie in real world can accept car, but cannot process event until able to communicate with renting branch).

- Take Reservation
- Walk-in Rental
  - for return to other branch
- Transfer Pick-up
  - cannot switch responsibility of ownership to receiving branch
- Book Service
  - cannot find out depot capacity on possible dates

What can other branches not do if a branch is cut off?

- Let the off-line branch know about changes of customer address
- Know about changes of customer address from the off-line branch

- Arrange Transfer

- Take Reservation

- Walk-in Rental
  - for delivery/return to the off-line branch

- Return from Rental
  - from the cut-off branch (ie in real world can accept car, but cannot process event until able to communicate with the off-line branch).

- Transfer Pick-up
  - cannot switch responsibility of ownership to cut-off branch

What can head office not do if a branch is cut off?

- Decide to close it
- Remove it
- Obtain movements history, car group history and customer history from it

What can a service depot not do if one of its branches is cut off?

- Obtain maintenance history of cars of the off-line branch

- Take booking for maintenance for car of the off-line branch
  - cannot check if car is available on possible dates

- Know about maintenance bookings cancelled by the branch
  - could be informed by phone or EMail

- Copy maintenance history data into branch aspect of service.

10.7 Option 3 - Partially Clustered Option

From the 'most-distributed' option we can develop more-clustered options. One possibility is to cluster data processing at high-throughput business locations. In EU-Rent we could make city branches serve garage and hotel branches. The effects of this would be:

- less expensive hardware and software at 700 garage and hotel branches

- more storage required at 200 city branches

- higher communications volume (and cost) and less robustness.

A minor change to the branch LDM is required, to show that some (city) branches provide data processing services to other (hotel and garage) branches, as shown in Figure 10.38.

Chapter 10
SSADM extensions applied to EU-Ren-

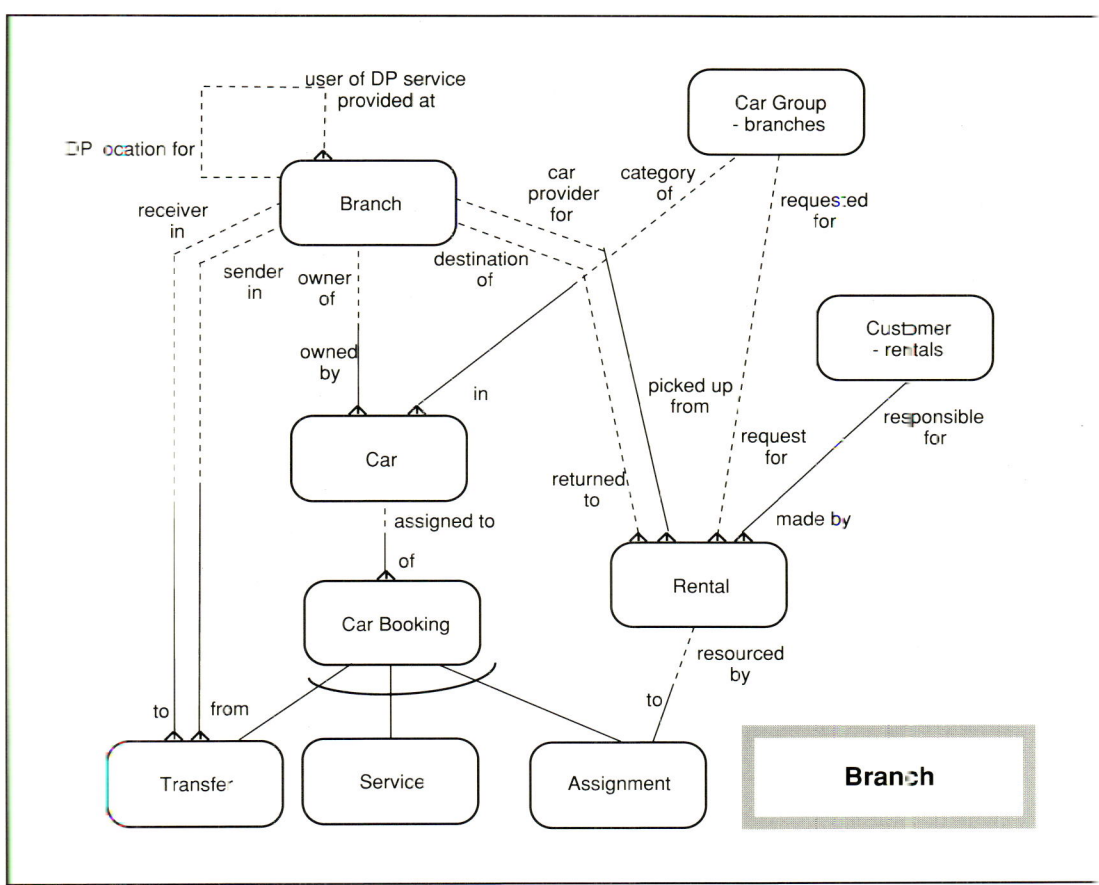

Figure 10.38: Branch Data Model for partially clustered option

This could be modelled more precisely with Branch subtypes as in Figure 10.39.

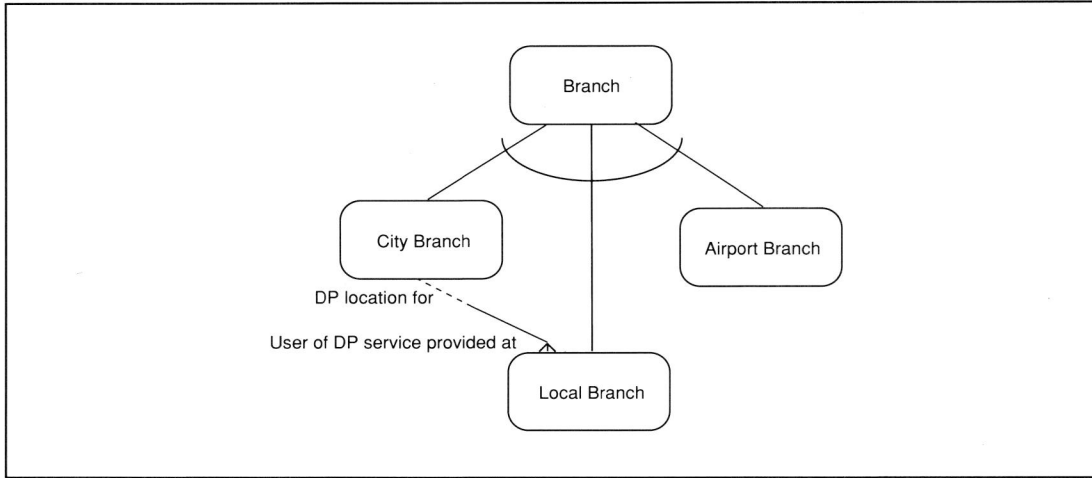

Figure 10.39: Branch subtypes

However, we shall not complicate the LDM with this extension. Whether or not the extension is shown on the LDM, some changes to the branch ELH will be needed: for example, when a city branch closes, the local branches it serves must be switched to other city branches.

Two points to note are:

- although the change is driven by implementation issues - cost and robustness - it has an impact on the business and should be shown on the LDM. If this design is selected, EU-Rent will have to allocate local branches to city branches, and users will need to take account of the relationships between branches

- we have assumed that each branch will be separately allocated to a service depot; ie that a local branch does not necessarily use the same service depot as the city branch that provides its DP services. In practice, if EU-Rent were assigning local branches to city branches, use of the same service depot might well be one of the criteria.

LDMs for service depot and head office are unchanged.

Chapter 10
SSADM extensions applied to EU-Rent

Communication Map The communication map developed for option 1 needs to be extended to show communication between the two types of branch as shown in Figure 10.40.

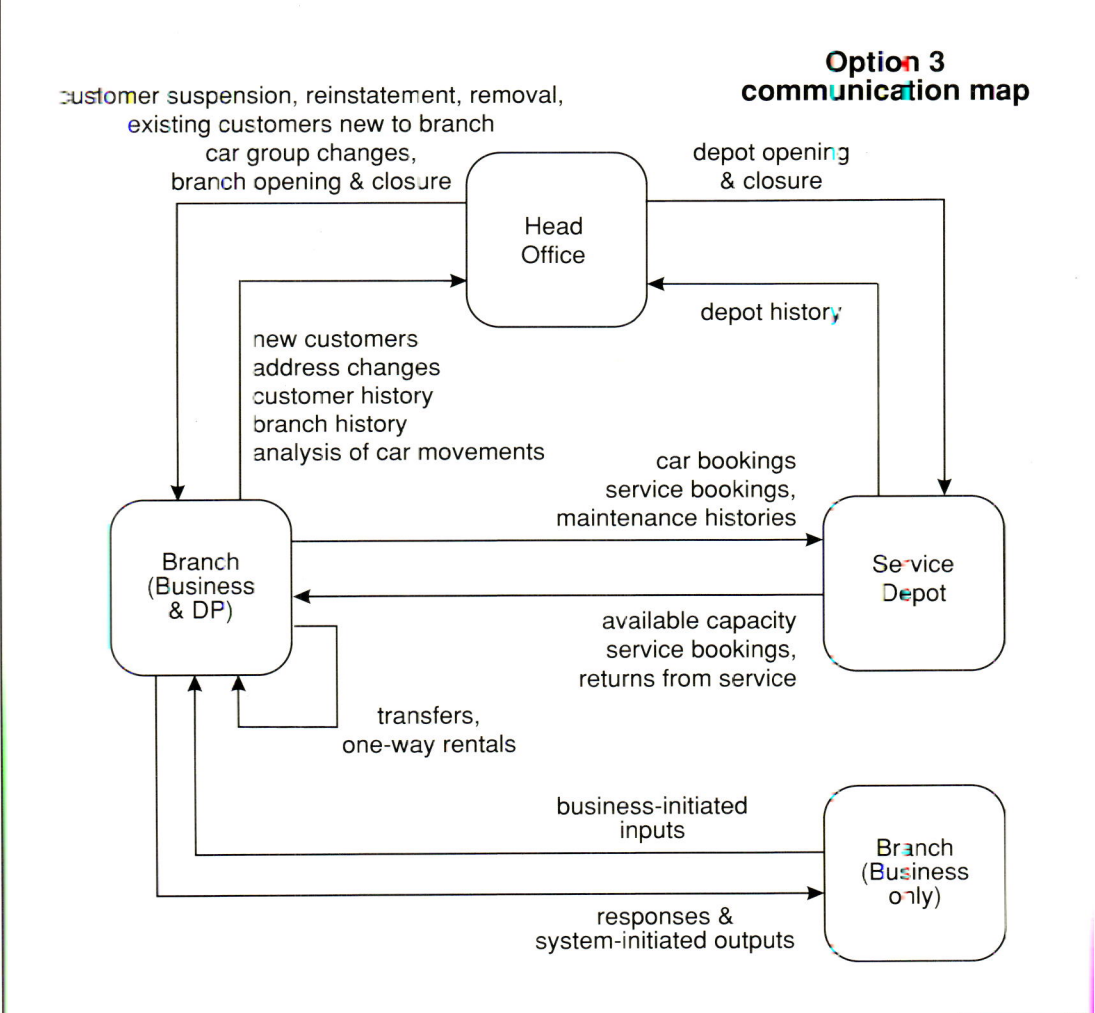

Figure 10.40: Communication map for partially clustered option

Summarise of communication between locations

The summary of communication developed in step 8 of the first-cut distribution rules has to be updated.

Each city branch (currently handling 750 bookings per week) will provide support for, on average, 3.5 garage and hotel branches (each handling 165 bookings per week).

Weekly load for each of 200 city branches
 = 750 + 165 x 3.5
 = 1,328 bookings

Weekly load for each of 100 airport branches
 = 1,344 bookings

Figures 10.41 to 10.44 show the volumes of communication traffic involved.

Aspect	Event/enquiry	No per week
Customer (copied down to say, 2 branches)	Customer approval Customer disapproval Customer history Customer removal	50 50 1 5,000
Customer - rentals	Reservation (new customer) Reservation (existing customer, new to branch) Reservation (change of address)	5,000 1,000 2,000
Car Group (copied down to 300 branches)	Group withdrawal Rate change Specification of Group	< 1 < 1 < 1
Service	Service booking Service cancellation	16,000 2,000
Service - service days	Car Maintenance History Return from service	14,000 14,000

Figure 10.41: Coordination of aspects (events/enquiries that affect both aspects of split entities)

Entity	Event/enquiry	No. per week
Car	Transfer Pick-up	450

Figure 10.42: Movable entities (entities moved from one location to another, assuming that 50% of movements are between branches served by the same DP location)

Entity	Event/enquiry	No per week
Branch (assumes that 25% of rentals for return to different branch are between branches served by the same DP location)	Reservation (different branch) Rental Cancellation (different branch) Walk-In Rental (different branch)	30,000 3,000 1,500
Branch (assumes that 50% of transfers are between branches served by the same DP location)	Transfer booking Transfer cancellation	500 50

Figure 10.43: Multiple relationships between master and detail (Creation/swapping/deletion of details that are related to different instances of the same master entity type, where the masters may be in different locations)

Function	No per week
Serving branch manager	
Cancel Transfer	300
Cancel Booking for Maintenance	300
Cars Returned to Other Branches	2,000
Purchase Car	600
Record Agreement for Transfer	300
Sell Car	600
Take Booking for Maintenance	2,400
Write Off Car	150
Serving booking clerk	
Book Car (batch output, 700 local branches, 6 days per week)	4,200
Cancel Reservation	12,000
Customer Pick-up	115,000
Check Late Returns (700 local branches, 6 days per week)	4,200
Return from Rental	115,000
Return from Service	4,000
Service Pick-up	4,000
Take Reservation	120,000
Transfer Delivery	300
Transfer Pick-up	300
Walk-In Rental	6,000
These numbers assume that local branches generate 30% of traffic, based on:	
100 airport branches with 1,344 rental per week	134,400
200 city branches with 750 rentals per week	150,000
700 local branches with 165 rentals per week	115,000

Figure 10.44: Access from local branches to data processing locations (city branches)

10.7.1 Option 3: Robustness Analysis

Head Office - as for option 2.

Service Depot - as for option 2.

City Branch - as for option 2, plus:
if city branch is cut off, its local branches (average 3.5) cannot do anything that requires DP support.

Local Branch - If a local branch is cut off it cannot access DP support directly.

However, if its city branch is running DP services the local branch could communicate by phone and fax (or EMail) and have transactions submitted at the city branch.

Variants on Option 3

Option 3a: Batch interface between local and city branches

With the exception of walk-in rentals (< 2 per local branch per day) and arranging transfers of car (< 1 per local branch per two weeks), local branches and city branches could communicate by exchanging batches of input and output. This would reduce communication costs with some loss of functionality. Batch sizes would be small. See Figure 10.45.

Function	No. per local branch per day
Serving branch manager	
Cancel Transfer	0.1
Cancel Booking for Maintenance	0.1
Cars Returned to Other Branches	0.5
Purchase Car	0.2
Sell Car	0.2
Take Booking for Maintenance	0.6
Write Off Car	0.1
Serving booking clerk	
Book Car (batch output, 700 local branches, 6 days per week)	1
Cancel Reservation	3
Customer Pick-up	29
Check Late Returns (700 local branches, 6 days per week)	1
Return from Rental	29
Return from Service	1
Service Pick-up	1
Take Reservation	30
Transfer Delivery	0.1
Transfer Pick-up	0.1

Figure 10.45: Modified volumes for batch interface between local and city branches

The main impact on business activity is that suspended customers would not be refused rentals when they made reservations, but rather when the batch response was returned, early the following day.

With small batch sizes such as these, shipping the transactions and responses via EMail should be evaluated as an alternative to installing communications software at local branches (provided that workarounds can be found for walk-in rentals and transfers).

Option 3b: Storing branch aspect of customer at head office

Customer-rentals, the branch aspect of customer, is modelled separately from the head office aspect. In option 2 customer-rentals is replicated at each branch where the customer is active (assumed 3 per customer). In option 3 customer-rentals is replicated at each DP branch (ie airport and city branch) where the customer is active (assumed 2 per customer).

Logical specifications are very little changed by this kind of change of data location placement. For example, in Figure 10.46, the partitioning of the ECD for reservation is shown, assuming that customer-rentals is stored at branch.

Chapter 10
SSADM extensions applied to EU-Rent

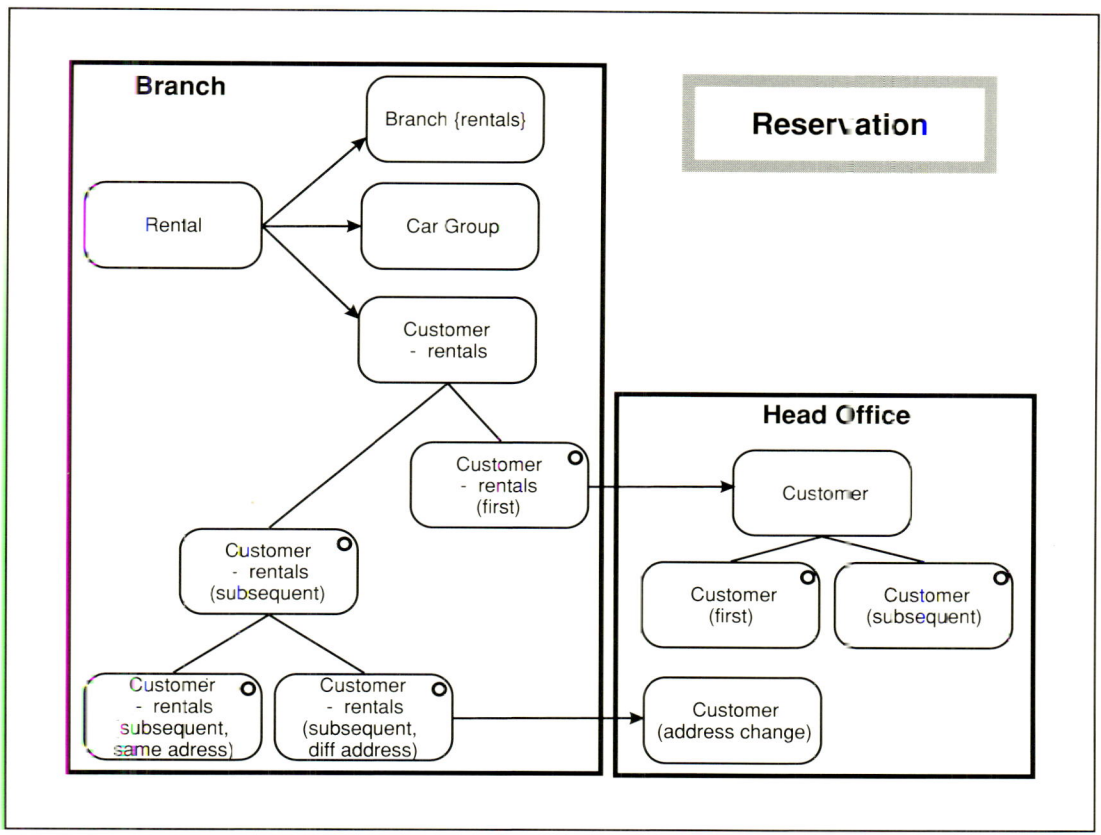

Figure 10.46: Reservation ECD - Customer-rentals stored at branch

If customer-rentals were stored at head office the ECD would have the same structure but would be partitioned differently as in Figure 10.47.

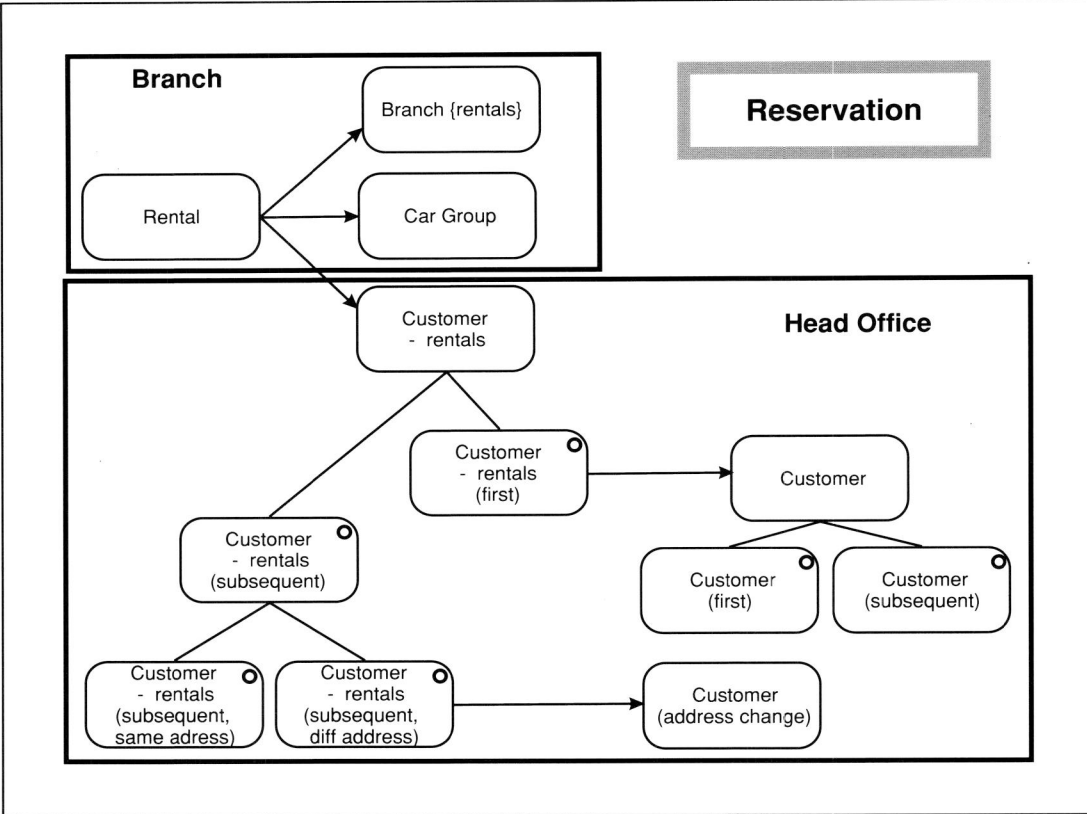

Figure 10.47: Reservation ECD - Customer-rentals stored at head office

The effects of this would be:

- customer-rentals would not be replicated: this would save data storage, and remove the requirement to distribute address changes and suspension status to branches

- communications would increase: every reference to customer would require access to head office. With customer-rentals at branch only customers who are new to branch or have changed their addresses require access to head office

- robustness of branches will be reduced: any functions requiring customer data will not be available at any branch if head office is cut off from the network

- branch databases will be less stable, since referential integrity between rental and customer will be maintained across separate locations.

These effects would probably mean that this option would not be taken forward. However, it does illustrate that logical specifications of both data and processing are fairly robust under changes of data placement.

10.8 Option Sizing & Costing

The purpose of option sizing and costing is to:

- investigate peak volumes of dominant transactions

- enable comparison of costs of options.

10.8.1 Peak Volume Analysis

This analysis is only carried out for the events car rental booking, customer car pick-up and customer car return since they overwhelmingly dominate the performance of the system. The fact that not all car bookings result in rentals is ignored in this analysis, for simplicity.

There are three types of branches:

branches in major airports

There are 100 such branches. They stay open 16 hours per days, 7 days per week. Business is spread uniformly across the day. The average number of rentals per airport branch per week is 1,344. See Figures 10.48 and 10.51.

branches in major cities

There are 200 such branches. They stay open 11 hours per day, 6 days per week. Nearly all pick-ups take place between 8 am and 11 am. Nearly all returns take place between 4 pm and 7 pm. Bookings are spread evenly through the day. The average number of rentals per major branch per week is 750. See Figures 10.49 and 10.52.

branches in local agencies such as hotels or garages

There are 700 such branches. Their transactions follow the same usage pattern as major city branches. The average number of rentals per hotel or garage branch per week is 165. See Figures 10.50 and 10.53.

The total volumes in the system by transaction type are shown in Figure 10.54.

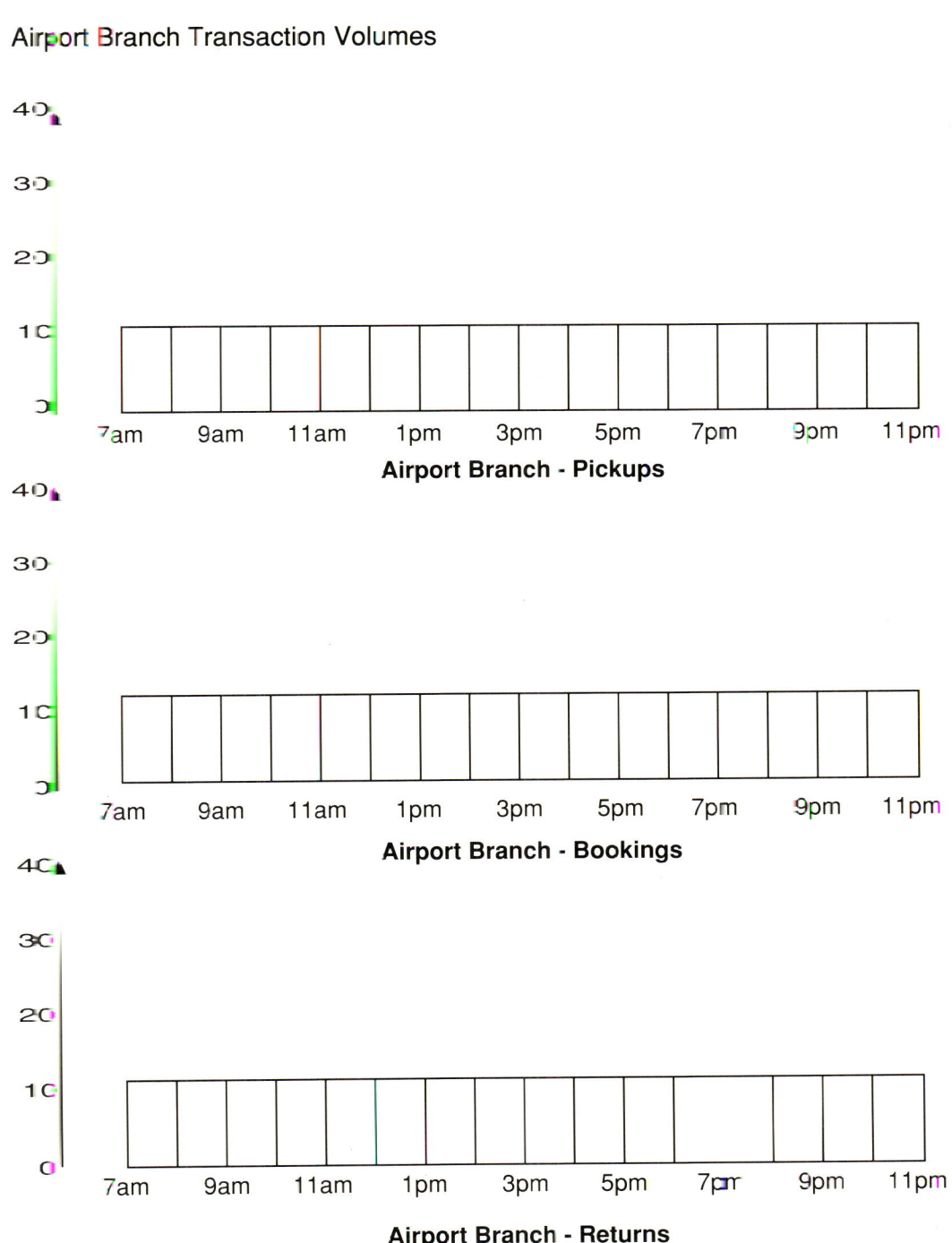

Figure 10.48: Airport branch transaction volumes

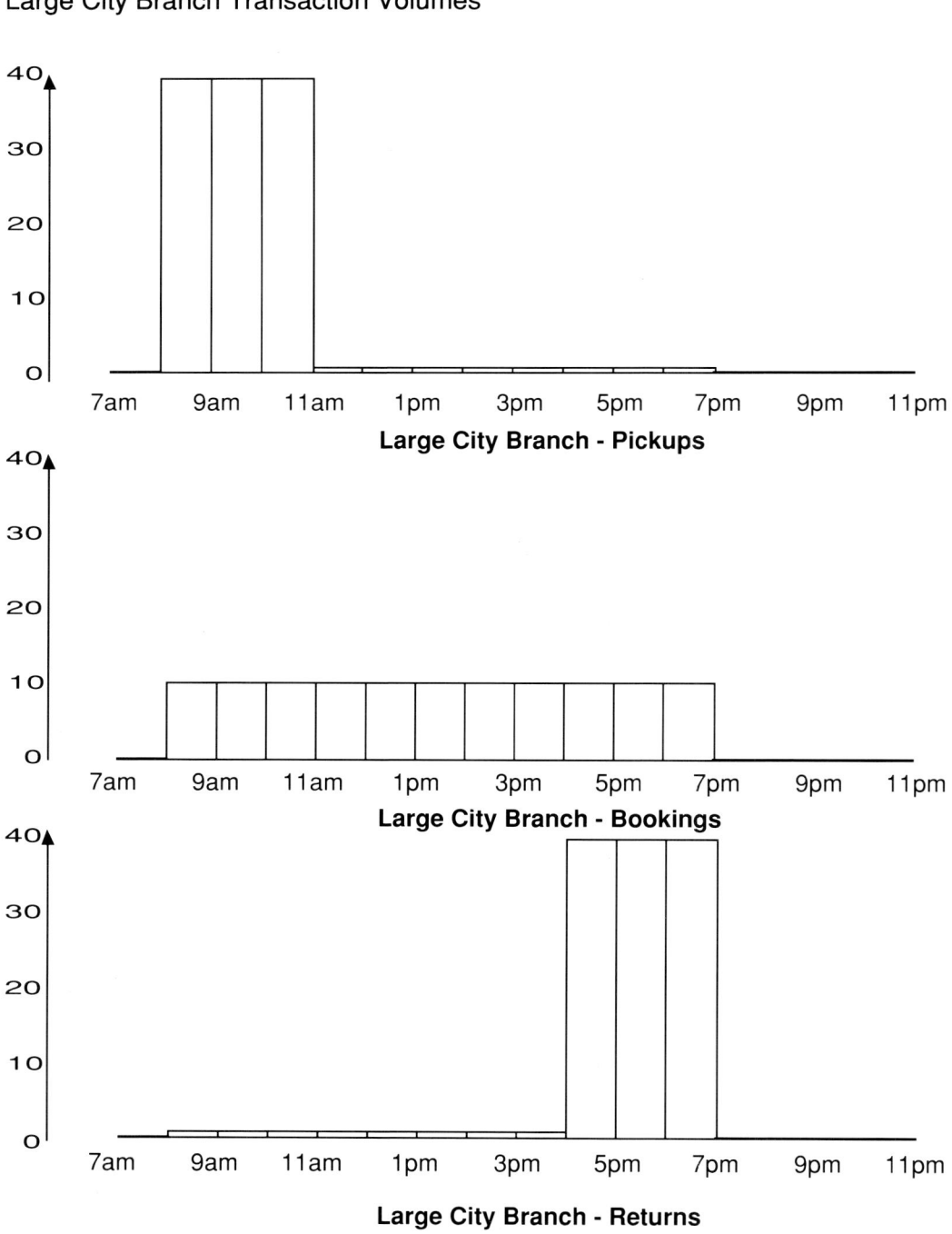

Figure 10.49: Large city branch transaction volumes

Garage (or Hotel) Branch Transaction Volumes

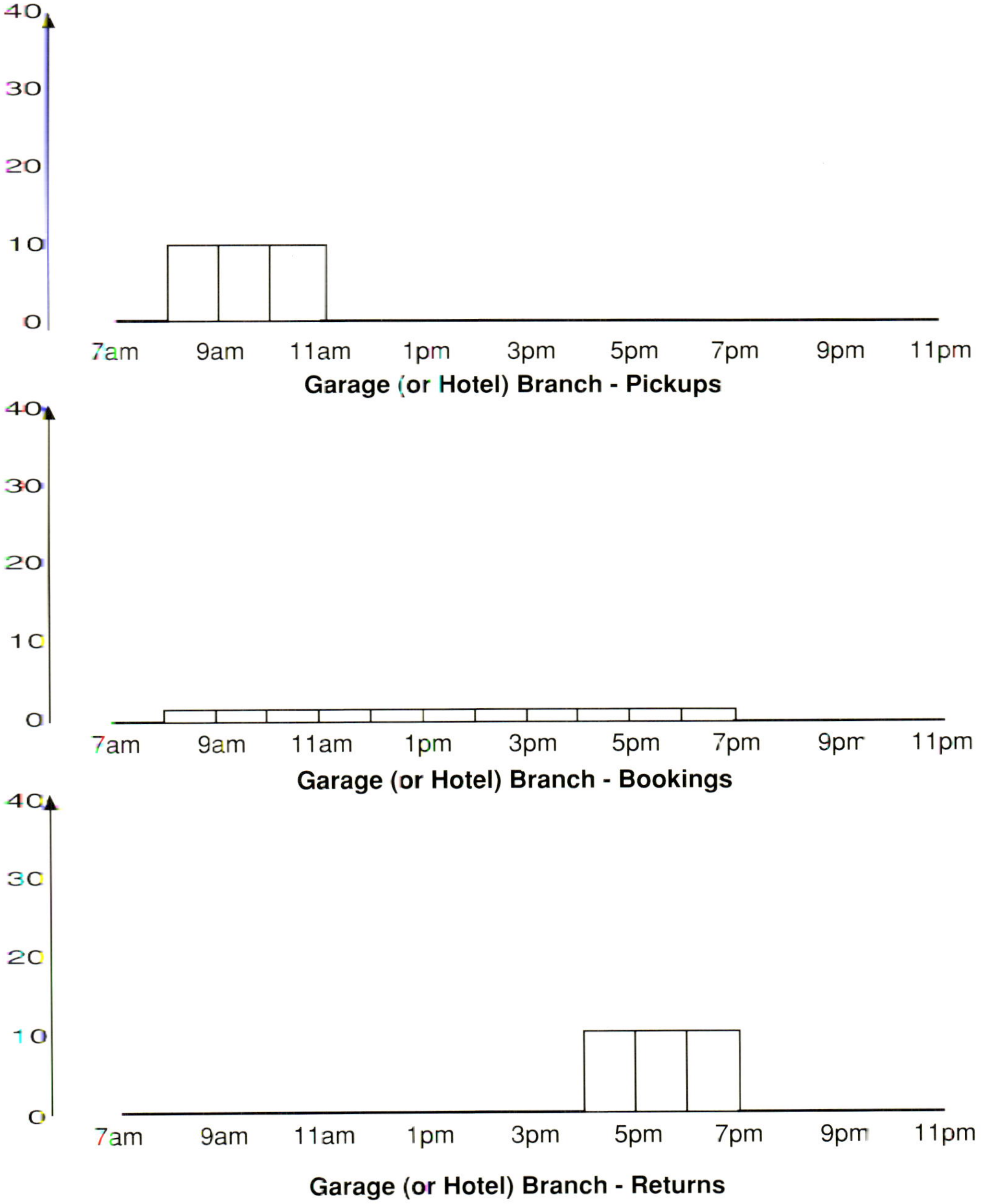

Garage (or Hotel) Branch - Pickups

Garage (or Hotel) Branch - Bookings

Garage (or Hotel) Branch - Returns

Figure 10.50: Garage (or hotel) transaction volumes

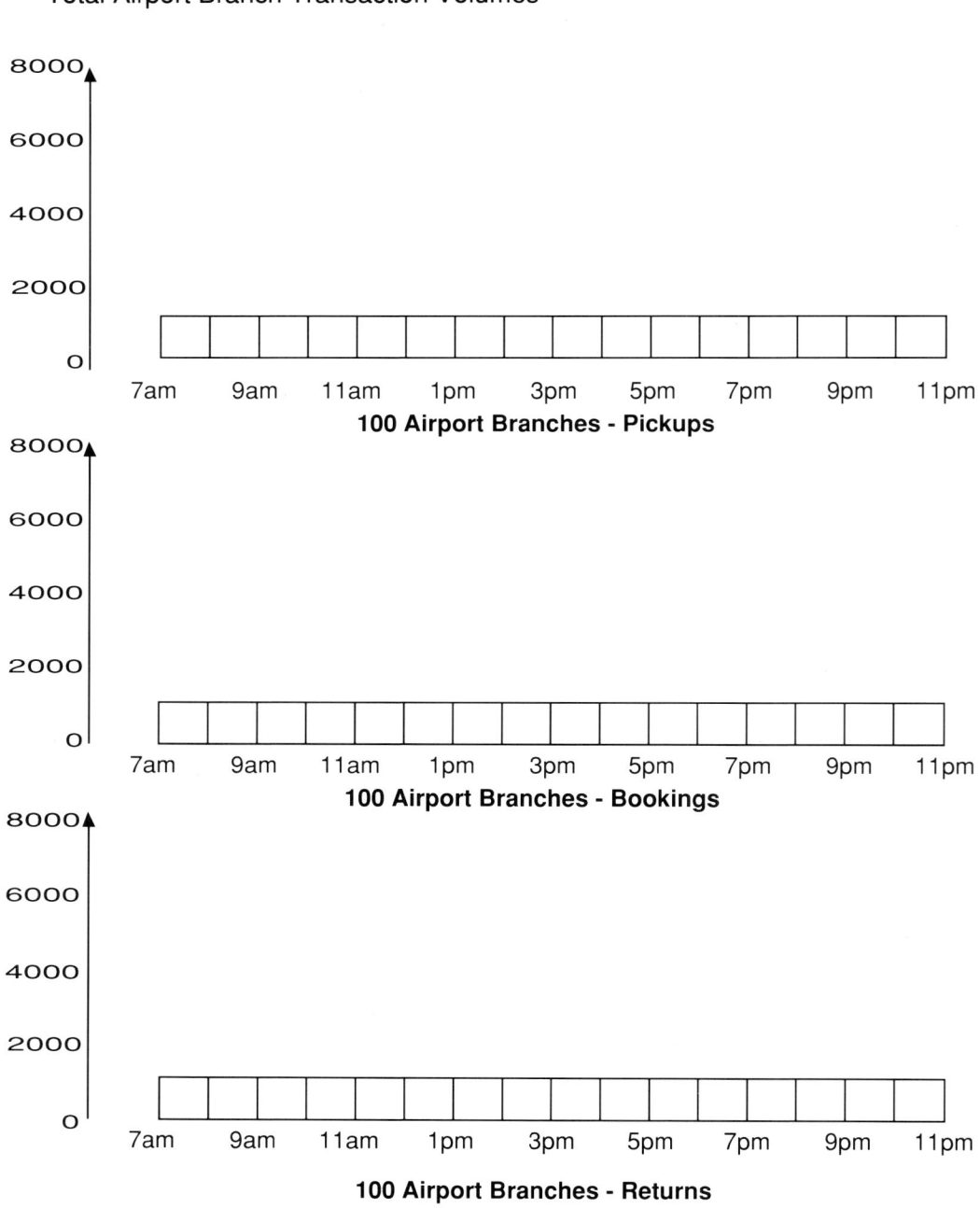

Figure 10.51: Total airport branch transaction volumes

Chapter 10
SSADM extensions applied to EU-Rent

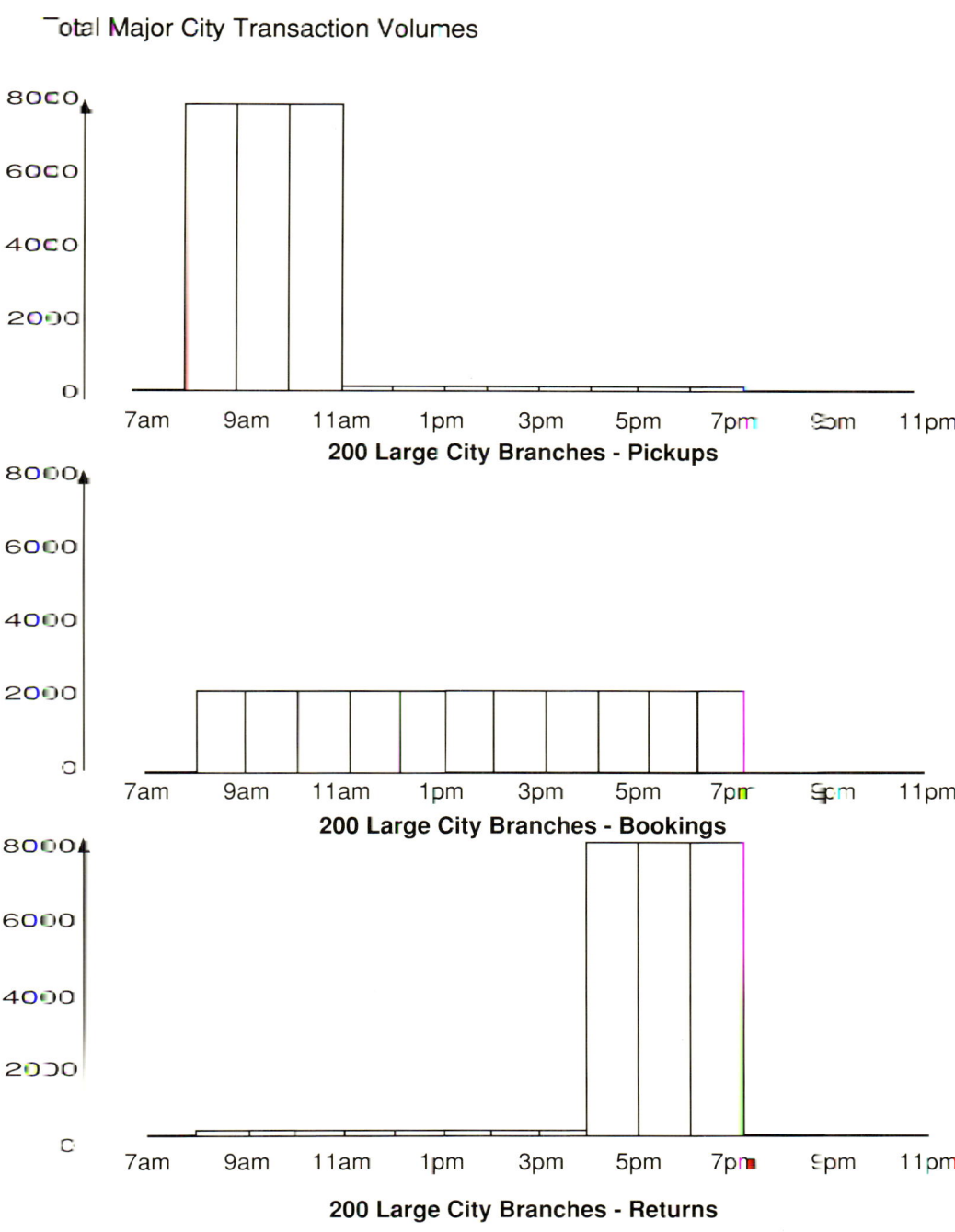

Figure 10.52: Total major city transaction volumes

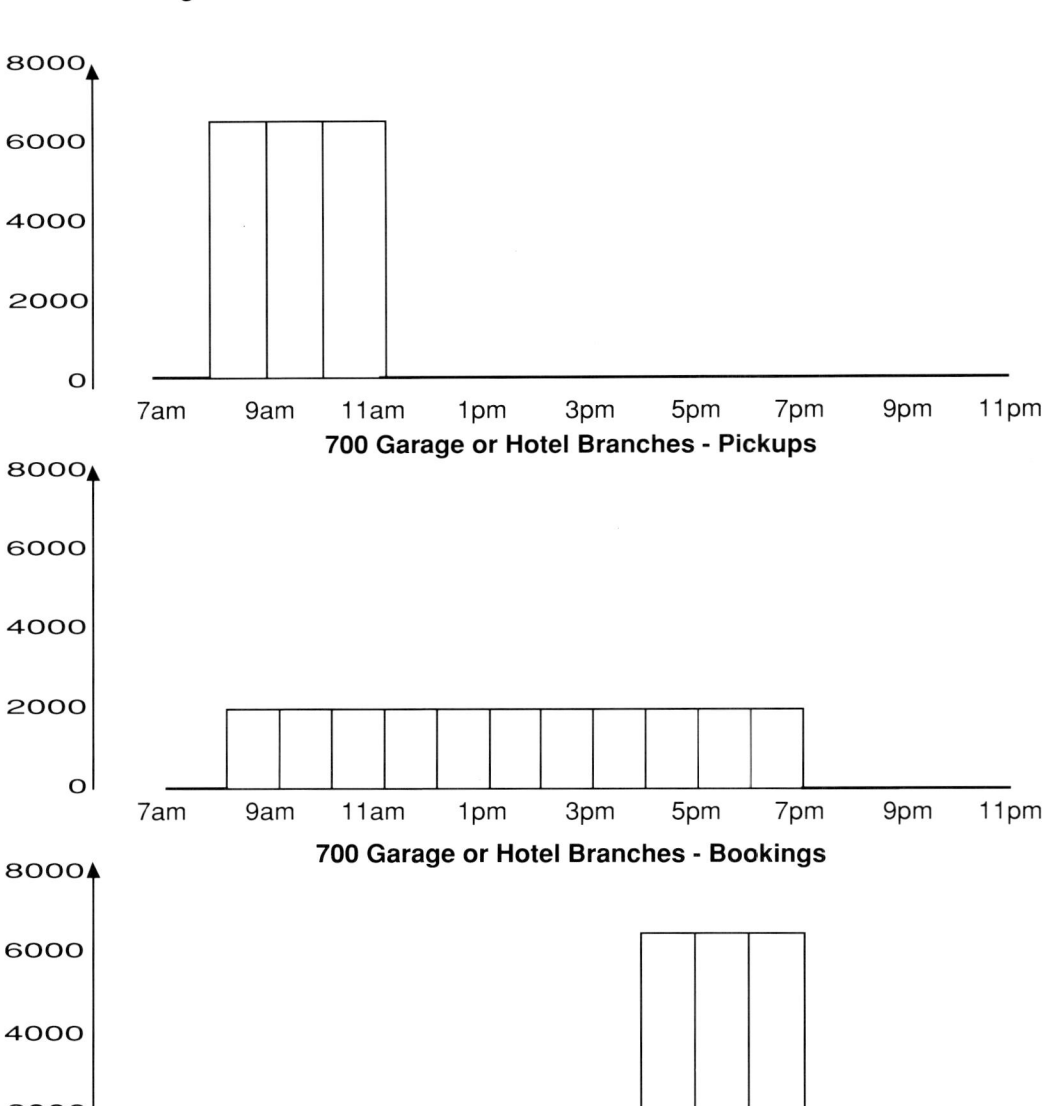

Figure 10.53: Total garage and hotel transaction volumes

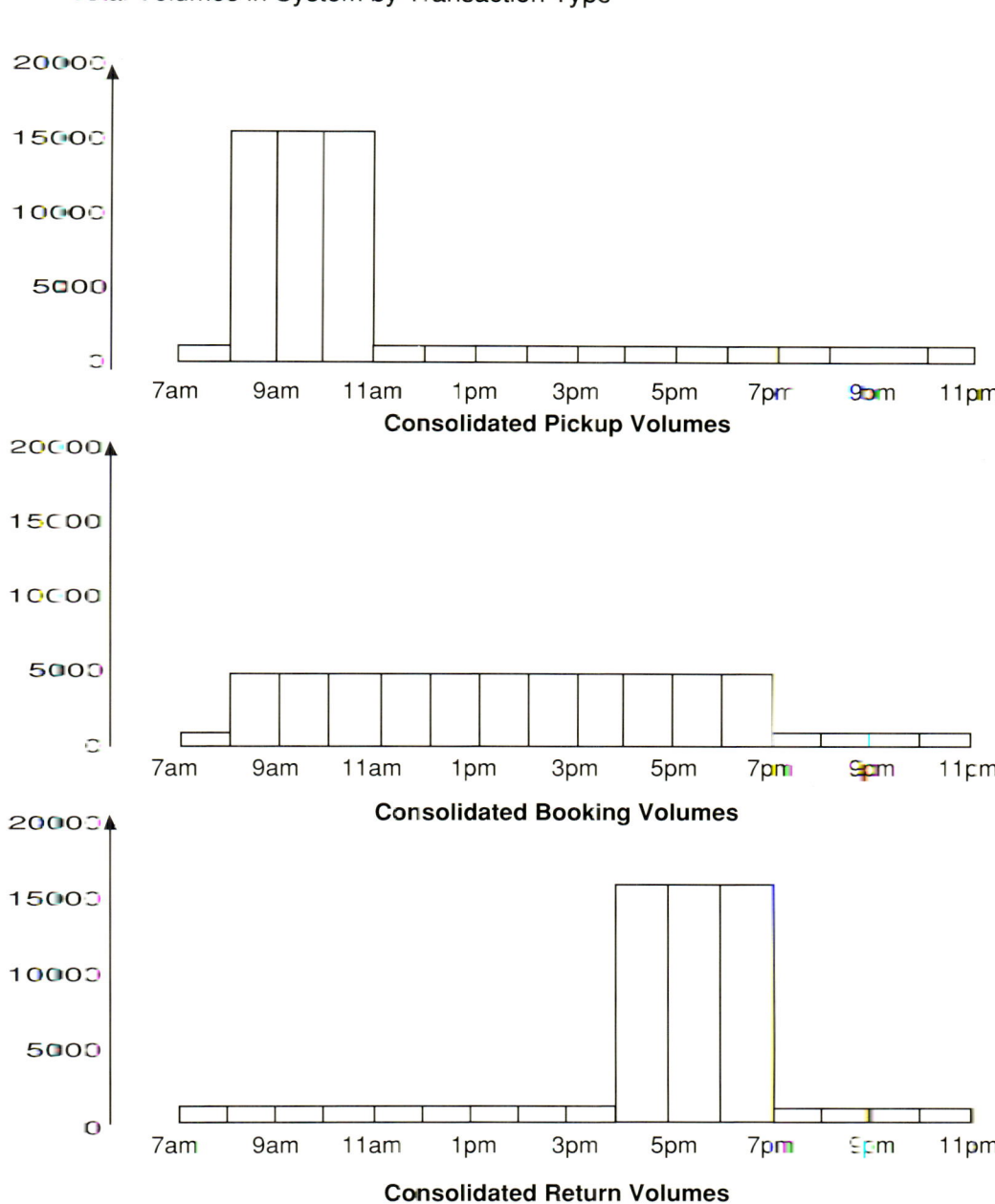

Figure 10.54. *Total volumes in system by transaction type*

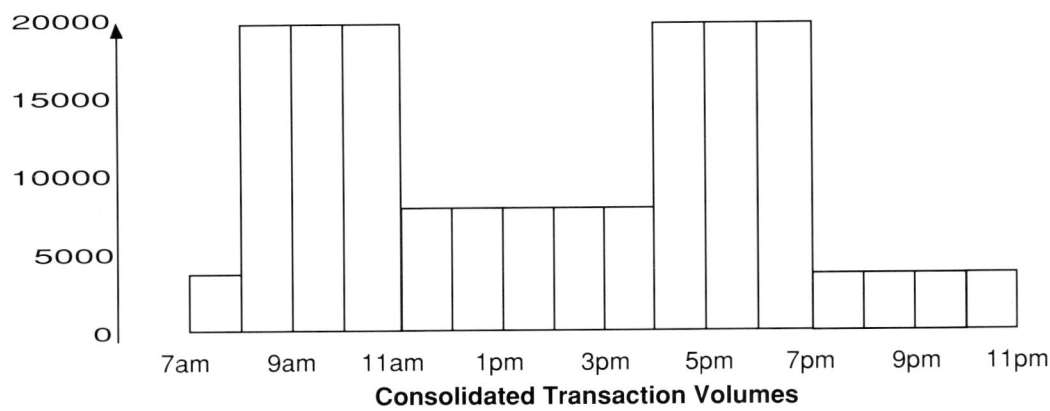

Figure 10.55: *Consolidated transaction volumes*

10.8.2 Centralisation versus Distribution

Finally, we provide some very rough costings of options.

Common Local Costs

We assume:

	Total Workstations
airport branches have 5 workstations (4 clerks, 1 manager)	500
major city branches have 7 workstations (6 clerks, 1 manager)	1,400
hotel or garage branches have 1.2 workstations	840
service depots have 1 workstation	400

Each workstation is a low cost personal computer plus an impact printer, say £1,000.

Total local workstation costs: £3,140,000.

Centralisation Costs

Telephone Connections:

400 x 50 x 1000 = 20,000,000 Bookings
400 x 50 x 1000 = 20,000,000 Pick-ups
400 x 50 x 1000 = 20,000,000 Returns

but of these 1,344 x 50 x 100 = 6,720,000 airport branch bookings are walk-ins where the booking and pick-up can be accomplished on the same telephone call.

Therefore there are approximately 53,000,000 connections per year.

We have assumed that a connection charge, independent of distance or duration across Europe is 5 pence.

Connection charges under this assumption are therefore £2,650,000 per annum.

The central hardware has to support a peak of about 21,000 transactions per hour, or 6 per second. The transactions aren't very complex: about 2 to 4 i/os. It's not obvious that this needs anything like mainframe power. Since connection charges seem likely to dominate mid to low end mainframe costs we haven't done any real capacity planning, but central hardware costs could be expected to be in the region of:

£220,000 low-end mainframe.
£30,000 disc drive
£50,000 for line controllers

totalling say £300,000 centrally.

Distribution costs (with no local copies of customer information)

Pick-ups can be handled without any telephone connection. This saves 20,000,000 - 6,720,000 = 13,280,000 connections per year = £664,000 per annum.

Transaction volumes are fairly light at each branch. Peak volumes in the major city branches are about 40 transactions per hour. The local personal computers seem quite capable of handling this load. The biggest amount of data for the average branch is 100 cars (say 1,000 bytes per car), 10,000 bookings (say 100 bytes per booking) and 50,000 booking days (say 20 bytes per booking day) = 2,100,000. The largest branches are about three times this size, say 7,000,000 bytes. This could easily be stored at a single workstation.

We might need about £200 for each of about 2,000 workstations (excluding service depots and garage and hotel branches with only one workstation) for local networking and extra memory, say £400,000.

Distribution costs (with local copies of customer information)

We will consider three variants of this option. For each of these, pick-ups can again be handled without any telephone connections, thus leaving a total of 46,720,000 connections per year for bookings, pick-ups and returns.

Local copies of all customer information, real-time updating

There are 5,000 customer removals every week (and by implication 5,000 rental bookings per week cause the creation of new customers, if the customer population is stable over time). If each customer change has to be broadcast to 1,000 sites this will result in 10,000,000 telephone calls per week, costing £500,000 per week, or £25,000,000 per annum.

This option saves nearly all of the remaining 46,720,000 calls per annum for bookings, pick-ups and returns.

Local copies of all customer information, batch updating

There are 5,000 customer removals every week (and by implication 5,000 rental bookings per week cause the creation of new customers, if the customer population is stable over time). If updating is done once per week to 1,000 sites this will result in 1,000 short duration telephone calls per week uploading data costing £50 per week, or £2,500 per annum, and 1,000 30 minute duration calls (say 100 bytes x 5,000 at 250 cps) download at, say, £1 per minute costing £1,000 per week or £50,000 per annum.

This option saves nearly all of the remaining 46,720,000 calls per annum for bookings, pick-ups and returns.

The option will cause some minor operating problems in the rare event that a new customer rents a car from more than one branch twice in a week.

Reinstatements and disapprovals could be transmitted in real time. Again there is a minor problem of what to do with a disapproval for a customer whose details haven't arrived yet.

Local copies of reinstatements and disapprovals only

Locally, we would keep locally only a data store of bad customers. Connection charges for this are negligible. However this option doesn't save the remaining 46,720,000 calls per annum because the customer entities are being connected to and disconnected from their booking entities on rental booking and car return. This raises the question of what the utility is of the implementation of these connections and disconnections. Essentially, they allow the implementation of a capability of navigating from customer to booking without broadcasting to the whole network. If we don't care about this, we can drop the connection and disconnection, saving 46,720,000 telephone connections, and improving system robustness.

A Meta model of distribution concepts

A.1 Meta modelling notation

This section describes in outline the notation used in the meta model (see Figure A.5).

Figure A.1: Entities 'A' and 'B' connected by a typical relationship

Entities are objects or concepts, either concrete or abstract, which are of interest in the domain being modelled. See Figure A.1. Relationships between entities are described from the perspective of both the entities they connect. See Figures A.2 and A.3.

Figure A.2: An occurrence of entity A *may* be related to *one or more* occurrences of entity B

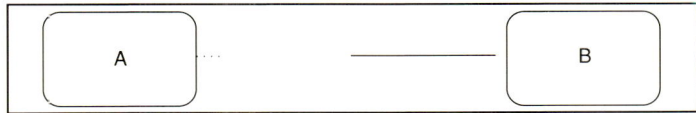

Figure A.3: An occurrence of entity B *must* be related to *one and only one* occurrence of entity A

An exclusion arc is placed across relationships where only one of the relationships between entity occurrences can exist at a time. See Figure A.4.

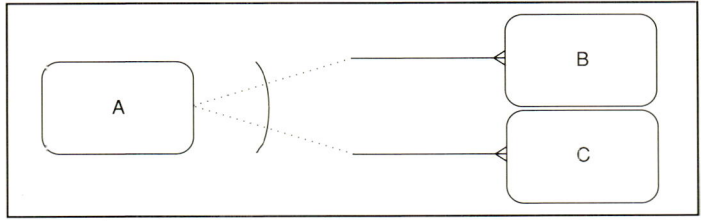

Figure A.4: An occurrence of entity A *may* be related to occurrences of either entity B or entity C but not both

A.2 Meta model of distribution concepts

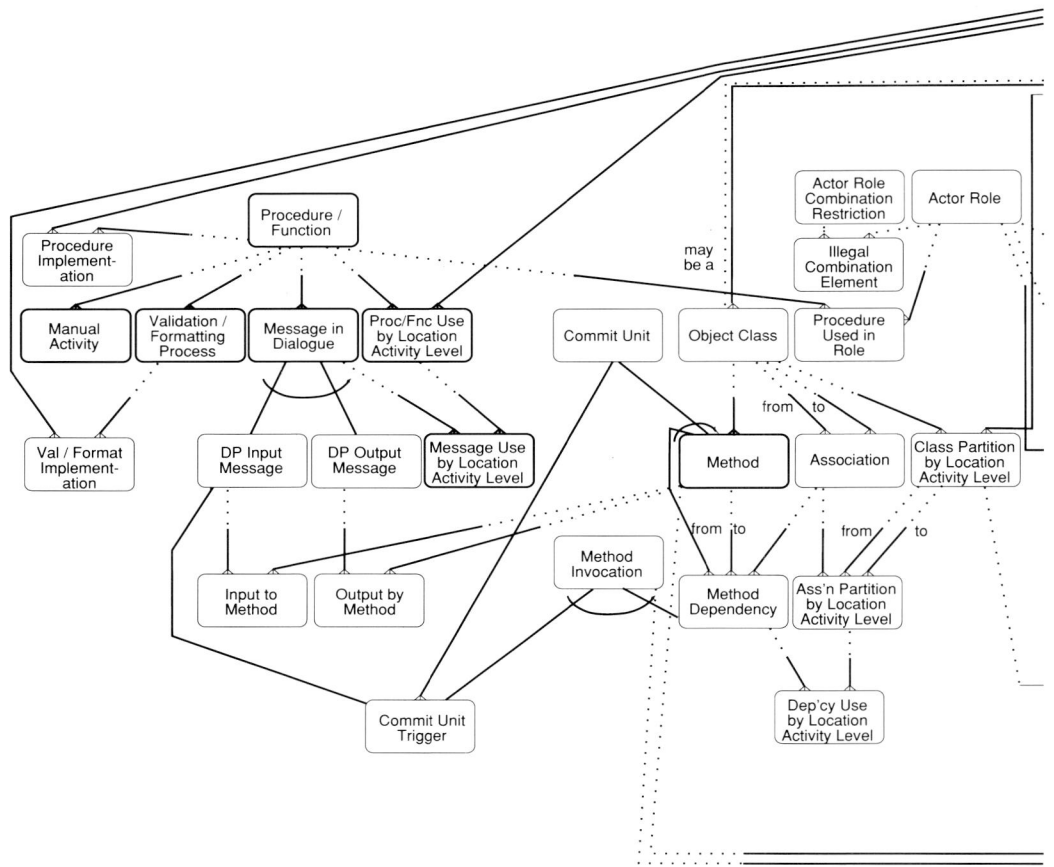

Figure A.5: Meta model of distribution concepts

Annex A
Meta model of distribution concepts

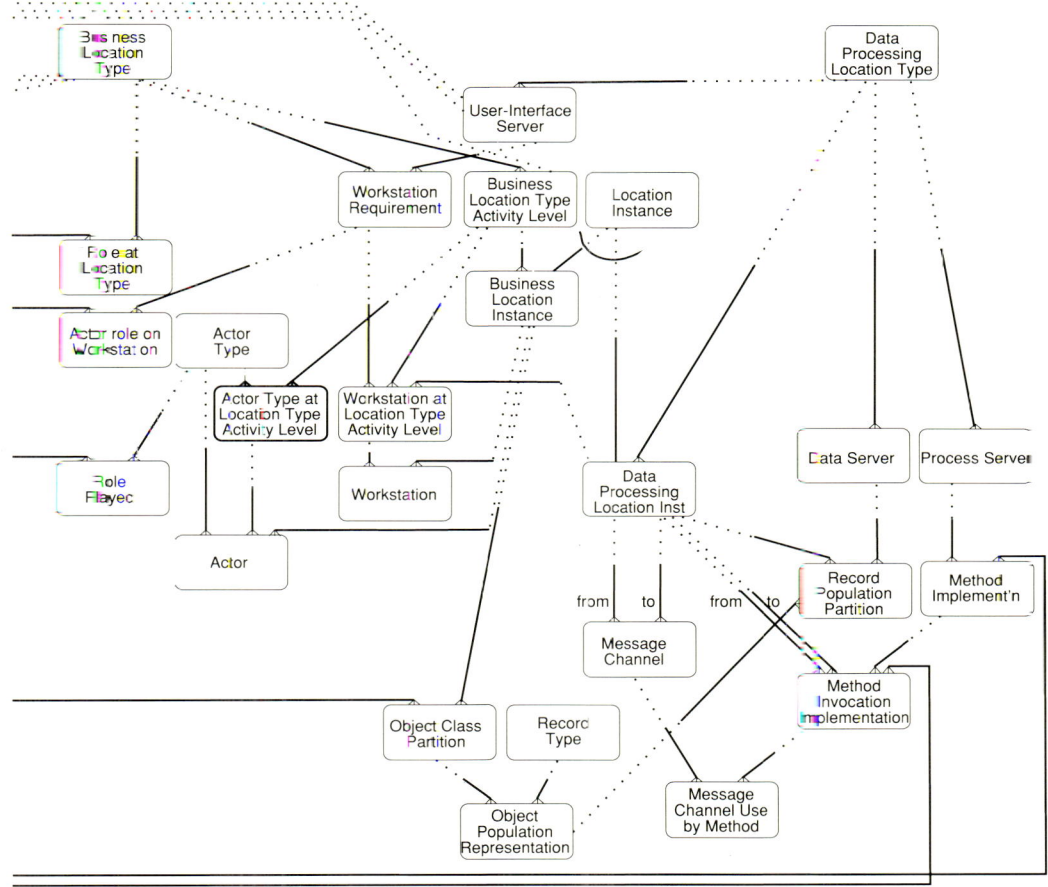

Annex B
Checklist for cost estimation

B Checklist for cost estimation

This annex contains a checklist of subjects for which system costs should be considered when costing a distributed system. Note that this list is not necessarily complete for all business or technical environments; neither will all the items on the list necessarily be relevant for all environments. There are a variety of options for supporting the operation and maintenance of distributed systems. Hence, there are some significant decisions to be taken when deciding upon a strategy for supporting a distributed system.

The costs are considered in three categories:

- costs per location
- inter-location communication costs
- support infrastructure costs.

Note that in particular costs of support and communication will vary according to the need for these services at different location types or even individual locations.

B.1 Costs per location

These costs apply to each location.

B.1.1 Initial costs

Hardware

Hardware includes both primary processor(s), storage and output facilities and local communications equipment.

Note that hardware could be either leased or purchased. Database management software may require additional storage devices for data security. Additional devices may be required for taking local backups if backups are not taken over the network.

385

Software	Proprietary software may be leased or purchased outright. Although proprietary software is usually costed on a 'per installation' basis, vendors often provide significant discounts for multiple licence usage.

Development and testing of bespoke software are generally costed as for a centralised system, but with the additional costs of performance and resilience testing. |
| Environment | Includes the acquisition and conversion of accommodation; air conditioning and if necessary conversion for a clean environment (although the latter is becoming less necessary as technology changes).

Environmental costs also include the provision of clean, smooth, uninterruptible power supplies and the installation of local communications facilities (wiring etc). This can be disruptive and expensive when the installation is in existing work areas. |
| Support | Support needs are likely to vary with the complexity of software being supported and the predicted impact on the business if problems are encountered during the system's operation. Typically however, the installation of sophisticated database or communication systems requires specialist support. A typical support provision is one support person per 50 - 100 users, depending on the sophistication of the end users and the variety and complexity of the software and systems involved.

Support options include:

- dedicated, trained, local support personnel

- initial support provided by a suitably trained on-site person backed-up by a central help desk and later mobile support staff. Such local support would probably not involve additional staff at the location but would involve changes to job descriptions

- some method of providing service monitoring and support remotely over the communications facility. |

Annex B
Checklist for cost estimation

To be effective such support generally requires wide band communications.

Distributing, installing and upgrading database and other system software usually requires tape (or increasingly CD-ROM) reading capability. Options are:

- to provide such hardware locally

- to provide such hardware when required from a pool (this may cause problems if several systems need to be installed or upgraded in a short time period, for example to keep DBMS versions in step)

- to have available sufficient communication bandwidth to down-load system software from a central location.

Additional on-site spare equipment may be required for resilience if front-line support is undertaken in-house.

Software installation — Installation of sophisticated software over a number of sites is likely to require phasing in over a period of time to reduce the demand for skilled installation staff.

Training — Decisions must be taken on whether to undertake user and local support staff training on-site or at a central location and whether the training should be undertaken internally or part or all of it contracted out.

On-site training may require the provision (and maintenance) of local training databases. Internal training may require specialised training facilities, comparable to those facilities that will be used during the operation of the system.

B.1.2 Recurrent costs

Depreciation — Depreciation on computer equipment should be according to the normal business rules for the organisation. Technical advances in computers mean

387

| | | that the effective life of a PC or workstation is around 5 years. After that time, upgrading, if possible, is not cost effective. |

Hardware maintenance   Contracted-out maintenance, at least for distant sites, may be a cheaper option than in-house provision.

Software maintenance   Software vendors usually publish price lists for support and upgrades. The per-site cost for this vendor-supplied support can frequently be reduced where multiple sites are involved or if the licensee agrees to channel support calls to the software vendor through a single contact point.

Local support   Local support includes staff and office costs of person(s) providing local support.

Operations   Includes costs associated with the use and operation of the system at a location, including power, consumables and user personnel.

There may be extra costs associated with system security. If local backups are taken, then there should be a provision for maintaining off-site copies.

B.2 Inter-location communication costs

Inter-location communication costs are those associated with communications infrastructure. Many of the costs depend on whether bandwidth is purchased from a value-added network service supplier or whether dedicated lines are installed. Dedicated communications are usually only cost effective when very high bandwidth is required or the distances involved are relatively short.

B.2.1 Initial costs

Unless dedicated lines are to be installed, initial costs (other than those associated with location specific wiring and communications hardware), are likely to be small, although there may be some initial licensing fees from the network service provider. Indeed, some network

Annex B
Checklist for cost estimation

providers require that certain interface hardware is provided by themselves. This is to facilitate tracing of network problems.

Where dedicated lines are to be installed then this is a major project in its own right, involving significant support implications. However, immediate costs include the purchase and installation of cabling or other media, together with any intermediate switches, routers and repeaters.

Some solutions may involve a mixture of dedicated and leased lines, depending on the traffic requirements.

B.22 Recurrent costs

For dedicated lines, support costs are recurrent.

In the case of leased lines, costs depend on many factors, including: amount of data transferred, distance between start and finish locations, time of transfer, required bandwidth and the required level of service availability. Because of the complexity in determining the applicable tariffs, cost estimation should be undertaken with the help of the network services supplier.

B.3 Support infrastructure costs

Support infrastructure is the provision of specialist support services to back up the local support provision. Generally, there will be a need for central help-desk provision. If on-site support is not contracted out for remote locations, then there will be a requirement for mobile support services. The organisation of mobile support services depends on the geographic area to be covered and not all locations or location types will necessarily be supported in the same way. Typically, if a large geographic area is to be covered by mobile support staff then these support staff are likely to be dispersed throughout the areas, probably based at the larger and more important locations.

In general, the larger and more complex the software involved, the more formal the support infrastructure will need to be. Systems distributed over few nodes and involving simple software will probably find relatively simple support arrangements satisfactory.

B.3.1 Initial costs

Initial costs of support infrastructure include:

- help-desk support

- recruitment and training of support personnel

- hardware and software comparable to that used at typical locations

- acquisition of telephone and general office equipment and other office set-up costs

- software for recording or tracking support calls

- mobile support

- transport (leased or purchased cars)

- test equipment and tools

- personal communications (portable telephones etc) for support personnel

- working spares inventory.

B.3.2 Recurrent costs

Recurrent costs include:

- help desk

- personnel

- consumables

- equipment rentals

- mobile support

- transport and communication costs

- consumables and replacement of spares

- depreciation on transport, tools and spares.

Bibliography

American National Standards Institute (ANSI)	'The ANSI/X3/SPARC DBMS Framework: Report of the Study Group on Data Base Management Systems.', edited by D.C. Tsischritzis and A. Klug, Information Systems 3 (1978).
CCTA Information Systems Engineering Library	Application Partitioning and Integration with SSADM, HMSO, 1994, ISBN 0 11 330622 9
	Reuse in SSADM using OO, HMSO, 1994, ISBN 0 11 330621 0
	SSADM and Client/Server Applications, HMSO, 1994, ISBN 0 11 330624 5
	Database Language SQL Explained, HMSO, 1993, ISBN 0 11 330583 4
CCTA IT Infrastructure Library	Management of Local Processes and Terminals, HMSO, 1992, ISBN 0 11 330550 8
	Network Services Management, HMSO, 1994, ISBN 0 11 330558 3
CCTA Information Management (IM) Library	Electronic Data Interchange in Government: The Business Opportunities, HMSO, 1994, ISBN 0 946683 73 5

ISE, IT Infrastructure and IM Library Volumes are available from:

HMSO Publications Centre
(Mail, fax and telephone orders only)
PO Box 276
London
SW8 5DT

Telephone orders from outside UK +44 171 873 9090
(from within UK 0171 873 9090)
General enquiries from outside UK +44 171 873 0011
(from within UK 0171 873 0011)
(queuing system in operation for both numbers).

	Alternatively, they may be purchased from HMSO Bookshops, HMSO's Accredited Agents and through good booksellers.
Consultative Committee on International Telephony and Telegraphy (CCITT)	X.25 Recommendations (1984) Wide Area Networks. (Now adopted as an ISO standard).
	X.400 Recommendations (1988) Message Handling System and Service Overview. (Now adopted as an ISO standard).
EMSC	The BOS Engineering Method, Version 1, 1993, EMSC Report.
	BOS Engineering Method reference manual, 1993, EMSC
	GRAPES - Language Description, edited by G. Held, Munich 1991
	GRAPES BM - Language Description, internal EMSC report, 1993
	GRAPES OO - Sprachdefinition, SNI, Munich, 1991
	Representation of work products, internal EMSC report, 1993.
Euromethod	Euromethod Delivery Planning Guide, Deliverable 2.3, EM-2.3-DPG, 1994, Euromethod Project
	Euromethod Concepts Manual 2 Deliverable Model, Deliverable 3.2, EM-3.2-DM, 1994, Euromethod Project
	Euromethod, CCTA IS Notice 71, 1994.
International Organization for Standardization (ISO)	ISO/IEC 9735:1990 Electronic data interchange for administration, commerce and transport (EDIFACT)
	ISO/IEC 10026-1: Information technology - Open Systems Interconnection - Distributed Transaction Processing (DTP) - Part 1: OSI TP Model, 15. Dec. 1992
	ISO/IEC 9579 - 1 Remote Database Access (RDA) - Part 1, Generic model, service and protocol

Bibliography

	ISO/IEC 9579 - 2 Remote Database Access - Part 2, SQL specialisation
	Information on ISO/IEC standards is generally available from national standards organisations. For example, in the UK contact British Standards Insitution (BSI) Publications, Linford Wood, Milton Keynes, MK14 6LE. Tel: 01908 221166.
Joint CCTA / EMSC publication	'SSADM & GRAPES: Two Complementary Major European Methodologies for Information Systems Engineering', edited by R. Duschl and N. C. Hopkins, 1992, Springer-Verlag, ISBN 3-540-55380-0
Object Management Group	Common Object Request Broker Architecture, (CORBA), OMG, Jan. 1992
SSADM	The SSADM V4 Reference Manuals (ISBN 1 85554 004 5) are published in the UK by NCC Blackwell Ltd and are available from The Publications Manager, National Computer Centre Ltd, Oxford Road, Manchester M1 7ED.
	An information pack on SSADM is available from the International SSADM Users Group (ISUG): tel: +44 1959 534337 (01959 534337 from within UK) and fax: +44 1959 534184 (01959 534184 from within UK).
	'Quits and Resumes on Entity Life Histories: A Comparison of Alternative Approaches', ISUG Technical Committee, 1993. This paper is available from the ISUG on the same numbers as above.
UK Government Open Systems Interconnection Profiles (GOSIP)	GOSIP Open Distributed Transaction Processing Subprofile, CCTA.
X/Open	Preliminary Specification: Remote Procedure Call, Oct. 93 (CAE Specification due during 4th quarter '94)
	Distributed Computing Services (XDCS) Framework, Nov. 1992
	Preliminary Specification: Distributed Transaction Processing (DTP): The XATMI Specification, Dec. 1992

CAE Specification: SQL Remote Database Access, Aug. 1993

X/Open Snapshot: Distributed Transaction Processing: The Peer-to-Peer Specification, Jan. 1993

X/Open publications are available from X/Open Company Ltd., Apex Plaza, Forbury Rd., Reading, Berkshire RG21 1AX. UK tel: 01734 508311

Glossary

All entries in the glossary are followed by a letter in brackets indicating the primary context in which the definition is meant to be applicable:

    i   method independent guidance
   m   meta model.

BOS Engineering Method and SSADM terms have been omitted as these are defined in the respective manuals.

3-schema Specification Architecture (i)
A framework for IT system specification and implementation, in which the IS services needed to support business activities are defined in a **conceptual model**. The mappings from the conceptual model to specific user organisations and implementation technologies are defined in an **external design** and an **internal design**.

Actor (m)
An Actor may be a human, a User and a DDP System, or in rare cases a DDP System only that carries out a task in an enterprise at a Business Location Instance.

Each Actor is uniquely assigned to a Business Location Instance. Humans who work at several Business Location Instances are treated as several Actors, each of which can be assigned uniquely to a Business Location Instance.

Actor Role (m)
An Actor Role is a set of Procedures, Functions which satisfy a set of closely related business tasks. Groups of tasks common to more than one job are amalgamated into single Actor Roles.

Actor Role on Workstation (m)
Assignment of an Actor Role to a Workstation to satisfy a Workstation Requirement.

Actor Type (m) An Actor Type is a classification of Actors according to the Actor Roles they undertake. The sets of Actor Roles of different Actor Types may overlap, ie, Actors of different Actor Types may have some Actor Roles in common.

Sometimes there are restrictions that prevent the combination of Actor Roles in the same Actor Type, such as where job descriptions support audit breaks or where legal constraints exist.

Actor Type at Location Type Activity Level (m) The number of Actors of a given Actor Type assigned to a Business Location Type Activity Level.

ANSI (i) American National Standards Institute.

AVIS (i) The car rental company with which the EU-Rent case study was verified.

architecture (i) The structure of the system software components that provide basic services to applications. This usage of 'architecture' is distinct as from the usage in the 3-schema Specification Architecture.

aspect (i) An application's view of a real-world entity type, which models part of the behaviour of the entity type. What is usually called 'an entity' on an logical data model is really an aspect, since it represents only a partial view of the real-world entity type. In most cases a real-world entity type has only one logical data model aspect; there is no confusion in referring to 'logical data model entities'. Aspects have to be distinguished only when there are multiple views of the same entity type that have to be coordinated in some way.

Association (m) A relationship type between two Object Classes (or one Object Class and itself). All relationship instances have to conform to their relationship type.

Association Partition by Location Activity Level (m) The number of Associations relative to a Business Location Type Activity Level.

Glossary

	The Association Partition by Location Activity Level depends on the Class Partition by Location Activity Level.
attribute (i)	A descriptive property of an **object class** or **entity** that can take different values. The values of the attribute can vary both with the instance of the object class or entity under consideration and with the time at which the instance is considered.
BOS (i)	A joint initiative for the development of trans-European information systems between Bull, Clivetti and Siemens Nixdorf.
BOS Engineering Method (i)	Version 1 of BOS Engineering Method was developed in parallel with this volume by the **EMSC** from DOMINO/GRAPES (Siemens Nixdorf), OMEGA (a variant of Merise from Bull) and MOiS (Olivetti).
business event (i)	An event that triggers business activities or procedures.
Business Location Instance (m)	A Location Instance at which business takes place and at which Actors carry out their jobs through Procedures/Functions. In general, human Actors require the services of a DDP System.
	The services of a DDP System (ie automated Procedures/Functions and Data) are provided at a Business Location Instance by a set of Workstations.
	Where the business taking place at certain Location Instances is negligible from a business point of view (eg just forwarding documents), it is often natural to treat these Location Instances together with a more dominant Business Location Instance as one.
Business Location Type (m)	A classification of Business Location Instances according to the Actor Roles undertaken at the Location Instances.
	The Actor Roles assigned to a Business Location Type indirectly specify the set of Procedures/Functions and Data that are needed at Business Location Instances.

	Each Business Location Type has a set of Workstation Requirements that result from the Actor Roles that make up this Business Location Type.
Business Location Type Activity Level (m)	A set of Business Location Instances with the same activity profile. An activity profile is defined by the frequency of Procedure/Function use, the number of Object Instances and the number of associated Actors.
business process view (BPV) (i)	A Euromethod term which describes a model of real-world business activities.
business reengineering (i)	The process of changing the way business is done.
CAE (i)	Common Applications Environment.
CASE (i)	Computer Assisted Software Engineering.
CCITT (i)	Consultative Committee for International Telephone and Telegraphy.
CCTA (i)	The Government Centre for Information Systems (UK).
CD-ROM (i)	Compact disc - read only memory.
centralised system (i)	A system with a single database, which is contained together with all conceptual processes at a one location. There may be workstations at other locations, but these would only have external processes and working data storage.
class (i)	See **Object Class**.
class hierarchy (i)	An object-oriented term for a hierarchy of Object Classes in which subtypes inherit the methods and attributes of their supertypes.
class instance (i)	See **Object Instance**.
Class Partition by Location Activity Level (m)	The number of Object Instances of a given Object Class belonging to a Business Location Type Activity Level.

Glossary

client/server service (i)	A service providing **process location transparency**, possibly for **commit unit** components to high-level structures of commit units.
client/server platform (i)	A platform providing a client/server service to an application.
client (i)	A client requests services from a **server**.
Commit Unit (m)	A set of Methods to be executed in accordance with the ACID properties:

- **a**tomic. Either all the Methods in the Commit Unit are executed or the Commit Unit is not executed at all

- **c**onsistency preserving. A Commit Unit either brings all the affected Objects into a new valid state or the states of the Objects are reset to the previous state if the Commit Unit is cancelled. (The resetting of states is sometimes referred to as 'rollback')

- **i**solated. During the execution of a Commit Unit the state changes imposed on Objects are not visible to other Commit Units. Only if a Commit Unit is completed successfully is its impact on the Object states transparent to other Commit Units

- **d**urable. The changes made by a successfully completed Commit Unit are not lost because of system breakdowns.

In a conventional database environment a Commit Unit corresponds to a transaction.

Each Commit Unit has a start Method, that is the Method invoked by a Commit Unit Trigger. A Commit Unit may have a set of Commit Unit Triggers.

The set of Methods which make up a Commit Unit is defined by the start Method of the Commit Unit and all Methods on which the start Method depends, either directly or indirectly.

Commit Unit Trigger (m)	The arrival of a DP Input Message, a defined point in time or the change of the internal state of the distributed system.
	A Commit Unit Trigger starts the execution of a Commit Unit by invoking the start Method in the Commit Unit.
	We assume update and enquiry processing to be done in the form of Commit Units. Enquiries which are not Commit Units may make sense in some applications, however, the problems involved are not specific to Distributed Information Systems and thus are not considered here.
conceptual model (i)	The **conceptual schema** in the **3-schema Specification Architecture**, called a *model* to emphasise that it is a partial model of the business, developed by a process of analysis and discovery. It specifies the required IT services as: information support needed by business activities; data needed to provide it; processes needed to keep the data up to date. It also defines which business activities are to be automated. It described the services independently of the user organisation structure and the technology for implementation.
conceptual process (i)	Any process that is part of the **conceptual model**.
conceptual schema (i)	See **conceptual model**.
cooperation service (i)	A service which supports interaction and coordination between application programs. Three principal types of cooperation service are identified within this volume: information exchange services; process cooperation services and security services.
corporate aspect (i)	An aspect stored on a server that is accessible by the whole organisation.
corporate entity (i)	An entity stored on a server that is accessible by the whole organisation.
Data (m)	A representation of information in a formalised manner suitable for communication, interpretation or processing by human beings or automated means.

Glossary

data location transparency (i)	The service whereby **conceptual processes** access data, without the conceptual processes having information about where the data is located.
data model (i)	A model of a business's data including data inter-relationships.
Data Processing Input Message (m)	A set of Data entered together into a DDP System via an input device, for example either a Record entered into a screen mask by keyboard or a scanned document.
	A DP Input Message may correspond to a Commit Unit Trigger, in which case it starts the execution of a Commit Unit. There are also DP Input Messages that do not correspond to a Commit Unit Trigger, for example a note sent to the screen of another User.
Data Processing Location Instance (m)	A Location Instance at which the services of a DDP System are provided. At a DP Location Instance hardware and system software are located, Data is stored and/or Procedure/Function Implementations, Method Implementations and Val/Format Implementations are executed.
Data Processing Location Type (m)	The classification of DP Location Instances according to the capability to store Data and execute application specific processes.
	A DP Location Type is defined by its ability to act as a data server, process server and user-interface server.
	The Workstation Requirements which need to be supported by DP Location Instances can be derived from the definition of their DP Location Type. This derivation is achieved by comparing the Data and processing needed by an Actor Role against the Data and processing provided by a DP Location Type.
	A DP Location Type defines the minimal hardware and system software requirements that have to be satisfied by its DP Location Instances.
Data Processing Output Message (m)	A set of Data, such as a screen print out, sent simultaneously to an output device of the DDP System.

Data Server (m)	A data server provides access services to records stored at the associated data-processing location.
data server (i)	An implementation of the **internal design**.
DBMS (i)	Acronym for database management system.
DDBMS (i)	Acronym for distributed database management system.
dedicated lines (i)	Communication lines installed solely for the use of the organisation paying for them.
Dependency use by Location Activity Level (m)	The Dependency Use by Location Activity Level defines how often an Association Partition by Location Activity Level is used per Method execution.
dialogue (i)	The part of the external design which handles on-line input and output between the actor and the system.
distributed architecture (i)	Within this volume, used synonymously with **architecture**.
distribution concept (i)	A concept, on one of several levels of abstraction, needed to classify and record facts during the analysis and design of a distributed system.
distributed application (i)	The part of a distributed system that implements the three schemata of the **3-schema Specification Architecture**.
Distributed Data Processing System (DDP System) (m)	A set of co-ordinated Data Processing Location Instances. A DDP System provides services, ie data storage and processing, for one or more DI Systems.
Distributed Information System (DI System) (m,i)	A DI System consists of a set of co-ordinated Business Location Instances. A DI System is usually supported by a DDP System. Sometimes it may be supported by several DDP Systems.
distributed object-oriented database (i)	A service providing process location transparency to an event manager and to the smallest decompositions of commit units, methods.

Glossary

distributed system (i)	See Distributed Information System.
distribution option (i)	An option for the logical assignment of data and procedure/functions to business and data processing locations. In terms of the generic development process, the decision to select a particular distribution option is taken during agree the information system specification. The selected option may have to be reviewed and modified after cost-benefit analysis.
distributed technical platform (i)	The part of a **distributed system** that provides **services** to the **distributed application**.
ECU (i)	European Currency Unit.
EML (i)	European Modelling Language.
EMSC (i)	European Methodology and System Center.
encapsulation (i)	An object-oriented term describing the property of objects whereby the methods of an object cannot access the attributes of any other object.
entity (i)	Each detailed type of business data is known as an entity.
entity aspect (i)	See **Aspect**.
enquiry trigger (i)	The data items that must be input to the DDP system to initiate an enquiry.
EU (i)	European Union.
EU-Rent (i)	A fictitious car rental company used to illustrate the points made in this volume. EU-Rent examples are also used in Euromethod and in several CCTA ISE Library Volumes published in the UK.
	The business of EU-Rent is car rentals, but this is largely irrelevant; it merely provides an easily understood context for examples. The business issues and user requirements of EU-Rent could be easily mapped to other systems. They include:

- the requirement to deliver a range of services (rental of cars of different quality and price) at many locations (rental branches), with different volumes of business and patterns of demand

- customers who may use more than one location, but whose business with the organisation as a whole should be tracked

- a well-defined organisational identity to be presented at all locations

- strong general policies set centrally (car models that may be used, rental tariffs, procedures for dealing with customers), but significant flexibility and authority for local managers (number of cars owned by branch, authority to override published tariff to beat competitors' prices)

- performance targets for local managers

- locally-managed sharing or swapping of resources

- an internal support structure (the maintenance depots) needed to maintain the resources and ensure that the product delivered to customers is of adequate quality

- a customer base that is shared with other, separate systems (EU-Stay hotels and EU-Fly airline), and possibilities of communicating or co-ordinating with these systems.

Many of EU-Rent's characteristics are common to other types of business; for example, health care, vocational training, social security, policing, retail chain stores, branch banking etc.

EURES (i)	EURopean Employment information System.
EDIS (i)	Electronic Data Interchange for the Social domain.
Euromethod (i)	A major EU initiative to provide a public domain 'framework' for the planning, procurement and

management of services for the investigation, development or amendment of information systems.

European Modelling Language (i) An EU-funded collaboration to develop a modelling language which will allow different developers to use different development methods at each stage of the development process, but require the IS experts acting on behalf of the customer of the information system to be familiar with only the European Modelling Language.

event manager (i) A process that handles the externally-input data, breaks it down into messages used to invoke objects, and consolidates the responses into the output expected by the external design.

external design (i) The **external schema** in the **3-schema Specification Architecture**, called a design to emphasise that it is developed by a process of design and engineering - there is no 'right' answer. The external schema passes update data and enquiry triggers to the **conceptual schema**, and receives update and enquiry output in response. There could be several different external designs for a single **conceptual schema**. The external schema is defined in: procedures [derived from DFDs and Requirements Catalogue Entries (SSADM) or Business Transactions (BOS Engineering Method) and ad-hoc enquiry specifications]; dialogues (which may have been developed via prototypes) and the batch input-output system.

external schema (i) See **external design**.

file server (i) A computer, usually in a network of PCs, used for storing and backing up files accessed from other computers.

generic development process (i) The generic development process provides a framework for decisions specific to the development of distributed systems. It is derived from the customer-supplier transformation and decision point concepts produced as part of the Euromethod project. The Euromethod decision point concepts were carefully chosen to allow compatibility with the development processes of existing European methods.

geographical distribution (i)	The distribution of computers and interconnections across physical locations.
GRAPES (i)	The graphical modelling language which supports BOS Engineering Method.
graphical user interface (i)	A user interface which makes use of menus and/or graphical objects, such as icons, for selection of options and usually has a windowing capability, enabling multiple window displays on the screen at the same time.
horizontal partitioning (i)	The process of splitting a data table horizontally into record subsets. It is used for allocating record instances to different locations.
IEC (i)	International Electrotechnical Commission. IEC entered into a cooperative agreement with ISO via Joint Technical Committee 1 to jointly publish information technology standards.
inheritance (i)	An object-oriented term describing the property of Object Classes which allows subtypes in a class hierarchy to automatically take on the methods and attributes of all their supertypes, before adding methods and attributes of their own.
Input to Method (m)	An assignment of a DP Input Message to a Method.
	Only those DP Input Messages that are processed by a Method correspond to an Input to Method. Other DP Input Messages, which are processed by system software, are not Inputs to Method.
instance variable (i)	See **attribute**.
interface style guide (i)	A guide describing the style of interface between users and the system.
internal design (i)	The **internal schema** in the **3-schema Specification Architecture**, called a design to emphasise that it is developed by a process of design and engineering - there is no 'right' answer. The logical data model in the **conceptual model** is mapped on to a data storage and access technology to produce a database design. Stored

Glossary

	data is presented to implemented update and enquiry processes by a process data interface, as if it were stored in the logical data model.
internal schema (i)	See **internal design**.
IS (i)	Information System.
ISAM-file	A file that is accessed via the index sequential access method.
ISE Library (s)	CCTA's Information Systems Engineering Library.
ISO (i)	International Organization for Standardization
IT (i)	Information Technology.
IT facilities (i)	A term used in this volume to collectively describe user-interface servers, process servers and data servers.
LAN	Local Area Network.
leased lines (i)	Communication lines leased from an organisation providing telecommunications services.
Location Instance (m)	A Location Instance is a location which can be identified uniquely.
	Usually Location Instances are sites that can be identified by their position on a map, their postal address and possibly position within that address. Sometimes, however, other identifiers for Location Instances are needed, for example, in the case of a taxi company it might be adequate to treat each taxi as a Location Instance identified by the taxi number.
locking (i)	The ability of a commit unit to prevent other commit units from accessing data which it is in the process of enquiring on or updating.
logical design (i)	The part of the design of an IT system that is independent of the technology on which it will be implemented.

loosely-coordinated activities (i)	Activities which can only be temporarily inconsistent before reverting to their consistent state. Loosely-coordinated activities form a single system.
Manual Activity (m)	A part of a Procedure/Function to be carried out manually by a human Actor or User
Message Channel (m)	A Message Channel is a point to point connection between two Data Processing Location Instances that is capable of transferring messages, for example, a modem connection or a Datex-P connection.
	A Message Channel is characterised by its transmission rate and transmission cost. The utilisation of a Message Channel is an important volumetric.
Message Channel Use by Method (m)	A Message Channel Use by Method records how often a Message Channel is used for a Method Invocation at a DP Location.
Message in Dialogue (m)	Either a DP Output Message or a DP Input Message.
message passing (i)	An object-oriented term describing the way in which objects communicate with each other.
Message use by Location Activity Level (m)	The number of Messages in Dialogue per Business Location Type Activity Level.
	The Message Use by Location Activity Level depends on the number of Messages in Dialogue per Procedure/Function and on the Procedure/Function Use by Location Activity Level. The number of Messages in Dialogue per Procedure/Function is given in the Procedure/Function definition.
meta model (i)	A model of modelling concepts and the relationships between them.
Method Dependency (m)	A Method Dependency exits, if one Method is invoked because of the execution of another.
	A Method Dependency may correspond to an Association between Object Classes.

Glossary

Method Implementation (m)	Program code that implements a Method.
Method Invocation (m)	A Method Invocation is the start of the execution of a Method. This usually involves the transfer of input parameters to the invoked Method and the takeover of the control by that Method.

A Method Invocation may be caused by a Commit Unit Trigger or by another Method. In the latter case the invoked Method depends on another Method, ie, there is a Method Dependency corresponding to this Method Invocation. |
| **Method Invocation Implementation (m)** | The implementation of a Method Invocation.

For example, a Method Invocation Implementation could be a message passed by a message exchange service from one DP Location Instance to another, or it might be a set of variables, which contain the input parameters of the Method to be invoked. Another possibility is to implement a Method Invocation by either a local or remote procedure call. In these cases there need to be mechanisms that allow the invoked Method to take over control. |
| **method (object-oriented) (m)** | The first of two usages of the term method within this volume. A Method is a function on the Data of an Object. As a side effect a Method may additionally cause changes on the data of other Objects because of a Method Dependency.

Changing the Data of an Object means changing the state of the Object.

Each Method belongs to a Commit Unit. A Method may be the start Method in a Commit Unit, in which case it is invoked by a Commit Unit Trigger, or it may depend on another Method. |
| **method (systems development) (i)** | The second of two usages of the term method within this volume. It implies a systematic approach to the development of IT systems. However, methods can usually be tailored to the needs of individual organisations or projects. The ease of use of most |

	methods is greatly enhanced by the use of a suitable CASE tool.
methodology (i)	See **method (systems development)**.
middleware (i)	Software that implements the services provided to an application.
network components (i)	See **IT facilities**.
object (i)	See Object Instance.
object attribute (i)	See **attribute**.
Object Class (m)	The classification of Objects according to similarity of structure and behaviour.
	The structure of an Object Class is defined by the structure of the Data of the Objects in the Object Class.
	A set of Methods defines the behaviour of Objects of an Object Class.
	A Business Location Type may correspond to an Object Class.
	An Object Class corresponds to an entity type or a set of closely related entity types in a conventional database environment.
	An Object Class may naturally belong to a Business Location Type. However, not all Object Classes naturally belong to a Business Location Type.
Object Class Partition (m)	An Object Class Partition is a set of Object Instances from a single Object Class that belong to a Business Location Instance.
	An Object Class Partition mirrors the fact that an Object Class naturally belongs to a Business Location Type. Usually each Object Instance has an attribute that denotes the Business Location Instance to which it naturally belongs. That means all the Object Instances

	belonging to the same Business Location Instance make up an Object Class Partition.
	Other Object Class Partitions result from design decisions which define the Business Location Instance to which a set of Object Instances belong.
object database (i)	A database which stores **objects**.
Object Instance (m)	Something, whether concrete or abstract, that is important to the Distributed Information System being investigated.
	An Object has a state, a behaviour and an identity.
	Objects are represented in the Distributed Data Processing System by Data and a set of Methods which manipulate these Data.
	In the simplest case, an Object corresponds to a single entity in a conventional database environment. It may, however, correspond to several entities.
Object Population Representation (m)	Mapping of Object Class Partitions onto Record Population Partitions.
	An Object Instance in a given Object Class Partition may map on to a set of Records, each of which may be stored at a different Data Processing Location Instance, ie, belong to a different Record Population Partition.
Output by Method (m)	Assignment of DP Output Message to Method.
	Those DP Output Messages that result from application specific Methods correspond to Outputs by Method.
partitioning of data (i)	The process of splitting data tables either horizontally or vertically into subsets of the data they contain.
PC (i)	Abbreviation for personal computer.
platform (i)	See **technical platform**.

Procedure Implementation (m)	Program code that implements a Procedure. A Procedure Implementation implements the chaining of the Messages in Dialogue and Validation/Formatting Processes that are assigned to a Procedure.
Procedure Used in Role (m)	Assignment of a Procedure/Function to an Actor Role.
Procedure/Function (m)	A set of business activities that is seen as a unit from the business point of view and which is carried out by a single Actor in a relatively small time interval. From the data processing point of view, a Procedure/Function consists of a set of Manual Activities, a set of Messages in Dialogue and a set of Validation/Formatting Processes and defines their possible sequences.
Procedure/Function use by Location Activity Level (m)	The frequency of Procedure/Function use per Business Location Type Activity Level.
process location transparency (i)	The service whereby the **external design** interacts with **conceptual processes**, without the external design having information about where the conceptual processes are located.
process server (i)	An implementation of the conceptual processes.
Process Server (m)	A process server provides execution capabilities for enquiries, updates specified in methods, and commit units.
program-data interface (i)	An interface between conceptual processes and data, which allows the conceptual processes to be implemented independently of how the data is physically stored.
RAM (i)	Abbreviation for Random Access Memory, which is computer memory used for the storage and rapid access of files whilst power is switched on.
Record (m)	A tuple of attribute values that conforms to a Record Type.

Record Population Partition (m)	Set of Records of a given Record Type actually stored at a Data Processing Location Instance.
	Each Record in a Record Population Partition has to coincide with a Record Type in a Record Type Storage Capability owned by the corresponding Data Processing Location Instance.
Record Type (m)	A named tuple of attribute names.
	Each Object Class is represented by one or more Record Types. Representing one Object Class by several Record Types corresponds to vertical partitioning
	Record Types with the same structure representing different Object Classes are considered as separate Record Types. One Record Type cannot represent several Object Classes. Storing Object Instances of several Object Classes together is not considered in this volume, because this is a physical design optimisation issue.
Record Type Storage Capability (m)	Assignment of the capability to store Records of a given Record Type to a DP Location Type
relation (i)	A logical file of records in a **relational database**. A relation must have a unique key; the order of the rows and columns is not significant; each column must have a unique name; no duplicate rows are allowed. A relation is more commonly referred to as a 'table'.
relational database (i)	A database in which records and data are stored as **relations**.
relationship (i)	A relationship between **entities**.
remote data access (i)	A service providing data location transparency to the process server.
remote procedure call (i)	A service providing process location transparency to the user-interface server.
repeater (i)	Equipment in a communications network.

replicated data (i)	Data that is reproduced, usually at more than one data processing location.
robustness (i)	The extent to which an IT system can keep operating when communication links to one or more of its data processing locations are out of action.
Role at Location Type (m)	Assignment of an Actor Role to a Business Location Type.
Role Played (m)	Assignment of an Actor Role to an Actor Type.
router (i)	Equipment in a communications network.
server (i)	A server provides services to a **client**.
service (i)	Work undertaken for one IT facility or network component by another.
service architecture (i)	Emphasises the view that architectures provide different combinations of services. See also **architecture**.
service layer (i)	Layers between IT facilities or network components that provide process or data location transparency.
SNI (i)	Siemens Nixdorf Informationssysteme AG.
SQL (i)	SQL, an abbreviation for Structured Query Language, was originally a language for the access, manipulation and querying of data in relational databases. It now has a much broader role and the title of its international standard, 'Database Language SQL' reflects this broader role.
SSADM V4 (i)	The fourth version of CCTA's Structured Systems Analysis and Design Method.
switch (i)	Part of a communications network.
system architecture (i)	See **architecture**.
table (i)	See **relation**.

Glossary

technical architecture (i)	See **architecture**.
tightly-coordinated activities (i)	Activities which are always consistent with one another when viewed by an external observer, independently of where those activities are located. Tightly-coordinated activities form a single system.
tuple (i)	A row in a database **table**.
uncoordinated activities (i)	Activities which can be inconsistent more than temporarily. Uncoordinated activities do not form a single system.
update data (i)	Data to be used to update that already contained in the database.
User (m)	A human who executes a set of Procedures/Functions with the aid of a DDP System.
User-Interface Server (m)	A User-Interface server provides capabilities for presentation of data to the user (dp-output message), control and forwarding of events (dp-input message) according to the associated implementations of procedures/functions. Additionally it provides capabilities for executing implementations of validation/format processes. It is not a server in the sense of client/server.
user-interface server (i)	An implementation of the **external design**.
Validation/Format Implementation (Val/Format Implementation) (m)	Program code that implements a Validation/Formatting Process.
Validation/ Formatting Process (m)	The processing required at the user interface for validation of input, eg, syntax check, type checking and presentation of output. A typical example for a Validation/Formatting Process is the processing carried out by a Graphical User Interface.

415

vertical partitioning (i)	The process of splitting a data table vertically into aspects. It is used for storing aspects at different locations.
Workstation (m)	A set of devices that allow a User to interact with a DDP System at a Business Location Instance.

Typically a Workstation consists of a keyboard, a mouse and a screen, sometimes a printer and a scanner.

Each Workstation is connected to a Data Processing Location Instance that provides computing power.

Thus a Workstation links a Business Location Instance to a DP Location Instance. The Business Location Instance and the DP Location Instance may correspond to the same Location Instance. |
Workstation at Location Type Activity Level (m)	The number of Workstations, corresponding to a given Workstation Requirement, at a Business Location Type Activity Level.
Workstation Requirement (m)	A set of Workstations that are capable of supporting the same set of Actor Roles.
X/Open (i)	An international public limited company promoting vendor and user interests in the area of open systems.

Index

3-schema Specification Architecture 17, 29, 34, 37, 45,
   59, 96, 124, 395, 396, 400, 402, 405, 406
  3-schema processing architecture 34, 35, 56
  ANSI Sparc 3-Schema Database Architecture 29, 120
abstract services 83, 85, 86, 94, 99
  abstract cooperation services 85
ACID 69, 399
  atomic 69, 399
  consistency preserving 69, 399
  durable 69, 399
  isolated 69, 399
activity 22, 46, 55, 87, 103, 104, 129, 130
  activities 21-25, 31, 33, 34, 38, 46, 51, 62, 66, 86, 87,
     395, 397, 398, 400, 408, 412, 415
  activity level 76-81, 396-398, 402, 408, 412, 416
  activity profile 76
  parallel activity 125
actor 33, 36, 38, 54-56, 60-64, 66, 71, 72, 76, 88, 395-398,
   401, 402, 408, 412, 414, 416
  actor/business location concepts 60, 61
  actor role 62, 395, 401, 412, 414
  actor role on workstation 395
  actor type 54, 63, 76, 396, 414
  actor type at location type activity level 76, 396
application partitioning 24, 112, 113, 391
architecture 56, 83, 85, 86, 89-92, 95-99, 102, 105, 110,
   111, 114, 116, 125, 393, 395, 396
  distributed architecture 16, 402
  independence of logical design 45, 52
  service architecture 414
  technical architecture 27, 52, 54, 131, 415
aspect 47, 51, 127, 396, 400, 403
  aspects 45, 47-51, 54, 60, 83, 87, 88, 100, 127, 396, 402,
     411, 416
  aspects and inheritance 51
association 65, 78, 79, 396, 397, 402, 408
association partition by location activity level 78, 79, 396,
   397, 402
attribute 33, 66, 72, 73, 397, 406, 410, 412, 413
  attributes 32, 47-50, 81, 398, 403, 406

417

BOS Engineering Method 15, 17, 18, 21, 30, 35, 42, 47,
    52, 55, 56, 137-140, 142, 147, 167, 392, 395, 397, 405,
    406
BOS Engineering Method extensions 137
  activity 141, 143, 149, 190, 208, 214
    activities 192
    manual activity 141
  actor 140, 152
    actor role 140
    actor role on workstation 140
    actor type 140
  architecture 139, 162
    technical architecture 139, 162
  aspects 138
  business 140-157, 177, 204, 206
    business location instance 140
    business location type 140, 143, 144, 146, 149-151,
      156, 192
    business locations 143-146, 149-153, 155-157, 160,
      165, 166, 168, 190, 192, 193, 199, 200
    business transaction 144, 145, 170-173, 186, 195
    business transaction definitions 172
    Business Context Model 167
    Business Organisation Model 167, 174, 185
    Business Service Model 167, 172
  cache volumes 158, 201
  CASE 165
  central system 155, 193, 196
  centralised option 196
  cluster server 210-215
  clustering 155
  commit unit 140
    commit unit trigger 140
  communication 138, 141, 145, 148, 150, 153, 155, 160,
      163-165, 167, 188, 193, 209, 212, 215
    communication diagram 165, 167, 188
    communication requests 163-165, 193
    internal communication protocols 148, 163, 164
    throughput analysis 207, 214, 215
    traffic 152
  consistency 148
    consistency rules 149, 165
  context definition 167
  cost 209
    communication costs 155

Index

BOS Engineering Method extensions
  cost contd.
    costs 154, 155, 178, 209
    operational costs 154
  customer 143, 152-154, 164, 168, 169, 171, 173, 180,
      185, 194, 198, 200-203, 205-208, 212-213
  data 139-141, 145-148, 151-162, 165, 168-170, 172, 173,
      177, 179-181, 183, 186, 189-193, 195, 195, 198-201,
      203, 204, 203-207, 210-215
    cached data 201
    Data Catalogue 162, 172
    data location transparency 161
    data server 140, 147
    data storage 155, 196
    data transfer 212-215
    data view 140, 146, 151, 181, 183, 191, 192
    data volumes 193, 207, 213
  database 140-142, 147, 153, 155, 160-165, 193, 195, 196,
      201, 203, 206, 208-213
  design 137, 147, 148, 152-155
  dialogue 141, 142
  distributed commit management 160
  distributed system 155, 167, 193, 196, 207
  distribution 137, 138, 140, 142, 144, 148, 150, 151, 153
      155, 165, 167, 188, 193, 196
  distribution of data 151
  dp-location instance 140
  dp-location type 140
  dp-system 146, 154, 196, 204, 211
  elementary tasks 174
  encapsulated 157
  enquiry 151, 152
  entity 141, 151, 152, 156, 157, 162, 165, 177, 199-202,
      207, 213
    entities 146, 151-153, 156, 178-181, 183, 186, 190, 199,
      201, 202
    entity type 152, 156, 199, 201, 202
  EU-Rent 137, 138, 142, 167-170, 174, 177, 180, 185, 190,
      193, 195-197, 210
    case study 165, 167, 170, 180, 186
  European Methodology and System Center 137
    EMSC 137, 138
  event 140, 174
  external partners 149-151, 167, 168, 173, 186

BOS Engineering Method extensions contd.
  first-cut 155, 160, 161, 201, 202
    first-cut storage concepts 201, 202
  fully distributed option 197, 210
  fully distributed system 193, 196, 207
  function 141
  generic development process
    agree the basis of an IS project in an application area 139
    agree the information system adaptation 139
    agree the information system architecture 139
    agree the information system requirements 139
    agree the information system specification 139
    agree the IT system architecture and the user/machine interface 139
    agree the specification of the computer system and manual procedures 139
    decision point 139
  geographical distribution 138, 144
    Geographical Business Structure 140-144, 148, 149, 151, 154, 155, 190
    Geographical DP-Structure 140, 141, 145, 146
  GRAPES 137-139, 165, 166
  hardware 155, 163, 197, 209
  implementation 139, 141, 142, 160, 163, 198
    Implementation Assignment 141, 142, 160, 163
  inconsistencies 203
  information resource 141, 151, 155-158, 160, 180-184
    Information Resource Definition 151
  Interface Tables 168, 170, 172
  IT system 139, 196, 197, 210
  keys 169, 171
  level 143, 144, 149, 157, 163, 165, 173
  Local Database Schemes 140-142, 155, 160
  location type 140, 142-144, 146, 147, 149-151, 156, 192, 194
    Location Data View 140, 146, 151, 191, 192
    location instance 140, 141, 145
    Location Interaction Diagram 144, 145, 166
    location transparency 161
  message 140-142, 161, 162, 164, 168, 170, 172, 188, 189
    external messages 172, 186, 188
    external message definitions 172
    internal messages 148, 161, 162, 186, 188
    Internal Message Definitions 161, 188

BCS Engineering Method extensions
  message contd.
    message channel 141
    message in dialogue 141
    messages 148, 151, 160-162, 168-170, 172, 186, 188, 192
  method 137-142, 147, 148, 160, 151, 167, 183
    input to method 141
    method dependency 141
    method invocation 1410
    method invocation implementation 141
    methods 138, 152, 160-162, 180, 181, 183, 186
    output by method 141
  module 141, 142
  network 159, 164, 193, 204, 206, 212
  object 141
    association 140, 165
    attributes 178, 179
    class 141, 182-184
    class template 182-184
    object class 141
    object class partition 141
  on-line 193, 196, 206, 211, 213
  option 196, 197, 210, 211, 213
  organisational units 142, 149, 150, 185
    Organisational Business Structure 140-143, 148, 149, 151, 185
    Organisational Interaction Definition 144, 149, 154
  ownership 156-159, 199, 201, 202, 205
  procedure 140-142, 148, 149, 151-155, 159-163, 186, 187, 194, 196, 198, 199, 204, 205
    critical procedures 206
    Procedure Definitions 140-142, 149, 151, 152, 154, 155, 159, 161, 163, 186
    procedure/function 141
    procedure implementation 141, 198
    procedure used in role 141
  process 141, 142, 168, 187, 196
    process cooperation services
    process implementation concepts
    process server 141, 196
  products 137, 138, 140, 142, 148, 149, 151-155, 159-161, 163
  record population partition 141
  record type 141, 142, 140, 156, 165

BOS Engineering Method extensions contd.
  relationship 177
  remote access frequency 156, 157, 159, 199, 200, 202
  remote data access 156
  remote database access 161, 164, 196
    rda 196
  remote processing 196
    rp 196
  replicate 158, 201
    replicated 201-203, 211-213
  requirements 137, 139, 142-144, 153
    requirements specification 139
  robustness 148, 152-154, 156-159, 199-202, 204, 205, 212
    robustness analysis 148, 152, 204, 205, 212
    robustness analysis and design for procedures 148, 152
  roles 142-144, 149, 150, 152, 174, 175, 185, 188, 190, 192
    role at location type 142
    role played 142
  rules 147-149, 154, 161, 165
  schema 141, 147, 170, 171
  server 140-142, 147, 193, 195, 196, 210-215
  specification 139, 148, 163-165
  step 152, 153, 156, 159-162
  storage concept 159, 202
  subtask 174-176, 175, 186
  subtypes 149
  support 162, 215
  table 144, 155, 158, 159, 170, 194, 198, 201
    tables 168, 170, 172
  transaction volumes 144, 145, 170-173, 186 195
  trigger 140, 170, 171, 173, 194, 195
    trigger frequencies 194, 195
    trigger/processing concepts
    trigger/result schema 170, 171
  user 139, 142, 196, 211
  user-interface server 142, 211
  validation/formatting process 142
    validation/formatting implementation 142
  volumes 156-159, 193, 199, 201, 202, 206, 207, 213
  workstation 140, 142-144, 196, 210
business 19-22, 24-26, 30-36, 38, 43, 47, 53-57, 59-66, 70, 76-81, 89, 110, 114, 116, 119, 120, 124-127, 129-134, 385-387, 391, 395-398, 400-405, 408, 410-412, 414, 416
  business activity 21, 34

business contd.
  business rule 24, 130
  business system 126
business location 54, 55, 57, 60-66, 70, 76-81, 125, 127,
    130-132, 395-398, 402, 408, 410-412, 414, 416
  actor/business location concepts 60, 61
  business location instance 54, 60-62, 64, 66, 70, 80, 395,
    397, 410, 411, 416
  business location type 54, 63-66, 76-81, 396-398, 408,
    410, 412, 414, 416
  business location type activity level 76-79, 81, 396,
    398, 408, 412, 416
  business location type activity levels 76, 79
  business locations 38, 56, 120, 127, 131-134
CASE 398, 410
centralised option 127
centralised solution 116, 125
centralised systems 15, 17, 59, 88, 116
class 43, 45, 51, 65, 66, 73, 74, 77, 78, 80, 107, 120,
    396-398, 406, 410, 411, 413
  class partition by location activity level 77, 78, 397,
    398
client/server 38, 40, 42-44, 96-98, 102, 103, 105-107, 125,
    391, 399, 415
  client 85, 92, 414
  client/server architecture 97, 98, 102, 103, 125
  CS 96, 99, 105
  server 20, 47, 48, 55, 71, 72, 74, 85, 91, 92,
    100, 124, 132, 134, 399-402, 405, 412-415
clustering 102, 127, 131
commit unit 39, 41-44, 87, 92-94, 399-401, 407, 409
  commit unit trigger 69, 70, 399-401, 409
communication 20, 22-25, 27, 40, 46, 48, 52, 57, 65, 66, 80,
    81, 85, 90, 93, 104, 105, 112, 115, 116, 118, 123, 131,
    133, 134, 385-388, 390, 400, 402, 407, 414
  bandwidth 90, 125, 387-389
  communication costs 80, 112, 115, 385, 388, 390
  communication protocols 104
  traffic 56, 81, 389
  See also: network.
conceptual model 34, 38, 84, 124, 131, 395, 400, 406
conceptual process 45, 133, 400
conceptual schema 29, 31, 34-37, 39, 40, 93, 120, 132, 133,
    400, 405

consistency 22, 25, 39, 46, 55, 69, 87, 91, 92, 99, 113, 114,
    116-120, 126, 128, 132, 399
consistent 22, 46, 47, 51, 112, 118, 119, 408, 415
coordinated activities 22, 24, 25, 408, 415
coordinated system 22, 24, 25, 45, 46, 52, 55, 112, 126
corporate aspect 400
corporate attributes 48
corporate entity 48, 49, 51, 400
corporate server 48
cost 15, 17, 27, 55, 81, 102, 105, 114-117, 122, 125, 128,
    130, 132, 385, 388, 389, 403, 408
cost-benefit analysis 403
cost estimates 116
costs 22, 48, 76, 80, 109, 112-116, 126, 127, 385-390
    maintenance and software upgrades 115
    operational costs 109, 115
    software costs 116
current system 21
customer 20, 22-26, 30, 31, 47-50, 90, 92, 94, 98, 109-111,
    129, 130, 404, 405
data 21-26, 29, 32-42, 44, 45, 47-57, 59, 60, 62, 64-67,
    70-74, 79-81, 83, 85-92, 94-97, 100-107, 110-112, 114,
    116-120, 122-134, 385, 389, 391, 392, 396-398, 400-416
    centrally-maintained reference data 128
    data clustering 127
    data history 128
    data implementation concepts 72, 73
    data location level 132
    data location transparency 38, 41, 86, 89, 100, 101, 132,
        401, 413, 414
    data location type 54, 70, 73, 401, 411, 413, 416
    data/object concepts 64
    data processing location instance 54, 70, 73, 401, 411,
        413, 416
    data processing locations 39, 56, 57, 83, 103, 104, 124,
        403, 414
    data replication 52, 53, 102
    data server 40-42, 71, 72, 125, 401, 402
    data storage 42, 92, 127, 131, 132, 398, 402, 406
    data storage location 42, 131, 132
    data view 110, 111
    horizontal partitioning 101, 102, 120, 121, 123, 127, 406
    locking 42, 88, 106, 107, 407
    low-usage data 128
    partitioning of data 42, 56, 411

data contd.
  stored data 34, 62, 131, 407
    vertical partitioning 73, 101, 120, 121, 123, 127, 413, 416
  database 29, 30, 39-41, 43-45, 48-50, 53, 64, 65, 69, 72, 83,
      85, 88-94, 97, 100-105, 107, 115, 120, 125, 132, 133,
      385-387, 391-394, 398, 399, 402, 406, 410, 411, 413-415
    database access level 132
    DBMS 37, 41, 102, 132, 387, 391, 402
    deadlock 27, 88, 106
    query optimisation 102
  Database administration 103
    DBA 103
  data processing location concepts 70
    dp input message 66, 69, 400, 401, 406, 408
    dp location type 71, 72, 79, 80, 401, 413
    dp output message 67, 408, 411
    dp-system 87-89, 93, 125
  dependency use by location activity level 78, 79, 402
  design 15, 16, 18, 22-25, 27, 29, 35-40, 43-46, 48, 52, 53,
      55-57, 59, 66, 76, 77, 79, 81, 84, 85, 90, 91, 93, 97, 107,
      109, 116, 117, 120, 124, 126, 128, 130, 131, 134, 395,
      402, 405-407, 411-415
    design approach 27, 45, 52, 56
    design principles 45
    design versus discovery 36
    discovery 33, 36, 400
  dialogue 62, 66, 74, 78, 402, 408, 412
    dialogues 35, 38, 405
  distributed database management systems 53, 54, 60, 85,
      87-89, 101, 402, 411
    DDBMS 89, 90, 92, 99, 101, 402
  distributed data processing system
    DDP System 60-62, 64, 66, 67, 69, 70, 72, 79, 81, 395,
      397, 401-403, 415, 416
  distributed information system 15, 16, 60, 402, 403, 411
    DI System 60, 62, 64, 76, 79, 402
  distributed system 19, 21, 23, 24, 29, 37, 38, 45, 46, 48,
      52, 54-56, 59, 83, 85-87, 89, 107, 111, 113-117, 119,
      120, 124, 125, 127, 385, 400, 402, 403
  distributed transaction processing 53, 87, 92-94, 104, 107,
      392-394
    DTP 92, 93, 99, 104, 392, 393

distribution 17, 25-27, 29, 45, 46, 49, 53-56, 59, 66, 83, 89, 92, 99, 103, 109, 112-114, 116, 117, 120, 124-127, 130, 381, 382, 402, 403, 406
   distribution of data 56, 120, 124, 126
   distribution of processing 56, 89, 124, 130
   distribution option 403
EDIFACT 95, 392
Electronic Data Interchange for the Social domain 15, 404
   EDIS 15, 404
Electronic Mail 53, 94, 95, 103
   EMail 40, 94-96, 99, 103, 104, 133, 134
encapsulation 403
   encapsulated 43
enquiry 34-36, 39, 43, 47, 49, 51, 90-92, 97, 100, 400, 403, 405, 407
   enquiries 34, 39, 47, 49, 50, 100, 101, 391, 400, 412
entity 32, 33, 41, 42, 45, 47-49, 51, 64, 65, 381, 393, 396, 397, 400, 403, 410, 411
   entities 32, 33, 36, 47, 64, 126-130, 381, 396, 411, 413
   entity aspect 47, 51, 403
   entity aspects 45, 47
   entity behaviour 51
   entity instance 51
   entity life histories 393
   entity type 33, 42, 47, 49, 65, 396, 410
   shared entity types 49
EU-Rent 19-24, 27, 30, 31, 34, 47, 49, 60-63, 65, 66, 70, 71, 76, 77, 80, 81, 90-92, 97, 127-130, 134, 396, 403, 404
   case study 17, 27, 396
Euromethod 109, 392, 398, 403-405
   Business Information View 110
   Business Process View 31, 110, 398
      BPV 31, 32, 36, 398
   Computer System Architecture View 111, 125
   Computer System Data View 110, 111
   Computer System Function View 110, 111
   Work Practice View 110
European employment information system 15, 404
   EURES 15, 404
European Methodology and System Center 403
   EMSC 392, 393, 397, 403
event 43, 44, 49, 51, 107, 397, 402, 405
   event manager 44, 402, 405
existing system 110

external design 35-40, 43, 44, 84, 93, 97, 124, 130, 131
    395, 402, 405, 412, 415
  external process 42
  external schema 29, 34-36, 38, 39, 120, 122, 405
first-cut design 126-128
function 36, 61, 62, 65-67, 74, 76, 78, 110, 111, 123, 393,
    401, 408, 409, 412
  functions 36-40, 61, 62, 64, 74, 88, 114, 123, 132, 133,
    395, 397, 403, 415
functional requirements 31, 55, 109, 113
generic development process 18, 109, 116, 403, 405
  agree the basis of an IS project in an application area
    110, 113, 114
  agree the information system adaptation 111
  agree the information system architecture 110, 116-
    120
  agree the information system specification 110, 403
  agree the information system requirements 110, 116
  agree the specification of the computer system and
    manual procedure 111
  agree the IT system architecture and the user/machine
    interface 111
  decision point 109, 405
geographical distribution 26, 27, 29, 406
GRAPES 15, 17, 18, 29, 392, 393, 397, 406
graphical user interface 68, 406, 415
  menus 37, 406
  MS-Windows 112
  X-Windows 112
help desk 386, 389, 390
implementation 26, 27, 29, 34, 36, 40, 48, 52, 57, 72-75,
    81, 85, 90, 91, 395, 400, 402, 409, 412, 415
  hardware 15, 20, 22, 53, 54, 70-72, 80, 84, 85, 100, 112,
    115, 116, 385, 387-390, 401
  inconsistent access speed 122
inconsistencies between uncoordinated systems 22
information exchange services 53, 83, 85, 400
  message exchange 53, 75, 83, 86, 409
    msg 86, 99
  remote database access 50, 53, 83, 85, 89, 91, 92, 100,
    101, 107, 132, 133, 392-394
    rda 85, 86, 89, 91, 92, 99, 101, 131, 134, 392
  transparency of data location 52, 53, 102
    dlt 86, 89, 99

information exchange services contd.
    transparency of data replication 53
        rt 86, 89, 99
inherit 51, 398
inheritance 51, 406
input to method 406
inputs to method 68, 406
instance variable 406
integration 24, 112, 113, 391
    integrated 49, 56
internal design 37, 38, 40, 84, 90, 91, 124, 128, 395, 402, 406, 407
internal schema 29, 34, 37, 120, 124, 406, 407
ISE Library 24, 112, 113, 403, 407
    Application Partitioning and Integration with SSADM 24, 112, 113, 391
    Reuse in SSADM using OO 391
IT system 20, 21, 31, 32, 34, 38, 111, 395, 407, 414
keys 129
layer 39, 41, 52, 84-87, 90, 91, 97, 414
level 16, 25, 27, 34, 36, 37, 43, 47, 54, 56, 57, 66, 72, 73, 75-81, 83, 85, 88, 101-103, 105, 107, 110, 119, 120, 132, 389, 396-399, 402, 408, 412, 416
location instance 54, 60-62, 64, 66, 70, 72, 73, 75, 80, 81, 395, 397, 401, 407, 409-411, 413, 416
location transparency 38-41, 86, 89, 100, 101, 105, 132, 399, 401, 402, 412-414
location type 49, 54, 63-66, 71, 72, 74, 76-81, 106, 126, 396-398, 401, 408, 410, 412-414, 416
logical data modelling 47
    logical data model 396, 406, 407
    subtype hierarchies 51
logical design 15, 16, 27, 45, 52, 53, 56, 57, 76, 77, 85, 97, 407
    logical design volumetrics 76
logical requirements 46, 53-55, 57
loosely-coordinated activities 24, 25, 408
manual activity 66, 408
merge 130
message 48, 53, 66, 67, 69, 75, 78, 81, 83, 86, 94, 95, 97, 392, 400, 401, 406, 408, 409, 411, 415
    messages 27, 36, 44, 48, 62, 66, 68, 69, 74, 78, 81, 86, 94, 107, 401, 405, 406, 408, 411, 412
    message channel 81, 408
    message channel use by method 81, 408

message contd.
  message in dialogue 66, 408
  message use by location activity level 78, 408
meta model 17, 59-61, 65, 381, 382, 395, 408
  meta model concepts 59, 60
method 15-18, 21, 30, 35, 42, 43, 47, 52, 55, 56, 65, 68-71, 74, 75, 78-81, 94, 124, 127, 386, 392, 395, 397, 399-402, 405-411, 414
  method dependency 65, 70, 408, 409
  method invocation 69, 70, 75, 80, 81, 408, 409
  method invocation implementation 75, 81, 409
  methods 15, 17, 26, 41-44, 64, 65, 68-70, 74, 80, 94, 109, 124, 398, 399, 402, 403, 405, 406, 409-412
most-distributed option 132
multi-location 26
network 29, 37-40, 42-44, 53, 79, 80, 88, 100, 103-105, 107, 112, 114, 115, 117, 119, 123, 125, 132, 385, 388, 389, 391, 405, 407, 410, 413, 414
  network bandwidth 125
  See also: communication.
notation 381
object 40, 43-45, 53, 59, 64-66, 69, 72-74, 76-78, 80, 107, 120, 393, 396-399, 402, 403, 406, 408-411, 413
  object class 43, 45, 65, 66, 73, 74, 77, 78, 80, 107, 120, 396-398, 410, 411, 413
  object class partition 66, 73, 410, 411
  object instance 64, 66, 72, 73, 398, 410, 411
  object-oriented 40, 43, 45, 53, 65, 107, 398, 402, 403, 406, 408, 409
  object-oriented distributed transaction processing 53, 54, 60, 83, 87, 88, 107, 402, 411
  object population representation 73, 411
  subtypes 398, 406
  supertypes 398, 406
off-line 103, 132, 133
on-line 133, 402
operation 25, 385-388, 391
optimisation 102, 105, 122, 413
option 56, 111, 114, 126, 127, 132, 133, 388, 403
output by method 411
ownership 128
performance 41, 48, 57, 102, 104-106, 122, 125-129, 132, 133, 386, 404
physical design 37, 57, 59, 76, 79, 81, 413
  physical design volumetrics 76, 79

policies 27, 41, 42, 44, 110, 399, 403, 411, 404
pre-project decisions 112
procedure 36, 40-42, 50, 61, 62, 66, 67, 72, 74-76, 78, 87,
    94, 95, 97, 99, 100, 103-106, 124, 131, 133, 393, 398,
    401, 403, 408, 409, 412, 413
  procedure implementation 74, 412
  procedure used in role 412
procedure/function 36, 61, 62, 66, 67, 74, 76, 78, 398, 401,
    408, 412
  procedures/functions 36, 38-40, 61, 62, 64, 395, 397,
    415
process 18, 23, 26, 27, 31, 33, 36, 38-45, 53-55, 67-69, 71,
    74, 75, 83, 85-87, 96, 97, 103, 105, 107, 109, 110, 114,
    116, 123-125, 131-133, 398-403, 405-407, 411-416
  inter-location processes 114
  intra-location processes 114
  process implementation concepts 74, 75
  process location transparency 38, 40, 105, 399, 402,
    412, 413
  process server 40, 41, 71, 74, 124, 125, 132, 401, 412,
    413,
process cooperation services 53, 83, 87, 400
  distributed commit management 27, 54, 83, 87, 92
    dcm 87, 89, 92, 99
  remote processing 53, 83, 87
    rp 87, 99
  security services 54, 83, 88, 400
    sec 88, 99
products 40, 41, 99, 100, 104, 105, 107, 109-111, 392
program-data interface 41, 42, 124, 132, 412
  PDI 100
project initiation document 110
project partitioning 48
RDA-oriented 131
real-world 30, 31, 49, 129, 130, 396, 398
record instance 72
record population partition 73, 411, 413
  record population partitions 72, 411
record type 72, 80, 412, 413
relationship 25, 47, 65, 78, 96, 118, 381, 396, 413
  relationship type 65, 396
relaxed semantics 25
remote data access 40, 41, 131, 413
remote database access with distributed commit 53, 92

remote database access with distributed commit
  management 92
 RDA+ 92, 99
remote database access without distributed commit 93
remote procedure call 40-42, 50, 87, 97, 133, 393, 409, 413
replication 40, 48, 52, 53, 56, 57, 83, 86, 89, 102, 107, 120,
  121, 123-126, 128
 replicate 41, 52, 57, 128, 133
 replicated 37, 52, 86, 102, 123, 128, 414
 replication transparency 83, 86, 89
requirements 15, 18, 22, 26, 27, 31, 35, 37, 40, 45-47,
  52-57, 64, 72, 79, 80, 87, 89, 105, 107, 109-113, 116-
  118, 120, 123, 126, 389, 398, 401, 403, 405
 requirements analysis 15, 26
 requirements catalogue 35, 405
 user requirements 403
robustness 25, 27, 40, 41, 45, 48, 52, 55-57, 86, 109, 113,
  114, 116-120, 125, 126, 128, 129, 131, 414
 robustness analysis 57
roles 33, 36-38, 56, 62-64, 71, 72, 395-398, 416
 role at location type 414
 role played 54, 414
RPC-oriented 131
rules 24, 37, 102, 126, 127, 387
schema 17, 29, 31, 34-40, 45, 56, 59, 93, 96, 120, 122, 124,
  132, 133, 395, 396, 400, 402, 405-407
security 19, 54, 83, 88, 122, 129, 130, 385, 388, 400, 404
 back-up vulnerability 123
 data theft 117
 propagation of corrupt data 123
 reliability 123, 134
service layer 39, 41, 52, 414
services 17, 18, 29, 34, 37-40, 46, 52-54, 57, 62, 70, 80, 83,
  85-89, 99, 103, 104, 385, 389, 391, 393, 395-397,
  399-405, 407, 410, 414
 mapping of services to architectures 99, 103
shared server 134
specification 17, 59, 85, 87, 91, 96, 110, 111, 124, 393, 394,
  395, 396, 400, 402, 403, 405, 406
SSADM V4 218, 219, 223, 227, 228, 230, 232-234, 236-
  238-242, 257, 262, 264, 269, 270, 274, 284, 308, 335,
  393, 414
SSADM V4 extensions
 3-schema Specification Architecture 226, 227, 241, 248
 actor 223

SSADM V4 extensions
  actor contd.
    actor role 223
    actor role on workstation 223
    actor type 223
  application partitioning 219, 220, 245
    disjoint partitioning 275, 337, 342
  architecture 222, 238, 279
  aspects 226, 241, 242, 253-256, 262-264, 266, 268-275,
      336-338, 340-344, 346-348, 351, 353, 356, 360, 364
    aspect type 248
    base aspect 247, 254, 255, 262, 271, 342-344
    dependent aspect 254
    developing required data model 236
    ELHs for aspects 254-257
    entity aspects 224, 227, 237, 248, 250, 253, 266, 268-
      270, 271
    first-cut data design 240
    modelling data types split across more than one dp
      location 244-246
    parallel lives modelled as separate aspects 262-264
    relational data analysis 247, 248
  association 218, 223
  attributes 231, 234-236, 244, 247-249, 252, 254, 267, 287,
      313, 315-317, 340, 341, 343, 346
  batch messages 241
  business 272, 289, 312, 332, 356, 358, 367
    business activity 227, 313-315, 364
    business events 250
    business location instance 223
    business locations 230, 233-235, 236, 243, 249, 253,
      273, 274, 276, 279, 310-312, 333, 335, 336, 349, 356
    business location type 223, 229, 233, 236, 253, 274,
      311, 312, 333, 336
    business option 226, 232, 234, 236
    business rules 264-266, 317, 341
  Business System Options 221, 222, 232-236, 249
    additional steps 234-236
    BSO-specific tables 249
    BSOs 249
    changes to validation of the LDM 244
    modifications to existing steps 233-234
    structural changes 225-226
    usage during Feasibility Study 228
  CASE 248

SSADM V4 extensions contd.
  centralised design 235
  centralised option 274, 287, 325, 326-328, 333, 336
  centralised solution 228, 229
  changes to modelling steps and techniques 225
  class 224, 269, 336
  client/server 242, 311
    server 226, 263
  clustered locations 241
    clustering 227, 235
    'most clustered' design 235
  commit unit 223
    commit unit trigger 223
  common components 241
  communication 227, 228, 230, 235, 240, 241, 272-274,
      281, 298, 336, 337, 349, 350, 351, 359, 360, 363
    batch communication 241
    traffic 245, 276, 332, 351, 360, 362
  communication map 273, 275, 276, 349, 359
    communication map - volumes table 278
  communications mapping 227
  conceptual model 226, 234, 242, 273, 310, 321
  conceptual process 310
  conceptual schema 239, 248, 269, 279, 342
  consistency 228, 229, 238, 241, 243, 272, 273, 300, 301,
      323
  consistent 235, 243, 248, 262, 263
  constraints on distribution 229, 244
  Core SSADM V4 232
  cost 227, 229, 233, 243, 276, 313, 316, 325, 333, 356,
      358, 376
    communication costs 272, 363
    cost-benefit analysis 233
    costs 236, 272, 279, 315, 363, 367, 376-378
  current system 231, 287-290, 292, 296, 299-301
  customer 240, 241, 245, 247, 248, 253-256, 263-265, 268,
      271-273, 277, 278, 280-282, 284, 285, 295, 296, 302,
      312, 314-316, 318, 321, 322, 324, 329, 332, 335, 336,
      340, 341, 343, 344, 351-355, 360, 362-366, 367,
      377-379
  data 224, 226-231, 234, 236-243, 244, 246, 247, 249, 250,
      254, 272-279, 282, 287, 289, 290, 293, 298, 300, 301,
      303, 315, 323, 324, 326, 327, 329-332, 335-337, 340,
      343-346, 348, 349, 353, 356, 357, 364, 366, 367,
      377-379

SSADM V4 extensions
  data contd.
    data location transparency 239, 247, 305, 333
    data processing location instance 223
    data processing locations 232, 234, 244, 275-277, 310, 349, 350, 362
    data processing location type 223
    data replication transparency 239, 242, 273
    data server 226
    data storage 272, 277, 310-311, 366
    data storage location 240, 310, 311
    partitioning of data 226
  database 219, 225, 226, 231, 234, 238-242, 250, 257, 263, 269, 272, 279, 283, 285, 301, 310, 311, 323, 326, 332, 349, 353
    database storage 240
    DBMS 240
    deadlock 323
    extension of classification system for storage and performance 240
    locking 242, 282
    referential integrity 323, 367
    selective locking 242
    timing forms 240
  data flow model 228-230
    DFD 228-230, 233, 246, 248, 253, 287-294, 297, 298, 303-309, 327, 328
    DFM 230
    logical DFM 230
    low-level DFD 230
  data flow modelling 229, 243, 246
  design 217-219, 226-231, 233-235, 239-243, 245-247, 265, 267, 271, 273, 274, 287, 299-301, 310, 312, 321, 323, 325, 333, 335, 336, 338, 342, 348, 349, 358
  dialogue 224
    dialogues 226, 239, 308
  disciplined quits 237
  discovery 248
  distributed commit service 278, 279
  distributed processing 238, 244
  distributed processing architecture 238
  distributed system 228, 229, 240, 242, 243, 246, 247, 257, 287, 300, 301
  distributed transaction processing 220, 279

SSADM V4 extensions contd.
    distributed transactions 240
    distribution 217, 219, 223, 225-229, 232-235, 240, 242,
        244, 245, 248, 273-276, 279, 287, 310, 335, 338, 359,
        376-378
        define distribution options 234, 236
        distribution of processing 242
        distribution option 226, 232, 236, 240, 273
    dominant transactions 367
    dp input message 224
    dp output message 224
    effect correspondence diagram 223, 224, 243, 279, 283
        directional correspondences 263
        ECD 224, 239, 268, 269, 279-281, 284, 364-365
        ECD fragment 279
        partitioning the ECD 239
    EMail 238, 274, 352-354, 356, 363, 364
    enquiry 219, 223, 224, 226, 231, 234, 235, 238, 239,
        241-243, 244, 249, 253, 265, 271, 276, 279, 321, 324,
        333, 340, 341, 344, 351, 352, 360, 361
        EAP 224, 279
        enquiries 231, 236, 242, 244, 247, 249, 253, 276, 300,
            310, 313, 315, 318, 320, 321, 323, 333, 335, 336, 343,
            351, 360
    enquiry process model 223
        EPM 242, 279
    entity 220, 223, 224, 226, 227, 230, 231, 235-237,
        240-243, 244-254, 257, 258, 262, 263, 266, 268-271,
        273-276, 279, 280, 282, 316-320, 323-325, 326,
        333-336, 341-343, 351, 352, 361
        entities 226, 230, 231, 234, 244-249, 253, 262, 269,
            274, 275, 283, 288, 290, 299, 317-320, 336, 337, 340,
            344, 348, 351, 360, 361, 379
        entity behaviour 279
        entity instance 241, 282
        entity type 223, 231, 236, 245, 250, 252, 268, 282, 323,
            324, 352, 361
        home entity 282
        multiple hits on an entity instance 282
        'one-of-a-kind' entities 348
    Entity Access Matrix 230, 231, 235, 237, 244, 248-253,
        318-320, 334-336
        creating the entity access matrix 249
        role in robustness analysis 273
        usage during first-cut distribution design 275-276

SSADM V4 extensions
  Entity Access Matrix contd.
    usage of spreadsheet 249
    volumes of events / enquiries by location 342, 343
  entity life history 224, 237, 243, 248
    ELH 248, 254-261, 263-267, 268, 358
    ELHs for aspects 254
    entity life histories 220, 237, 248
    parallel life 262, 263
    parallel lives 246, 256, 262, 263
    quits and resumes 220, 237, 393
  entity life history analysis 237, 243, 248
  EU-Rent 230, 238, 254, 263, 268, 271, 277, 287, 288, 310, 313, 315, 318, 353, 356, 358
    case study 230, 274, 287, 300, 326, 333
  event 223, 224, 226, 230, 231, 234, 235, 241, 242, 244, 246, 249-253, 257-259, 262, 264-266, 268, 270, 271, 281-283, 292, 315, 317-319, 321, 323, 326, 333, 351, 352, 355, 360, 361, 378
    event identification 230, 231, 244, 249, 315, 317, 318, 333
    event manager 242, 283
  external design 226, 230, 231, 233, 242, 246, 247, 310, 321, 333
  external entities 230, 246, 253, 288, 290, 299
  feasibility study 222, 227-229
    feasibility report 228
  first-cut 227, 235, 240, 273-275, 335, 336, 338, 359
  first-cut data design 227, 240
  first-cut distribution 227, 235, 273-275, 335, 338, 359
  first-cut distribution design 227, 273, 274, 335, 338
  first-cut distribution rules 235, 275, 359
  fully distributed option 325, 335
  function 223-225, 235, 241, 242, 253, 279, 289, 308, 311-313, 321, 324, 333, 362, 363
  function/business location type matrix 311, 312
  function component implementation map 241
    FCIM 241
  functional design 226
  functional requirements 227, 229, 232, 233, 236, 243, 249
  functions 226, 232-235, 237, 242, 246, 252, 253, 276, 300, 308, 310-313, 321, 323, 329, 333, 335, 367

SSADM V4 extensions contd.
  generic development process
    agree the basis of an IS project in an application area 222
    agree the information system adaptation 222
    agree the information system architecture 222
    agree the information system requirements 222
    agree the information system specification 222
    agree the specification of the computer system and manual procedures 222
  Government Centre for Information Systems 218
  hardware 220, 356, 377
  histories 220, 237, 248, 344, 353
  history 224, 234, 237, 243, 248, 250, 275, 277, 278, 296, 299, 312, 314, 315, 322, 329, 337, 341, 342, 344, 351-353, 355, 356, 360
  I/O structure 224, 241
  implementation 218, 219, 222, 224, 225, 239, 241, 269, 278, 279, 283, 358, 379
    conventional programming implementation 283
  inconsistencies 235, 236, 301
  input to method 224
  integration 219, 220, 245
    integrated 254
  internal design 226, 234, 243, 271, 310
  investigation of current environment 221, 229
  ISE Library 219, 220, 245
    Application Partitioning and Integration with SSADM 219, 220, 245
    Reuse in SSADM using OO 219, 220, 245, 263
  IT system 252
  keys 237, 247, 252
  laws of nature 264, 265
  least-dependent-occurrence rule 274, 336
  level 219, 230, 233, 236, 241, 253, 267, 287-289, 303, 304, 308, 327-329, 333, 342
  location instance 223, 224
  location transparency 239, 247, 278, 279, 305, 333
  location transparency service 278, 279
  location type 223, 225, 226, 233, 236, 253, 273, 274, 311, 312, 333, 336
  logical data model 226, 231, 249
    LDM 223, 224, 226, 230, 231, 234-236, 244, 245, 248-250, 252, 253, 262, 268, 269, 274, 313, 315, 317, 326, 330-333, 336, 346-348, 356, 358

SSADM V4 extensions
  logical data model contd.
    partitioning the LDM 234, 253
    subtype 267, 316
    subtypes 257, 266, 267, 357, 358
    validating the LDM 231, 244
  logical data modelling 243, 244
  logical data structure 303, 327
  logical design 221, 222, 239, 240, 323
  logical system specification 221
  manual activity 224
  menus 308
  message 224, 242, 245, 268, 270, 277, 279, 283, 284
    message channel 224
    message in dialogue 224
    message traffic 245
    messages 241, 242, 276, 277, 279, 282, 283
  method 218, 224, 239, 240, 248, 256, 279-283, 285
    method dependency 224
    method invocation 224, 279, 280, 282, 283
    method invocation implementation 224
    methods 279, 281, 285
  module 220, 225, 227
  network 235, 240, 242, 245, 247, 257, 272, 273, 276, 300,
    301, 323, 332, 348, 367, 379
  non-functional requirements 227, 229, 243
  notation 228, 229, 246, 262, 263, 268, 290, 293
  object 217, 219, 224, 239, 242, 245, 263, 269, 278, 279,
    281, 282
    object class 224, 269
    object class partition 224
    object-oriented 217, 219, 239, 269, 278, 279
    object-oriented distributed transaction processing
      279
    object-oriented implementation 239, 269, 278, 279
    object population representation 224
  off-line 238, 355, 356
  on-line 238
  operation 238, 251, 252, 257, 300, 301
  optimisation 242, 256, 257, 260, 262
  optimised states 237, 258, 260
  option 226-229, 232-234, 236, 240, 244, 272-274, 277,
    287, 300, 301, 326-328, 332, 333, 335, 336, 344, 348,
    349, 352, 362-364, 367, 378, 379
  output by method 224

SSADM V4 extensions contd.
  ownership 290, 292, 295, 302, 315, 324, 355
  ownership of data 227, 229, 243
  partially clustered option 325, 356, 357, 359
  performance 228, 229, 240, 241, 243, 272, 273, 276, 313, 333, 344, 367
  physical data design 240, 241
  physical design 221, 222, 240, 241, 243, 267, 273, 274, 336, 342, 348, 349
  physical design volumes
  physical geography 226
  policies 265
  procedure 224, 225, 228-234, 236-240, 270, 271, 273, 279, 295, 296
  procedure/function 225
  procedure implementation 225
  procedure used in role 225
  process 223, 225, 226, 228, 230, 231, 238, 239, 242, 243, 246-248, 268-273, 281, 284, 285, 287-294, 297, 298, 300, 305-309, 310, 329, 333, 355
    inter-location processes 300
    intra-location processes 300, 301
  process-data interface 273
    PDI 226, 239, 242, 267, 269, 277
  process location transparency 239
  process server 226, 242
  products 217, 223, 226, 227, 233
  project initiation document 218, 227-229
  real-world 245
  record instance 242
  record population partition 225
  record type 225, 242, 267
  relational data analysis 237, 243, 247
  relationship 223, 245, 251, 252, 317, 348, 349
  remote data access 333
  remote database access 238, 239, 311
    rda 278
  remote procedure call 270, 271, 279
  replication 239, 242, 272, 273, 275, 337, 342, 348
    replicate 234, 241
    replicated 236, 240, 241, 254, 343, 364, 366
    replication transparency 239
  required system DFDs 246, 248

SSADM V4 extensions contd.
  requirements 217, 221, 222, 225-229, 232, 233, 236-239,
      242, 243, 244, 249, 278, 287, 299-301, 313, 323, 325,
      326, 333
    definition of requirements 221
    requirements analysis 221, 222
    requirements catalogue 228
    requirements definition 229, 243
    requirements list 300, 301
    requirements specification 221, 222, 236, 237
  result 257, 302, 318, 319, 325, 367, 378
  reuse 219, 220, 245, 263
  robust operation 238
  robustness 227-229, 234, 235, 241, 243, 272, 273, 300,
      301, 323, 326, 332, 333, 348, 352, 356, 358, 362, 367,
      379
    robustness analysis 227, 235, 273, 332, 352, 362
  roles 223, 230, 231, 233, 237, 246, 290
    role at location type 225
    role played 225
  rules 235, 237, 240, 256, 260, 262, 264, 265, 275, 315,
      317, 359
  schema 226, 227, 239, 241, 248, 269, 279, 342
  select distribution option 236
  services 217, 218, 220, 230, 232, 238, 240, 278, 279, 315,
      342, 348, 349, 356, 358, 363
  specification 218, 221, 222, 225-227, 236, 237, 241, 242,
      248, 289, 322, 351, 360
  splitting entity types 244
  stability of design 228, 229, 243
  stage 225, 229, 232, 236-240, 273, 276
  state optimisation 227, 256, 257, 260, 262
  step 229-231, 233, 234, 236-243, 248, 274-276, 297, 301,
      338-342, 344, 345, 349, 359
  structural model 217, 227
  Structured Systems Analysis and Design Method 218
  success unit 223
  supertype 267
  support 217, 230, 231, 234, 238, 239, 244, 248, 249, 275,
      279, 301, 309, 313-315, 329, 341, 359, 362, 377
  table 240, 242, 267, 276, 278
    tables 240, 249, 343
  technical system options 221, 238, 239
  technique 227, 230, 231, 237, 239, 244, 253, 268, 270,
      271

SSADM V4 extensions contd.
  techniques 217, 218, 225, 227, 228, 235, 237, 243, 273, 326, 333
    additional techniques 217, 273
  temporary inconsistency 234
    temporary inconsistencies 235
  TNF relation 247
  transaction volumes 220, 274, 279, 332, 368-377, 369-374, 376, 377
  trigger 223
  two-phase commit 257, 281, 282
  UK Government Centre for Information Systems 218
    CCTA 217-219
  undisciplined quits 237
  unlocking 283
  update process 223, 243, 269-271, 273, 284, 285
  update process model 223, 284, 285
    consolidated UPM 239
    local UPMs 239
    UPM 239, 242, 270, 271, 278, 279
    UPM / EPM interface 242
    UPM fragment 279
  user 218, 219, 222-226, 228, 230-237, 239, 300, 308
    user dialogues 239
    user interface server 226
    user role 223, 225, 230, 232, 235, 236, 308
    user role/function matrix 223, 308
    users 223, 226, 229, 300, 301, 333, 358
  validation/formatting process 225
    validation/formatting implementation 225
  volumes
    communication volumes between aspects 275, 336
    communication volumes between locations 227, 241
    dominant functions 311
    effect of more clustering on volumes 356
    in communication map - volumes table 278, 351-352, 360-362, 363
    in Entity Access Matrix 235, 249, 252, 333-335, 343
    in Function/Business Location Type Matrix 312
    peak volume analysis 367-368
    of enquiries and events by location 342-343
    used in costing 376-377
    use in reviewing placement of shared LDM details 339
  workstation 223, 225, 230, 246, 376-378

441

stability of design 55, 109, 116, 117
   data theft 117
   load fluctuation 117
   system changes 117
stage 405
state optimisation 90, 92, 104, 126, 392, 414
step 27, 387
storage of 55
Structured Systems Analysis and Design Method 414
support 15, 16, 18, 26, 30-34, 37, 41, 53-55, 57, 60, 71, 76, 79, 83, 85, 86, 89, 92, 99-105, 115, 116, 126, 133, 385-390, 395, 396, 400, 404
synchronization 88, 123
tables 54, 99, 101-103, 102, 120, 121, 406, 411, 413-416
technical platform 403, 411
tightly-coordinated system 22, 24, 25
trigger 66, 67, 69, 70, 74, 94, 103, 399-401, 403, 409
two-phase commit 105, 106
UK Government Centre for Information Systems 218, 398
   CCTA 391-393, 398, 403, 407, 414
uncoordinated activities 22, 23, 126, 415
users 29, 30, 34, 36-41, 43, 45, 52, 55-57, 61, 62, 66-70, 72, 74, 83, 86, 88, 94, 96-98, 100, 103-105, 111, 112, 114, 117-119, 122, 124-126, 130, 131, 386-388, 393, 395, 400, 401, 403, 406-408, 413, 415, 416
   costs and benefits to users of loosely-coordinated systems 25
   costs and benefits to users of tightly-coordinated systems 22
user-interface server 40, 41, 55, 72, 74, 96-98, 105, 401, 413, 415
validation/formatting process 67, 74, 415
   validation/format process implementation 74
volumes 76, 77, 79, 88, 105, 404
   low volumes 130, 134
   transaction volumes 26, 53, 69, 87, 89, 92-94, 97, 101, 103-107, 134, 392-394, 399
volumetrics 76, 79, 80
workstation 38, 54, 57, 64, 70-72, 81, 90, 92, 98, 103, 388, 395, 398, 401, 416
   workstation at location type activity level 416
   workstation requirement 71, 81, 395, 416
X/Open 85, 87, 91-93, 99, 100, 393, 394, 416